frontiers of democratic theory

RANDOM HOUSE NEW YORK

frontiers of democratic theory

EDITED BY **HENRY S. KARIEL** UNIVERSITY OF HAWAII

Library of Congress Catalog Card Number: 79–97585

MANUFACTURED IN THE UNITED STATES OF AMERICA BY
THE BOOK PRESS INC., BRATTLEBORO, VT.

9 8 7 6 5 4 3 2

We have frequently printed the word Democracy.
Yet I cannot too often repeat that it is a word the
real gist of which still sleeps, quite unawakened,
notwithstanding the resonance and the many angry
tempests out of which its syllables have come, from
pen or tongue. It is a great word, whose history,
I suppose, remains unwritten, because that history has
yet to be enacted.

—WALT WHITMAN, *Democratic Vistas*, 1871

contents ❧

part three ☐ challenges to democratic revisionism

part four ☐ strategies for normative, empirical, and analytical work

index

introduction ✍

Shortly after World War II, a world-wide UNESCO survey showed the concept of democracy to be sufficiently elastic to allow every nation to applaud it. The principles of democracy found universal acclaim. Today the democratic ideology is in fact so pervasive that it has become easy to see mankind as having reached the end of ideological conflict. Eulogizing political equality, we readily assume that at least one ideal preoccupying previous generations of political thinkers—the ideal of widespread popular participation in political processes—has finally ceased to be controversial. Increasingly, we agree that men should participate in formulating whatever policies affect their lives—at least to the extent that participation will not threaten political stability, orderly economic growth, and industrial development. And since men everywhere appear to want the large-scale industrial society (or at least the comforts it promises), the remaining political problems, so it would seem, are merely practical ones. They are problems not of principle but of social engineering. It becomes sufficient to engage in empirical inquiry, to ask how to attain a maximum of "democracy" without sacrificing the obvious benefits of industrialism.

Accepting an industrial order, we feel bound to consent to the social discipline it entails. Having moved from a predominantly agrarian to a predominantly industrial economy, we have agreed on the way the labor of individuals must first be divided and then controlled within hierarchically structured organizations. We have realized that we cannot dispense with inequality: efficient mass production calls for specialists who must be coordinated by superiors who in turn must be governed in what we see as a social chain of command.

The organizational characteristics of industrial society are widely accepted as "given"; they are assumed to lie in the very nature of industrialism, a manifestation of its inner logic. As a consequence, we are prepared to adapt ourselves and our beliefs to our industrial environment. We inquire not how industrialism might be geared to democratic ideals but rather how democratic ideals might be geared to industrialism. For us, the hierarchical organization of an industrial society has somehow become *real*, and to accept it is to be "realistic." We believe that it makes demands and that men respond, or must be made to respond. Accordingly, we trim and adjust and revise the ideals that come into conflict with the demands of industrialism—the demands that labor be divided, that the control of men and machines be centralized, and that the few at the top be empowered to make the decisions for the many at the bottom. A stable, large-scale industrial society is said to imply the surrender of democratic principles—personal autonomy, equality in decision making, fraternity.

If we nevertheless continue to uphold the ideals of self-government and self-determination, this is because they are seen as relevant to, but a restricted part of, the policy-making process. The conditions for democracy, so we affirm with relief, are satisfied so long as men have the opportunity to vote periodically in free elections. It seems sufficient to control the elites that govern us. Should we reject such democratic elitism and desire more personal participation, more intimate and continuous involvement, this must occur in private groups, within associations unconcerned with the major issues of public policy. We thus come to believe that plans for extensive political participation are unrealistic. It becomes merely sentimental to insist on direct popular involvement when dealing with such matters as economic and industrial development, urban planning, and social welfare. Government by the people—as opposed to government for them—is regarded as wasteful and inefficient; it is perceived as a threat to our industrial order. Though not always expressed in these terms, this would appear to be the prevailing consensus.

One purpose of this collection of readings is to show that there is considerable disagreement about the place, significance, and promise of democracy in modern life. Rousseau, Paine, Babeuf, and Jefferson remain the adversaries of Burke, Bonald, Madison, and Tocqueville. Without being explicitly formulated, different theories of democracy continue to compete. They make different claims on us as citizens and impose differing societal arrangements. To embrace one or another theory of democracy is in fact to entertain different expectations of human capacities and social possibilities. Insofar as various theories compete and challenge one another, ideological conflict persists—however much it is disguised when it assumes the austere form of contemporary academic methodological disputes.

Although one conception of democracy has emerged as dominant today, offering itself as the most realistic and least sentimental, its specific implications are not readily apparent. This volume should help define the dominant theory more sharply, first by revealing how it has adjusted older conceptions to present-day needs and then by contrasting it with competitors that seek to recall us to the fundamentals of democracy. The readings should therefore bring the contemporary theories into sharper focus while disclosing the outlines of a continuing conflict. Dramatizing opposing points of view, they should enable us to evaluate their respective claims. Finally, they should provide us with an intelligible basis for moving beyond the present theoretical situation. Becoming clear about the present condition of democratic theory, we may find it easier to formulate and test our own vision of possibilities.

In view of these aims, the strategy this volume offers for dealing with the relevant material should be evident: Part One highlights elements of a normative theory of democracy that, though largely derived from eighteenth-century sources, continues to ring true. Part Two presents efforts to adjust the ideal to the demands of modern organizational life in the name of realism. Part Three presents a variety of empirical and analytical critiques of the prevailing realism. The concluding Part Four offers suggestions for transcending the existing theoretical predicaments, that is, programs for analysis and research designed to shift the current debate to a new level.

Considerable current debate relating to democratic theory has found no place in this volume. There is nothing, for example, to indicate the prodemocratic impulse implicit in contemporary Chinese assaults on the cult of the military, industrial, medical, and cultural expert. Polish and Yugoslavian efforts to use the "essential" Marx as a weapon against established bureaucracies are ignored. There are no examples of those defenses of one-party democracies that are broadcast today in some of the developing nations. Nor are there intimations of the stirrings on the fringe of

American politics, the efforts to make a coherent case for "industrial democracy" and "participatory democracy." To have provided samples of these would have detracted from one of the underlying purposes of this volume: to lead the student to discover the ideological content implicit in various scientific approaches to understanding the subject matter of politics.

This volume would be less concerned with the methodological issues troubling the practitioners of political science if methodological conflicts did not conceal substantive conflicts about the ideal organization of society. Because the study of politics as a self-consciously scientific movement is predominantly American, most of the material included is drawn from American sources. The result is bound to appear parochial. The final justification for such selectivity, not to say bias, is that the readings should do more than simply expose the student to explicit ideological messages. They should also enable him to become aware of the forms that contain the messages—the methodologies which themselves are permeated by the ideals they serve. If we wish to appreciate matters of style, form, procedure, posture, and method—recognizing their *value*—the specific limits of this volume should require no further apology.

A significant impetus to the thinking that underlies this collection, it should be acknowledged, was given by Lane Davis' analysis, "The Cost of Realism: Contemporary Restatements of Democracy," which appeared in 1964 and is here reprinted. Davis (along with Graeme Duncan and Steven Lukes) was one of the first to imply that ideological struggles about the meaning of democracy may be buried in the work of social scientists. The selected readings stress the implicit conflict between, for example, Robert A. Dahl and Robert E. Agger rather than between Tocqueville and Rousseau largely because of Davis' seminal essay.

This project would have been pursued less vigorously had it not been for two publishers who rejected it because (they rightly claimed) it betrayed a bias against democratic elitism, "realism," and "pluralist theory." It has also benefited from the encouragement, practical direction, and editorial help of Dennis F. Thompson, Charles A. McCoy, John Playford, and Kirk Thompson. They have inspired and all but compiled this anthology. It was thus left to the editor merely to edit, and to assume responsibility for errors of judgment.

H. S. K.

Honolulu, Hawaii
January, 1970

part one ❧

the
democratic
ideal

There has never been much enthusiasm for drawing the mass of men into the political arena. Since classical antiquity, the case for democracy has been more often met with critical doubts than approval. Although Pericles in his famous Funeral Oration extolled the virtues of popular participation in politics, celebrating the "happy versatility" of the Athenian democracy, he made no case for having *all* men experience its rewards. And Aristotle, having discussed the implications of democratic regimes, saw them as nothing more than a perversion of the most practicable state, the polity. The polity, he wrote, was to allow neither the poor nor the wealthy to rule. Essentially government by and for the middle classes, it was to give a measure of recognition to the claims of all interests; it was to bring man's diverse desires and ideals into a state of balance. While such a state might not bring out the best in men, neither would it allow the outbreak of the worst. If men were to live at least a moderately decent life, not everyone could be admitted to the political stage. In view of limited material resources, it was simply not prudent to encourage the development of everyone's potentialities by permitting full-scale participation in public affairs.

I

Although the great benefits of politics could thus be fully appreciated (as they are in Hannah Arendt's essay), they were reserved on the most practical of grounds for the few, namely, those qualified by birth or property ownership to take part in politics. To provide the education in civic virtue that would make it safe for the mass of men to enter the public stage seemed to be economically and psychologically impossible. It appeared irrelevant to speculate about a regime enabling each individual to develop his potentialities by participating in a process in which he could bring his own egoism and altruism into balance.

The case for authentic self-government did not become generally compelling until it was conceived of as practicable, or at least until aristocratic orders began to realize that it would no longer be prudent to remain intransigent opponents of democratic tendencies. Not until the eighteenth century (which dates it perhaps too precisely) was the case for democratic participation in the process of government made so tellingly that it forced those in power to react.

As absolutist government and older economic and religious establishments were assailed, the case was made for the democratization of politics. The initial theoretical thrust came from such English Puritans of the left as the Diggers and Levellers. The classic democratic statement was ultimately to be provided by John Locke's attack on the doctrine that kings ruled by divine right. Locke sought to free the individual person from arbitrary government and establish him as an independent, sovereign being who would be guided by his conscience, by "right reason." Governments were to derive their authority from the free consent of the governed. Those in power were to be curbed by a society of equals.

The equalitarian component of democratic theory was developed in the writings of Jean-Jacques Rousseau, who saw man as a community-building animal, naturally communicative, inclined toward cooperation and fraternity. Attacking the conventions and restraints imposed on men by the society of his day, he postulated a state in which all men would accept only such restraints as they themselves participated in formulating.

While these philosophers provided us with the foundation for a plausible conception of democratic politics, they scarcely pushed their thinking to logical conclusions. Understandably, they were always inhibited by what they believed to be possible in practice. Locke not only limited the franchise but also rejected direct participation in policy making. And Rousseau, suspecting that man's fraternal impulses would not express themselves spontaneously, insisted on an imposed civil religion to help maintain the consensus, assure altruism, and enforce patriotic sentiments. Nor were such individualists as Thomas Jefferson,

Jeremy Bentham, or John Stuart Mill prepared to radicalize the case for democracy and argue that it alone would ensure the full development of man's diverse capacities. The need for external discipline, a system of constitutional checks, was stressed by all but a few liberal anarchists. And these could readily be dismissed as utopians.

Yet there was an acknowledgement, sometimes merely implicit, that a democratic regime is desirable not only because it produces public policies that express a widespread consensus, not only because democracy compels the leadership to attend to the wishes of the electorate, but also because it makes participating in a common undertaking intrinsically rewarding. Mill came closest to advancing a view of democracy as an end in itself—not simply as a means for enriching one's private life. So did Karl Marx as he briefly sketched out his communist ideal. The selections by Ernest Barker and John Dewey make this point most explicitly.

The essays in this section should contribute to a normative conception of democracy as a procedure for promoting the development of all men by inducing them to identify their interests and test their values. Ideally, a democratic regime will maintain public stages on which men can become aware of themselves and of one another. On such stages, men will feel encouraged to perform, to try out various parts and reveal their ability to master them. They will play mutually conflicting roles and seek to govern their diverse impulses in the process. Including others in the drama of their existence, meeting others on terms of equality, they will necessarily enlarge the range of their sympathies. "The peculiar characteristic of civilized beings," John Stuart Mill wrote in *Principles of Political Economy* (1848), "is the capacity of cooperation; and this like other faculties tends to improve by practice, and becomes capable of assuming a constantly wider sphere of action." In action, incorporating the interests of others, individuals will display their capacity for continual growth. A political order that aspires to anything less, the following essays imply, must embarrass us.

1 ❧ ON PUBLIC HAPPINESS

HANNAH ARENDT

... Americans knew that public freedom consisted in having a share in public business, and that the activities connected with this business by no means constituted a burden but gave those who discharged them in public a feeling of happiness they could acquire nowhere else. They knew very well, and John Adams was bold enough to formulate this knowledge time and again, that the people went to the town assemblies, as their representatives later were to go to the famous Conventions, neither exclusively because of duty nor, and even less, to serve their own interests but most of all because they enjoyed the discussions, the deliberations, and the making of decisions. What brought them together was "the world and the public interest of liberty" (Harrington) and what moved them was "the passion for distinction," which John Adams held to be "more essential and remarkable" than any other human faculty: "Wherever men, women, or children, are to be found whether they be old or young, rich or poor, high or low, wise or foolish, ignorant or learned, every individual is seen to be strongly actuated by a desire to be seen, heard, talked of, approved and respected by the people about him, and within his knowledge." The virtue of this passion he called "emulation," the "desire to excel another," and its vice he called "ambition" because it "aims at power as a means of distinction."[1]

* * *

Jefferson himself—in a paper for the Virginia Convention of 1774 which in many respects anticipated the Declaration of Independence—had declared that "our ancestors" when they left the "British dominions in Europe" exercised "a right which nature has given all men . . . of establishing new societies, under such laws and regulations as to them shall seem most likely to promote public happiness."[2] If Jefferson was right and it was in quest of "public happiness" that the "free inhabitants of the British dominions" had emigrated to America, then the colonies in the New World must

FROM *On Revolution*, by Hannah Arendt, pp. 115, 123–124, 127–28, 259. Copyright © 1963 by Hannah Arendt. Reprinted by permission of The Viking Press, Inc.
[1] *Discourses on Davila, Works* (Boston, 1851), VI, 232–233.
[2] See "A Summary View of the Rights of British America, 1774," in *The Life and Selected Writings* (New York: Modern Library), pp. 293 ff.

have been the breeding grounds of revolutionaries from the beginning. And, by the same token, they must have been prompted even then by some sort of dissatisfaction with the rights and liberties of Englishmen, prompted by a desire for some kind of freedom which the "free inhabitants" of the mother country did not enjoy. This freedom they called later, when they had come to taste it, "public happiness," and it consisted in the citizen's right of access to the public realm, in his share in public power—to be "a participator in the government of affairs" in Jefferson's telling phrase[3]— as distinct from the generally recognized rights of subjects to be protected by the government in the pursuit of private happiness even against public power, that is, distinct from rights which only tyrannical power would abolish. The very fact that the word "happiness" was chosen in laying claim to a share in public power indicates strongly that there existed in the country, prior to the revolution, such a thing as "public happiness," and that men knew they could not be altogether "happy" if their happiness was located and enjoyed only in private life.

*　　*　　*

If the ultimate end of revolution was freedom and the constitution of a public space where freedom could appear, the *constitutio libertatis,* then the [Jeffersonian system of] wards, the only tangible place where everyone could be free, actually were the end of the great republic whose chief purpose in domestic affairs should have been to provide the people with such places of freedom and to protect them. The basic assumption of the ward system, whether Jefferson knew it or not, was that no one could be called happy without his share in public happiness, that no one could be called free without his experience in public freedom, and that no one could be called either happy or free without participating, and having a share, in public power.

*　　*　　*

Jefferson's true notion of happiness comes out very clearly (without any of the distortions through a traditional, conventional framework of concepts which, it turned out, was much harder to break than the structure of the traditional form of government) when he lets himself go in a mood of playful and sovereign irony and concludes one of his letters to Adams as follows: "May we meet there again, in Congress, with our ancient Colleagues, and

---

[3] In the important letter on the "republics of the wards" to Joseph C. Cabell, February 2, 1816. *Ibid.,* p. 661.

receive with them the seal of approbation 'Well done, good and faithful servants.' "⁴ Here, behind the irony, we have the candid admission that life in Congress, the joys of discourse, of legislation, of transacting business, of persuading and being persuaded, were to Jefferson no less conclusively a foretaste of an eternal bliss to come than the delights of contemplation had been for medieval piety. For even "the seal of approbation" is not at all the common reward for virtue in a future state; it is the applause, the demonstration of acclaim, "the esteem of the world" of which Jefferson in another context says that there had been a time when it "was of higher value in my eye than everything in it."⁵

2 ✣ DEMOCRACY AS ACTIVITY

ERNEST BARKER

. . . The individual personality of man alone has intrinsic and ultimate worth, and having also the capacity of development has also an intrinsic and ultimate claim to the essential condition of its development. Liberty will then be that essential condition; and the essence of liberty will be that it is a condition, or status, or quality, which individual personality must possess in order that it may translate itself from what it is to what it has the capacity of becoming.

The personality which has this capacity of development, of translating itself from its present self to a future and higher self is moral personality. It is something more than psychological personality—the personality which consists in being aware of sensations, and in determining action thereby. It is a moral personality

---

⁴ Letter of April 11, 1823, in L. J. Cappon (ed.) *The Adams-Jefferson Letters* (Chapel Hill, 1959), p. 594.
⁵ See the letter to Madison, June 9, 1793.
From Ernest Barker, *Reflections on Government* (London: Oxford University Press, 1942), pp. 15–19; *Principles of Social and Political Theory* (Oxford: Clarendon Press, 1951), pp. 203–209.

which consists in being conscious of conceptions—conceptions of some possible good—and in determining action in the light of such conceptions. The liberty which such a personality claims is therefore a moral liberty. It is a liberty which consists in possessing the status or condition or quality of determining one's own action by one's own conception of the good. The essential ground for claiming such liberty is that personality only develops, and disengages its intrinsic worth, if it determines itself by its own conceptions in the process of that development. If it were not self-determined, but other-determined, it would simply stay, in itself, on its own existing level, even if its acts, considered simply as acts, were raised to another level. Moral personality can only develop through the moral liberty of a personal will which wills for itself the conceptions which it has itself embraced.

But no moral personality exists *in vacuo*. A moral personality could not exist or act unless it existed and acted in a society of other such personalities. It lives by acting upon those who are like itself and of the same substance as itself, and by being acted upon by them in turn. If we abolish the notion of this interplay of like agents, we abolish the very idea of moral action, and we thus extinguish moral personality, which exists in and by such action. Two consequences follow from this fact that the existence of moral personality implies a society of such personalities. The first conclusion is formal. Because the personalities are like in their nature—of the same substance and the same worth—each must respect in the others what it values in itself, and each must allow, and indeed claim, for the others the same liberty of self-determination which it also claims for itself. Each being an end in himself, and for himself, the society of all must be necessarily based on the formal rule that each shall be treated by all as a free moral agent, and any social control—any adjustment of personal relations intended to ease their possible friction—must be compatible with this rule. In other words, such control or adjustment must be intended in the interest of moral liberty; must seek to remove obstacles to that liberty; must serve, not to diminish, but to defend and extend, the area of self-control.

The second conclusion is more substantial. If all are beings of a like nature, seeking alike to determine their action by a like conception of the good, we must not conceive them merely as existing in juxtaposition: we must also conceive them as acting in collaboration. They will exchange ideas, and thus clarify their conception of the good: they will borrow impulses, and thus corroborate their will for its attainment. The process of moral life, as it unfolds itself in a society, is thus a process by which the idea of the good becomes an idea of social thought and the will for the good becomes a matter of social volition. We must indeed, each of us severally, *appropriate* the idea: we must make it our own, and will it, as our own, with an effort of our own will; we must even, if we can, go beyond the idea as it stands at any given moment, adding some new thought of our own, seeking to realize it in our own lives, and offering it for incorporation in the general social stock. But always, behind ourselves, stands the society of ourselves—the general bank and capital of common thought and common will, to which we have all contributed and on which we can all draw, but which never absolves us from the duty of keeping our own account.

This society, and its great inherited deposit, are facts which we must never ignore. Equally, they are facts which we must never exaggerate. It is easy to fall into the idea that the society of ourselves, being so majestical, is something other than ourselves—higher, transcendent, a being beyond our beings. But the common thought and will which the society of ourselves precipitates is not a something above us, or in any way separate from us. We ourselves have made it, and are making it still: it is our own creation, and the work of our own minds. So far as it controls us, consistently with our nature as moral persons, it controls us from within, and not with the force of an external presence; it controls us as freely accepted and genuinely appropriated thought, which is part of our own personality. And as we must freely accept it if we are ourselves to be free, so we may also be bound, in hours of crisis and ultimate decision, to reject it freely for just the same reason. There are times and seasons when we may feel it our duty, and our true liberty, to guide ourselves by a conception of good which is beyond social thought and social will, and proceeds immediately from our own deepest self. Resistance is part of liberty, as well as acceptance. But the ground and the source of resistance is the same as that of acceptance.

Upon this basis we may attain some conception of the relation of man and the state, and of the place of liberty in that conception. The moral personality of the individual, determining itself by its own conception of a good, is the beginning from which we start and the end with which we conclude. But this is not all. There is a middle as well as a beginning and an end. If we made the beginning and the end everything—if we refused to interpose a middle term, and to recognize that society intervenes between the beginning and the end—we should be compelled to embrace the gospel of anarchism. But the middle exists, and we need not embrace that gospel. The society of selves is a fact as well as the self, and the two are not independent but interdependent facts. We may even say that the society of selves exists with a double existence— existence by formal rule, and existence by dynamic process which produces a substance or content.

So far as the society of selves exists by formal rule, it exists as a scheme for the adjustment of relations. Under this scheme all alike are recognized as free agents; the conditions of their free agency are guaranteed; and while each is thereby limited for the sake of the freedom of all, each is also secured in a guaranteed freedom of action which he would not otherwise possess. This involves a system of law, intended to secure free agency and the conditions of such agency; and thus liberty—of the sort which we have termed by the name of personal or civil—is the end (as it is also the source) of the system of law which expresses the existence of the society by the method of formal rule.

So far as the society exists by dynamic process, it exists for and by the mutual interchange of conceptions and convictions about the good to be attained in human life and the methods of its attainment. It thus exists for and by a system of social discussion, under which each is free to give and receive and all can freely join in determining the content or substance of social thought— the good to be sought, and the way of life in which it issues. Now such discussion is also, as we have seen, the essence of democracy. It is the core of that political, or constitutional, liberty which exists under a system of democracy.

* * *

If the state can be regarded as mediating social thought about justice to its members, and as expressing in its law the product of such thought, we may draw from that premise the conclusion that the state should itself correspond, in its own nature and operation, to the process of social thought which it mediates, and should thus be a broad open channel for the flow of the product which it expresses. The process of social thought is a process in which all the members of society can freely share, and to which they can all contribute freely. It follows that, if there is to be correspondence and a broad open flow, the process of the activity of the state should also be a process in which all its members can freely share and to which they can all freely contribute. We may argue that this demand is satisfied, and satisfied only, by the democratic state. . . .

* * *

To find a firm basis for a theory of the democratic method of government in the modern state, we must go back to the process of social thought from which the state issues and to which it always remains attached. The process of social thought is naturally and necessarily a process of discussion. Ideas emerge here and there: each emergent idea becomes a magnet which attracts a clustering group of adherents: the various ideas, and the various groups they attract, must either engage in a war of competition with one another to achieve a victory, or attempt a method of composition which fuses and blends them together in peace. The military idea of a war of competition between ideas is prominent in the philosophy of Hegel. His dialectical idealism (which Marx turned upside down or as he preferred to say, "right side up again," in his dialectical materialism) assumes a war of ideas, in which "one shrewd thought devours another": a battle of thesis and antithesis in which each side fights for itself. But even Hegel's military conception of the war of ideas ends in a sort of composition between thesis and antithesis; or, more exactly, it ends by producing the synthesis of a higher truth in which the partial truths of the thesis and the antithesis are abolished and transcended. It has thus, after all, some approach to the principle of discussion; but Hegel's theory of discussion is rather that of a logical process inside a solitary mind (even if that mind be conceived as the "objective" mind of a whole society) than that of a social process among and between a number of minds. The theory which is implied in Aristotle's *Politics* is much nearer to the idea of such a social process. Instead of assuming a war of two conflicting ideas, to be ended by a transcendent and triumphant synthesis, he assumes a plurality of social ideas, to be fused and blended together in a "scheme of composition." Just as it takes all sorts of men to make a world, so it takes all sorts of ideas to produce a "catholic" and all-round view. Aristotle applies this conception to the field of culture and the province of artistic judgment: here, he says, "some appreciate one aspect, and some another but all together appreciate all." But he also applies it generally to the whole field of social thought; and he applies it, in particular, to matters of political judgment. The many, he holds, "when they meet together" and put their minds fairly to one another can achieve a composition of ideas which gives their judgment a general validity.

If we follow the guidance of Aristotle, we shall say that social thought proceeds by the way of a plurality of ideas, by the way of debate and discussion between the different ideas, "when they meet together" and come into contact with one another and by the way of a composition of ideas attained through such debate and discussion. We shall also say that this social way must also be, and also is, the political way: in other words it must also be, and also is, the method of the state's government and the way of the state's operation. This is not only because the state should be true to the society from which it comes and on which it continues to rest: it is also because the way of society (the way of plurality of ideas, debate among them, and composition of them) is right in itself and universally right—right for society, right for the state, and right wherever men are gathered together and have to act together. The one way to get at practical truth, the right thing to do, the straight line of action is, in any form of group, the way of thinking things over together and talking them over together, with a view to finding some composition of the different threads of thought. It is the way of the Friends, when they seek what they call "the sense of the meeting." It is the way of democracy, which is not a solution, but a way of seeking solutions—not a form of state devoted to this or that particular end (whether private enterprise or public management), but a form of state devoted, whatever its end may be to a single means and method of determining that end. The core of democracy is choice and not something chosen; choice among a number of ideas, and choice, too, of the scheme on which those ideas are eventually composed. Democracy is incompatible with any form of one-idea state because its essence is hospitality to a plurality of ideas, and because its method (which is also its essence) consists in holding together a number of different ideas with a view to comparison and composition of their differences. The democratic criticism of the one-idea state is not a criticism of its object (which may also be the object of the democratic state, or at any rate part of its object): it is a criticism of its whole process of life.

The last phrase, "process of life," suggests a further consideration which is of vital importance in the theory of democracy. One of the archbishops of Canterbury, Frederic Temple, once said that there were two schools of political thought: one which held that politics existed for the production of a result, or the *ergon* school; and another which held that politics was valuable in itself as a process of activity, or the *energeia* school. The school of production judged politics by the results which it produced: the school of process preferred to judge on a different basis, and it was content, and more than content, if the process of the political life of a community elicited and enlisted for its operation the minds and wills of its members, thus aiding, and indeed in its measure constituting, the development of their capacities as persons. The distinction here suggested, which goes back to Aristotle,[1] is a just and pregnant distinction. We are naturally apt to think of politics in terms of making, rather than of doing, as if our political activity were directed wholly to achieving an object outside itself (and not immanent in itself), such as a scheme of legal order, or an adjustment of economic relations, or some other similar structure. But this is not the whole of the matter, or even the greater part. It is certainly true, and indeed it has already been urged in the course of our argument, that the state as a legal association must necessarily produce a result: it must produce a scheme of declared and enforced law which gives expression to the idea of justice. But there are two other things which must also be borne in mind. First, the ultimate purpose behind justice, and therefore behind law, is the development of the capacities of human personality in as many persons as possible to the greatest possible extent. That is the final result which the state must produce—or rather help to produce; for the result produces itself in each person through his own internal activity, even if it needs help, in the way of removal of hindrances and the offering of opportunities, in order to produce itself fully. This first reflection naturally leads to the second. If we hold that behind and beyond the *production* of law by the state there is a *process* of personal activity and personal development in its members, we may go on to say that the production should itself be drawn into the process. In other words we may argue that the productive effort of the state, the effort of declaring and enforcing a system of law, should also be a process in which, and through which, each member of the state is spurred into personal development, because he is drawn into free participation in one of the greatest of all our secular human activities.

These reflections suggest a second main justification of the democratic system. Not only is it justified, as we saw at the beginning of this section, by the fact that it makes the state true to the method of general discussion and composition of ideas which is the method of society; it is also justified, as we now see, by the fact that it makes the state, in the very process of its own operation, true to the fundamental purpose which lies behind its operation, the purpose of the development in action of the capacities of personality.

---

[1] The distinction between production (*poiesis*) and action (*praxis*) is discussed in the *Ethics*, Book VI, cc. iii–v. The gist of the argument is that "Production has an end other than itself: action cannot have; for good action is itself its own end."

3 ❧ DEMOCRACY AS A WAY OF LIFE

JOHN DEWEY

Democracy is much broader than a special political form, a method of conducting government, of making laws and carrying on governmental administration by means of popular suffrage and elected officers. It is that, of course. But it is something broader and deeper than that. The political and governmental phase of democracy is a means, the best means so far found, for realizing ends that lie in the wide domain of human relationships and the development of human personality. It is, as we often say, though perhaps without appreciating all that is involved in the saying, a way of life, social and individual. The keynote of democracy as a way of life may be expressed, it seems to me, as the necessity for the participation of every mature human being in formation of the values that regulate the living of men together: which is necessary from the standpoint of both the general social welfare and the full development of human beings as individuals.

Universal suffrage, recurring elections, responsibility of those who are in political power to the voters, and the other factors of democratic government are means that have been found expedient for realizing democracy as the truly human way of living. They are not a final end and a final value. They are to be judged on the basis of their contribution to end. It is a form of idolatry to erect means into the end which they serve. Democratic political forms are simply the best means that human wit has devised up to a special time in history. But they rest back upon the idea that no man or limited set of men is wise enough or good enough to rule others without their consent; the positive meaning of this statement is that all those who are affected by social institutions must have a share in producing and managing them. The two facts that each one is influenced in what he does and enjoys and in what he becomes by the institutions under which he lives, and that therefore he shall have, in a democracy, a voice in shaping them, are the passive and active sides of the same fact.

The development of political democracy came about through substitution of the method of mutual consultation and voluntary agreement for the method of subordination of the many to the few

FROM John Dewey, "Democracy and Educational Administration," in Joseph Ratner (ed.), *Intelligence in the Modern World* (New York: Random House, 1939), pp. 400–404.

enforced from above. Social arrangements which involve fixed subordination are maintained by coercion. The coercion need not be physical. There have existed, for short periods, benevolent despotisms. But coercion of some sort there has been; perhaps economic, certainly psychological and moral. The very fact of exclusion from participation is a subtle form of suppression. It gives individuals no opportunity to reflect and decide upon what is good for them. Others who are supposed to be wiser and who in any case have more power decide the question for them and also decide the methods and means by which subjects may arrive at the enjoyment of what is good for them. This form of coercion and suppression is more subtle and more effective than are overt intimidation and restraint. When it is habitual and embodied in social institutions, it seems the normal and natural state of affairs. The mass usually become unaware that they have a claim to a development of their own powers. Their experience is so restricted that they are not conscious of restriction. It is part of the democratic conception that they as individuals are not the only sufferers, but that the whole social body is deprived of the potential resources that should be at its service. The individuals of the submerged mass may not be very wise. But there is one thing they are wiser about than anybody else can be, and that is where the shoe pinches, the troubles they suffer from.

The foundation of democracy is faith in the capacities of human nature; faith in human intelligence and in the power of pooled and cooperative experience. It is not belief that these things are complete but that if given a show they will grow and be able to generate progressively the knowledge and wisdom needed to guide collective action. Every autocratic and authoritarian scheme of social action rests on a belief that the needed intelligence is confined to a superior few, who because of inherent natural gifts are endowed with the ability and the right to control the conduct of others, laying down principles and rules and directing the ways in which they are carried out. It would be foolish to deny that much can be said for this point of view. It is that which controlled human relations in social groups for much the greater part of human history. The democratic faith has emerged very, very recently in the history of mankind. Even where democracies now exist, men's minds and feelings are still permeated with ideas about leadership imposed from above, ideas that developed in the long early history of mankind. After democratic political institutions were nominally established, beliefs and ways of looking at life and of acting that originated when men and women were externally controlled and subjected to arbitrary power persisted in the family, the church, business, and the school, and experience shows that as long as they persist there, political democracy is not secure.

Belief in equality is an element of the democratic credo. It is not, however, belief in equality of natural endowments. Those who proclaimed the idea of equality did not suppose they were enunciating a psychological doctrine, but a legal and political one. All individuals are entitled to equality of treatment by law and in its administration. Each one is affected equally in quality if not in quantity by the institutions under which he lives and has an equal right to express his judgment, although the weight of his judgment may not be equal in amount when it enters into the pooled result to that of others. In short, each one is equally an individual and entitled to equal opportunity of development of his own capacities, be they large or small in range. Moreover, each has needs of his own, as significant to him as those of others are to them. The very fact of natural and psychological inequality is all the more reason for establishment by law of equality of opportunity, since otherwise the former becomes a means of oppression of the less gifted.

While what we call intelligence may be distributed in unequal amounts, it is the democratic faith that it is sufficiently general so that each individual has something to contribute, and the value of each contribution can be assessed only as it enters into the final pooled intelligence constituted by the contributions of all. Every authoritarian scheme, on the contrary, assumes that its value may be assessed by some *prior* principle, if not of family and birth or race and color or possession of material wealth, then by the position and rank a person occupies in the existing social scheme. The democratic faith in equality is the faith that each individual shall have the chance and opportunity to contribute whatever he is capable of contributing and that the value of his contribution be decided by its place and function in the organized total of similar contributions, not on the basis of prior status of any kind whatever.

I have emphasized in what precedes the importance of the effective release of intelligence in connection with personal experience in the democratic way of living. I have done so purposely because democracy is so often and so naturally associated in our minds with freedom of *action,* forgetting the importance of freed intelligence which is necessary to direct and to warrant freedom of action. Unless freedom of individual action has intelligence and informed conviction back of it, its manifestation is almost sure to result in confusion and disorder. The democratic idea of freedom is not the right of each individual to *do* as he pleases, even if it be qualified by adding "provided he does not interfere with the same freedom on the part of others." While the idea is not always, not often enough, expressed in words, the basic freedom is that of freedom of *mind* and of whatever degree of freedom of action and experience is necessary to produce freedom of intelligence. The modes of freedom guaranteed in the Bill of Rights are all of this nature: freedom of belief and conscience, of expression of opinion, of assembly for discussion and conference, of the press as an organ of communication. They are guaranteed because without them individuals are not free to develop and society is deprived of what they might contribute.

4 ❧ THE CITIZEN AS PUBLIC AGENT

JOSEPH TUSSMAN

If I had to select a figure of speech which, upon analysis, would reveal the basic dilemma of our political life, I would choose the "marketplace of ideas." "The best test of truth," one of our sages has told us, "is the power of the thought to get itself accepted in the competition of the market." (How I wish some genius had thrown equal light on another dark area of our lives by proclaiming that the best test of virtue is "the power of a desire to get itself accepted in the competition of the market." But we must work with what we have and regretfully I leave the marketplace of virtue and take up my drier theme.)

The marketplace of ideas! Do we appreciate enough the revolutionary daring of that conception? At one bold stroke it identifies the deliberative and the bargaining arts, turns the scientist into a businessman, the sage into the salesman. This is the most significant triumph of a business civilization. Or it would be, if it did

FROM Joseph Tussman, *Obligation and the Body Politic*, pp. 104–121. Copyright © 1960 by Oxford University Press, Inc. Reprinted by permission of Oxford University Press, Inc.

not ensure disaster. For, unfortunately, we need the product of deliberation, and, however difficult it may be for us to recapture the sense of difference, deliberating and bargaining are not the same, neither in process nor in result. Education turns on this difference. The school, said one of the Popes, is either a Temple or a Den. It is, I would agree, either the nurturer of the deliberative animal or, failing that, a bordello of the mind.

The aristocratic theory of government, whatever its shortcomings in practice, also rests upon this distinction. It sees governing as a difficult art or profession requiring a high order of intelligence, discipline, and character. Its basic assertion is that only a few are capable of meeting the demands of this form of deliberative life. The democrat, when democracy was a creed that mattered, did not disagree about the difficulty of governing. He argued, rather, that all (or most) men have deliberative and moral potentiality and that given the proper education and environment, each could take his place in the deliberative forum and share the responsibilities of sovereignty. And why should he do this? Not simply in order to get more, but primarily in order to develop his deliberative and moral character and to achieve the dignity of being a ruler of the society of which he is a member. For this is the genuine democratic urge, impervious to all the cornucopias of the most benevolent paternalism.

With both misgivings and hopes we gingerly extended the franchise and launched into mass education. But where is the optimist today who has not shaken his head over apathy and private preoccupation, over the growing complexity of public issues, over the shortcomings of public education, and the mind-destroying uses of mass communication. Have we not been brought, if we think about these matters, to consider again whether the life of politics is indeed the life for everyone, whether there are not also other paths than the political to dignity and self-realization?

The essential feature of a democratic polity is its concern for the participation of the member in the process by which the community is governed. It goes beyond the insistence that politics or government be included among the careers open to talent. It gives to each citizen a public office, a place in the sovereign tribunal and, unless it is a sham, it places its destiny in the hands of that tribunal. Here is the ultimate decision-maker, the court of last appeal, the guardian of the guardians, government "by the people." The significance of democracy as an ideal rests on the significance of participation in the sovereign tribunal; for the democrat, being tribunal-worthy is what being a rational animal means, and the character we bring to the office of the citizen is the crucial test of culture. It is not clear that we are passing that test.

It is altogether possible that we may drift increasingly in the direction of ritualistic democracy. We will feel little pain and the portrait of Lincoln will not come crashing from the wall. But popular participation in politics may become increasingly meaningless, popular mandates increasingly directionless, as we seek to protect the "responsible" institutions of government from the effects of mindless participation and clamor. Without too much imagination we can see the Presidential Sweepstakes becoming the main event, combining the excitement of a national lottery with the thrill of a coronation. We will redouble our efforts and turn out the votes, but the vote will decide less and less as we move deeper into the morass of public relations, the projection of images, and the painless engineering of consent. Perhaps this path is inevitable for us, but it is not democracy—only its tragic parody.

The alternative is difficult indeed. It demands the reshaping of the electorate into a genuinely deliberative tribunal capable of dealing responsibly with fundamental issues. It would require vastly more and better education than we have yet been able to achieve, and would require a revolution in our habits and institutions of communication. We would need to transform ourselves from domestic into political animals. The task seems overwhelming.

It is here, as we gird ourselves for heroic effort, that the temptation appears—not the aristocratic temptation to which the Grand Inquisitor succumbed but a temptation which parades itself as democratic. It is the temptation of the marketplace. Why, it whispers, dream of impossible tribunals manned by thoughtful, devoted, disinterested angels deliberating about the common good? There is a better plan, which takes men as they are and asks of them only what is possible and pleasant. We know this story well: the unleashing of competitiveness, the guiltless assertion of self-interest, the eternal selling of everything—our products and services, our programs and ideas, ourselves. Why man a tribunal when we can have a market instead? Come, let us bargain together.

It would be a major task to trace and assess the impact of the marketplace upon our culture. I cannot be concerned here even with the broad range of its effect upon our political life. But the attempt to understand the problems of political democracy in America today involves us inescapably in the struggle between the life of the marketplace and the life of the forum or tribunal.

We do not, of course, hear much of this struggle in our public education. The received doctrine beds down the lion with the lamb. But our attempts at education for democracy, for participation in public life, are hopelessly perplexed by the divergent demands of marketplace and tribunal. How, for example shall we teach our children to communicate with the necessary respect for the integrity of language, and for each other, when we support (almost as culture heroes) a large class of professional liars to hail with impartial sincerity the claim of any client? This is not intended as a "personal" remark; the point is precisely that advertising is a respectable profession in our marketplace culture. But how, supporting such a profession, can we really make the point that the integrity of communication is the wellspring of a community's life? It is no answer to say that we have learned to defend ourselves by not believing what we hear, or that propaganda will counter propaganda and the truth will prevail even though no one tells it. We are poisoning the wells, and we cannot live on antidotes.

Add to our prevailing style of communication the familiar emphasis on individualism, private interest, and private enterprise and the story of our education for democracy is almost told. We teach men to compete and bargain. Are we to be surprised, then, at the corruption of the tribunal into its marketplace parody?

Democratic political life turns upon the office of the citizen and upon the demands of that office. The citizen is, in his political capacity, a public agent with all that that implies. He is asked public, not private questions: "Do we need more public schools?" not "Would I like to pay more taxes?" He must, in this capacity, be concerned with the public interest, not with his private goods. His communication must be colleagial, not manipulative. He must deliberate, not bargain. This is the program. And it is simply the application of tribunal manners to the electoral tribunal. Nothing is more certain than that the abandonment of this conception spells the doom of meaningful democracy.

And we are abandoning it. But do we care? We prosper. More people have more things and give thanks in more churches than ever before. Our complex political institutions operate. This, at long last, seems to be it. Here and there a critic strikes a mild Veblenian note (and we chuckle with him), or bemoans the lonely crowd, the organization man, the road to Miltown, the move to the suburbs, the rise in mental ills. But for these critics we have a delicious phrase—merchants of doom and gloom—and we are not buying any.

The voice of doom needs to be louder before we hear it. Apparently it speaks Russian. In the Thirties the social critic spoke against the background of internal economic collapse. For the Fifties, and perhaps the Sixties, the Russians take the place of unemployment. The test is "will it solve them?" It is an external standard which leaves the quality of our own lives out of the picture. But it is a convenient test. Enough scientists and engineers is simply "more than they have"; the right rate of capital invest-ment is "more than theirs." Ominous statistics seem now to threaten free enterprise as nothing else has. We are, sporadically, shaken by glimpses of the future. But we do very little.

In these cold-war circumstances the prospects for the revitaliza-tion of the popular tribunal are rather slim. We seem, in fact, to be giving up even on the hope that our legislative bodies will be able to transform themselves from bargaining assemblies into competent policy-making tribunals and turn more and more to the Executive for salvation. But if the outcome is some form of ritualis-tic or plebiscitic democracy let us not put the blame too quickly on human nature or on the Russians. For our own ideas will have done more than anything else to corrupt the popular tribunal and turn the hope of democratic government to ashes. We will, I hope, soon learn that it is bootless to drive the money-changer from the Temple only to let him set up shop in the Forum.

Let me deal briefly with some of the conceptions or misconcep-tions which plague us.

That Government Should Give Us What We Want

The contrast between what we want and what is good for us is certainly familiar enough. Every child knows the force of this distinction and, no doubt, looks forward to the day of freedom when he can at last do what he wants. But parental, and social, authority exerts itself to ensure that by the time the child moves out to govern his own life he too will honor by observance the con-trast between what he wants and what he thinks best.

The relation between "good" and "desire" is the oldest theme of moral reflection, and it is still a lively theme. Variations run from the complete identification of good and desire to complete separa-tion, and it would be pointless to be dogmatic here. It is difficult, however, to see how the conception of "good" for an animal, of whatever kind, can avoid ultimate involvement with his needs, wants, desires. But at the same time not even a wholehearted hedonism can quite deny that indulging a particular desire at some particular time might be bad. Even if the good is taken as happiness, happiness as pleasure, pleasure as the satisfaction of desire, it is still the case that the satisfaction of a particular desire may turn out not to be good. In one way or another we come to recognize that immediacy or urgency is not a sufficient guide, that impulse may need checking, and that, at times, there is a difference between what we happen to want and what is good for us. Governing ourselves is not doing what we want; it is doing what we think best.

This is no less the case for our political lives. Government is purposive, but it is a mistake to suppose that its purpose is simply to give us what we want, to conform its action to what happens at any particular time to be the state of popular feeling or desire. Political tribunals, including the electorate, are not simply clumsy, prescientific devices for determining the state of community desire; nor, in intention, are they the servants of that desire, even if it could be determined. We recognize this when we reserve our greatest admiration for the statesman, who seldom gives us what we want, and condemn the politician who fails to do what is needed because of "public opinion."

We mislead ourselves when we talk of government as the servant of the people. What, in a democracy, can that mean? Whose servant is the electorate? And what are we supposed to give ourselves? A democracy had better take as its slogan: "It is not the aim of government to give us what we want." It needs this reminder more than it needs an urge to self-indulgence. Government is not the tool of our impulsiveness but the instrument of our deliberate selves; it is people doing as they think best, and this is not always "what they want."

But here we see the divergent tendencies of the forum and the marketplace. Our schools, if they do their work, strengthen our deliberate and deliberative selves. Between the impression and the conviction, between the impulse and the action we learn to pause and to consider. But out of school we spend enormous sums to undo this work. We advertise. We put our knowledge of the mind to work against reflection, to make the impression deeper and indelible, to trigger impulse into action. The teacher and the salesman are the deadliest of enemies, one fighting to strengthen, the other to weaken, the human mind.

The product of advertising, we are told, is "consumer demand." And what is that but public opinion or the will of the people? In making us see the "will of the people" as a version of consumer demand, popular sovereignty as consumer sovereignty, the marketplace view of life strikes a fundamental blow at the conception of self-government. It transforms the citizen from ruler to consumer and substitutes for the habits of responsibility the arts of acquisition and enjoyment.

That Self-interested Competition Between Individuals, Interests, and Factions Promotes the General Good.

This popular creed is not unrelated to what has just been mentioned. Its significance for us here lies in what it does to the popular tribunal. It boldly converts what has generally been regarded as political disease into the model of proper political function, harnessing the power of private vice to the chariot of public virtue. Or so it is hoped. How deep is our conviction that in pursuing each his own interest, merging for greater effectiveness into interest-groups, we are acting as moral agents of the public weal. Oh, kindly invisible hand who has made virtue so easy! Each knows what he wants and labels it "good" and chases it. And all the little goods add up to one great big public good. We run for fun and make the treadmill go.

Self-interest and competitiveness are ancient facts of life and not the inventions of political theorists. But there is something novel and bold in seeing them not as tendencies to be curbed but as powers to be encouraged and harnessed. The case we have made for competitive individualism is familiar enough; it has two main features.

First, it is claimed that to encourage competition is to spur individuals to greater creative effort to heighten their energies, develop their powers and skills, and, in general, to increase the quantity and raise the quality of human achievement.

And second, it is held that the energies thus released are essentially self-corrective in their operation, that excesses are offset, and that a competitive system has inherent balance and moves in a desirable direction. Progress, in short, through conflict; the competitor the agent of progress.

There is little doubt that competition is a spur. We are so imbued with its spirit that we find it difficult to imagine another motive for effort and achievement. We think of the desire to achieve as the desire to succeed, the desire to succeed as the desire to surpass others, to win the race, to climb to the top. No one, I suppose, has had a keener eye for our emulative proclivities than Veblen but, as he pointed out, there is, besides the desire to master others, the desire to master tasks or problems, the sense of craftsmanship. The craving to excel others is only a corrupt form of the craving for excellence.

But competition is a cheap source of motive power, and we can turn almost anything into a competitive sport. We can turn "learning" into competition for grades; but we should not be surprised if the victims grow into competitors without a love for learning. Competition, in short, produces competitors. But competitiveness is as likely to be an obstacle as a spur to genuine creativity. We need, I think to re-examine the assumption that the energies released by self-interested competition are productive of excellence. The conception of life as a competitive game is not the profoundest conception of the human situation.

As for the self-regulating features of a competitive system, the belief in which gives to the competitor the moral assurance that he is still playing a necessary social role as he looks out for himself—this is, of course, an echo of the metaphysical optimism expressed in doctrines of evolution through natural selection and of the inevitability of progress. The massive growth of regulation, however, testifies to the end of general faith in non-regulation. And, in any case the staunchest believer in "fitness will flourish" can have nothing to object to in the spectacle of the flourishing of government. Faith in factionalism is, I believe, dying out, and although we sometimes give ourselves the dialectical reassurance that every power contains within itself the seeds of its own countervailing power, our hopes rest increasingly not upon the matched giants in the marketplace but upon the institutions of the "public sector."

Still, competitive individualism lingers as a creed and partly shapes our character. To the extent that this is the case we man the public tribunal with a spirit alien to its demands and find ourselves acting the ruler with the manners of the marketplace. Invited to cooperative deliberation we respond with competitive bargaining.

That Compromise Is a Reasonable and Democratic Way of Dealing With Controversy.

The roots of the doctrine of compromise go deep and it would, I think, be a mistake to treat it simply as—what it nevertheless is —the marketplace conception of "being reasonable." It draws its theoretical strength from cognitive skepticism and what used to be called moral or ethical relativism. To claim infallibility is to take the path of fanaticism; to impose our own values on others makes us zealots and tyrants. Fanatics and zealots are always at each other's throats and unless they mend their ways the issue comes to force and war. So we must begin with the recognition that our beliefs and our values are only "ours," overcome vanity and self-righteousness, and acknowledge that those who disagree with us about what we believe in or cherish most deeply are not necessarily fools or scoundrels but mortals caught up, as we are, in the inevitable partialities and limitations of the human animal.

Some such views as these (dare we say truths?) lie behind the defense of compromise. How can we resolve our differences when the assurance of cognitive or moral certitude is only an illusion fathered by a wish? Nor can we appeal to an "arbitrary" standard if all do not accept it as the arbiter. What, then, can we do but seek accommodation, give and take, strike a bargain and accept it with good grace? To do this is to be modest, tolerant, skeptical, sociable, civilized, humane, reasonable. Otherwise we are arrogant, intolerant, dogmatic, antisocial, barbaric, inhumane, irrational. This should do to suggest the division of persons into those with whom we can do business and those beyond the pale, the compromising and the uncompromising.

Unfortunately, the doctrine fails us in several respects. It does not seem to apply where things really matter; nor does it produce anything really satisfactory. It is, as a political doctrine, a sort of weary congressional view of things. It may "contain" conflict and quiet the House but it contains very little else, and certainly does not contain the art of governing.

Disagreement in belief and in attitude is a familiar fact of life, and we are all cognitive and moral security risks, or at least we cannot be sure who is not. But it does not follow from the recognition of our fallibility and partiality that our salvation lies in the compromise or the bargain. Where has it saved us or created what we value? Scientists disagree, but does science move by compromise? Is great art the product of compromise? Has compromise given Socrates or Jesus to the world—Crito and the Compromise on the Mount? Whom shall we advise to bargain? Is it for lovers or for friends, for families or colleagues, for priests or teachers? Bargaining is the death of any fellowship.

But what, then, shall we do? We come together and must decide and act; but we disagree. As we consider this situation we must recognize that it has two related but distinct aspects. First, there is the problem of holding the group or enterprise together in the face of disagreement which threatens disintegration. But second, there is the need to meet the problem or challenge with which the group is faced. There is thus both an internal and an external problem, and we must not lose sight of either.

When we think of problem-solving or decision-making as an individual matter our attention is usually focused on the external problem and on the adequacy of the solution. But when a group is confronted with a problem and its members disagree our attention is caught by this aspect of the situation and we become involved in group dynamics and "interpersonal relations." Saving the group becomes the problem with priority, and we nourish the arts of reducing heat, smoothing rough edges, and keeping everyone involved and happy. This is desirable and even necessary. It becomes dangerous, however, when we seek to achieve harmony by techniques which purchase this harmony at the expense of adequate solution of the external problem. Among them is the technique of compromise.

The case for compromise is that it is better than warfare and that it holds a group together. No one gets everything he wants but everyone gets something, and, getting something, is content to go along. This is, after all, what the bargaining transaction involves; each gives up something and each gets something. But how does cohesiveness thus purchased leave the external problem? Has the bargain solved it? The answer, unfortunately, is that it has not. The result of the pulling and hauling, the gains and the concessions, is all too often the elimination of just those elements of clarity, simplicity, imagination, and daring which are needed. We never describe an improvement in a plan as a compromise. Nor is a compromise the "best that is possible." Everyone involved thinks that it is worse than something else, and most are probably right. The only consolation is that it could be worse; it is a lesser evil as it is also a lesser good. But, as Pascal pointed out, if the lesser evil is a kind of good it is also true that a lesser good is a kind of evil.

To approach decision in the bargaining spirit is to confuse "solving" with "getting." This confusion is part of the pathology of the governing process. It has the odd result of making two heads worse than one, and it makes a committee utterly hopeless. There is a place for bargaining in life, but it is an impostor in the tribunal. To enshrine it, as the process of compromise, in the political forum is to ensure that the political process will fail to meet its challenge and will indeed become a "second best" way of dealing with secondary issues. This is a degradation we cannot afford; if we fail now in politics what else is there to turn to?

The art of common deliberation is not an easy one. It calls on all the powers of the mind. It demands honesty, courage, objectivity, and self-discipline in the presence of passionate commitment. It is a co-operative not a competitive activity and, in spirit, utterly alien to the bargaining temper of the marketplace.

But the belief in compromise goes hand in hand with the belief in consumer sovereignty, competitive individualism, and the invisible hand. And these are the notions which have subverted the authentic conception of democratic political life and brought us helpless and bemused into our age of anxiety—Hamlets in supermarkets.

I do not argue, although I may seem to, that democracy demands the abdication of the private pursuit of private goods. But it does involve each of us in two discontinuous roles and this duality is the source of much perplexity. Plato, in the *Republic*, limits the governing function to a small class. To these rulers Plato does, so far as possible, deny a private life. The guardians have no private homes, no families, no private property. Those outside the ruling class, on the other hand, have only private lives. The rulers and the subjects constitute two separate classes and each class has its own way of life. The one does not meddle in politics; the other does nothing else. Each person has only a single role to play.

Marketplace democracy also, in its own way, gives to each person only a single role. For it asserts the essential continuity of private and public. The citizen is thought of primarily as a private person pursuing his own ends, and the political arena is only another setting for the same game. There, as elsewhere each is the guardian of his own interests.

With both these forms of the denial of duality the authentic theory of democracy takes issue. Its basic assertion is that every citizen has two distinct roles to play. Each citizen is a member, a subject, a private person free within the common limits to pursue his own ends. But each is also an agent of the body politic, a ruler, a manner of the sovereign tribunal with all of the duties, obligations, and responsibilities that go with that role. It is the confusion of these roles which trouble us today.

We are familiar enough with the "conflict of interest" situation and, in the case of ordinary tribunals, quite concerned to protect the public function against the intrusion of private distraction. But the office of the citizen is harder to protect. John Stuart Mill expressed reservations about the wisdom of the secret ballot. He feared that in its protective darkness men might be tempted to favor their private interests and come to regard the franchise as a private opportunity, forgetting that it is a public office. It is this sense of public office that we need most to recapture. Why are we indignant when someone sells his vote for a few dollars? Has he behaved any better if he sells or betrays it to his private self?

Internal conflict is inevitable since we have public roles as well as private lives. We must be disinterested while we are involved, objective where we are interested parties. And democratic government is not helped by theories which obscure or deny the duality of our situation and dissolve public duties into private privileges. We need, rather, a clearer view of the electoral tribunal, of the people acting, as Alexander Meiklejohn has taught us, as the Fourth Branch of Government. As a member of that fourth—and basic—branch the citizen must learn to move within a framework of ideas and habits appropriate to the ultimate agent of the body politic.

The theory and practice of the Fourth Branch is crucial to the life of a democracy. But the difficulty here is a strange one. The problem is not that of introducing or gaining acceptance for a novel doctrine; it is rather that of getting us to take seriously a doctrine that is so familiar that we have forgotten to believe it. "We, the People . . ."—of course. "Government by the People . . ." —naturally. "The sovereign citizens . . ."—certainly. Does this really mean that in addition to the legislative, executive, and judicial branches of our government there is another part of the government, manned by the citizens, charged with the responsibility for making crucial political decisions—a real, concrete tribunal behind the Fourth of July phrase? If it does not mean this it means nothing.

But few things reveal us to ourselves as do our attempts in recent years to interpret and embody in our public life the significance of the Bill of Rights. And what we have revealed is how little a part the conception of the Fourth Branch plays in our daily reckoning. We tend to see the Bill of Rights as designed merely to protect the subject against government, as staking out an area of private rights. We ask, under stress and with regret, whether the necessities of government in an age of peril do not justify some restriction of private freedom. The issue, as we pose it, is between government and the individual, and by "government" we mean the legislative or the executive branch.

But what is overlooked is that the citizen not only has rights as a private person but has rights or powers as a public official as well. His political powers belong to him as a member of the electoral tribunal, and curbing or infringing those powers radically alters the relation of the Fourth Branch to the other, subordinate, branches of government. For Congress or the Executive to "supervise" the political activity of the citizen—his speech or his advocacy, his reading or writing—is not simply to assert the priority of public necessity over private expression but to violate the "separation of powers" at the expense of the independence and dominance of that very tribunal to which we pay such empty rhetorical tribute. There is no greater anomaly in a democracy than the assumption by legislative committees of the role of guardian of the public mind, meddling officiously in the political life of the citizen, wielding its "un-American" stamp of excommunication. Our toleration of this sort of practice is a measure of our failure to understand the meaning of "government by the people." We are quicker to defend our private rights than the integrity of our public function.

There is more to life than politics, even for the political animal. But there is more, also, than the private pursuit of happiness; and nothing is more central to the spirit of democracy than this conviction. The democrat turns his back resolutely on the temptation to divide men into pursuers of happiness and bearers of responsibility. He summons every man to his place in the public forum. To "life, liberty and the pursuit of happiness" he adds the "dignity" which is found in sharing the colleagial life of the rulers of the human city. The threat to that conception of human dignity takes many forms. But none is more deadly than the temptation of the marketplace.

for further study

BAY, CHRISTIAN. *The Structure of Freedom*. Stanford, 1958.
DEWEY, JOHN. *The Public and Its Problems*. New York, 1927.
FOLLETT, MARY PARKER. *The New State*. New York, 1920.
FRANKEL, CHARLES. *The Democratic Prospect*. New York, 1962.
FROMM, ERICH. *The Sane Society*. New York, 1955.
LINDSAY, A. D. *The Modern Democratic State*. London, 1943.
MACPHERSON, C. B. *The Real World of Democracy*. Oxford, 1966.
MARX, KARL, and FRIEDRICH ENGELS. *The German Ideology*. New York, 1939.
MILL, JOHN STUART. *On Liberty*. London, 1859.

————. *Representative Government.* London, 1861.

PENNOCK, J. ROLAND. *Liberal Democracy: Its Merits and Prospects.* New York, 1950.

SHAULL, RICHARD. "Revolution: Heritage and Contemporary Option," in Carl Oglesby and Richard Shaull, *Containment and Change.* Part II. New York, 1967.

SPITZ, DAVID. *Democracy and the Challenge of Power.* New York, 1958.

part two ❦

the
democratic
revisionists It is not surprising that

a theory of democracy that gives the ideal of personal participation a
central place should be challenged. How realistic is it to expect individuals to be directly involved in politics? Can the mass of men really
bear the strain of playing public roles? Will liberty not be destroyed as
men seek to escape the burden of having to make their own decisions,
of having to bring the variety of their impulses under rational control
unaided by an externally imposed discipline? In short, is self-government possible?

These questions are understandably provoked by a model of an ideal
democratic regime whose members are expected to discover and display
their interests, to play their parts and govern themselves. Such a regime
ideally aims at no less—and no more—than to serve those who actively
participate in it. Its participants are presumed to be in action not for
some ulterior purpose, not for some transcending abstract cause, but
exclusively to promote their personal development. They give the system their loyalty insofar as their own experiences confirm its value to
them: it enables them progressively to actualize their potentialities, to
design their lives and in effect make something of themselves.

This idealized conception of democracy assumes that all men are basically disposed to participate, that they have the natural capacity for playing a multiplicity of mutually conflicting roles, and that they are capable of weighing the consequences of their actions. It is expected that they will remain careful not to jeopardize others or the positions they might themselves take in the future. Their overriding interest will be in the continuity of the common play. It is assumed, moreover, that the economic resources exist to enable men to become rational, responsible citizens, that it is possible to provide the material conditions that enable men to feel sufficiently secure to take part in the drama of their existence. Men are not driven to lose their patience and can therefore remain in control of themselves.

These central premises—the belief in the individual's capacity for responsible action and in the economy's capacity for sustaining him—have been challenged by generations of thinkers determined to bring the idealists to their senses by calling attention to empirical reality. What specifically has disturbed the realists, driving them finally to revise the theory of democracy?

The classic revisionist statement remains that of the aristocrat Alexis de Tocqueville, who, in the 1830s, reacted against the way democratic tendencies seemed to be working themselves out in the United States. Referring to the American experience, he tried to demonstrate that a universal leveling would have disastrous consequences for civilization and culture. Equality would necessarily destroy liberty. His close look at America revealed that unless democratic tendencies were deflected, the sciences and the arts, commerce and industry, morality and manners would all be degraded and corrupted. Men would be stupefied and manipulated by demagogues even as their material needs were satisfied. While Tocqueville saw egalitarianism as an historically inevitable development, he nevertheless maintained that its evil consequences were avoidable. To save democracy from its excesses, it was necessary to support the federal organization and the functional separation of powers, to encourage voluntary associations and grassroots government—whatever institutions would frustrate the emergence of a nationwide egalitarian society.

Although no mere polemicist—he wrote as a detached social scientist analyzing an emergent society—on an ideological level Tocqueville's work served as an argument for the preservation of inequalities. In his analysis, support of a plurality of private hierarchies of power, of religious institutions, of private property, and of restrictions on governmental activity by constitutional checks and balances was the price that had to be paid to meet the dangers of majoritarianism, equality, and what came to be known pejoratively as the mass society.

Tocqueville's sweeping diagnosis and prescription were to be refined by later thinkers. Reacting to the specific social consequences not only of the French Revolution but also of the Industrial Revolution, they were impressed by the destruction of natural social ties and the loss of community values. With different accents Durkheim, Le Bon, Freud, Spengler, Ortega y Gasset, Mayo, Eliot, Niebuhr, Mumford, Talmon, and Lippmann expressed the belief that a common culture had been subverted by protestantism, capitalism, individualism, and the mechanization of industry. In their view, man—who came to be referred to as mass man—is left isolated by revolutionary movements, which cut the organic bonds of primary and local groups. Becoming mobile and restless, innocent of "values," he compulsively watches his neighbors and envies them. He searches for his lost place in the order of things; suffering from status anxiety, he is forever trying to find himself and learn his proper role. But having no sense of either place or self, he quests for identity. He seeks faith and leadership—and in the end gratefully embraces whoever promises salvation. Disoriented, displaced, and anxious, he seeks to escape his freedom and voluntarily delivers himself to extremists who promise him relief from the burden of politics. He is done with openness to possibilities; he becomes intolerant of ambiguity and acquires authoritarian character traits. When he does not turn to fascism, he turns to populist, egalitarian, totalitarian democracy and submits to the tyranny of "public opinion." In this theory, the destruction of the old order has led to the submissiveness, conformity, and intolerance of mass man, so that ultimately he becomes the victim of an irresponsible elite that exploits him for its own purposes.

The reality that appears to make this theory of the mass society creditable has been described by countless contemporary social scientists. In empirical terms, they have spelled out what they believe to be the political, organizational, and psychological implications of both industrialism and democracy, and they have recurrently concluded that democratic ideals must be revised to accord with the new reality.

What became overwhelmingly clear to them was that the industrial organization of society demanded so much specialization and hierarchical, bureaucratic control that demands for democratic participation in decision making were simply unrealistic. The Italian sociologist Roberto Michels in particular addressed himself to the organizational imperatives inherent in modern industrial society. Even associations sincerely aspiring to live up to their democratic claims, as Michels reported in detail, could not escape what he called the iron law of oligarchy. Mass organization requires elite rule. As he wrote in his *Political Parties* (1915), "The majority of human beings, in condition of eternal tutelage, are predestined by tragic necessity to submit to the dominion of a small minority, and must be content to constitute the pedestal of an oligarchy." The established leadership that conservative political thinkers such as Carlyle, Coleridge, Ruskin, and Arnold thought of as morally desirable, Michels (as well as Pareto and Mosca) regarded as an empirically inescapable necessity. Robert A. Dahl merely summed up the findings of several generations of social scientists when he remarked in his *Preface to Democratic Theory* (1956), "The making of governmental decisions is not a majestic march of great majorities united upon certain matters of basic policy. It is the steady appeasement of relatively small groups."

This situation does not inspire pessimism among the new realists. True, men might not be responsible, rational participants in a common enterprise. They might not be capable of integrating a diversity of roles. But what individual men cannot do, the political system might accomplish. The assumption of individual rationality can be dispensed with, provided the political system generates acceptable policies. It was Joseph A. Schumpeter who offered the most concise formula, in *Capitalism, Socialism and Democracy* (1942), arguing that his theory, which he called democratic, was at least truer to life than the classical theory of democracy. According to him, "The democratic method is that institutional arrangement for arriving at political decisions in which individuals acquire the power to decide by means of a competitive struggle for the people's vote." Elite competition would fully satisfy the conditions for democracy. "Democracy," Schumpeter affirmed, "means only that the people have the opportunity of accepting or refusing the men who are to rule them."

Such redefining of democracy was to make it inviting to conclude, as Anthony Downs did in his *Economic Theory of Democracy* (1957), that the main purpose of popular participation is to select a government, and that consequently individual rationality becomes uneconomical. So long as elites are compelled to remain responsive to the electorate and so long as individual voters have the opportunity to express their feelings at election time, the body politic is healthy. To expect more participation and rationality, as Gabriel A. Almond and Sidney Verba point out in their essay reprinted in this section, might itself be quite irrational. Or as Bernard Berelson, James Buchanan, and Gordon Tulloch have maintained, the *system's* performance fortunately compensates for the limits of the individual's performance.

If democratic revisionism is an impressive doctrine, this is not because it expresses a fear of equality or betrays resentment toward new groups who might enter the political arena. It is rather because its proponents, as empirical social scientists, have paid disciplined attention to things as they are; they have come to terms with behavior patterns that are manifestly present in the modern world. They have identified what is established and viable. Knowing the population of industrial societies to be disorganized, ignorant, and apathetic, they have seen government by the people to be impossible and denied the meaningfulness of such terms as "public interest" or "common good," recognizing them as façades behind which private interests pursue their own good. They have thus argued for the balance of private interests within a constitutional system of government.

Not demanding much of the individual citizen, not expecting him to be generous or fraternal or altruistic, the revisionists redefine democracy in terms of system maintenance. Although they fail to reveal what the mass of men may yet be capable of—how underdeveloped individuals may yet be rational and responsible—they expose with stunning precision and methodological rigor what political systems have achieved so far. They encourage their readers to appreciate the values of orderly constitutional government, political stability, and electoral systems that successfully make elites accountable to the more visible parts of body politic.

5   DEMOCRACY AS ELITE COMPETITION

JOSEPH A. SCHUMPETER

The eighteenth-century philosophy of democracy may be couched in the following definition: the democratic method is that institutional arrangement for arriving at political decisions which realizes the common good by making the people itself decide issues through the election of individuals who are to assemble in order to carry out its will. Let us develop the implications of this.

FROM Joseph A. Schumpeter, *Capitalism, Socialism, and Democracy*, 3rd ed., 1950, pp. 250–254, 269–273. Copyright © 1942, 1947 by Joseph A. Schumpeter. Copyright © 1950 by Harper & Brothers. Reprinted by permission of Harper & Row, Publishers, and George Allen & Unwin, Ltd.

It is held, then, that there exists a Common Good, the obvious beacon light of policy, which is always simple to define and which every normal person can be made to see by means of rational argument. There is hence no excuse for not seeing it and in fact no explanation for the presence of people who do not see it except ignorance—which can be removed—stupidity and anti-social interest. Moreover, this common good implies definite answers to all questions so that every social fact and every measure taken or to be taken can unequivocally be classed as "good" or "bad." All people having therefore to agree, in principle at least, there is also a Common Will of the people (= will of all reasonable individuals) that is exactly coterminous with the common good or interest or welfare or happiness. The only thing, barring stupidity and sinister interests, that can possibly bring in disagreement and account for the presence of an opposition is a difference of opinion as to the speed with which the goal, itself common to nearly all, is to be approached. Thus every member of the community, conscious of that goal, knowing his or her mind, discerning what is good and what is bad, takes part, actively and responsibly, in furthering the former and fighting the latter and all the members taken together control their public affairs.

It is true that the management of some of these affairs requires special aptitudes and techniques and will therefore have to be entrusted to specialists who have them. This does not affect the principle, however, because these specialists simply act in order to carry out the will of the people exactly as a doctor acts in order to carry out the will of the patient to get well. It is also true that in a community of any size, especially if it displays the phenomenon of division of labor, it would be highly inconvenient for every individual citizen to have to get into contact with all the other citizens on every issue in order to do his part in ruling or governing. It will be more convenient to reserve only the most important decisions for the individual citizen to pronounce upon—say by referendum—and to deal with the rest through a committee appointed by them—an assembly or parliament whose members will be elected by popular vote. This committee or body of delegates, as we have seen, will not represent the people in a legal sense but it will do in a less technical one—it will voice, reflect or represent the will of the electorate. . . .

As soon as we accept all the assumptions that are being made by this theory of the polity—or implied by it—democracy indeed acquires a perfectly unambiguous meaning and there is no problem in connection with it except how to bring it about. Moreover, we need only forget a few logical qualms in order to be able to add that in this case the democratic arrangement would not only be the best of all conceivable ones, but that few people would care to consider any other. It is no less obvious, however, that these assumptions are so many statements of fact every one of which would have to be proved if we are to arrive at that conclusion. And it is much easier to disprove them.

There is, first, no such thing as a uniquely determined common good that all people could agree on or be made to agree on by the force of rational argument. This is due not primarily to the fact that some people may want things other than the common good but to the much more fundamental fact that to different individuals and groups the common good is bound to mean different things. This fact, hidden from the utilitarian by the narrowness of his outlook on the world of human valuations, will introduce rifts on questions of principle which cannot be reconciled by rational argument because ultimate values—our conceptions of what life and what society should be—are beyond the range of mere logic. They may be bridged by compromise in some cases but not in others. Americans who say, "We want this country to arm to its teeth and then to fight for what we conceive to be right all over the globe" and Americans who say, "We want this country to work out its own problems, which is the only way it can serve humanity" are facing irreducible differences of ultimate values which compromise could only maim and degrade.

Secondly, even if a sufficiently definite common good—such as, for instance, the utilitarian's maximum of economic satisfaction—proved acceptable to all, this would not imply equally definite answers to individual issues. Opinions on these might differ to an extent important enough to produce most of the effects of "fundamental" dissension about ends themselves. The problems centering in the evaluation of present versus future satisfactions, even the case of socialism versus capitalism, would be left still open, for instance, after the conversion of every individual citizen to utilitarianism. "Health" might be desired by all, yet people would still disagree on vaccination and vasectomy. And so on.

The utilitarian fathers of democratic doctrine failed to see the full importance of this simply because none of them seriously considered any substantial change in the economic framework and the habits of bourgeois society. They saw little beyond the world of an eighteenth-century ironmonger.

But, third, as a consequence of both preceding propositions, the particular concept of the will of the people or the *volonté générale* that the utilitarians made their own vanishes into thin air. For that concept presupposes the existence of a uniquely determined common good discernible to all. Unlike the romanticists the utilitarians had no notion of that semi-mystic entity endowed with a will of its own—that "soul of the people" which the historical school of jurisprudence made so much of. They frankly derived their will of the people from the wills of individuals. And unless there is a center, the common good, toward which, in the long run at least, *all* individual wills gravitate, we shall not get that particular type of "natural" *volonté générale*. The utilitarian center of gravity, on the one hand, unifies individual wills, tends to weld them by means of rational discussion into the will of the people and, on the other hand, confers upon the latter the exclusive ethical dignity claimed by the classic democratic creed. *This creed does not consist simply in worshiping the will of the people as such* but rests on certain assumptions about the "natural" object of that will, which object is sanctioned by utilitarian reason. Both the existence and the dignity of this kind of *volonté générale* are gone as soon as the idea of the common good fails us. And both the pillars of the classical doctrine inevitably crumble into dust.

Of course, however conclusively those arguments may tell against this particular conception of the will of the people, they do not debar us from trying to build up another and more realistic one. I do not intend to question either the reality or the importance of the socio-psychological facts we think of when speaking of the will of a nation. Their analysis is certainly the prerequisite for making headway with the problems of democracy. It would, however, be better not to retain the term because this tends to obscure the fact that as soon as we have severed the will of the people from its utilitarian connotation we are building not merely a different theory of the same thing, but a theory of a completely different thing. We have every reason to be on our guard against the pitfalls that lie on the path of those defenders of democracy who while accepting, under pressure of accumulating evidence, more and more of the facts of the democratic process, yet try to anoint the results that process turns out with oil taken from eighteenth-century jars.

But though a common will or public opinion of some sort may still be said to emerge from the infinitely complex jumble of individual and group-wise situations, volitions, influences, actions, and reactions of the "democratic process," the result lacks not only rational unity but also rational sanction. The former means that, though from the standpoint of analysis, the democratic process is not simply chaotic—for the analyst nothing is chaotic that can be brought within the reach of explanatory principles—yet the results would not, except by chance, be meaningful in themselves—as for instance the realization of any definite end or ideal would be. The latter means, since *that* will is no longer congruent with any "good," that in order to claim ethical dignity for the result it will now be necessary to fall back upon an unqualified confidence in democratic forms of government as such—a belief that in principle would have to be independent of the desirability of results. As we have seen, it is not easy to place oneself on that standpoint. But even if we do so, the dropping of the utilitarian common good still leaves us with plenty of difficulties on our hands.

In particular, we still remain under the practical necessity of attributing to the will of the *individual* an independence and a rational quality that are altogether unrealistic. If we are to argue that the will of the citizens *per se* is a political factor entitled to respect, it must first exist. That is to say, it must be something more than an indeterminate bundle of vague impulses loosely playing about given slogans and mistaken impressions. Everyone would have to know definitely what he wants to stand for. This definite will would have to be implemented by the ability to observe and interpret correctly the facts that are directly accessible to everyone and to sift critically the information about the facts that are not. Finally from that definite will and from these ascertained facts a clear *and prompt* conclusion as to particular issues would have to be derived according to the rules of logical inference—with so high a degree of general efficiency moreover that one man's opinion could be held, without glaring absurdity, to be roughly as good as every other man's. And all this the modal citizen would have to perform for himself and independently of pressure groups and propaganda, for volitions and inferences that are imposed upon the electorate obviously do not qualify for ultimate data of the democratic process. The question whether these conditions are fulfilled to the extent required in order to make democracy work should not be answered by reckless assertion or equally reckless denial. It can be answered only by a laborious appraisal of a maze of conflicting evidence. . . .

* * *

I think that most students of politics have by now come to accept the criticisms leveled at the classical doctrine of democracy . . .

I also think that most of them agree, or will agree before long, in accepting another theory which is much truer to life and at the same time salvages much of what sponsors of the democratic method really mean by this term. Like the classical theory, it may be put into the nutshell of a definition.

It will be remembered that our chief troubles about the classical theory centered in the proposition that "the people" hold a definite and rational opinion about every individual question and that they give effect to this opinion—in a democracy—by choosing "representatives" who will see to it that that opinion is carried out. Thus the selection of the representatives is made secondary to the primary purpose of the democratic arrangement, which is to vest the power of deciding political issues in the electorate. Suppose we reverse the roles of these two elements and make the deciding of issues by the electorate secondary to the election of the men who are to do the deciding. To put it differently, we now take the view that the role of the people is to produce a government, or else an intermediate body which in turn will produce a national executive or government. And we define: the democratic method is that institutional arrangement for arriving at political decisions in which individuals acquire the power to decide by means of a competitive struggle for the people's vote.

Defense and explanation of this idea will speedily show that, as to both plausibility of assumptions and tenability of propositions, it greatly improves the theory of the democratic process.

First of all, we are provided with a reasonably efficient criterion by which to distinguish democratic governments from others. We have seen that the classical theory meets with difficulties on that score because both the will and the good of the people may be, and in many historical instances have been, served just as well or better by governments that cannot be described as democratic according to any accepted usage of the term. Now we are in a somewhat better position partly because we are resolved to stress a *modus procedendi* the presence or absence of which it is in most cases easy to verify.

For instance, a parliamentary monarchy like the English one fulfills the requirements of the democratic method because the monarch is practically constrained to appoint to cabinet office the same people as parliament would elect. A "constitutional" monarchy does not qualify to be called democratic because electorates and parliaments, while having all the other rights that electorates and parliaments have in parliamentary monarchies, lack the power to impose their choice as to the governing committee: the cabinet ministers are in this case servants of the monarch, in substance as well as in name and can in principle be dismissed as well as appointed by him. Such an arrangement may satisfy the people. The electorate may reaffirm this fact by voting against any proposal for change. The monarch may be so popular as to be able to defeat any competition for the supreme office. But since no machinery is provided for making this competition effective, the case does not come within our definition.

Second, the theory embodied in this definition leaves all the room we may wish to have for a proper recognition of the vital fact of leadership. The classical theory did not do this but, as we have seen, attributed to the electorate an altogether unrealistic degree of initiative which practically amounted to ignoring leadership. But collectives act almost exclusively by accepting leadership—this is the dominant mechanism of practically any collective action which is more than a reflex. Propositions about the working and the results of the democratic method that take account of this are bound to be infinitely more realistic than propositions which do not. They will not stop at the execution of a *volonté générale* but will go some way toward showing how it emerges or how it is substituted or faked. What we have termed Manufactured Will is no longer outside the theory, an aberration for the absence of which we piously pray; it enters on the ground floor as it should.

Third, however, so far as there are genuine group-wise volitions at all—for instance, the will of the unemployed to receive unemployment benefits or the will of other groups to help—our theory does not neglect them. On the contrary, we are now able to insert them in exactly the role they actually play. Such volitions do not as a rule assert themselves directly. Even if strong and definite they remain latent, often for decades, until they are called to life by some political leader who turns them into political factors. This he does, or else his agents do it for him, by organizing these volitions, by working them up and by including eventually appropriate items in his competitive offering. The interaction between sectional interests and public opinion and the way in which they produce the pattern we call the political situation appear from this angle in a new and much clearer light.

Fourth, our theory is of course no more definite than is the concept of competition for leadership. This concept presents similar difficulties as the concept of competition in the economic sphere, with which it may be usefully compared. In economic life competition is never completely lacking, but hardly ever is it perfect. Similarly, in political life there is always some competition, though perhaps only a potential one, for the allegiance of the people. To simplify matters we have restricted the kind of competition for leadership which is to define democracy, to free competition for a free vote. The justification for this is that democracy seems to imply a recognized method by which to conduct the competitive struggle, and that the electoral method is practically the only one available for communities of any size. But though this excludes many ways of securing leadership which should be excluded, such as competition by military insurrection, it does not exclude the cases that are strikingly analogous to the economic phenomena we label "unfair" or "fraudulent" competition or restraint of competition. And we cannot exclude them because if we did we should be left with a completely unrealistic ideal. Between this ideal case which does not exist and the cases in which all competition with the established leader is prevented by force, there is a continuous range of variation within which the democratic method of government shades off into the autocratic one by imperceptible steps. But if we wish to understand and not to philosophize, this is as it should be. The value of our criterion is not seriously impaired thereby.

Fifth, our theory seems to clarify the relation that subsists between democracy and individual freedom. If by the latter we mean the existence of a sphere of individual self-government the boundaries of which are historically variable—*no* society tolerates absolute freedom even of conscience and of speech, *no* society reduces that sphere to zero—the question clearly becomes a matter of degree. We have seen that the democratic method does not necessarily guarantee a greater amount of individual freedom than another political method would permit in similar circumstances. It may well be the other way around. But there is still a relation between the two. If, on principle at least, everyone is free to compete for political leadership by presenting himself to the electorate, this will in most cases though not in all mean a considerable amount of freedom of discussion *for all*. In particular it will normally mean a considerable amount of freedom of the press. This relation between democracy and freedom is not absolutely stringent and can be tampered with. But, from the standpoint of the intellectual, it is nevertheless very important. At the same time, it is all there is to that relation.

Sixth, it should be observed that in making it the primary function of the electorate to produce a government (directly or through an intermediate body) I intended to include in this phrase also the function of evicting it. The one means simply the acceptance of a leader or a group of leaders, the other means simply the withdrawal of this acceptance. This takes care of an element the reader may have missed. He may have thought that the electorate controls as well as installs. But since electorates normally do not control their political leaders in any way except by refusing to re-elect them or the parliamentary majorities that support them, it seems well to reduce our ideas about this control in the way indicated by our definition . . .

Seventh, our theory sheds much needed light on an old controversy. Whoever accepts the classical doctrine of democracy and in consequence believes that the democratic method is to guarantee that issues be decided and policies framed according to the will of the people must be struck by the fact that, even if that will were undeniably real and definite, decision by simple majorities would in many cases distort it rather than give effect to it. Evidently the will of the majority is the will of the majority and not the will of "the people." The latter is a mosaic that the former completely fails to "represent." To equate both by definition is not to solve the problem. Attempts at real solutions have, however, been made by the authors of the various plans for proportional representation.

These plans have met with adverse criticism on practical grounds. It is in fact obvious not only that proportional representation will offer opportunities for all sorts of idiosyncrasies to assert themselves but also that it may prevent democracy from producing efficient governments and thus prove a danger in times of stress. But before concluding that democracy becomes unworkable if its principle is carried out consistently, it is just as well to ask ourselves whether this principle really implies proportional representation. As a matter of fact, it does not. If acceptance of leadership is the true function of the electorate's vote, the case for proportional representation collapses because its premises are no longer binding. The principle of democracy then merely means that the reins of government should be handed to those who command more support than do any of the competing individuals or teams. And this in turn seems to assure the standing of the majority system within the logic of the democratic method, although we might still condemn it on grounds that lie outside that logic.

6 ❧ OLIGARCHY AS AN ORGANIZATIONAL IMPERATIVE

ROBERT MICHELS

A prendre le terme dans la rigueur de l'acception il n'a jamais existé de véritable démocratie, et il n'en existera jamais. Il est contre l'ordre naturel que le grand nombre gouverne, et que le petit soit gouverné.

J. J. ROUSSEAU, *Contrat Social*

Leadership is a necessary phenomenon in every form of social life. Consequently it is not the task of science to inquire whether this phenomenon is good or evil, or predominantly one or the other. But there is great scientific value in the demonstration that every system of leadership is incompatible with the most essential postulates of democracy. We are now aware that the law of the historic necessity of oligarchy is primarily based upon a series of facts of experience. Like all other scientific laws, sociological laws are derived from empirical observation. In order, however, to deprive our axiom of its purely descriptive character, and to confer upon it that status of analytical explanation which can alone transform a formula into a law, it does not suffice to contemplate from a unitary outlook those phenomena which may be empirically established; we must also study the determining causes of these phenomena. Such has been our task.

Now, if we leave out of consideration the tendency of the leaders to organize themselves and to consolidate their interests, and if we leave also out of consideration the gratitude of the led toward the leaders, and the general immobility and passivity of the masses, we are led to conclude that the principal cause of oligarchy in the democratic parties is to be found in the technical indispensability of leadership.

The process which has begun in consequence of the differentiation of functions in the party is completed by a complex of qualities which the leaders acquire through their detachment from the mass. At the outset, leaders arise *spontaneously;* their functions are *accessory* and *gratuitous.* Soon, however, they become *profes-*

FROM Robert Michels, *Political Parties* (New York: Free Press, 1915), pp. 416–425.

44

sional leaders, and in this second stage of development they are *stable* and *irremovable*.

It follows that the explanation of the oligarchical phenomenon which thus results is partly *psychological;* oligarchy derives, that is to say, from the psychical transformations which the leading personalities in the parties undergo in the course of their lives. But also, and still more, oligarchy depends upon what we may term the *psychology of organization itself,* that is to say, upon the tactical and technical necessities which result from the consolidation of every disciplined political aggregate. Reduced to its most concise expression, the fundamental sociological law of political parties (the term "political" being here used in its most comprehensive significance) may be formulated in the following terms: "It is organization which gives birth to the dominion of the elected over the electors, of the mandataries over the mandators, of the delegates over the delegators. Who says organization, says oligarchy."

Every party organization represents an oligarchical power grounded upon a democratic basis. We find everywhere electors and elected. Also we find everywhere that the power of the elected leaders over the electing masses is almost unlimited. The oligarchical structure of the building suffocates the basic democratic principle. That which *is* oppresses *that which ought to be.* For the masses, this essential difference between the reality and the ideal remains a mystery. Socialists often cherish a sincere belief that a new elite of politicians will keep faith better than did the old. The notion of the representation of popular interests, a notion to which the great majority of democrats, and in especial the working-class masses of the German-speaking lands, cleave with so much tenacity and confidence, is an illusion engendered by a false illumination, is an effect of mirage. In one of the most delightful pages of his analysis of modern Don Quixotism, Alphonse Daudet shows us how the "brav' commandant" Bravida, who has never quitted Tarascon, gradually comes to persuade himself, influenced by the burning southern sun, that he has been to Shanghai and has had all kinds of heroic adventures.[1] Similarly the modern proletariat, enduringly influenced by glib-tongued persons intellectually superior to the mass, ends by believing that by flocking to the poll and entrusting its social and economic cause to a delegate, its direct participation in power will be assured.[2]

[1] Alphonse Daudet, *Tartarin de Tarascon* (Paris: Marpon et Flammarion, 1887), p. 40.

[2] Militant democrats will not admit this publicly. According to them

The formation of oligarchies within the various forms of democracy is the outcome of organic necessity, and consequently affects every organization, be it socialist or even anarchist. Haller long ago noted that in every form of social life relationships of dominion and of dependence are created by Nature herself.[3] The supremacy of the leaders in the democratic and revolutionary parties has to be taken into account in every historic situation present and to come, even though only a few and exceptional minds will be fully conscious of its existence. The mass will never rule except *in abstracto*. Consequently the question we have to discuss is not whether ideal democracy is realizable, but rather to what point and in what degree democracy is desirable, possible, and realizable at a given moment. In the problem as thus stated we recognize the fundamental problem of politics as a science. Whoever fails to perceive this must, as Sombart says, either be so blind and fanatical as not to see that the democratic current daily makes undeniable advance, or else must be so inexperienced and devoid of critical faculty as to be unable to understand that all order and all civilization must exhibit aristocratic features.[4] The great error of socialists, an error committed in consequence of their lack of adequate psychological knowledge, is to be found in their combination of pessimism regarding the present, with rosy optimism and immeasurable confidence regarding the future. A realistic view of the mental condition of the masses shows beyond question that even if we admit the possibility of moral improvement in mankind, the human materials with whose use politicians and philosophers cannot dispense in their plans of social reconstruction are not of a character to justify excessive optimism. Within the limits of time for which human provision is possible, optimism will remain the exclusive privilege of utopian thinkers.

The socialist parties, like the trade unions, are living forms of

the power of the masses is unlimited. This unrealistic view, in its application to political elections, will be found in a number of socialist writings, although its expression is apt to be somewhat veiled. It is only in the work of Dr. P. Coullery, of La Chaux-de-Fonds, a somewhat eccentric Swiss internationalist, that we find a categorical expression of the thought: "Par le suffrage universel le peuple des travailleurs devient tout-puissant" (Coullery, *Jésus le Christ et sa Vie, sa Doctrine morale, politique, économique et sociale. Les Lois naturelles et la Socialisme* [Schweizer, Bienne, 1891], p. 303). In its application to party organization this same notion makes no closer approximation to the real facts of the case.

[3] Ludwig von Haller, *Restauration der Staatswissenschaften* (Winterthur, 1816), I, pp. 304 ff.

[4] Werner Sombart, *Dennoch!*, ed. cit., p. 90. Cf. also F. S. Merlino, *Pro e contro il Socialismo*, ed. cit., pp. 262 ff.

social life. As such they react with the utmost energy against any attempt to analyze their structure or their nature, as if it were a method of vivisection. When science attains to results which conflict with their apriorist ideology, they revolt with all their power. Yet their defense is extremely feeble. Those among the representatives of such organizations whose scientific earnestness and personal good faith make it impossible for them to deny outright the existence of oligarchical tendencies in every form of democracy endeavor to explain these tendencies as the outcome of a kind of atavism in the mentality of the masses, characteristic of the youth of the movement. The masses, they assure us, are still infected by the oligarchic virus simply because they have been oppressed during long centuries of slavery, and have never yet enjoyed an autonomous existence.[5] The socialist regime, however, will soon restore them to health, and will furnish them with all the capacity necessary for self-government. Nothing could be more antiscientific than the supposition that as soon as socialists have gained possession of governmental power it will suffice for the masses to

[5] Such an opinion has been expressed by the syndicalist theorists in especial, as, for instance, by Enrico Leone ("Divenire Sociale," vol. v, Nos. 18, 19) in a criticism of my own preliminary studies on this theme, and by Adolpho Momigliano ("Propaganda," Naples, December 2, 1910). Many of the reformists give utterance to a similar opinion. In a lengthy critical examination of my views (whose justice he by no means denies) Fausto Pagliari comes to the conclusion that the oligarchical tendencies of the socialist movement are not indications of what is going to continue in the future, but merely transitional forms of a movement which is still walking in darkness; signs of youth, not of age (*Oligarchia e Democrazia nell' Organizzazione operaia*, "Critica Sociale," February 1, 1909). Others, like the syndicalist Sergio Panunzio, accept my proposition without reserve but fail to apply its consequences to their own theory (*Syndicalisme et Représentation Ouvrière*, "Mouvement Socialiste," anno xii, No. 221). Eduard Bernstein, who also fails to rebut my demonstrations (cf. *Die Demokratie in der Sozialdemokratie*, "Soziale Monatshefte," 1908, fasc. 18 and 19), reproaches me with overstressing the psychological note, but does not himself fall into the error of the Marxists and syndicalists. He continues to hold today the realistic conception of the future which he expressed in 1897, when he compared the process of internal democratic administration with that of industrial production, writing: "At the door of the workshop we may be equal, but are equal no longer when we have gone inside. Here the engineer must issue his orders, and the various subordinate workmen must carry them out. The stoker cannot act according to his own fancy and draw the fires whenever it pleases him" (*Das demokratische Prinzip und seine Anwendung*, "Neue Zeit," anno xix, p. 25 [1897]). Bernstein, however, has not attained to clearness of vision regarding the results of the division of labor and of the differences in technical competence among the democratic masses. Consequently he remains faithful to a concept of democracy which has little more than the name in common with the democracy advocated by the great democratic thinkers of the eighteenth century and the socialists of the nineteenth.

exercise a little control over their leaders to secure that the interests of these leaders shall coincide perfectly with the interests of the led.[6] This idea may be compared with the view of Jules Guesde, no less antiscientific than anti-Marxist (though Guesde proclaims himself a Marxist), that whereas Christianity has made God into a man, socialism will make man into a god.[7]

The objective immaturity of the mass is not a mere transitory phenomenon which will disappear with the progress of democratization *au lendemain du socialisme.* On the contrary, it derives from the very nature of the mass as mass, for this, even when organized, suffers from an incurable incompetence for the solution of the diverse problems which present themselves for solution— because the mass *per se* is amorphous, and therefore needs division of labor, specialization, and guidance. *L'espèce humaine veut être gouvernée; elle le sera. J'ai honte de mon espèce,* wrote Proudhon from his prison in 1850.[8] Man as individual is by nature predestined to be guided, and to be guided all the more in proportion as the functions of life undergo division and subdivision. To an enormously greater degree is guidance necessary for the social group.

From this chain of reasoning and from these scientific convictions it would be erroneous to conclude that we should renounce all endeavors to ascertain the limits which may be imposed upon the powers exercised over the individual by oligarchies (state, dominant class, party, etc.). It would be an error to abandon the desperate enterprise of endeavoring to discover a social order which will render possible the complete realization of the idea of popular sovereignty. In the present work, as the writer said at the outset, it has not been his aim to indicate new paths. But it seemed necessary to lay considerable stress upon the pessimist aspect of democracy which is forced on us by historical study. We had to inquire whether, and within what limits, democracy must remain purely ideal, possessing no other value than that of a moral criterion which renders it possible to appreciate the varying degrees of that oligarchy which is immanent in every social regime. In other words, we have had to inquire if, and in what degree, democracy is an ideal which we can never hope to realize in practice. A further aim of this work was the demolition of some of the facile and superficial democratic illusions which trouble science and

[6] Cf. Léon Trochet (deputy of Liège), *Socialdémocratie et Anarchisme,* Discours, Brussels-Ghent-Liège, 1902, p. 42.

[7] Jules Guesde, *La Problème et la Solution,* Libr. du Parti Socialiste, Paris, p. 17.

[8] Charles Gide et Charles Rist, *Histoire des Doctrines économiques depuis les Physiocrates jusqu'a nos jours,* Larose et Tenin, Paris, 1909, p. 709.

lead the masses astray. Finally, the author desired to throw light upon certain sociological tendencies which oppose the reign of democracy, and to a still greater extent oppose the reign of socialism.

The writer does not wish to deny that every revolutionary working-class movement, and every movement sincerely inspired by the democratic spirit, may have a certain value as contributing to the enfeeblement of oligarchic tendencies. The peasant in the fable, when on his death bed, tells his sons that a treasure is buried in the field. After the old man's death the sons dig everywhere in order to discover the treasure. They do not find it. But their indefatigable labor improves the soil and secures for them a comparative well-being. The treasure in the fable may well symbolize democracy. Democracy is a treasure which no one will ever discover by deliberate search. But in continuing our search, in laboring indefatigably to discover the indiscoverable, we shall perform a work which will have fertile results in the democratic sense. We have seen, indeed, that within the bosom of the democratic working-class party are born the very tendencies to counteract which that party brought into existence. Thanks to the diversity and to the unequal worth of the elements of the party, these tendencies often give rise to manifestations which border on tyranny. We have seen that the replacement of the traditional legitimism of the powers-that-be by the brutal plebiscitary rule of Bonapartist parvenus does not furnish these tendencies with any moral or aesthetic superiority. Historical evolution mocks all the prophylactic measures that have been adopted for the prevention of oligarchy. If laws are passed to control the dominion of the leaders, it is the laws which gradually weaken, and not the leaders. Sometimes, however, the democratic principle carries with it, if not a cure, at least a palliative, for the disease of oligarchy. When Victor Considérant formulated his "democratico-pacificist" socialism, he declared that socialism signified not the rule of society by the lower classes of the population, but the government and organization of society in the interest of all, through the intermediation of a group of citizens; and he added that the numerical importance of this group must increase *pari passu* with social development.[9] This last observation draws attention to a point of capital importance. It is, in fact, a general characteristic of democracy, and hence also of the labor movement, to stimulate and to strengthen in the individual the intellectual aptitudes for criticism and control. We have seen how the progressive bureaucratization of the demo-

[9] Victor Considérant, *Principes du Socialisme. Manifeste de la Démocratie au xix Siècle*, Librairie Phalanstérienne, Paris, 1847, p. 53.

cratic organism tends to neutralize the beneficial effects of such criticism and such control. Nonetheless it is true that the labor movement, in virtue of the theoretical postulates it proclaims, is apt to bring into existence (in opposition to the will of the leaders) a certain number of free spirits who, moved by principle, by instinct, or by both, desire to revise the base upon which authority is established. Urged on by conviction or by temperament, they are never weary of asking an eternal "Why?" about every human institution. Now this predisposition toward free inquiry, in which we cannot fail to recognize one of the most precious factors of civilization, will gradually increase in proportion as the economic status of the masses undergoes improvement and becomes more stable, and in proportion as they are admitted more effectively to the advantages of civilization. A wider education involves an increasing capacity for exercising control. Can we not observe every day that among the well-to-do the authority of the leaders over the led, extensive though it be, is never so unrestricted as in the case of the leaders of the poor? Taken in the mass, the poor are powerless and disarmed vis-à-vis their leaders. Their intellectual and cultural inferiority makes it impossible for them to see whither the leader is going, or to estimate in advance the significance of his actions. It is, consequently, the great task of social education to raise the intellectual level of the masses, so that they may be enabled, within the limits of what is possible, to counteract the oligarchical tendencies of the working-class movement.

In view of the perennial incompetence of the masses, we have to recognize the existence of two regulative principles:

1. The *ideological* tendency of democracy toward criticism and control;

2. The *effective* countertendency of democracy toward the creation of parties ever more complex and ever more differentiated— parties, that is to say, which are increasingly based upon the competence of the few.

To the idealist, the analysis of the forms of contemporary democracy cannot fail to be a source of bitter deceptions and profound discouragement. Those alone, perhaps, are in a position to pass a fair judgment upon democracy who, without lapsing into dilettantist sentimentalism, recognize that all scientific and human ideals have relative values. If we wish to estimate the value of democracy, we must do so in comparison with its converse, pure aristocracy. The defects inherent in democracy are obvious. It is nonetheless true that as a form of social life we must choose democracy as the least of evils. The ideal government would doubtless be that of an aristocracy of persons at once morally good and technically efficient. But where shall we discover such an aristocracy? We may find it sometimes, though very rarely, as the outcome of deliberate selection; but we shall never find it where the hereditary principle remains in operation. Thus monarchy in its pristine purity must be considered as imperfection incarnate, as the most incurable of ills; from the moral point of view it is inferior even to the most revolting of demagogic dictatorships, for the corrupt organism of the latter at least contains a healthy principle upon whose working we may continue to base hopes of social resanation. It may be said, therefore, that the more humanity comes to recognize the advantages which democracy, however imperfect, presents over aristocracy, even at its best, the less likely is it that a recognition of the defects of democracy will provoke a return to aristocracy. Apart from certain formal differences and from the qualities which can be acquired only by good education and inheritance (qualities in which aristocracy will always have the advantage over democracy—qualities which democracy either neglects altogether, or, attempting to imitate them, falsifies them to the point of caricature), the defects of democracy will be found to inhere in its inability to get rid of its aristocratic scoriæ. On the other hand, nothing but a serene and frank examination of the oligarchical dangers of democracy will enable us to minimize these dangers, even though they can never be entirely avoided.

The democratic currents of history resemble successive waves. They break ever on the same shoal. They are ever renewed. This enduring spectacle is simultaneously encouraging and depressing. When democracies have gained a certain stage of development, they undergo a gradual transformation, adopting the aristocratic spirit, and in many cases also the aristocratic forms, against which at the outset they struggled so fiercely. Now new accusers arise to denounce the traitors; after an era of glorious combats and of inglorious power, they end by fusing with the old dominant class; whereupon once more they are in their turn attacked by fresh opponents who appeal to the name of democracy. It is probable that this cruel game will continue without end.

7 ❧ POLYARCHY

ROBERT A. DAHL AND
CHARLES E. LINDBLOM

Polyarchy and the First Problem of Politics

From about the time of the American Revolution until the First World War the prevailing mood of partisans of democracy was one of unlimited confidence. The "iron law" of oligarchy was intellectually repealed, and political equality was looked upon as certain to prevail in an inevitable victory of democracy over tyranny. Marx and Engels were as much in the grip of this tradition as Lincoln and Gladstone.

There were important critics of this view, yet their impact was slight. But since the First World War, and more notably since the Second, a great tidal shift in attitude by Western intellectuals reflects a new awareness of the strength of tendencies to inequality. Contrast the intellectual mood of today with that of a half-century ago—let us say during the period of the great Liberal reforms in England after the 1906 elections. To be sure there were some, like Dicey, who professed to see in the advance of the welfare state—or socialism, as he called it—a genuine threat to liberty. But it is no great exaggeration to say that the Fabians more nearly reflected the predominant intellectual mood of the day. Shaw, the Webbs, H. G. Wells were the intellectual advance guard; and the great Liberal politicians and administrators, like Balfour, Lloyd George, the young Churchill, and Haldane, were—we can now see—not far behind. The central tenets of that Liberal-Labor creed were two. A larger measure of welfare, security, and equality could and should be extended to the masses by means of government power—an extension which would strengthen, not weaken, the advance to democracy. Only reactionaries and a few anarchists really doubted the validity of this creed. In the United States this intellectual mood and the political forces upholding it were not dominant for another generation, and in France the intellectual and political power of the Popular Front coincided roughly with the reform period of the New Deal in the United States.

FROM Robert A. Dahl and Charles E. Lindblom, *Politics, Economics, and Welfare*, Torchbook edition, 1963, pp. 272–275, 277–278, 309, 312, 314. Copyright © 1953 by Harper & Row, Publishers. Used by permission of the publishers.

It may now be justly charged against those intellectuals that they played down, or even missed, what may well be called the First Problem of Politics. This is the antique and yet ever recurring problem of how citizens can keep their rulers from becoming tyrants. As one looks through the writings of the Fabians and their counterparts in the United States and France, one finds curiously little concern with that problem. Perhaps they believed that it was virtually solved.

The belief that the First Problem of Politics is still unsolved and that those earlier optimists who believed otherwise were quite fundamentally wrong seems to mark off our time from one so shortly past. For now it has become possible to believe that *1984,* if a caricature, is at least a caricature of a quite possible future and, indeed, for much of the earth's surface a quite visible present. One has only to compare the inverted utopias written today with those of the past to realize the void between us and our predecessors; take Orwell's *1984,* or the *Animal Farm,* or Koestler's *The Age of Longing* and compare these with, say, Bellamy's *Looking Backward.*

A few years ago, it was still possible for E. F. M. Durbin to write: "It is . . . important to realize that a growth in the economic power of the State need not compromise our political liberty since it rests in the hands of a democratically elected Parliament, and the guarantee of our freedom remains where it always did, in the *political* constitution and practice of our society."[1] It is not so much that Durbin's statement is wrong; what strikes us today is the inadequacy of the syllogism.

What has brought about this change of mood? One can, of course, hardly underestimate the force of a few anarchists and critics like Orwell or ex-communists like Koestler. *1984* and *Darkness at Noon* have been profoundly influential political tracts. Bertrand de Jouvenal's *Power*[2] has persuasively (if, as we believe, inaccurately) argued the thesis that the whole history of man is one of the continued growth in control by government. Still, what has happened to generate and give plausibility to views of this kind? Five things, mainly.

First, in the USSR what at one time evidently seemed to many intellectuals a vast step toward social justice, equality, and a new democracy eventuated in rank injustice; incredible inequality of

[1] E. F. M. Durbin, *Problems of Economic Planning,* Routledge and Kegan Paul, Ltd., London, 1949, p. 60. It is only fair to say that Durbin had assayed the political problem much more comprehensively in his *Politics of Democratic Socialism,* G. Routledge and Sons, Ltd., London, 1940.

[2] Bertrand de Jouvenal, *On Power,* New York, The Viking Press, 1949.

control, status, security, and income; and an arbitrary tyranny of a scope and power probably never before experienced by mankind.

Second, the growth and expansion of dictatorship, not merely in the Soviet Union but in Germany, Italy, Spain, Portugal, Argentina, and its defeat of polyarchy in some of these countries, no longer permits us to believe that democracy is somehow the normal or inevitable condition of men, and tyranny abnormal. Even a left-wing democratic socialist like R. H. S. Crossman now finds it necessary to conclude that:

Slavery of the acquiescent majority to the ruthless few is the hereditary state of mankind. It is not power itself, but the legitimation of the lust for power, which corrupts absolutely. So, the rulers of the free society must be rendered impotent to indulge their natural instincts by an elaborate system of social indoctrination. The Western tradition has fashioned a breed of political eunuchs, parliamentarians whose aim is no longer to destroy their opponents but to defeat them in argument, no longer to enslave the masses but to serve them responsibly. Democracy of this kind is as unnatural as a well-kept flower bed; totalitarianism as natural as the jungle of weeds and suckers which overrun our garden when we leave it untended for a single season.[3]

No antidemocratic intellectual, neither Pareto, nor Mosca, nor Michels ever put the case more strongly than this representative of English democratic socialism!

Third, the temptations of control in modern society are enormous. Frank Knight once wrote that the probability that the people in control would be individuals who would dislike the possession and exercise of control is on a level with the probability that an extremely tender-hearted person would get the job of whipping master on a slave plantation. In every society there are potential tyrants, and positions of control tend to attract the potential tyrants.

Fourth, the rise of secret police, torture, and the concentration camp as normal instruments of rulership over much of the world calls attention to fundamental changes in social technique. In attempting to discover the sociological basis of majority rule, one sociologist has written: "What, finally, is the ultimate ground for the power which the majority exercises? The answer is so deceptively simple as to discourage ready acceptance. It rests in the elemental fact . . . that the majority is stronger than the minority

[3] R. H. S. Crossman, "Know Thine Enemy," *The New Statesman and Nation,* April 21, 1951, p. 453.

or, in Simmel's words, 'das die Vielen mächtiger sind als die Wenigen.' . . . Given the same organization, the larger number can always control the smaller, can command its services, and secure its compliance."[4] But this statement is no longer valid. Because relatively simple firearms gave supremacy to foot soldiers between the American Revolution and, perhaps, the First World War, it was roughly true during this short historical period that the greater number could, on a showdown, defeat the lesser number; and even if this fact alone could not explain the existence of majority rule, it became evident that majority rule was finally enforceable by the expectation of physical force and severe punishment.[5] But it is no longer true that the majority can bring every minority to heel by the threat of force and punishment. On the contrary, as the history of the past generation has so vividly illustrated, it is now quite possible for small minorities to subjugate large majorities, and to maintain them indefinitely in subjection.[6]

Fifth, from a rare, abnormal, and even extinguishable event war has come to appear as a recurring probability that can only be avoided, in our lifetime at least, by a permanent mobilization of manpower and resources such as, in the immediate past, took place only during periods of war.

In sum, it is now terrifyingly clear that the drive away from equality of control in modern society is extraordinarily powerful. Despite this drive, however, in some societies the democratic goal is still roughly and crudely approximated, in the sense that nonleaders exercise a relatively high degree of control over leaders. The constellation of social processes that makes this possible we call polyarchy. Polyarchy, not democracy, is the actual solution to the First Problem of Politics. . . .

* * *

Characteristics and Conditions of Polyarchy

So far the term "polyarchy" has not been given much operational significance. It is very easy to say that the USSR is not a polyarchy and the United States, Great Britain, Canada, New Zealand, Aus-

[4] Arnold Bierstadt, "The Sociology of Minorities," *American Sociological Review,* December, 1948, pp. 709–710.

[5] S. B. McKinley, *Democracy and Military Power,* Vanguard Press, New York, 1934.

[6] Karl Mannheim, *Diagnosis of Our Time,* Kegan Paul, Trench, Trubner and Co., Ltd., London, 1943, pp. 2–3; also, Karl Mannheim, *Man and Society in an Age of Reconstruction,* Kegan Paul, Trench, Trubner and Co., Ltd., London, 1940, p. 48.

tralia, France, Norway, Sweden, Denmark, Mexico, and Israel (to take some important representative examples) are. For it is correct to say that in these latter countries nonleaders exercise a high degree of control over governmental leaders, and in the USSR they do not. But to make "a high degree of control" meaningful some additional criteria are needed. The most important ones are these:

1. Most adults in the organization have the opportunity to vote in elections with no significant rewards and penalties directly attached either to the act of voting or to the choice among candidates.
2. In elections the vote of each member has about the same weight.
3. Nonelected officials are subordinate to elected leaders in making organization policy. That is, when they so wish, elected leaders can have the last word on policy with nonelected officials.
4. Elected leaders in turn are subordinate to nonleaders, in the sense that those in office will be displaced by alternative leaders in a peaceful and relatively prompt manner whenever a greater number of voters cast their votes for alternative leaders than for those in office.
5. Adults in the organization have available to them several alternative sources of information, including some that are not under significant unilateral control by government leaders. "Available" in this context means only that members who wish to do so can utilize these sources without incurring penalties initiated by government leaders or their subordinates.
6. Members of the organization who accept these rules have an opportunity, either directly or through delegates, to offer rival policies and candidates without severe penalties for their doing so.

One could debate many of the terms in each of these criteria. Political theorists do so endlessly.[7] How many adults is "most"? What are "severe" penalties? How equally weighted must votes be to have "about the same weight"? For example, does the federal system in the United States permit this country to qualify fully as

[7] The extraordinary difficulty of handling terms related to democracy and polyarchy is vividly illustrated in "Analytical Survey of Agreements and Disagreements," by Arne Naess and Stein Rokkan, based on the replies of 100 scholars to a UNESCO questionnaire on the meaning of democracy, in Richard McKeon (ed.), *Democracy in a World of Tensions: A Symposium Prepared by UNESCO*, University of Chicago Press, Chicago, 1951, pp. 447 ff.

a polyarchy? How soon is "relatively prompt"? Just how sub-ordinate must nonelected officials be? No doubt further oper-ational criteria could be set up for each of these shorthand symbols, but the important quarrels over the application of the criteria will arise over factual disputes, not over definitional ques-tions. If the authors' view of the facts—a view shared by most noncommunist antifascists—is correct, then clearly the Soviet Union and Spain lack all the characteristics of a polyarchy; so do most large American corporations; and many trade unions and some boss-ridden municipalities lack several important ones.

Each of the criteria can therefore be expressed in terms of a continuum. For example, because the voters of Nevada elect the same number of senators as all the voters of New York State, the American national government meets the second criterion of poly-archy less fully than does, say, Great Britain. Moreover, a process is polyarchal only with respect to a given membership. Before women were permitted to vote in France, French national govern-ment was a polyarchy for men only. In the United States, the South as a whole has never been a polyarchy for Negroes or indeed even for many poor whites. But for registered Democrats in the South the party primary is a polyarchal process. . . .

Polyarchy also requires a relatively high degree of political activity. That is, enough people must participate in the govern-mental process so that political leaders compete for the support of a large and more or less representative cross section of the popu-lation.

* * *

In practice, then, the democratic goal that governmental de-cisions should accord with the preferences of the greater number of adults in the society is extraordinarily difficult to approximate, and rarely, if ever, is it closely approximated. For the greater num-ber of people often do not have definite preferences on a given is-sue; or when they do, often they do not act on them; or their prefer-ences are often so ambiguous and conflicting that one set of "preferences of the greater number" violates another set of "pref-erences of the greater number" which for some reason were not acted on.

* * *

A considerable measure of political inactivity is not *by itself* a sign that the democratic goal is not being roughly approximated by a polyarchy. . . .

The question, then, is not so much whether citizens are active but whether they have the opportunity to exert control through activity when they wish to do so. . . .

* * *

Nevertheless, many policy decisions cannot actually reflect any specific preferences of the greater number. About the most that can be said for polyarchy is that, if the opportunities for political action are kept open to a representative section of the adult population, specific policies will rarely violate highly ranked, intense, stable, and relatively broad preferences of the greater number for a longer period than about the interval between elections. That is, a very great deal of government policy is bound to reflect the specific preferences of small minorities rather than majorities. But so long as the opportunity for political action is kept open to the greater number, such policies will be determined within broad and often vague limits set by widely shared norms and the expectations of policy makers that they will activate the greater number against them whenever, in placating minorities, they exceed the boundaries set by the highly ranked, intense, and stable preferences of the greater number.

8 🐚 THE NEW POLITY

GABRIEL A. ALMOND AND SIDNEY VERBA

. . . Is there a democratic political culture—a pattern of political attitudes that fosters democratic stability, that in some way "fits" the democratic political system? To answer this question we must look at the political culture in the two relatively stable and successful democracies, Great Britain and the United States. . . . the political cultures of these two nations approximate the civic culture. This pattern of political attitudes differs in some respects

FROM Gabriel A. Almond and Sidney Verba, *The Civic Culture: Political Attitudes and Democracy in Five Nations* (1963), pp. 473–475, 481, 483, 487, 493. Reprinted by permission of Princeton University Press.

from the "rationality-activist" model, or the model of political culture which, according to the norms of democratic ideology, would be found in a successful democracy. Civics texts would have us believe that the problem facing the citizen in a democracy is, to quote the title of a recent book in the field, *How to Be an Active Citizen*.[1] According to this rationality-activist view, a successful democracy requires that citizens be involved and active in politics, informed about politics, and influential. Furthermore, when they make decisions, particularly the important decision of how to cast their vote, they must make them on the basis of careful evaluation of evidence and careful weighing of alternatives. The passive citizen, the nonvoter, the poorly informed or apathetic citizen—all indicate a weak democracy. This view of democratic citizenship stresses activity, involvement, rationality. To use the terminology we have developed, it stresses the role of the participant and says little about the role of the subject or parochial.

Recent studies of political behavior call the rationality-activist model into question, for it is becoming clear that citizens in democracies rarely live up to this model. They are not well informed, not deeply involved, not particularly active; and the process by which they come to their voting decision is anything but a process of rational calculation.[2] Nor does this model accurately represent the civic culture we have found in Britain and the United States. It is true—and this point is both substantively important as well as indicative of the usefulness of comparative data—that the informed, involved, rational, and active citizen is more frequently found in the successful than in the unsuccessful democracies. The characteristics of the rationality-activist model of democratic citizenship are indeed components of the civic culture; but the point to be stressed here is that they are only *part* of that culture.

The civic culture is a mixed political culture. In it many individuals are active in politics, but there are also many who take the more passive role of subject. More important, even among those performing the active political role of the citizen, the roles of subject and parochial have not been displaced. The participant role has been added to the subject and parochial roles. This means that the active citizen maintains his traditional, nonpolitical ties, as

[1] Paul Douglass and Alice McMahon, *How to Be an Active Citizen*, Gainesville, Fla., 1960.

[2] See, for instance, Berelson *et al.*, *Voting*, chap. xiv; Campbell *et al.*, *The American Voter*, chap. x; and Julian L. Woodward and Elmo Roper, "Political Activity of American Citizens," *American Political Science Review*, XLIV (1950), pp. 872–85.

well as his more passive political role as a subject. It is true that the rationality-activist model of the citizen does not imply that participant orientations replace subject and parochial ones; but by not mentioning the latter two roles explicitly, it does imply that they are irrelevant to the democratic political culture.

Actually, these two orientations do more than persist: they play an important part in the civic culture. In the first place, the parochial and subject orientations modify the intensity of the individual's political involvement and activity. Political activity is but one part of the citizen's concerns, and usually not a very important part at that. The maintainance of other orientations limits the extent of his commitment to political activity and keeps politics, as it were, in its place. Furthermore, not only do the parochial and subject orientations persist side by side with the participant orientations, but they penetrate and modify the participant orientations. Primary affiliations, for instance, are important in the patterns of citizen influence. In addition, a diffuse set of social attitudes and interpersonal attitudes tends to affect the content of the political attitudes—to make them less intense and divisive. Penetrated by primary group orientations and by general social and interpersonal attitudes, political attitudes are not solely the results of articulated principle and rational calculation.

How can we explain the discrepancy between the ideals of the rationality-activist model and the patterns of political attitudes we actually find, even in the more stable and successful democracies? One possible explanation, and the one most often found in the literature on civic education, is that this discrepancy is evidence for the malfunctioning of democracy. Insofar as people do not live up to the ideal of the active citizen, democracy is a failure. If one believes that the realities of political life should be molded to fit one's theories of politics, such an explanation is satisfactory. But if one holds to the view that theories of politics should be drawn from the realities of political life—a somewhat easier and probably more useful task—then this explanation of the gap between the rationality-activist model and democratic realities is less acceptable. From the latter point of view, one would probably argue that the gap exists because the standards have been set unreasonably high. Given the complexity of political affairs, given the other demands made upon an individual's time, and given the difficulty of obtaining information necessary for making rational political decisions, it is no wonder that the ordinary citizen is not the ideal citizen. In the light of an individual's nonpolitical interests, it might be quite irrational to invest in political activity the time and effort needed to live up to the rationality-activist model. It may just not be worth it to be that good a citizen.

*   *   *

The comparative infrequency of political participation, its relative lack of importance for the individual, and the objective weakness of the ordinary man allow governmental elites to act. The inactivity of the ordinary man and his inability to influence decisions help provide the power that governmental elites need if they are to make decisions. But this maximizes only one of the contradictory goals of a democratic system. The power of the elites must be kept in check. The citizen's opposite role, as an active and influential enforcer of the responsiveness of elites, is maintained by his strong commitment to the norm of active citizenship, as well as by his perception that he can be an influential citizen. This may be in part a myth, for it involves a set of norms of participation and perceptions of ability to influence that are not quite matched by actual political behavior. Yet the very fact that citizens hold to this myth—that they see themselves as influential and as obligated to take an active role—creates a potentiality of citizen influence and activity. The subjectively competent citizen . . . has not necessarily attempted to influence the government, but he is *more likely* to have made such attempts than is the citizen who does not consider himself competent.[3]

A citizen within the civic culture has, then, a reserve of influence. He is not constantly involved in politics, he does not actively oversee the behavior of political decision makers. But he does have the potential to act if there is need. . . . The citizen is not a constant political actor. He is rarely active in political groups. But he thinks that he can mobilize his ordinary social environment, if necessary, for political use. He is not the active citizen: he is the potentially active citizen. . . .

That politics has relatively little importance for citizens is an important part of the mechanism by which the set of inconsistent political orientations keeps political elites in check, without checking them so tightly as to make them ineffective. For the balance of inconsistent orientations would be more difficult to maintain if the issues of politics were always considered important by the citizens. If issues arise that individuals consider important, or if some relatively severe dissatisfaction with government occurs, the individual will be motivated to think about the topic and thus will be

[3] On the importance of the democratic myth, see V. O. Key, Jr., *Public Opinion and American Democracy*, New York, 1961, p. 547.

under greater pressure to resolve the inconsistency—to make attitudes and behavior consonant with each other. One way he may do this is to bring his behavior into line with norms and perceptions by becoming politically active. Thus the inconsistency between attitudes and behavior acts as a latent or potential source of political influence and activity.

* * *

Elite responsiveness can be enforced while the activity and involvement of the ordinary citizen remain low. The pattern of citizen influence is not always or even predominantly, one of stimulus (the citizen or group of citizens make a demand) followed by response (the governmental elite acts to satisfy the demand). Rather, the well-known "law of anticipated reactions" may operate here. A good deal of citizen influence over governmental elites may entail no activity or even conscious intent of citizens. On the contrary, elites may anticipate possible demands and activities and act in response to what they anticipate. They act responsively, not because citizens are actively making demands, but in order to keep them from becoming active.

Within the civic culture, then, the individual is not necessarily the rational, active citizen. His pattern of activity is more mixed and tempered. In this way he can combine some measure of competence, involvement, and activity with passivity and noninvolvement. Furthermore, his relationship with the government is not a purely rational one, for it includes adherence—his and the decision maker's—to what we have called the democratic myth of citizen competence. And this myth has significant consequences. For one thing, it is not pure myth: the belief in the influence potential of the average man has some truth to it and does indicate real behavioral potential. And whether true or not, the myth is believed. . . .

In sum, the most striking characteristic of the civic culture . . . is its mixed quality. It is a mixture in the first place of parochial, subject, and citizen orientations. The orientation of the parochial to primary relationships, the passive political orientation of the subject, the activity of the citizen, all merge with the civic culture. The result is a set of political orientations that are managed or balanced. There is political activity, but not so much as to destroy governmental authority; there is involvement and commitment, but they are moderated; there is political cleavage, but it is held in check. Above all, the political orientations that make up the civic culture are closely related to general social and interpersonal orientations. Within the civic culture the norms of interpersonal relationships, of general trust and confidence in one's social environment, penetrate political attitudes and temper them. The mixture of attitudes found in the civic culture, we have argued, "fits" the democratic political system. It is, in a number of ways, particularly appropriate for the mixed political system that is democracy.

9 🍀 THE TWO-PARTY SYSTEM

JAMES Q. WILSON

The changes which the amateur Democrat proposes to make in the structure and functions of American political parties are not trivial; they are fundamental. Even the pseudo-amateur who seeks only power and office is compelled, by his position of leadership in an amateur club, to play his part in a major effort to alter radically the local organizations of American political parties. Although the successes of the amateurs will probably be limited to a few localities, their proposals for a new party politics deserve serious attention.

Most generally, the amateur believes that political parties ought to be programmatic, internally democratic, and largely or entirely free of a reliance on material incentives such as patronage. A programmatic party would offer a real policy alternative to the opposition party. A vote for the party would be as much, or more, a deliberate vote for a set of clear and specific proposals, linked by a common point of view or philosophy of government, as it would be a vote for a set of leaders. The programmatic basis of one party would, to some extent, compel an expression of purpose by the opposing party and thus lead toward the realignment of both parties nationally, with liberals in one and conservatives in the other. Elec-

FROM James Q. Wilson, *The Amateur Democrat: Club Politics in Three Cities* (University of Chicago Press: 1962), pp. 340–344, 346, 358–359. Copyright © 1962 by the University of Chicago Press. Reprinted by permission of the University of Chicago Press.

tive officials would be bound by their party to put into effect at least the more important of the policies of the party and would be held responsible for failure to do so. Otherwise, programs and platforms of the new party politics would be as meaningless as those of the traditional parties—i.e., designed to win votes but not to influence government. Thus, a commitment to a programmatic party implies a commitment to a disciplined party. In order to insure that party leaders are responsive to the rank and file, the parties would be internally democratic, with party members choosing party leaders and holding them accountable. Candidates for public office and platforms would be ratified, after some meaningful debate and with real opportunities for choice, by the membership. Although the possibilities of material gain would not necessarily be foreclosed, the strength of the party would not rest on patronage and favoritism but on the freely given consent of the members and their voluntary contributions of time, effort, and money. Party leaders might legitimately aspire to high appointive office (for here policy can be made and it is important to have good men in office, committed to programs in which you believe) but not to lesser appointive posts which exist not to make policy but to reward workers for service and to compel their loyalties.

The value of this conception of a new party politics is rarely discussed by the amateur Democrats; instead, it is largely taken for granted. Despite the conspicuous parallels between the amateurs' proposals and the recommendations of certain scholars who are also critical of traditional political practices, no amateur interviewed ever referred to these writings and no one ever called attention to any systematic defense of the goals of the club movement.[1] And yet these goals, insofar as they refer to party structure and function, can be questioned at almost every point. Many theoretical criticisms have been made of the abstract proposals for party reform; the amateur clubs offer an opportunity to evaluate such proposals on the basis of the actual experience of party organization.[2]

[1] Proposals for party reform include E. E. Schattschneider, *Party Government* (New York: Farrar & Rinehart, 1942); Committee on Political Parties of the American Political Science Association, *Toward a More Responsible Two-Party System* (New York: Rinehart, 1950); Stephen K. Bailey, *The Condition of Our National Political Parties* (New York: Fund for the Republic, 1959); Thomas K. Finletter, *Can Representative Government Do the Job?* (New York: Reynal & Hitchcock, 1945).

[2] Criticisms of party reforms include Pendleton Herring, *The Politics of Democracy* (New York: W. W. Norton, 1940); Herbert Agar, *The Price of Union* (Boston: Houghton Mifflin, 1950); Austin Ranney, "Toward a More Responsible Two-Party System: A Commentary" *American Political Science*

The two crucial proposals of the amateurs are that parties be internally democratic and that they be committed to certain substantive goals. There is a serious question whether it is either desirable or feasible for American parties to be either internally democratic or the source of programs and issues.

The answers to these questions depend on one's conception of the nature of democracy generally. The view held by the amateurs implies that in a large and heterogeneous society the probability of government being "democratic" is increased significantly by political arrangements which broaden popular participation in the making of political decisions. Democracy, in this view, is the method for realizing the common good by allowing the people to decide issues through the election of individuals who assemble to carry out the popular will. If this is the case, then clearly the selection of elective officials ideally must be as democratic as possible from the very first—i.e., the selection of candidates by political parties must be as democratic as the election of officeholders by the voters. And the formulation of the popular will ideally must begin as soon as possible in the political process—i.e., policies must be stated explicitly by the rank-and-file members of the parties and not merely inferred from the vague "mandate" of the electorate when it has chosen a president or governor. In a general election, the choice of the electorate is limited, in the typical case, to two candidates and two party platforms. Government will be more democratic if as many people as possible can participate in the choice of those candidates and the writing of those platforms.

An alternative theory of democracy rejects this view as unrealistic. This second theory takes into account the fact that people have many fundamental disagreements which cannot be reduced to two simple choices no matter how elaborate the party system may be; that these people are by and large uninformed on all but the most dramatic and fundamental issues; that many of the politically relevant views of people are emotional and even irrational; and that therefore there is no way—and there *should not* be any way—to arrive at decisions on all important matters or at some conception of the common good by algebraically adding the likes and dislikes of the voters. The implication of this view is that, far from increasing public participation in the choice of candidates and issues, democracy is best served by reducing and simplifying those choices to a single elemental choice—that of the principal

---

Review, XLV (June 1951), 488 ff.; Edward C. Banfield, "In Defense of the American Party System," paper prepared for the Public Affairs Conference Center, University of Chicago, 1961 (mimeographed).

elective officials. The democratic system is defined, in this theory, not as some method by which "the people rule," but as "that institutional arrangement for arriving at political decisions in which individuals acquire the power to decide by means of a competitive struggle for the people's vote."[3] A political party, therefore, is a group "whose members propose to act in concert in the competitive struggle for political power."[4]

The amateur Democrats hold a view of democracy which implies that many—if not most—people are similar in character to the amateurs themselves and thus equipped to operate issue-oriented parties by democratic means in the interests of the common good. The alternative view of democracy implies that most voters are radically unlike the amateurs, and that their interests will be better served by a party system which asks them to make a single fundamental choice rather than to participate in a kind of party town meeting. The amateurs believe that America's governing institutions are best served if there is democracy within the political parties as well as between them; the adherents of the alternative view argue that while *inter*party democracy is essential, *intra*party democracy is not and, indeed, that the success of the former is reduced by the extent of the latter.

Although they are not given to theorizing or even to disinterested reflection, professional politicians by and large act as if they subscribed to this second view of democracy. Its advantage for their purposes is manifest: if a popular choice between competing leaders is all that we can or should reasonably expect of the voters, then a democratic society (and perhaps the public interest) can be served by men who act selfishly. The ends of government (public policies) need not provide the motives for undertaking political action. Further, the party can attempt to give the voters whatever they seem to want without concerning itself with whether what is offered conforms to some particular ideology or was shaped by the votes of party members. Internal democracy and a commitment to substantive programs would be as irrelevant to the selection of candidates and issues by a party as they would be to the choice of merchandise and sales programs by department stores.[5] . . .

If democracy involves the choice of leaders rather than policies,

---

[3] The phrase and, of course, the theory, are from Joseph A. Schumpeter, *Capitalism, Socialism, and Democracy* (London: George Allen & Unwin Ltd., 1954), p. 269.

[4] *Ibid.*, p. 283.

[5] E. E. Schattschneider, who advocates more programmatic political parties but opposes making them internally democratic, has used the same metaphor. *Op. cit.*, p. 60.

then the possibilities of statesmanship free from the vetoes of uninformed opinion are greater. Votes for leaders can be won with
a variety of appeals, including personality, sectional and ethnic
loyalties, traditional party allegiances, patronage, and the inculca-
tion of a general belief that the candidate "will do a good job."
Votes for policies, on the other hand, can only be won by persuading people to agree to those policies, and for this the old issueless
appeals are of little value. Further, obtaining agreement on anything but the most general (and most vague) issues is usually impossible. To the extent that amateur politicians have as their model
a political party which concerns itself entirely with appeals to
issues, they are working for the creation of a system which will
have enlarged powers for imposing vetoes on the judgment of
elected officials. And, even with the most optimistic allowances
for the ability of the new party to inform its workers and followers
and generate thoughtful proposals, there can be little doubt that,
with the inherently superior sources of information at the disposal
of the officials and their inherently greater sense of the realities of
the situation within which they must act, these officials will find a
programmatic party a burdensome constraint. If a weakness of
democratic government is that its crucial decisions are subject to
uninformed popular vetoes, then the problem will be made worse
by converting parties into plebiscitiary mechanisms for taking
those decisions into the marketplace.

* * *

. . . No society, certainly not one as complex and dynamic as
ours, can cope with its problems or even cohere *solely* on the basis
of reason and concern for the public welfare: elements that are not
reasonable and public-spirited must somehow help to hold it together and make it "work." A society must, in other words, depend
to some extent upon essential social functions being performed by
accident or, at least, without being intended, on the chance that
motives that are not public-regarding will give rise to long-run, indirect benefits that will help maintain the society. To destroy in
the name of reason and morality the mechanisms, the remote and
indirect consequences of which may be indispensable to the
maintenance of social order, might be disastrous.

The American party system, there is some reason to think, may
be such a mechanism. As Schumpeter and others have observed,
the very basis of it is a competitive struggle for people's votes, not
a reasonable discussion of the common good. American political
parties have by and large been a source of social integration rather

than of political cleavage (or even on occasion of political choice); some students have found this their greatest virtue; others have seen it as their principal vice.[6] The thrust of the amateur's involvement has been to attempt to convert the two-party system from an integrative to a divisive agency. . . .

10 ❧ SURVIVAL THROUGH APATHY

BERNARD BERELSON

. . . Political theory written with reference to practice has the advantage that its categories are the categories in which political life really occurs. And, in turn, relating research to problems of normative theory would make such research more realistic and more pertinent to the problems of policy. At the same time, empirical research can help to clarify the standards and correct the empirical presuppositions of normative theory. . . .

Perhaps the main impact of realistic research on contemporary politics has been to temper some of the requirements set by our traditional normative theory for the typical citizen. "Out of all this literature of political observation and analysis, which is relatively new," says Max Beloff, "there has come to exist a picture in our minds of the political scene which differs very considerably from that familiar to us from the classical texts of democratic politics."

Experienced observers have long known, of course, that the in-

---

[6] We may note some of the historians who have interpreted American politics in part in terms of the role of parties in promoting consensus. These include Daniel J. Boorstin, *The Genius of American Politics* (Chicago: University of Chicago Press, 1953); Louis Hartz, *The Liberal Tradition in America* (Boston: Houghton Mifflin, 1955); and David M. Potter, *People of Plenty* (Chicago: University of Chicago Press, 1954). The older historians who saw American politics in terms of conflict rather than consensus included Vernon Parrington and Charles Beard. A critical review of the "consensus" school is John Higham, "The Cult of the 'American Consensus,'" *Commentary*, XXVII (February 1959), 93–100.

From Bernard Berelson, Paul Lazarsfeld, and William McPhee, *Voting* (University of Chicago Press: 1954), pp. 306–307, 311–323. Copyright © 1954 by the University of Chicago Press. Reprinted by permission of the University of Chicago Press.

dividual voter was not all that the theory of democracy requires of him. As Bryce put it:

How little solidity and substance there is in the political or social beliefs of nineteen persons out of every twenty. These beliefs, when examined, mostly resolve themselves into two or three prejudices and aversions, two or three prepossessions for a particular party or section of a party, two or three phrases or catch-words suggesting or embodying arguments which the man who repeats them has not analyzed.

While our data do not support such an extreme statement, they do reveal that certain requirements commonly assumed for the successful operation of democracy are not met by the behavior of the "average" citizen. . . .

If the democratic system depended solely on the qualifications of the individual voter, then it seems remarkable that democracies have survived through the centuries. After examining the detailed data on how individuals misperceive political reality or respond to irrelevant social influences, one wonders how a democracy ever solves its political problems. But when one considers the data in a broader perspective—how huge segments of the society adapt to political conditions affecting them or how the political system adjusts itself to changing conditions over long periods of time—he cannot fail to be impressed with the total result. Where the rational citizen seems to abdicate, nevertheless angels seem to tread.

The eminent judge Learned Hand, in a delightful essay on "Democracy: Its Presumptions and Reality," comes to essentially this conclusion.

I do not know how it is with you, but for myself I generally give up at the outset. The simplest problems which come up from day to day seem to me quite unanswerable as soon as I try to get below the surface. . . . My vote is one of the most unimportant acts of my life; if I were to acquaint myself with the matters on which it ought really to depend, if I were to try to get a judgment on which I was willing to risk affairs of even the smallest moment, I should be doing nothing else, and that seems a fatuous conclusion to a fatuous undertaking.

Yet he recognizes the paradox—somehow the system not only works on the most difficult and complex questions but often works with distinction. "For, abuse it as you will, it gives a bloodless measure of social forces—bloodless, have you thought of that?— a means of continuity, a principle of stability, a relief from the paralyzing terror of revolution."

Justice Hand concludes that we have "outgrown" the conditions assumed in traditional democratic theory and that "the theory has ceased to work." And yet, the system that has grown out of classic democratic theory, and, in this country, out of quite different and even elementary social conditions, does continue to work—perhaps even more vigorously and effectively than ever.

That is the paradox. *Individual voters* today seem unable to satisfy the requirements for a democratic system of government outlined by political theorists. But the *system of democracy* does meet certain requirements for a going political organization. The individual members may not meet all the standards, but the whole nevertheless survives and grows. This suggests that where the classic theory is defective is in its concentration on the *individual citizen*. What are undervalued are certain collective properties that reside in the electorate as a whole and in the political and social system in which it functions.

The political philosophy we have inherited, then, has given more consideration to the virtues of the typical citizen of the democracy than to the working of the *system* as a whole. Moreover, when it dealt with the system, it mainly considered the single constitutive institutions of the system, not those general features necessary if the institutions are to work as required. For example, the rule of law, representative government, periodic elections, the party system, and the several freedoms of discussion, press, association, and assembly have all been examined by political philosophers seeking to clarify and to justify the idea of political democracy. But liberal democracy is more than a political system in which individual voters and political institutions operate. For political democracy to survive, other features are required: the intensity of conflict must be limited, the rate of change must be restrained, stability in the social and economic structure must be maintained, a pluralistic social organization must exist, and a basic consensus must bind together the contending parties.

Such features of the system of political democracy belong neither to the constitutive institutions nor to the individual voter. It might be said that they form the atmosphere or the environment in which both operate. In any case, such features have not been carefully considered by political philosophers, and it is on these broader properties of the democratic political system that more reflection and study by political theory is called for. In the most tentative fashion let us explore the values of the political system, as they involve the electorate, in the light of the foregoing considerations.

Underlying the paradox is an assumption that the population is homogeneous socially and should be homogeneous politically: that everybody is about the same in relevant social characteristics; that, if something is a political virtue (like interest in the election), then everyone should have it; that there is such a thing as *"the"* typical citizen on whom uniform requirements can be imposed. The tendency of classic democratic literature to work with an image of *"the"* voter was never justified. For, as we will attempt to illustrate here, some of the most important requirements that democratic values impose on a system require a voting population that is not homogeneous but heterogeneous in its political qualities.

The need for heterogeneity arises from the contradictory functions we expect our voting system to serve. We expect the political system to adjust itself and our affairs to changing conditions; yet we demand too that it display a high degree of stability. We expect the contending interests and parties to pursue their ends vigorously and the voters to care; yet, after the election is over, we expect reconciliation. We expect the voting outcome to serve what is best for the community; yet we do not want disinterested voting unattached to the purposes and interests of different segments of that community. We want voters to express their own free and self-determined choices; yet, for the good of the community, we would like voters to avail themselves of the best information and guidance available from the groups and leaders around them. We expect a high degree of rationality to prevail in the decision; but were all irrationality and mythology absent, and all ends pursued by the most coldly rational selection of political means, it is doubtful if the system would hold together.

In short, our electoral system calls for apparently incompatible properties—which, although they cannot all reside in each individual voter, can (and do) reside in a heterogeneous electorate. What seems to be required of the electorate as a whole is a *distribution* of qualities along important dimensions. We need some people who are active in a certain respect, others in the middle, and still others passive. The contradictory things we want from the total require that the parts be different. This can be illustrated by taking up a number of important dimensions by which an electorate might be characterized.

How could a mass democracy work if all the people were deeply involved in politics? Lack of interest by some people is not without its benefits, too. True, the highly interested voters vote more, and know more about the campaign, and read and listen more, and participate more; however, they are also less open to persuasion and less likely to change. Extreme interest goes with extreme partisanship and might culminate in rigid fanaticism that could destroy democratic processes if generalized throughout the community. Low affect toward the election—not caring much—underlies the resolution of many political problems; votes can be resolved into a two-party split instead of fragmented into many parties (the splinter parties of the left, for example, splinter because their advocates are *too* interested in politics). Low interest provides maneuvering room for political shifts necessary for a complex society in a period of rapid change. Compromise might be based upon sophisticated awareness of costs and returns—perhaps impossible to demand of a mass society—but it is more often induced by indifference. Some people are and should be highly interested in politics, but not everyone is or needs to be. Only the doctrinaire would deprecate the moderate indifference that facilitates compromise.

Hence, an important balance between action motivated by strong sentiments and action with little passion behind it is obtained by heterogeneity within the electorate. Balance of this sort is, in practice, met by a distribution of voters rather than by a homogeneous collection of "ideal" citizens.

A similar dimension along which an electorate might be characterized is stability-flexibility. The need for change and adaptation is clear, and the need for stability ought equally to be (especially from observation of current democratic practice in, say, certain Latin American countries).

How is political stability achieved? There are a number of social sources of political stability: the training of the younger generation before it is old enough to care much about the matter, the natural selection that surrounds the individual voter with families and friends who reinforce his own inclinations, the tendency to adjust in favor of the majority of the group, the self-perpetuating tendency of political traditions among ethnic and class and regional strata where like-minded people find themselves socially together. Political stability is based upon social stability. Family traditions, personal associations, status-related organizational memberships, ethnic affiliations, socioeconomic strata—such ties for the individual do not change rapidly or sharply, and since his vote is so importantly a product of them, neither does it. In effect, a large part of the study of voting deals not with why votes change but rather with why they do not.

In addition, the varying conditions facing the country, the varying political appeals made to the electorate, and the varying dispositions of the voters activated by these stimuli—these, combined with the long-lasting nature of the political loyalties they instill, produce an important cohesion within the system. . . .

* * *

What of flexibility? Curiously, the voters least admirable when measured against individual requirements contribute most when measured against the aggregate requirement for flexibility. For those who change political preferences most readily are those who are least interested, who are subject to conflicting social pressures, who have inconsistent beliefs and erratic voting histories. Without them—if the decision were left only to the deeply concerned, well-integrated, consistently-principled ideal citizens—the political system might easily prove too rigid to adapt to changing domestic and international conditions.

In fact, it may be that the very people who are most sensitive to changing social conditions are those most susceptible to political change. For, in either case, the people exposed to membership in overlapping strata, those whose former life-patterns are being broken up, those who are moving about socially or physically, those who are forming new families and new friendships—it is they who are open to adjustments of attitudes and tastes. They may be the least partisan and the least interested voters, but they perform a valuable function for the entire system. Here again is an instance in which an individual "inadequacy" provides a positive service for the society: the campaign can be a reaffirming force for the settled majority and a creative force for the unsettled minority. There is stability on both sides and flexibility in the middle.

Closely related to the question of stability is the question of past versus future orientation of the system. In America a progressive outlook is highly valued, but, at the same time, so is a conservative one. Here a balance between the two is easily found in the party system and in the distribution of voters themselves from extreme conservatives to extreme liberals. . . .

* * *

A balance (between preservation of the past and receptivity to the future) seems to be required of a democratic electorate. The heterogeneous electorate in itself provides a balance between liberalism and conservatism; and so does the sequence of political events from periods of drifting change to abrupt rallies back to the loyalties of earlier years.

* * *

Similarly there are required *social* consensus and cleavage—in effect, pluralism—in politics. Such pluralism makes for enough consensus to hold the system together and enough cleavage to make it move. Too much consensus would be deadening and re-strictive of liberty; too much cleavage would be destructive of the society as a whole.

Consider the pictures of the hypothetical relationships between political preference (e.g., party support) and a social character-istic as presented in this chart:

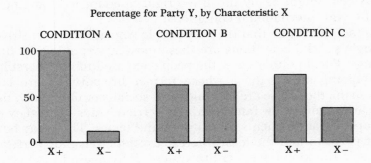

Percentage for Party Y, by Characteristic X

In Condition A there is virtual identity between the character-istic and political preference; all the people of type $X+$ vote one way, and all the people of $X-$ vote the other way. In Condition B the opposite is the case, and there is no relationship between vote and the characteristic; both parties are supported equally by peo-ple of the two types. In Condition C there is neither a complete relationship nor a complete absence; more $X+$'s than $X-$'s are partisans of a given side, but there are some members of each type in each political camp.

Now a democratic society in which Condition A was intensified would probably be in danger of its existence. The issues of politics would cut so deeply, be so keenly felt, and, especially, be so fully reinforced by other social identifications of the electorate as to threaten the basic consensus itself. This might be called "total politics"—a conception of politics, incidentally, advanced by such leading theorists of National Socialism and Communism as Carl Schmitt and Lenin. This involves the mutual reinforcement of political differences and other social distinctions meaningful to the citizen. The multiplication of Condition B, on the other hand, would suggest a community in which politics was of no "real" importance to the community, in which it was not associated with special interests. Condition C is a combination of Conditions A and B—that is, a situation in which special interests are of some but not of overriding importance. It portrays neither the extremist or fanatical community like A nor the "pure" or utopian community like B. . . .

*   *   *

Thus again a requirement we might place on an electoral system—balance between total political war between segments of the society and total political indifference to group interests of that society—translates into varied requirements for different individuals. With respect to group or bloc voting, as with other aspects of political behavior, it is perhaps not unfortunate that "some do and some do not."

Lord Bryce pointed out the difficulties in a theory of democracy that assumes that each citizen must himself be capable of voting intelligently:

Orthodox democratic theory assumes that every citizen has, or ought to have, thought out for himself certain opinions, i.e., ought to have a definite view, defensible by argument, of what the country needs, of what principles ought to be applied in governing it, of the man to whose hands the government ought to be entrusted. There are persons who talk, though certainly very few who act, as if they believed this theory, which may be compared to the theory of some ultra-Protestants that every good Christian has or ought to have . . . worked out for himself from the Bible a system of theology.

In the first place, however, the information available to the individual voter is not limited to that directly possessed by him. True, the individual casts his own personal ballot. But, as we have tried to indicate, . . . that is perhaps the most individualized action he takes in an election. His vote is formed in the midst of his fellows in a sort of group decision—if, indeed, it may be called a decision at all—and the total information and knowledge possessed in the group's present and past generations can be made available for the group's choice. Here is where opinion-leading relationships, for example, play an active role.

Second, and probably more important, the individual voter may not have a great deal of detailed information, but he usually has picked up the crucial *general* information as part of his social learning itself. He may not know the parties' positions on the tariff, or who is for reciprocal trade treaties, or what are the differences on Asiatic policy, or how the parties split on civil rights, or how many security risks were exposed by whom. But he cannot live in an American community without knowing broadly where the parties stand. He has learned that the Republicans are more conservative and the Democrats more liberal—and he can locate his own sentiments and cast his vote accordingly. After all, he must vote for one or the other party, and, if he knows the big thing about the parties, he does not need to know all the little things. The basic role a party plays as an institution in American life is more important to his voting than a particular stand on a particular issue.

It would be unthinkable to try to maintain our present economic style of life without a complex system of delegating to others what we are not competent to do ourselves, without accepting and giving training to each other about what each is expected to do, without accepting our dependence on others in many spheres and taking responsibility for their dependence on us in some spheres. And, like it or not, to maintain our present political style of life, we may have to accept much the same interdependence with others in collective behavior. We have learned slowly in economic life that it is useful not to have everyone a butcher or a baker, any more than it is useful to have no one skilled in such activities. The same kind of division of labor—as repugnant as it may be in some respects to our individualistic tradition—is serving us well today in mass politics. There is an implicit division of political labor within the electorate.

In short, when we turn from requirements for "average" citizens to requirements for the survival of the total democratic system, we find it unnecessary for the individual voter to be an "average citizen" cast in the classic or any other single mold. With our increasingly complex and differentiated citizenry has grown up an equally complex political system, and it is perhaps not simply a fortunate accident that they have grown and prospered together.

But it is a dangerous act of mental complacency to assume that conditions found surviving together are, therefore, positively "functional" for each other. The apathetic segment of America probably has helped to hold the system together and cushioned the shock of disagreement, adjustment, and change. But that is not to say that we can stand apathy without limit. Similarly, there must be some limit to the degree of stability or nonadaptation that a political society can maintain and still survive in a changing world. And surely the quality and amount of conformity that is necessary and desirable can be exceeded, as it has been in times of war and in the present Communist scare, to the damage of the society itself and of the other societies with which it must survive in the world.

How can our analysis be reconciled with the classical theory of liberal political democracy? Is the theory "wrong"? Must it be discarded in favor of empirical political sociology? Must its ethical or normative content be dismissed as incompatible with the nature of modern man or of mass society? That is not our view. Rather, it seems to us that modern political theory of democracy stands in need of revision and not replacement by empirical sociology. The classical political philosophers were right in the direction of their assessment of the virtues of the citizen. But they demanded those virtues in too extreme or doctrinal a form. The voters does have some principles, he does have information and rationality, he does have interest—but he does not have them in the extreme, elaborate, comprehensive, or detailed form in which they were uniformly recommended by political philosophers. Like Justice Hand, the typical citizen has other interests in life, and it is good, even for the political system, that he pursues them. The classical requirements are more appropriate for the opinion leaders in the society, but even they do not meet them directly. Happily for the system, voters distribute themselves along a continuum.

*   *   *

And it turns out that this distribution itself, with its internal checks and balances, can perform the functions and incorporate the same values ascribed by some theorists to each individual in the system as well as to the constitutive political institutions!

11 ⚜ THE DEMOCRATIC CALCULUS

JAMES M. BUCHANAN AND
GORDON TULLOCH

Compared with the more standard works in political science, our analysis may seem to involve a "pessimistic" view of human nature. For scientific progress, however, it is essential that all conceivable assumptions about human behavior be tested. If our models provide some explanations of real-world events, and we believe that they do, our assumptions must have some empirical validity, quite apart from the "attractiveness" of the human characters that inhabit our hypothetical model world.

In one sense our approach taken as a whole is more "optimistic" than that taken by standard writers in political theory. Our assumptions about human nature may be judged "pessimistic," but our conception of the political process, as such, is surely more congenial to those seeking "sweetness and light," "peace," and all such good things than the conception usually implicit in political discourse. We view collective decision making (collective action) as a form of human activity through which mutual gains are made possible. Thus, in our conception, collective activity, like market activity, is a genuinely *cooperative* endeavor in which *all* parties, conceptually, stand to gain. By contrast, much of orthodox political thought seems to be based on the view that the collective-choice process reflects a partisan struggle in which the beneficiaries secure gains solely at the expense of the losers. If the political "game" should be, in fact, similar to that conception which seems to be implicit in much discussion, especially that concerned with the doctrine of majority rule, the maintenance of political order must depend, in fact, on the strength of moral restraints placed on human actors. If, by contrast, a broader and, we think, a more "correct" conception of political choice is adopted, there need be less reliance on moral restraints of individuals.

* * *

Market organization . . . is based on the idea that individuals will tend, by and large, to seek their own interest. This does not suggest that each and every participant in the market place is assumed to try to exert the maximum effort to secure short-run gains. It does suggest that the social philosophy of market organization recognizes this behavior as a possibility and that the organizational norms are based on the view that this sort of behavior can be channeled in such a direction that it becomes beneficial rather than detrimental to the interests of all members of the community. These organizational norms are misunderstood and grossly misrepresented in much of the critical discussion of the market order. This order is not, in any sense, organized on the principle that self-seeking activity is morally "good." There is no conflict between the philosophy of the market, which is a philosophy of social organization, and that of Christianity, which is a philosophy of individual behavior. The market order is founded on the empirical reality that not *all* men renounce self-interest, and that, because of this, the pursuit of private gain should be put to social use where this is possible.

. . . Can the pursuit of individual self-interest be turned to good account in politics as well as in economics? . . . Empirical evidence does seem to point toward this pursuit as an important element in modern democratic process. Our approach is based on the idea that, insofar as this pursuit of self-interest does take place, it should be taken into account in the organization of the political constitution. Only in this way can the institutional setting for collective choice-making be constructed so as to confine the exploitation of man by man within acceptable limits. We are convinced that man can organize his political society better by putting checkreins on his behavior in advance, checkreins which effectively restrain the behavior of the deviant from the "moral way"—behavior that may be observed only occasionally and temporarily but which may also be quite characteristic of real-world human beings.

To the extent that the individual, in his capacity as decision maker for the group, is able to divorce himself from his own interests (his own set of values) and to take a broadly based attitude of Kantian scope, the external costs that any decision-making rule is expected to impose are reduced. We do not deny this possibility or even the common appearance of such an attitude on the part of individual electors or on that of legislators and administrators. Moreover, insofar as this attitude exists, somewhat fewer constitutional constraints on the operation of ordinary rules for collective choice may be dictated than would otherwise be indicated as rational. It should be stressed that moral restraint is a substitute for institutional-constitutional restraint, and in a society with more of the former there will be less need for the latter, and vice versa. Our quarrel with those who would rely primarily on the moral restraint of individuals to prevent undue exploitation of individuals and groups through the political process is, therefore, at base, an empirical one. The assessment of the nature of man himself will, or should, determine the respective importance that is placed on institutional-constitutional restraint and on moral limitations on the behavior of individuals in political society.

The assessment of human nature that is required here cannot, however, be limited to an observation of man's activity in the political process to the exclusion of his activity elsewhere. The modern critic of constitutional democracy who calls for more direct operation of majority rule cannot, at the same time, rationally condemn modern man for his attention to selfish and short-run interests in the nation's market place. If modern man is unduly interested in the emoluments of the affluent society (in creature comforts), he is not likely to shed this cloak merely because he is placed in a slightly different institutional complex. A shift of activity from the market sector cannot in itself change the nature of man, the actor in both processes. The individual who seeks short-run pleasures through his consumption of modern "luxury" items sold in the market is precisely the same individual who will seek partisan advantage through political action. The man who spends his time at the television set or in his automobile in private life is not the man who is likely to vote for more taxes to finance libraries, concerts, and schools. This simple point seems to have been almost entirely overlooked in the so-called "great debate" of the 1960s.

It is not surprising that our conception of the "good" political society should resemble that held by the philosophers of the Enlightenment. Our analysis marks a return to an integration of the political and the economic problems of social organization, and constitutional democracy in its modern sense was born as a twin of the market economy. With the philosophers of the Enlightenment we share the faith that man can rationally organize his own society, that existing organization can always be perfected, and that nothing in the social order should remain exempt from rational, critical, and intelligent discussion. Man's reason is the slave to his passions, and recognizing this about himself, man can organize his own association with his fellows in such a manner that the mutual benefits from social interdependence can be effectively maximized.

12 ȷ THE FUNCTIONAL SYSTEM
LESTER W. MILBRATH

Most Americans have been told, and have come to believe by the time they reach adulthood, that in order for democracy to flourish, it is essential for citizens to be interested in, informed about, and active in politics. If democracy is going to be rule "of the people, by the people, and for the people," the people, by definition, must be interested and active. Many citizens believe that a decision made by all the people is better than a decision made by only part of the people. When only part of the people participate, the government is likely to be directed so as to violate the interests of the nonparticipators. Disinterest and apathy are not approved because, should they become widespread, power could easily be usurped and the quality of government seriously decline. An important preventive is to have a societal norm proclaiming a duty for all citizens to be interested, informed, and active.

. . . Very few United States citizens measure up to that prescription. Although the data are not quite so good for other countries, those we do have suggest that very few persons living in Western democracies measure up to it either. Is there reason, then, to fear for the future of democracy? This question has received a good deal of attention by some eminent political scientists in recent years. (Almond and Verba, 1963, Ch. 15; Berelson, 1952; Berelson, et al., 1954, Ch. 14; Campbell, et al., 1960, Ch. 20; Dahl, 1954; Dahl, 1961, Bk. VI; Duncan and Lukes, 1963; Eckstein, 1961; Key, 1961, Ch. 21; Lane, 1959, Ch. 22; Lane, 1962; Lipset, 1960b, Ch. 13; McClosky, 1964; Prothro and Grigg, 1960). Although these scholars are not in total agreement in their analyses, none expresses great concern about the future of democracy. One reason for this lack of intense concern is that these scholars are confronted by evidence from many societies, accumulated over a considerable period of time, that, despite the low level of political interest and activity, democratic governments continue to flourish and provide reasonably satisfactory governance for their citizens.

In reconciling the fact of low participation with the fact of adequately functioning democracies, political scientists have enlarged their understanding of the political process and of the role of the average citizen in that process. The role of the citizen has

From Lester W. Milbrath, *Political Participation* (Chicago: Rand McNally, 1965), pp. 142–154.

evolved into something different from that envisaged by classical democratic theorists such as John Locke. He had in mind a small homogeneous society where most persons were engaged in primary economic activities (agriculture, forestry, fishing, and the like) and where any average man was considered qualified to hold public office and to resolve public issues (which usually were much simpler than those confronting society today). Each man was expected to take an active role in public affairs.

Modern society, in contrast, has evolved a very high division of labor, not only in the economic sector but also in politics and government. Political roles have become highly differentiated and specialized. This enables some men (elected and appointed officials) to devote their full attention to the complex public issues facing modern society. This division of labor allows other men (most of the citizens) to pay relatively little attention to public affairs. Politics and government are a peripheral rather than a central concern in the lives of most citizens in modern Western societies. As long as public officials perform their tasks well, most citizens seem content not to become involved in politics.

The fact of indifference to politics by many citizens should not be taken to mean that government would function well if citizens ignored it completely. In order to keep public actions responsive to the wishes and desires of the people, citizens must at least participate in the choice of their public officials. The institutions of modern democracies have so evolved that policy leadership is left in the hands of elected officials who at periodic intervals go before the people at an election to see which of two or more competing elites will have policy leadership in the next ensuing period. Both the leaders and the public acknowledge the essentiality of this electoral link between the public and its governing elite.

The burden upon the citizen is much less if he is called upon only to select who his rulers will be than if he is asked to decide the pros and cons of an abstract policy. Furthermore, choices of public officials confront the citizen only at periodic elections, thus taking very little of his time. Society has evolved helpful mechanisms, called political parties, to simplify further the choice between alternative sets of public officials. Instead of having to become informed about a number of individual candidates, the citizen can manage simply by knowing the record and reputation of the political parties under whose labels the candidates run. Parties also are helpful in calling the voter's attention to the failures of the opposition party and to their own successes. The citizen does not need to dig for information, it is literally thrust at him.

Another device for keeping public officials responsive to the people is to require and ensure open channels of communication, so that citizens who so wish can be heard or consulted when public officials are making policy decisions. In part, this is achieved by constitutional provisions for freedom of speech, press, assembly, and petition. Society also has evolved social institutions, such as interest groups and the mass media, which keep citizens informed of what public officials are doing and public officials informed of what citizens want. The fact that top officials are placed there by election is very significant in ensuring that channels of communication stay open between the public and their leaders. If an official should refuse to listen (thus closing the channel), he would probably pay for his folly by losing his position at the next election.

As we think about the role of the average citizen, then, we should not expect him to give a lot of attention to, and be active in resolving, issues of public policy. Nor should we expect him to stand up and be counted on every issue that comes along. The most we can expect is that he will participate in the choice of decision makers and that he will ask to be heard if an issue comes along that greatly concerns him or on which he can make some special contribution. Many citizens do not even vote or speak up on issues, yet their passive role has the consequence of accepting things as they are. Indeed, it is impossible to escape at least a passive role in the choice of decision makers. The choice process can proceed and government can continue to function even if many citizens choose to be so inactive as to fail to vote.

In evaluating citizen roles, we should keep in mind that citizens play two roles at once. At the same time that they try to make the government respond to their wishes, citizens also must play the role of obedient subjects of the regime under which they live. The participant and subject roles pull in opposite directions, and it is important that they be kept in balance. It is difficult for a compliant subject also to question the performance of his rulers and to try to influence their policy decisions. Similarly, it is difficult for a very active and intense participant in politics to subject himself readily to every policy and law decided on by the government. Most citizens work out a balance between the two roles in their daily lives, although there are individual differences in emphasis; some lean more toward the subject role, and others lean more toward the participant role. The moderately active, rather than the highly active person, is more likely to achieve satisfaction in balancing the two roles.[1]

A similar type of balance needs to be achieved at the system level, too. We want a government that is responsive to the wishes of the people but, at the same time, we want an effective government that is able to carry policies through to completion. There is a high probability of conflict between these two objectives. A government overly responsive to every whim of the public cannot pursue a consistent policy. The Fourth French Republic, which saw twenty changes of government in the twelve years following World War II, is a good example of a government made ineffective by responding too readily to every fluctuation in public opinion. Conversely, a government which pursued a given program without paying any attention to the wishes and desires of the public would be thought of as autocratic and unsatisfactory. Most dictatorships are in this latter category. In maintaining a balance between responsiveness and the power to act, the system is aided by the efforts of individual citizens to balance their participant and subject roles. As subjects, they tend to allow a government to develop and pursue a policy for a certain period before passing judgment. As participants, they scrutinize the actions of officials, communicate their policy desires to the officials, and prepare to replace them with other officials if they do not perform adequately. The system balance is further aided by the fact that some individuals prefer to emphasize the role of subject, while others prefer to emphasize the role of participant. If everyone were highly active in politics, or if everyone were passively obedient, it would be more difficult to maintain system balance between responsiveness and power to act.

Moderate levels of participation help societies find another type of balance, that between consensus and cleavage.[2] It is in the very nature of politics that disputes will arise concerning issues and candidates, thus producing cleavages in the society. These must be bridged in some manner, however, if the society is to cohere and function adequately. Agreement on some large principle, even though it is vague and platitudinous, often helps to bridge a cleavage.[3] Resolution of a conflict by peaceful means, such as an election, facilitates movement toward consensus. The im-

---

[1] Much of this argument is indebted to Almond and Verba (1963).

[2] Berelson (1952) and Almond and Verba (1963) have made this point.

[3] McClosky (1964) has argued that agreement on large abstract principles is functional for political society, even if there is little agreement on specific applications of those principles.

portant point here is that societies having large numbers of people who are intensely interested and active in politics (it is virtually impossible to have high activity without intense interest) tend to have wide and deep cleavages that are very difficult to bridge. A current example is the controversy over civil rights in the American South. The intense feelings on both sides of that issue have assuredly stimulated active participation in politics by many who were formerly apathetic, but their political activities have also served to deepen the cleavage between the contending forces, making consensus increasingly remote. It is much easier to forget about past disputes or to take a broad perspective on present ones if those disputes are not considered vital by the participants. It is paradoxical that the kind of issue that stimulates widespread participation in politics is also the kind of issue likely to create wide cleavages in society.

Although it must be conceded that governments continue to function adequately with moderate to low levels of participation in politics, would they function even better if many more people became highly active? Although it can be argued that participation in politics develops character,[4] there is doubt that the society as a whole would benefit if intense interest and active involvement in politics became widespread throughout the population.

We would expect to find, in a society where most adults are intensely interested and involved in politics, that political concerns have moved from the periphery to the center of life interests for most persons. Probably most social relationships, in such a society, would become politicized. Some of the new African one-party states, Ghana, for example, are characterized by high politicization of social relationships. In a highly politicized society, political considerations determine a person's opportunities for education, for a job, for advancement on the job, for a place to live, for goods to enjoy. Furthermore, politics determines the thoughts a citizen can express, the religion he follows, his chances for justice. Such a permeation of politics into all aspects of life is antithetical to the basic principle of limited government in a constitutional democracy. . . .

Knowing the boundaries of politics is basic to the ability of citizens to discriminate legitimate from illegitimate actions by their rulers. Being able to discriminate legitimate from illegitimate actions is, in turn, basic to the ability of a body politic to act in concert

---

[4] Duncan and Lukes (1963) have cited this as a reason for holding to high participation as a democratic norm.

to forestall tyrannous actions by their rulers. The social wisdom which enables a body politic to discriminate areas rightfully governed by politics from areas rightfully outside politics has evolved slowly and painfully over many centuries in Western society. Such boundaries would be difficult to maintain if a high percentage of citizens should become intensely interested and involved in politics. A study of participation rates and of the factors stimulating participation suggests that there is little likelihood that intense political interest and involvement will develop so long as government functions adequately, enabling citizens to keep politics as a peripheral concern in their lives.

The point that high levels of political interest and participation may not be beneficial to constitutional democracy should not be taken to mean that moderate levels of participation automatically guarantee the maintenance of constitutional democracy. A special burden of responsibility for the maintenance of the system rests on the shoulders of the political elites. If these elites are to perform their roles adequately, it is important that they array themselves into two or more competing groups (usually called political parties). As these elites compete for the support of the voters, they perform functions of vigil and criticism *vis-à-vis* their opponents that moderately interested and active citizens might not perform for themselves. Partisan criticism functions best if it is tempered by the realization that after the next election the elite currently in the role of critic may be called upon to govern. This tempered criticism not only gives the party in power a chance to carry a program through to completion and stand responsible for it, but it also enables bridging of cleavages and helps maintain overall coherence of the society.

Several conditions are critical to the adequate functioning of a system of competitive elites in a constitutional democracy.[5] It is important that the elites be committed to democratic values and believe in the rules of the game. It must be taken for granted, for example, that the elites will compete for mass support and that expression of that support in an election will determine which elite will rule for the ensuing period. Several bits of research suggest that participation in politics builds a commitment to democratic values and that elites are much more likely to understand and adhere to specific applications of general democratic principles than are average citizens (Almond and Verba, 1963; McClosky, 1964; Prothro and Grigg, 1960). An elite in power must

---

[5] This section is largely indebted to Key (1961, Ch. 21).

have a live-and-let-live policy *vis-à-vis* its opponents out of power;
elite political actors should be gladiators but not revolutionaries.
Property rights may be important to ensure that opponents out of
power have some way to support themselves until they can regain
power. From another perspective, no elite will readily relinquish
power, should it be defeated in an election, if it has no alternative
base of economic support. That base might be income-earning
property, practice of a profession, jobs in industry not controlled
by the government, and so forth. An elite also will be reluctant to
relinquish power if it is convinced that its opponents will destroy
the group, perhaps by imprisonment or other harassment, once
the opponents have been given power.

In order that the interests of all sectors of society be adequately
taken care of by the government, it is important that each elite
recruit from many sectors of society. An elite from a single class
or group would have difficulty gaining the confidence of the people,
and competitive elites would be reluctant to entrust it with the
reins of power. New recruits should have easy access to the center
of power in the elite to prevent the inner group from getting out of
touch with the people. It is vital that the recruits be socialized to
elite norms and customs, especially basic democratic principles
and the rules of the political game.

The system demands much less from the political beliefs and
behavior of the mass of the citizens than from the elites. To perform its role, the attentive public must believe in the right of the
public to watch and to criticize the behavior of the elites. It also
needs a minimal sense of involvement in public matters and a
sense of loyalty to the whole community rather than to only a segment of the society. It must perform the minimal chore of selecting
among the elites at election time. This low level of attention and
control by the mass of the public leaves a wide latitude to the
elected elite for creative leadership.

. . . It is important to continue moral admonishment for citizens
to become active in politics, not because we want or expect great
masses of them to become active, but rather because the admonishment helps keep the system open and sustains a belief in the right
of all to participate, which is an important norm governing the
behavior of political elites.

The democratic myth of citizen competence . . . has significant consequences. For one thing, it is not pure myth: the belief in the influence
potential of the average man has some truth to it and does indicate

real behavioral potential. And whether true or not, the myth is believed (Almond and Verba, 1963, p. 487).

It is a curious social fact that a norm, such as that which says citizens should be interested and active in politics, which is violated wholesale, still can be an important ingredient in the functioning of the political system. Should that norm wither or vanish, it would be much easier for unscrupulous elites to seize power and tyrannize ordinary citizens. Elites believing in that norm are more likely to welcome new recruits, are more likely to relinquish office easily when defeated in an election, are more likely to try to inform and educate their followers, are more likely to keep communication channels open and listen to the desires of the people, than are elites not believing in that norm. Perhaps one of the reasons the norm remains viable is that elites realize a decline of the norm could spell their own doom as they compete for the power to govern.

Recapitulation of the foregoing argument, in brief form, may help the reader to see where it is leading. (1) Most citizens in any political society do not live up to the classical democratic prescription to be interested in, informed about, and active in politics. (2) Yet, democratic governments and societies continue to function adequately. (3) It is a fact that high participation is not required for successful democracy. (4) However, to ensure responsiveness of officials, it is essential that a sizable percentage of citizens participate in choosing their public officials. (5) Maintaining open channels of communication in the society also helps to ensure responsiveness of officials to public demands. (6) Moderate levels of participation by the mass of citizens help to balance citizen roles as participants and as obedient subjects. (7) Moderate levels of participation also help balance political systems which must be both responsive and powerful enough to act. (8) Furthermore, moderate participation levels are helpful in maintaining a balance between consensus and cleavage in society. (9) High participation levels would actually be detrimental to society if they tended to politicize a large percentage of social relationships. (10) Constitutional democracy is most likely to flourish if only a moderate proportion of social relationships (areas of life) are governed by political considerations. (11) Moderate or low participation levels by the general public place a special burden or responsibility on political elites for the successful functioning of constitutional democracy. (12) Elites must adhere to democratic norms and rules of the game and have a live-and-let-live attitude toward their opponents. (13) A society with widespread apathy could easily be dominated by an unscrupulous elite; only continuous vigilance by at least a few concerned citizens can prevent tyranny. (14) Elite recruitment and training is an especially important function. (15) To help ensure final control of the political system by the public, it is essential to maintain an open communications system, to keep gladiator ranks open to make it easy for citizens to become active should they so choose, to continue moral admonishment for citizens to become active, and to keep alive the democratic myth of citizen competence.

It would be difficult to prove the validity of the above argument with research findings. For lack of evidence, many of the asserted relationships must remain hypothetical for the time being. Certain norms or preferred states for society have had to be posited (e.g., that governments should be both responsive and effective); others might disagree with those preferences. The points were put forward with the hope that they will stimulate discussion leading all of us to a clearer understanding of the dynamics of democracy. If this analysis is correct, present levels and patterns of participation in politics do not constitute a threat to democracy; they seem, in fact, to be a realistic adjustment to the nature of modern society. The political processes of that democracy may not be close to the ideal of the classical theorists, but they may well be the best possible approximation to popular control of government that can be achieved in modern, industrialized, mobile, mass society.

references

ALMOND, GABRIEL, and SIDNEY VERBA. *The Civic Culture*. Princeton: Princeton University Press, 1963.

———. "Democratic Theory and Public Opinion," *Public Opinion Quarterly*, XVI (Fall 1952), 313–330.

BERELSON, BERNARD R., PAUL F. LAZARSFELD, and WILLIAM N. McPHEE. *Voting*. Chicago: University of Chicago Press, 1954.

CAMPBELL, ANGUS. "Surge and Decline: A Study of Electoral Change," *Public Opinion Quarterly*, XXIV (Fall 1960), 397–418.

DAHL, ROBERT A. *A Preface to Democratic Theory*. Chicago: University of Chicago Press, 1954.

———. *Who Governs? Democracy and Power in an American City*. New Haven: Yale University Press, 1961.

DUNCAN, GRAEME, and STEVEN LUKES. "The New Democracy," *Political Studies*, XI (June 1963), 156–177.

ECKSTEIN, HARRY. *A Theory of Stable Democracy*. Research Monograph No. 10. Princeton: Princeton University, Woodrow Wilson School of Public and International Affairs, Center of International Studies, 1961.

KEY, V. O., JR. *Public Opinion and American Democracy*. New York: Alfred A. Knopf, 1961.

LANE, ROBERT E. *Political Life: Why People Get Involved in Politics*. New York: The Free Press, 1959.

———. *Political Ideology: Why the American Common Man Believes What He Does*. New York: The Free Press, 1962.

LIPSET, SEYMOUR MARTIN. *Political Man*. Garden City, N.Y.: Doubleday, 1960.

McCLOSKY, HERBERT. "Consensus and Ideology in American Politics," *American Political Science Review*, LVIII (June 1964), 361–382.

PROTHRO, JAMES W., and CHARLES M. GRIGG. "Fundamental Principles of Democracy: Bases of Agreement and Disagreement," *Journal of Politics*, XXII (May 1960), 276–294.

13 ❧ PREVENTIVE POLITICS

HAROLD D. LASSWELL

. . . Political demands probably bear but a limited relevance to social needs. The political symbol becomes ladened with the residue of successive positive and negative identifications, and with the emotional charge of displaced private motives. This accumulation of irrelevancy usually signifies that tension exists in the lives of many people, and it may possess a diagnostic value to the objective investigator. The individual who is sorely divided against himself may seek peace by unifying himself against an outsider. This is the well-known "peacefulness of being at war." But the permanent removal of the tensions of the personality may depend upon the reconstruction of the individual's view of the world, and not upon belligerent crusades to change the world.

The democratic state depends upon the technique of discussion to relieve the strains of adjustment to a changing world. If the analysis of the individual discloses the probable irrelevance of what the person demands to what he needs (i.e., to that which will produce a permanent relief of strain), serious doubt is cast upon the efficacy of the technique of discussion as a means of handling social problems.

The premise of democracy is that each man is the best judge of his own interest, and that all whose interests are affected should be consulted in the determination of policy. Thus the procedure of a democratic society is to clear the way to the presentation of various demands by interested parties, leaving the coast clear for bargain and compromise, or for creative invention and integration.

The findings of personality research show that the individual is a poor judge of his own interest. The individual who chooses a political policy as a symbol of his wants is usually trying to relieve his own disorders by irrelevant palliatives. An examination of the total state of the person will frequently show that his theory of his own interests is far removed from the course of procedure which will give him a happy and well-adjusted life. Human behavior toward remote social objects, familiarity with which is beyond the personal experience of but a few, is especially likely to be a symptomatic rather than a healthy and reflective adjustment. . . .

FROM Harold D. Lasswell, *Psychopathology and Politics* (1930), in *The Political Writings of Harold D. Lasswell* (New York: Free Press, 1949, 1951), pp. 193–197.

In a sense politics proceeds by the creation of fictitious values The person who is solicited to testify to his own interest is stimulated by the problem put to him to commit himself. The terms in which he couches his own interest vary according to a multitude of factors, but whatever the conditioning influences may be, the resulting theory of his interest becomes invested with his own narcissism. The political symbol is presumably an instrumental makeshift toward the advancement of the other values of the personality; but it very quickly ceases to be an instrumental value, and becomes a terminal value, no longer the servant but the co-equal, or indeed the master. Thus the human animal distinguishes himself by his infinite capacity for making ends of his means.

It should not be hastily assumed that because a particular set of controversies passes out of the public mind that the implied problems were solved in any fundamental sense. Quite often the solution is a magical solution which changes nothing in the conditions affecting the tension level of the community, and which merely permits the community to distract its attention to another set of equally irrelevant symbols. The number of statutes which pass the legislature, or the number of decrees which are handed down by the executive, but which change nothing in the permanent practices of society, is a rough index of the role of magic in politics.

In some measure, of course, discontent is relieved in the very process of agitating, discussing, and legislating about social changes which in the end are not substantially affected. Political symbolization has its catharsis function, and consumes the energies which are released by the maladaptations of individuals to one another.

But discussion often leads to modifications in social practice which complicate social problems. About all that can be said for various punitive measures resorted to by the community is that they have presently broken down and ceased to continue the damage which they began to inflict on society.

Generalizing broadly, political methods have involved the manipulation of symbols, goods, and violence, as in propaganda, bribery, and assassination. It is common to act on the assumption that they are to be applied in the settlement of conflicting demands, and not in the obviation of conflict. Insofar as they rest upon a philosophy, they identify the problem of politics with the problem of coping with differences which are sharply drawn.

The identification of the field of politics with the field of battle, whether the theater be the frontier or the forum, has produced an unfortunate warp in the minds of those who manage affairs, or those who simply think about the management of affairs. The contribution of politics has been thought to be in the elaboration of the methods by which conflicts are resolved. This has produced a vast diversion of energy toward the study of the formal etiquette of government. In some vague way, the problem of politics is the advancement of the good life, but this is at once assumed to depend upon the modification of the mechanisms of government. Democratic theorists in particular have hastily assumed that social harmony depends upon discussion, and that discussion depends upon the formal consultation of all those affected by social policies.

The time has come to abandon the assumption that the problem of politics is the problem of promoting discussion among all the interests concerned in a given problem. Discussion frequently complicates social difficulties, for the discussion by far-flung interests arouses a psychology of conflict which produces obstructive, fictitious, and irrelevant values. The problem of politics is less to solve conflicts than to prevent them; less to serve as a safety valve for social protest than to apply social energy to the abolition of recurrent sources of strain in society.

This redefinition of the problem of politics may be called the idea of preventive politics. The politics of prevention draws attention squarely to the central problem of reducing the level of strain and maladaptation in society. In some measure it will proceed by encouraging discussion among all those who are affected by social policy, but this will be no iron-clad rule. In some measure it will proceed by improving the machinery of settling disputes, but this will be subordinated to a comprehensive program, and no longer treated as an especially desirable mode of handling the situation.

for further study

DAHL, ROBERT A. *A Preface to Democratic Theory.* Chicago, 1956.
————. *Who Governs?* New Haven, 1961.
DOWNS, ANTHONY. *An Economic Theory of Democracy.* New York, 1957.
LIPPMANN, WALTER. *The Phantom Public.* New York, 1925.
LIPSET, S. M. *Political Man.* Garden City, N.Y., 1959.
MAYO, H. B. *An Introduction to Democratic Theory.* New York, 1960.
MEDDING, PETER Y. " 'Elite' Democracy: An Unsuccessful Critique of a Misunderstood Theory," *Journal of Politics,* Vol. 31 (August 1969), 641–654.
MERELMAN, RICHARD M. "On the Neo-Elitist Critique of Community Power," *American Political Science Review,* Vol. 62 (June 1962), 451–460.

PLAMENATZ, JOHN P. "Electoral Studies and Democratic Theory," *Political Studies*, Vol. 6 (February 1958), 1–9.

POLSBY, NELSON W. " 'Pluralism' in the Study of Community Power, or, Erklärung before Verklärung in der Wissenssoziologie," *The American Sociologist*, Vol. 4 (May 1969), 118–122.

SARTORI, GIOVANNI. *Democratic Theory*. New York, 1965.

SCHUMPETER, JOSEPH A. *Capitalism, Socialism and Democracy*. New York, 1942, Part IV.

SELZNICK, PHILIP. *Leadership in Administration*. Evanston, Ill., 1957.

part three ❧

challenges to democratic revisionism

As the preceding selections indicate, the overriding concern of the democratic revisionists—the new realists—is to remain close to the facts of political life. Above all, the revisionists seek to describe prevailing patterns of behavior as accurately as scientific methods allow. Given their empirical orientation, it is understandable that their work should be questioned on empirical grounds. What has encountered criticism are their methods for studying political behavior and, more significantly, the assumptions that sustain their methods. The main target of the attack has been their alleged "realism," their acceptance of a conception of democracy that squares with the existing political reality, a conception that identifies democracy with limited participation, government by competing elites, and political stability.

The critics of the revisionist position have been more preoccupied with exposing the empirical and logical limitations of so-called realistic studies than with affirming "unrealistic" cases of their own. They have scarcely argued explicitly for bringing the less visible and audible parts of society into the political arena. Their attacks, therefore, seem to be as free from an ideological commitment as the work of their opponents. Both appear merely to share a commitment to the empirical temper.

That more is involved, however, is revealed by the tone and polemical thrust of the selections that follow. Such revisionists as Schumpeter, Michels, Lippmann, Almond, and Dahl are accused of generalizing from limited instances. They are charged with the failure to see that arrested human development and elitism are inevitable only under special conditions—conditions that themselves are far from inevitable. It is claimed that the "iron law" of oligarchy, the "imperatives" of industrial development, or the "inner logic" of bureaucratic organization need not be regarded as inescapable. Men have options, and their norms rather than some given reality can determine which option they exercise.

There is pathos, Alvin W. Gouldner contends, in the readiness of the "realists" to resign themselves to elite competition, the pluralism of economic groups, or the hierarchical control of human labor. Whether or not these arrangements are functional depends, as Wayne Hield shows, on the research designs of social scientists. It is determined by one's goals, not by the nature of things. Moreover, the specific behavior of individuals, man's seemingly boundless acquisitiveness, is not simply "human nature" but the consequence of the way elites organize the economic system. No doubt, irrational competitiveness, unlimited acquisitiveness—what C. B. Macpherson has called possessive individualism—are virtually universal in a consumer-oriented market economy and an industrial system designed to cater to it. But such human traits result from the way resources are distributed and industry is organized. They are not preordained. Consequently, the revisionists' empirical findings about man's inability to control his acquisitive impulses may well be descriptively accurate. But these findings would appear in a different light if the revisionists embraced different norms, if they expected more of man and politics, if, in other words, their conception of human nature and political systems were a more generous one.

The critics of revisionism imply that man is mature and society genuinely political only when incentives and opportunities for participation exist in all dimensions of life. For them, it is not sufficient for the political system to generate widely acceptable public policies, however necessary that may be. They do not see a system as fully democratic unless all individuals are actively involved in the process of decision making. And they see man as an authentic citizen only when he himself brings the variety of his desires under control, only when he governs himself because he derives intrinsic satisfaction from the very process of accommodating his mutually conflicting interests.

Yet if this position is merely implied by the antirevisionists, this is because, like the revisionists, they cast their studies in empirical terms. They do not speak as prophets or write as utopian visionaries. To them, it appears pointless to attempt a change in outlook without first effecting a change in institutions. And most of them see the prevailing institutions as so formidable and so well established that experimental action designed to demonstrate the feasibility of a democratic system appears doomed to fail. The times are not ripe for the kind of idealism which gives life to theory.

To be sure, proposals abound for rehabilitating politics. There are programs for (1) realigning political parties so as to produce ideologically-oriented oppositions; (2) stimulating middle-class youth or blacks or unions or all of these in a coalition in order to rejuvenate politics; (3) imposing, as Arthur Miller and Earl Latham have argued, a constitutional order and a bill of rights on corporations, unions, and professional associations so that their membership can meaningfully participate in their internal affairs; (4) developing forms of democracy at the place of industrial work; (5) promoting neighborhood associations for local self-government; and more broadly (6) choosing a revolutionary style of life and disrupting the power structures of society in what Richard Shaull has called a "political equivalent to guerrilla war."

All these may be intended as practical proposals for democratizing politics; they may in effect be seen as large-scale experimental designs. But it has been difficult to think of them as practicable. Insofar as they still appear unrealistic, the persistent academic style of antirevisionist writing may be understandable. It should not be surprising that the critique of revisionism is a methodological one, that those who believe in a more capacious democracy should be content to say as clearly as they can what the empirical work of their opponents consists of, showing how confined and confining it is.

Furthermore, it should be understandable why some critics of revisionism have lost their patience and gone beyond exposing the scientific fallacies of the revisionists—namely, their failure to state conclusions in hypothetical terms, their failure to imply that science can establish nothing conclusively, their failure to concede that their findings have but limited applicability. Some of the critics have gone beyond making such points and assailed the very ideals of empiricism, indicting empirical methods indiscriminately. Men impatient with what they regard as needlessly oppressive political institutions have thus questioned the technique by which such institutions may be understood and controlled. At least some of those who advocate extending democracy have simply assaulted the behavioral study of politics. True, there have also been polemical attacks of behavioralism from the right (for example, Russell Kirk's or Francis Wilson's); their authors have been more in favor of paralyzing politics than extending it. But other critiques (for example, Mulford Sibley's or Wright Mills') are clearly left-wing, implicitly expressing their authors' moral drive to increase participation in politics.

Although these left-wing attacks are formulated as academic methodological critiques, they may be seen as an indirect manifestation of the persistence of ideological conflict. So long as the environment in industrially developing nations is experienced as impervious to change, ideological conflict is not likely to find more direct expression. Under such conditions, most men will mindlessly pressure one another, some will articulate potentially relevant programs, and a few will express themselves in the tortured prose of the social sciences.

14 ❧ THE STRESS ON STABILITY

WAYNE HIELD

One of the more significant changes in the social sciences today is the way the subject of "social change" is being redefined for investigation. In the eighteenth and nineteenth centuries social scientists were interested in the problem of how to mold a society characterized by rational order and progress for all. The assumption of human nature underlying the theories of such figures as Marx and Lester Ward, for example, lay in the belief that man was fundamentally a rational being capable of coming to grips with the laws of social reality as they perceived them and resolutely working for the change of broad social and political structures. Their theoretical systems were designed to demonstrate the possibility of man's controlling his physical and social environment for human betterment. As such their theoretical positions presented alternative programs and methods for the patterning of societal action.[1]

FROM Wayne Hield, "The Study of Change in Social Science," *British Journal of Sociology*, 5 (March 1954), 1–11.

[1] Cf. Reinhard Bendix, "The Image of Man in the Social Sciences," *Commentary*, February 1951, for a discussion of earlier theorists in this connection.

Today, social scientists are predominantly occupied with the reverse emphasis of how to help man successfully adjust to the existing social and political order. The theoretical basis of research begins with the Hobbesian problem of how to maintain social control. The subject of change as treated by Talcott Parsons and Robert K. Merton, undoubtedly the leading social theorists in the field of sociology today, is defined as a by-product in the malfunctioning of social control or order. Though both theorists have made notable contributions to our understanding of the mechanisms involved in social control, their approach is similar to the earlier anthropologists Malinowski and Radcliffe Brown, both of whom were primarily concerned with maintaining a stable, integrated, and harmonious social equilibrium. By taking as their research problem the task of explaining how it is that various social institutions of preliterate societies function interdependently in an integrated whole, these earlier anthropologists either neglected the question of change in direction or control of institutional structures or studied social change as evidence of breakdown in social control and consequently studied means by which control was restored. Thus in the study of certain laws and customs of these preliterate societies, attention was centered in the conditions leading to the perpetuation of codes of behavior and to the impact of crime or delinquency, for example, in either strengthening or serving to reinforce societal sanctions. Interest in the stability and order of such communities tended to preclude study of social and political change, and particularly, changes of the distribution of power.

The skeletal framework of this anthropological approach has become central to the theoretic formulations of Parsons and Merton by addressing the problem for research to the investigation of social control, to the conditions contributing to the structured form and content of social control, and to the analysis of deviance, as for example, crime, delinquency, radical movements, with its repercussions on the social order.[2] Their systematic theory in outlining logical steps for the analysis of social control is the "structural-functional" orientation. By "structure" is meant the relatively stable patterning of social relationships in such a way that it may be treated as structured from the point of view of the system; an example of "structure" would be "institutionalization,"

2 Talcott Parsons, *The Social System* (Routledge & Kegan Paul, 1953); Talcott Parsons, *Essays in Sociological Theory* (Glencoe: The Free Press, 1949); Robert K. Merton, *Social Theory and Social Structure* (Glencoe: The Free Press, 1949); Talcott Parsons, E. A. Shils, *et al.*, *Toward a General Theory of Action* (Cambridge: Harvard University Press, 1951).

in which the attitudes and behaviors of a number of people have enough similarity to be treated as a unit in further analysis. While "structure" is the more static category defining the unit for investigation at a descriptive level, "function" refers to the more dynamic aspect of what the "structure" means to the actors in either fulfilling or failing to satisfy certain biological or socially induced needs. Certain conditions, processes, or pressures may then be analyzed in the sense that they either contribute to the functional perpetuation of the structural system or are "dysfunctional" in that they detract from the integration and effectiveness of the system.[3] This system currently in use in biological theory, particularly in physiology, sets forth a logically interrelated set of constructs to serve as a guide in the study of social action. The system is an elaborate attempt to systematize the scattered theories and methods of the social sciences under one embracing rubric of logically constructed categories for the purpose of further analytic research. In research, the "structural-functional" orientation is a set of methodological tools for the study of social control, deviance, and "re-equilibration."

Although Parsons and Merton in their stress on the problem of "social control" claim to be equally interested in social deviance insofar as this increases our understanding of the mechanisms of permanence and change, the perhaps unforeseen consequence of this theoretic position is leading to a deluge of inquiries of various forms of social adjustment, or how it is that man adapts himself to certain institutional structures exercising social control. This may be due in part to the way they define their system of "structural-functional" analysis. Much of the systematic elaboration of this system involves the formulation of "normative patterns" of behavior or ideal-types representing alternative ways that people might think or behave when confronted with certain structural or institutional settings. One pattern variable, for example, ostensibly taken from Parsons' study of the medical profession, is that of "universalistic" behavior, in which the actor exhibits an equalitarian concern for all persons, as against "particularism," or interest in a few as against others. The ethical code of the medical profession would adhere to the position of "universalism" in that the doctor treats all cases according to professional standards regardless of race, creed, or other background factors of the patient. In this instance "particularistic" behavior would represent a "dysfunctional" form of behavior insofar as the professional ethics

[3] Parsons, *Essays in Sociological Theory*, chaps. I and II.

code is violated. Similar listings of logical forms of behavior provide categories for the study of role orientation in institutional environments. They are primarily intended for studying alternative ways of adjusting to certain "structural" or institutional settings. Given a condition of "social control" as exemplified in the universalistic behavior of the doctor, the research question is to seek factors explaining the origins and perpetuation of the code and to pressures contributing to deviant or "dysfunctional" interpretations and practices in violation of the code; finally, Parsons would be interested in the interplay of reactions of the deviant case and those who support the ethical code of universalism. It becomes the task of the social scientist to investigate means of maintaining social control or reducing tensions or conflicts to restore a condition of harmony and equilibrium. By defining in this way what is problematic in research, deviant attitudes and behaviors become speculatively interesting if somewhat pathological consequences of certain "dysfunctional" elements in social order. Where deviance presents itself, the theoretic concern is with the processes involved in restoring or re-equilibrating a condition of equilibrium or social control.

Essentially this position in sociology is following the tradition of the psychologists, social psychologists, and anthropologists in their emphasis on social adjustment. Mental hygienists are busy in smoothing over the sharp, asocial edges of the personality to allow its successful marketability in the white-collar world.[4] The flood of interest in "psychologizing" now explains away the curious idea systems of the deviant, the abnormal, the malcontent, as "personality" problems. Such deviants are not to be taken at their face value when continued demands are made for wage raises, for example; rather are their statements taken as symptoms of underlying exaggerated personality needs requiring the therapy of understanding the "psychological" reasons for their fixated ideas in order to be "saved" and turned back into society without them.

Industrial sociologists, in the tradition of Elton Mayo, are dishing out the morning coffee and the morale-building essay contest on "My Job and Why I Like to Work Here" to better adjust the morale of the worker to his business of tending the machine. The work of Kurt Lewin in dynamics of small-group behavior has been followed by J. L. Moreno's sociometric methods utilized for tracking down the "social isolate" or other deviants to adjust them to

[4] See Kingsley Davis, "Mental Hygiene and the Class Structure," *A Study of Interpersonal Relations*, edited by Patrick Mullahy (New York: Hermitage Press, 1949).

the larger whole, be it the schoolroom, factory, church, or the armed forces.

In much the same vein, countless studies of housing projects are under way in the social sciences investigating how tenants get along together and how they adapt themselves to their new environment. Generally, studies of biracial housing units demonstrate that Negroes and whites living in the same area manage to live down their previously held race prejudices. The problem of "race prejudice" is seen as one of interpersonal relationships at the lowest rung in the social hierarchy instead of looking at the various policies of those who establish such housing units and who are the real decision makers in predetermining to a large extent what kinds of adjustment will be made by their tenants. Such studies typically take the existing circumstances of social relationships as the given; the problem is how to adjust the tenants or participants in that institutional setting.

In the field of sociology, the relatively new phenomenon of systematic "content analysis" of every conceivable type of mass communication is studied to ascertain its effect on mass audiences. The larger magazine publishers in our society are anxious to know what kind of people are reading their publication and why. Industrial enterprises are hiring social scientists to assess the effects of sales appeals on their customers. Given the product, the problem is how to make the people buy it. The entire range of public-opinion-polling research in much the same manner asks how the man on the street feels or thinks about various social issues or certain radio and TV programs. Thus, the researcher poses the problem: "How is the ordinary man adjusting to society these days?"

Again in the area of social class studies, Lloyd Warner and his followers in their surveys of social circles in various small towns, have offered their findings as a means for aiding those who are not contented with their lot to fit into the desired stratum. Their "subjective" approach to social class leads to generalizations that one's class position is somehow equated with whatever level the person feels he is in; if you think of yourself as middle-class, you are middle-class. Typically the focus of this type of research is the attitudes of the "average" small-town man. What people think or feel about each other is now regarded as more important than the "objective" approach by Marx in the study of economic position or relation to the means of production as index of class. Thus Parsons gives this definition of stratification: "The ranking system in terms of esteem is what we may call the system of stratification of the society."[5] While paying lip service to "objective" elements in determining class position, Parsons together with the Lloyd Warner school devote little attention to the consideration of economic or technological variables in the study of social class or to the distribution of economic and political power in determining the bases of stratification.

For the most part, the reaction to Marx manifest in the reliance on the works of Max Weber has resulted in an orientation stressing the role of ideologies or value orientations as motivating factors of behavior in such a manner that economic and technological variables are by-passed. The study of how people feel about other people in their work or in their community position is creating an imbalance and a one-sided "social psychological view in the field of sociology. This is not meant to deny the noteworthy and long overdue attempt to embrace what is useful in social psychological constructs within the realm of sociological theory. Earlier sociological works particularly in the twenties and early thirties were devoid of social psychological mechanisms so necessary in explaining the motivation of human behavior. The swing away from previous descriptive studies of the forms of social behavior to the intensive investigation of what certain attitudes or behaviors *really mean* to the actors is conducive to the plethora of small group studies today. The amenability of small groups to neatly formulated research designs capable of relatively accurate measure necessarily limits the magnitude and certainly the significance of one's inquiry. Not surprisingly, a recent work by George C. Homans in the comparative study of small groups comes up with the general hypothesis, confirmed in those few, diverse groups he studied, that the more people associate together the more they like each other."[6]

Throughout these works, the "man on the street," or the worker in the factory, or the soldier in the armed forces becomes the central object of investigation. The mass man becomes the irrational object to be manipulated by the social scientist or by outside interests through the aid of social science techniques in adjusting his personality needs to the desired condition of conformity or harmony. It does not take much vision to realize that the human

[5] Parsons, *The Social System*, p. 132. See also his *Essays in Sociological Theory*, chap. VII.

[6] George C. Homans, *The Human Group* (Routledge & Kegan Paul, 1951).

relations experts of the next fifty years are, however unintended, going to constitute the main drift in this area with their new-found occupation of building the morale of the disenchanted, fitting the unfit, and adjusting the maladjusted.

Social Adjustment in Social Science Theory

The key theoretical concepts in social psychology and sociology preordain the nature of these studies of social adjustment. In both fields there is a convergence of theory with suggestions for research proceeding from nearly identical theoretical constructs: the tension-need theory of behavior. In this view, as developed through the works of the gestaltists Lewin, Tolman, H. A. Murray, and more recently, Kretch and Crutchfield, the personality is ideally conceptualized in his most restful moments as being in a state of "psychic homeostasis," or a relative absence of needs. The basic postulate of this approach is that a need does not become dominant in a personality if there is no obstruction to its satisfaction. When the person does not receive enough affection, for example, a tension develops in the personality and we speak of a *need* for affection. Resulting behavior constitutes an attempt to release tension; all obstructions to need satisfactions, or reduction in tension, are considered to be hedonically negative, while the "greatest pleasure seems to be associated with a relatively rapid lowering of need tension." Normal functioning is linked with the state of "psychic homeostasis."

In research, the logical question to be asked follows: "What social conditions give rise to a state of exaggerated need-tension and how can such tension be reduced to a state of homeostasis?" From this one can see that it is readily adapted to any condition or scene of conflict representing tension, and to the means by which such conflict may be attenuated. The problem of change is that of reducing intensified need-dispositions or altering the expectations of the subjects with the interest in restoring a condition of equilibration or social order. Illustrative case studies of this method are provided by Kretch and Crutchfield and by Kurt Lewin in considering conflict between management and labor to be the reflection of certain underlying social tensions and needs not met in the work situation. Remedies for these conditions hark back to those of Elton Mayo, T. N. Whitehead, and Burleigh Gardner by suggesting the use of more psychological rewards, praise and recognition, as a means for reducing conflicts between labor and management.[7]

The tension-need theory has now been incorporated in the major theoretical works of Talcott Parsons. In his recent work, *The Social System*, the basic problem outlined is that of explaining the adjustment of individuals or social groups to one another. As Parsons indicates, the social system is characterized by a plurality of individual actors who interact with each other in terms of a tendency to the "optimization of gratification." The focus of his work is that of the "gratification-deprivation" balance of the ego personality (me) in relation to alter (you). Motivation is defined as orientation to improvement of the "gratification-deprivation" balance of the actor.[8] Thus, his thesis develops from the same hedonistic calculus found in the tension-need theory of behavior. Deviant behavior, for Parsons, is defined as the abnormal in psychological terms:

We may say that the need for *security* in the motivational sense is the need to preserve stable cathexes of social objects, including collectivities. Tendencies to dominance or submission, aggressiveness or compulsive independence, then, may be interpreted as manifestations of insecurity. The need for a feeling of *adequacy* on the other hand, we may say, is the need to feel able to live up to the normative standards of the expectation system, to conform in that sense. The compulsive enforcer, the perfectionist, the incorrigible and the evader, then, could be interpreted as motivated by a sense of inadequacy.[9]

With this operational definition of deviance as "insecurity" and "inadequacy," Parsons stresses ways in which deviance can be mitigated. In this he offers explanations for the origins of deviant behavior; the genesis of value orientations making for conflict between ego and alter; discussion of conflicts in roles; and possible structural determinants of deviance. In each case he proceeds to means for re-equilibrating the system of order. It is no accident,

[7] Kretch and Crutchfield, *Theory and Problems of Social Psychology* (New York: McGraw Hill, 1948), chap. XIV; Kurt Lewin, *Resolving Social Conflicts* (New York: Harpers, 1948), chap. 8.

[8] The opposite thesis is, of course, equally plausible that real gratification is found particularly in the state of tension or in various states of deprivation. While this hypothesis has not been the subject of research, it would seem that extensive documentation of the idea could be found in such societies as our own that thrive on a constant high level of tension in "interpersonal" relationships to say nothing of the consistent tensions evident in international diplomacy. For a suggestive consideration of this problem, see Fyodor Dostoevsky, "Notes from Underground," *The Short Novels of Dostoevsky* (edited by Thomas Mann), (New York: Dial Press, 1951), pp. 129–156.

[9] Parsons, *The Social System*, p. 261.

then, that Parsons' discussion of the "Mechanisms of Social Control" follows that of his treatment of deviant behavior.

In light of the foregoing, it is hardly a surprise that Parsons draws upon an extensive analogy of social control to the role of psychotherapy as a means illustrating suggested treatment of deviance. He states that psychotherapy may serve "as a prototype of the mechanisms of social control."[10] As the modern-day Elton Mayo he lists the four conditions of successful therapy which may serve as prototypes as corresponding parts in other mechanisms of social control: support, permissiveness for the expression of deviant expectations, denial of reciprocity for these deviant expectations, and conditional manipulation of sanctions, notably, the relational rewards, in this connection. That is, the individual deviant is to be given cathectic support while the therapist or social controller takes the "responsibility for upholding of the normative pattern."

This view corresponds with the tension-need theory in that "tension" is operationally equated with the "deviance" component of Parsons' theory of social control. Both theories tend to assume normality to be a successful adjustment on the part of the individual to the socially approved norms of our society. For Parsons, in discussing the problem of socialization in our society, the mature adult is one who can adapt to "an autonomous achievement orientation, the capacity for effective neutrality, for universalism and for functional specificity independent of the direct gratification interests of childhood, especially in affectively neutral contexts." In other words, the mature adult is one who competes for success without letting his dependency needs get the best of him, keeps his feelings to himself or at least well under control, plays the game according to the rules laid out for him, and is expected to know a lot about a little rather than a little about a lot. In short, the ideal-type personality in our culture is still the embodiment of the Protestant ethic and Parsons suggests that it would be interesting to find out why it is that some groups deviate from these norms and what methods, as for example, psychotherapy, may be utilized to bring the deviant back to the sanctity of "re-equilibration."

All this fits into the larger societal trends Parsons anticipates in our society. As a student of Max Weber, Parsons sees a growing rationalization of our societal life, a strain toward objectivity, systematization, and organizational efficiency in the calculation of appropriate means to achieve desired goals. While both Weber and Parsons agree in recognizing this vast directional factor in the

10 Parsons, *The Social System*, p. 301.

nature of modern life, their evaluations of this trend are quite different. Weber was appalled by the implications for human freedom in this development of rationalization in bureaucratic structures. Bureaucratization, as Weber studied it, proceeds hand in hand with a growing concentration of economic and political power at the apex of large organizational structures together with the economic and social leveling of the masses. The important policy-making functions of the modern bureaucratic organization are appropriated by the top officials of the hierarchy while below an army of technicians and clerks perform routine tasks of administration carrying out decisions made at higher levels. The immediate implication perceived by Weber is the threat of such concentration of authority to the democratic process as those who are governed find themselves leveled to a state of apathetic mediocrity. It was to this problem of how to maintain freedom or independent exercise of discretion in modern life that Weber devoted much of his writing and his activity in political life:

This passion for bureaucracy, as we have heard it expressed here, is enough to drive one to despair. It is as if in politics the spectre of timidity—which has in any case always been rather a good standby for the German—were to stand alone at the helm; as if we were deliberately to become men who need "order" and nothing but order, who become nervous and cowardly if for one moment this order wavers, and helpless if they are torn away from their total incorporation in it. That the world should know no men but these: it is in such an evolution that we are already caught up, and the great question is therefore not how can we promote and hasten it, but what can we oppose to this machinery in order to keep a portion of mankind free from this parcelling-out of the soul, from this supreme mastery of the bureaucratic way of life.[11]

In contrast to Weber, who constantly asked this question above of how to regulate and control bureaucratic machinery in maintaining the dignity of man, Parsons neglects this as a basic problem to be dealt with by social scientists. Instead he seems to agree with the big change and direction of these changes in modern life. The nature of modern scientific investigation in its objective quest for laws of human behavior is considered a prime leader in this respect. There are certain nonempirical elements such as philosophy, ideologies, and religious beliefs which will in turn act back on the progress of rationalization in science as obstacles in its development. . . . "Making this allowance for this factor, however, we

[11] From a lecture by Max Weber on bureaucratization in J. P. Mayer, *Max Weber and German Politics* (Faber & Faber, Ltd., 1943), p. 97.

may speak of the process of rationalization with considerable confidence as a general directional factor in the change of social systems."[12]

At one point, Parsons recognizes certain conflicts between his "virtual certainty" that there is an "inherent factor of the general directionality of change in the process of rationalization" and certain expressive symbols of our age. The forced "affective neutrality" of our technological and bureaucratic system finds release in spectator amusements: comics, TV, radio, movies. Technological change, says Parsons, forces new reward systems and new distributions of roles, however: "It is probable that the strains imposed by these processes much more than any inherent 'conflict of interests' is the primary factor in the genesis of so-called 'class-conflicts' in modern Western society."[13]

In a few brief paragraphs the "dysfunctional" elements in the rationalization of our society are accounted for and brushed aside. For the most part, Americans are getting along well enough; if there are occasional conflicts and disturbances, these are epiphenomena. Thus we may infer from Parsons' position that frustration in our society is explained as a momentary zigzag in the course of progressing rationalization. It only remains to adjust our societal groups to the "normative pattern."

Since "adjustment" is the major problem in question, suggestions for research center on ideologies, beliefs, and expectations in their proper structural-functional settings in the analysis of conformity or deviance of social groups from societal norms, for, operating with the assumptions of the psychotherapeutic process, these are what must be changed by the therapists in maintaining social control. The researcher of late in his study of small-group behavior and of the mass man wants to know who and what the subject is thinking about when he expresses a certain attitude or behavior; this is what is referred to as "reference group" theory in the social sciences.[14] What determines the extent of internalizing certain attitudes of parents, peers, or authority figures and how is this reflected in behavior? Through an understanding of the ego-cathected identifications of the individual, the applied scientist can work toward changing the subject's identifications with people who have been significant to him and thereby change the way in which he defines the situation.

[12] Parsons, *The Social System*, p. 499.
[13] Parsons, *ibid.*, p. 513.
[14] See T. H. Newcomb, *Social Psychology* (Tavistock Publications, 1952), p. 225 ff., for elaboration of this theoretical construct.

This position is closely similar to John Dewey's description of the conservative mentality who thinks of changing society through first changing the individual, purifying the heart, and when this is done, the change of institutions will follow of itself.[15] The other school, continues Dewey, denies the efficacy of this subjective approach and asserts that man's nature is determined by his relation to the forces of environment; first, man must change society's institutions, then "human nature" will follow. Contemporary social scientists are, for the most part, taking the institutional structures in which people work and live out their lives as the constant given; the problem is that of how to alter attitudes by doling out more recognition and praise to subjects or to change the ego-identification pattern of the subject from one cathected group or person to another.

In this orientation, theorists have turned to the concepts of "status" and "role" developed by the anthropologist Ralph Linton as valuable tools for examining how people adjust to their formally prescribed positions in various institutional or social settings. "Status," as defined by Linton, refers to a place in a social structure recognized by society such as age, sex, occupation, position in family unit, and so forth. "Role" designates the behavior expected by society or certain groups or individuals in carrying out one's status position. The concept of "role" is the dynamic aspect of "status" suggesting analysis of how the individual interprets his status position.[16]

These concepts originally employed in the study of small, relatively static preliterate communities imply a state of stability and definity which is hardly present in "status" and "role" positions in our highly complex and changing society. One can, of course, formally delimit certain "status" positions for the purpose of defining what is to be studied in an organizational structure. However, this imputed concreteness to position in an organization is misleading and tends to neglect the fact that definitions of behavior expected in certain "status" and "role" positions are continually changing not only in the minds of those who perform them but in the expectations of those who recruit and control the behavior of subordinates. As these concepts have been defined, the aspect of "role" which is the dynamic interpretation by the subject of his "status" position leads the scientist to the investigation of back-

15 John Dewey, *Human Nature and Conduct* (New York: The Modern Library, 1930). See Introduction.

16 Ralph Linton, *The Cultural Background of Personality* (Routledge & Kegan Paul, 1946), pp. 77–82.

ground factors, ideologies, or other elements brought to his present "status" position resulting in more or less successful adjustment to the defined constant variable, his "status" position. In this, the interacting effect of change in the expectations of the leaders and the led as they influence one another is avoided by devoting attention essentially to the adjustment of the subordinate to the superordinate. Should the actors manifest so-called "deviant" or "dysfunctional" behavior in a more dynamic interpretation of their position, the very labels employed in the approach of Parsons appear to assume that the given set of institutional norms or the given power structure is the normal and correct state of affairs. Man is a helpless creature to be adapted and adjusted to the *status quo* or what is called "social control." Evidence of conflict or tension or anything which might be considered "compulsive" and motivated by a sense of inadequacy prompts the social scientist to fit him into the ubiquitous "social equilibrium." Such deviants, by definition, are "dysfunctional" to the larger order of harmony.

The study of change has thus been obscured by the formulation of theoretical constructs stressing order and stability. While it is interesting and useful to learn how a complex society manages to get along without complete chaos, our society among others, is, in the meantime, moving in the direction of more centralized controls over the areas of human freedom. In the opinion of the writer, the problem of modern society is not altogether that of Plato, Machiavelli, Hobbes, Locke, Rousseau and others who sought the foundations of a stable order to restrain what appeared to be impending societal chaos. Social control *today* is on the increase as large-scale bureaucracy proceeds to engulf modern man in the struggle to hold such structures accountable to society. It is this very rigidity and inflexibility of the bureaucracy and the consequent apathy of the employee that is now beginning to stimulate interest in "The Lonely Crowd" and in "Man for Himself."[17]

Research is needed in the problem of how to make man a rational being, an agent of change with the power to effect deliberate modification of his own environment rather than to view him as an irrational, passive adjuster to the contemporary scene. Problems for research would investigate, for example, the conditions for developing a personality with the "nerve of failure" to withstand pressures for ethical and behavioral conformity without being morally destroyed. What kind of family, peer group, or occu-

---

[17] David Riesman, *The Lonely Crowd* (New Haven: Yale University Press, 1950); Erich Fromm, *Man for Himself* (New York: Rinehart and Company, 1947).

pational background is conducive to the active and autonomous individual who has the moral strength or actual power to act back upon pressures for conformity.[18] Under what conditions do individuals or groups become active and effective in altering the given definition of the situation. What contributes to the recognition and acceptance of alternative views within and between large-scale organizations.[19] How are significant changes in policy made and carried out in large-scale bureaucracy. Such questions necessarily involve a consideration of the bases of power to accomplish change while assuming a certain amount of tension or conflict to be "normal" and perhaps inevitable in the study of change.

15 ❧ THE DENIAL OF OPTIONS

ALVIN W. GOULDNER

The conduct of a polemic focuses attention on the differences between two points of view to the neglect of their continuity and convergences. No modern polemic better exemplifies this than the controversy between the proponents of capitalism and of socialism. Each tends to define itself as the antithesis of the other; even the uncommitted bystander, rare though he be, is likely to think of the two as if they were utterly alien systems.

There have always been some, however, who have taken exception to this sharp contrast between socialism and capitalism and who have insisted that there are significant similarities between the two. One of these, the French sociologist Emile Durkheim, maintained that socialism like capitalism involved an overbearing

[18] For specific propositions in research along these lines, see Marie Jahoda, "Toward a Social Psychology of Mental Health," *Problems of Infancy and Childhood*, Fourth Conference Supplement II (Josiah Macy, Jr., Foundation, New York: 1950).

[19] Seymour M. Lipset deals with this problem in *Union Democracy*, (Glencoe, Ill.: Free Press, 1956).

FROM Alvin W. Gouldner, "Metaphysical Pathos and the Theory of Bureaucracy," *American Political Science Review*, 49 (June 1955), 496–507. The article has been retitled by the editor.

preoccupation with economic interests. In both socialist and capitalist societies, Durkheim argued, economic concerns were at the center of attention. In Durkheim's view, neither capitalism nor socialism deemed it necessary to bridle materialistic ends; neither society subordinated pecuniary interests to some higher, governing, moral norms. Therefore, "from Durkheim's point of view," writes Talcott Parsons, "socialism and laissez-faire individualism are of the same piece."[1]

Bertrand Russell came to similar conclusions on the basis of a trip to the then newly established Soviet Republic: ". . . the practical difference between socialism and capitalism is not so great as politicians on both sides suppose. Certain features will appear in the early stages of industrialism under either system; and under either system certain other features will appear in its later stages."[2]

Without doubt, though, the most sophisticated formulation of this view was that conceived by the German sociologist Max Weber. To Weber, the distinguishing characteristic of modern capitalism was the "rational organization of free labor." The pursuit of private gain, noted Weber, was well known in many earlier societies; what distinguishes present-day capitalism, he held, is the peculiar organization of the production unit, an organization that is essentially bureaucratic. This conception of capitalism, writes Parsons, "has one important concrete result; in contradistinction to Marx and most 'liberal' theories, it strongly minimizes the differences between capitalism and socialism, emphasizing rather their continuity. Not only would socialistic organization leave the central fact of bureaucracy untouched, it would greatly accentuate its importance."[3]

While Marx had dwelt largely on the interrelations *among* production units, that is, their market ties, Weber focused on the social relations *within* the industrial unit. If social relations inside of

[1] Talcott Parsons, *The Structure of Social Action* (New York 1937), p. 341. For Durkheim's own statement, see his *Le Socialisme* (Paris, 1908), especially Ch. 2.

[2] Bertrand and Dora Russell, *Prospects of Industrial Civilization* (New York, 1923), p. 14. Compare this with the discussion of Stalinist Communism by a postwar Russian refugee, G. F. Achminow, *Die Macht im Hintergrund: Totengräber des Kommunismus* (Ulm, 1950), which is discussed in Hans Gerth and C. Wright Mills, *Character and Social Structure* (New York, 1953), p. 477.

[3] Parsons, p. 509. See also the provocative fuller development of this argument as it applies to industrial organization: George C. Homans, "Industrial Harmony as a Goal," in *Industrial Conflict*, eds. Kornhauser, Dubin, and Ross (New York, 1954).

socialist and capitalist factories are fundamentally alike, in that they are both bureaucratic, then, asked Weber, does a socialist revolution yield very much of an improvement for the capitalist proletarian?

If Marx argued that the workers of the world had nothing to *lose* by revolting, Weber contended that they really had nothing to *gain*. "For the time being," he declared, "the dictatorship of the official and not that of the worker is on the march." Capitalism and socialism are thus placed under the same conceptual umbrella—bureaucracy—with the important practical result that the problem of choosing between them loses much of its point.

It is for this reason that the discussions of bureaucratic organization which are heir to the Weberian analysis must be understood as being, in part, a displacement of the controversy over socialism. Weber made it clear that questions of economic choice could no longer be treated in isolation from questions of administration. From Weber's time forward, administrative and economic choices were seen to be but two facets of the same hard problem. This has been recognized even by socialists, at least when they have been unencumbered by Communist party orthodoxy. For example, Oskar Lange once remarked, with a frankness that we hope he will never be compelled to regret, ". . . the real danger of socialism is that of bureaucratic organization of economic life. . . ."[4]

It is sometimes assumed today that the Weberian outlook is at bottom anti-socialist. In effect, the argument runs, Weber's viewpoint devitalizes the myth-like appeal of socialism, draining off its ability to muster immense enthusiasms. Weber's theses are therefore held to be an "ideology" serviceable for the survival of capitalism, while Weber himself is characterized as the "Marx of the bourgeoisie."

Now all this may be true, but it is only a partial truth; for, in actuality, Weber's theories cut two ways, not one. If it is correct that this theory of bureaucracy saps the fervor of the socialist offensive, it also undermines the stamina of the capitalist bastions. If socialism and capitalism are similar in being bureaucratic, then not only is there little *profit* in substituting one for the other, but there is also little *loss*.

Considered only from the standpoint of its political consequences then, the Weberian outlook is not anti-socialist alone, nor anti-capitalist alone, it is both. In the final analysis its political

[4] Oskar Lange and Fred M. Taylor, *On the Economic Theory of Socialism,* ed. Lippincott (Minneapolis, 1948), p. 109.

slogan becomes "a plague on both your houses." If Weber is to be regarded as an "ideologist," he is an ideologist not of counter-revolution but of quiescence and neutralism. For many intellectuals who have erected a theory of group organization on Weberian foundations, the world has been emptied of choice, leaving them disoriented and despairing.

That gifted historian of ideas, Arthur O. Lovejoy, astutely observed that every theory is associated with, or generates, a set of sentiments which those subscribing to the theory could only dimly sense. Lovejoy called this the "metaphysical pathos" of ideas, a pathos which is "exemplified in any description of the nature of things, any characterization of the world to which one belongs, in terms which, like the word of a poem, evoke through their associations and through a sort of empathy which they engender, a congenial mood or tone of feelings."[5]

As a result, a commitment to a theory often occurs by a process other than the one which its proponents believe and it is usually more consequential than they realize. A commitment to a theory may be made because the theory is congruent with the mood or deep-lying sentiments of its adherents, rather than merely because it has been cerebrally inspected and found valid. This is as true for the rigorous prose of social science as it is for the more lucid metaphor of creative literature, for each has its own silent appeal and its own metaphysical pathos.

Furthermore, those who have committed themselves to a theory always get more than they have bargained for. We do not make a commercial contract with a theory in which we agree to accept only the consignment of intellectual goods which has been expressly ordered; usually we take also the metaphysical pathos in which the theory comes packaged. In the end, the theory reinforces or induces in the adherent a subtle alteration in the structure of sentiments through which he views the world.

So too is it with the theory of organization. Paradoxically enough, some of the very theories which promise to make man's own work more intelligible to himself and more amenable to his intelligence are infused with an intangible metaphysical pathos which insinuates, in the very midst of new discoveries, that all is lost. For the metaphysical pathos of much of the modern theory of group organization is that of pessimism and fatalism.

[5] Arthur O. Lovejoy, *The Great Chain of Being* (Cambridge, Mass., 1948), p. 11.

I. Explanations of Bureaucracy

Nowhere does the fatalism of the theory of organization become more articulate than in its efforts to account for the development of bureaucratic behavior. One of the less challenging explanations, for example, premises a supposedly invariant human nature. Thus in an otherwise illuminating analysis, one political scientist remarks: "Civil servants are ordinary mortals; they have the defects and weaknesses typical of human nature. Each loves, as Shakespeare said, 'his brief moment of authority.' "[6]

This, however, is difficult to reconcile with recurrent complaints, from civic leaders or business managers, that it is often hard to persuade people either to run for political office or to accept positions as foremen. Apparently there are some people who do not hanker after their brief moment of authority.

In any event, it does not seem possible to account for bureaucracy in any of its forms as an outgrowth of "human nature." This explanation cannot cope with the rudimentary fact that in some times and in some places there is much bureaucracy, but in other times and places there is little. Leaving aside the question of the validity of the argument, its practical results are again all too evident. For if bureaucracy is rooted in human nature then all hope for a remedy must be abandoned.

Much more serious as goads to pessimism are theories explaining bureaucracy as the end-product of increased size and complexity in organizations. This is by far the most popular of the interpretations. Marshall Dimock and Howard Hyde, for example, in their report to the Temporary National Economic Committee (TNEC), state: "The broadest structural cause of bureaucracy, whether in business or in government, is the tremendous size of the organization. Thus with capital or appropriations measured in hundreds of millions and in billions of dollars and personnel in tens and hundreds of thousands, it is difficult to avoid the obtrusion of the objectionable features of bureaucracy."[7]

While suggesting varied causes for the development of bureaucracy, Max Weber also interpreted it as a consequence of large size. For example, in discussing the ubiquity of bureaucratic forms

[6] John A. Vieg, "Bureaucracy—Fact and Fiction," in *Elements of Public Administration*, ed. Fritz Morstein Marx (New York, 1946), p. 52.

[7] Monograph #11, Temporary National Economic Committee, *Bureaucracy and Trusteeship in Large Corporations* (Washington, D. C., 1940), p. 36.

Weber adds: "The same [bureaucratic] phenomena are found in the large-scale capitalistic enterprise; and the larger it is, the greater their role."[8] He underscores the role of size by emphasizing that "only by reversion in every field—political, religious, economic, etc.—to small-scale organization would it be possible to escape its influence."[9] Despite his consideration of other possible sources of bureaucracy, these comments suggest that Weber regarded organizational size as the controlling factor in the development of bureaucracy.

Weber's emphasis on size as the crucial determinant of bureaucratic development is unsatisfactory for several reasons. First, there are historic examples of human efforts carried out on an enormous scale which were not bureaucratic in any serious sense of the term.[10] The building of the Egyptian pyramids is an obvious example. Second, Weber never considers the possibility that it is not "large size" as such that disposes to bureaucracy; large size may be important only because it generates other social forces which, in their turn, generate bureaucratic patterns.

Of course, in every analysis there are always intervening variables—the unknown "x"—which stand between any cause and effect. Scientific progress depends, in part, on moving away from the gross causes and coming closer to those which are more invariably connected with the object of interest. The point is that when a social scientist accepts "size" as an explanatory factor, instead of going on to ask what there is *about size* that makes for bureaucracy, he is making an analytic *decision*. It is not a formulation unavoidably dictated by the nature of the data itself.

Significantly, though, it is a decision that leads once again to bleak pessimism. For to inform members of our society that the only way out of the bureaucratic impasse is to return to the historical past and to trade in large for small-scale organizations is, in effect, to announce the practical impossibility of coping with bureaucracy. Moreover, many people in our society believe that

8 Max Weber: *The Theory of Social and Economic Organization*, translated and edited by A. M. Henderson and Talcott Parsons (New York, 1947), p. 334.
9 *Ibid.*, p. 338.
10 See Reinhard Bendix, "Bureaucracy: The Problem and Its Setting," *American Sociological Review*, Vol. 12, pp. 502–7 (Oct., 1947). On the other hand, there are theoretically significant cases of small organizations which are highly bureaucratized, for example, the Boulton and Watt factory in 1775–1805. This "case illustrates the fact that the bureaucratization of industry is not synonymous with the recent growth in the size of business enterprises." Reinhard Bendix, "Bureaucratization in Industry," in *Industrial Conflict*, p. 166.

"bigness" symbolizes progress; to tell them that it also creates bureaucracy is to place them on the horns of a dilemma which gores no matter which way they turn. In such a position the most pointless response is inaction.

Underlying this conception of the matter there is a Hegelian dialectic in which "good" and "bad" are viewed as inseparably connected opposites; bureaucracy, "the bad thing," is represented as the inescapable price that has to be paid for the good things, the efficiency and abundance of modern life. One social scientist clearly puts it this way: "Assembly line techniques offer marked advantages over those of custom craftsmanship. They also have their price. They entail the imposition of an order of progression, the fixing of a rate or rhythm of operation, and the discipline of a regular routine. Set order, fixed pace, and adherence to routine— these are the very stuff of which red tape is made. Yet they are of the essence of system, too."[11] However true or false, there can be little doubt that this is an outlook which is convenient and comfortable for bureaucrats—if not for many others.

II. The Structural-Functionalists

The fuller ramifications of this approach to bureaucracy can best be explained by turning to the analyses of industrial organization made by some of the "structural-functionalists." This is a comparatively new and vigorous school of American sociologists, which has grown directly out of the theories of Durkheim, Weber, and others, and whose most elaborate expression is to be found in the work of Talcott Parsons.

Parsons' recent analyses of industrial bureaucracy are of sufficient importance to be quoted in full. "Though with many individual exceptions [which he does not examine], *technological advance* almost always leads to increasingly *elaborate division of labor* and the concomitant requirement of increasingly elaborate organization." He continues:

The fundamental reason for this is, of course, that with elaborate differentiation of functions the need for *minute coordination* of the different functions develops at the same time. . . . There must be a *complex organization of supervision* to make quite sure that exactly the right thing is done. . . . Feeding the various parts into the process, in such a way that a modern assembly line can operate smoothly, requires very *complex organization* to see that they are available in just

[11] Vieg, pp. 5–6.

the right quantities at the right times and places. . . . One of the most important phases of this process of change is concerned with the necessity for *formalization* when certain points of complexity are reached. . . .

Smaller and simpler organizations are typically managed with a high degree of particularism (i.e., personal consideration) in the relations of persons in authority to their own subordinates. But when the "distance" between points of decision and of operation increases, and the number of operating units affected by decisions with it, uniformity and coordination can be attained *only* by a high degree of formalization. . . .[12]

Surprisingly enough, this is an atavistic recurrence of technological determinism in which characteristic bureaucratic traits—such as an elaborate division of labor, complex organization, and formulation—are held to stem directly from technological advance. This is a form of *technological* determinism because bureaucracy is seen as the result of technological change, without inquiring into the motives and meanings which these changes have for the people involved, and without wondering whether technological change would have a different impact on the formal organization of a group that had a high motivation to produce and therefore did not require close supervision. This is a form of technological *determinism,* because no alternative solutions are appraised or deemed possible and coordination is seen as attainable "*only* by a high degree of formalization. . . ."

Here once again we are invited to draw the conclusion that those who want modern technology must be prepared to pay for it with a minute and even stultifying division of labor.

All this, though, is a theoretical tapestry devoid of even the plainest empirical trimmings. Even on logical grounds, however, it is tenuous indeed. For it is evident that organizational patterns, such as a high division of labor, are found in spheres where modern technology has made comparatively little headway. This, in fact, is a point that Weber was at pains to insist upon. And if, as he maintained, bureaucratic forms are also found in charitable, political, or religious organizations—and not solely in industry—then they certainly cannot be explained as a consequence of modern machine technology.

Beyond these logical considerations, there are also some *empirical* grounds for questioning the adequacy of Parsons' analysis. Peter Drucker, for example, became extremely doubtful about the necessity of a minute division of labor while observing large-scale

[12] Talcott Parsons, *The Social System* (Glencoe, Illinois, 1951), pp. 507–8. Italics added.

American industry during World War II. (This is crucial for Parsons' argument, because he holds that it is through increased specialization that technology evokes the other elements of bureaucratic organization.) Drucker comments that "we have learned that it is neither necessary nor always efficient to organize all mass production in such a manner as to have the majority of workers confine themselves to doing one and only one of the elementary manipulations. . . . It was impossible [because of wartime shortages of skilled labor] to 'lay out' the job in the usual assembly-line fashion in which one unskilled operation done by one unskilled man is followed by the next unskilled man. The operation was broken down into its unskilled components like any assembly-line job. *But then the unskilled components were put together again with the result that an unskilled worker actually performed the job of a highly skilled mechanic*—and did it as reliably and efficiently as had been done by skilled men."[13]

In short, lower degrees of specialization than those normally found in large-scale industry are not necessarily forbidden by modern technology. Drucker's observations must, at the very least, raise the question as to how much of the minute division of labor is attributable to technological causes. Parsons, though, gives no consideration to other factors contributing to an extreme division of labor. However, Carl Dreyfuss, a German industrial sociologist, has advanced an array of keen observations and hypotheses which meet this question directly. He writes: "The artificial complication of the rank order . . . permits numerous employees to feel that they hold high positions and are to a certain extent independent." Moreover, he notes that a complicated division of labor is "with its unwarranted differentiations, telescoped positions, and ramifications, diametrically opposed to efforts of rationalization."[14] In other words, Dreyfuss suggests that much of the complex division of labor today is not to be explained by technological requirements, but rather in terms of the prestige satisfactions, the "psychic income," that it presumably provides workers.

In Dreyfuss' view, the "minute division of labor" also stems from management's needs to *control* workers and to make themselves independent of any specific individual or group of workers. A high division of labor, said Dreyfuss, means that "individual workers

---

[13] Peter Drucker, *Concept of the Corporation* (New York, 1946), pp. 183–84.
[14] Carl Dreyfuss, *Occupation and Ideology of the Salaried Employee*, trans. Eva Abramovitch (New York, 1938), p. 17.

and employees can be exchanged and replaced at any time.[15] Through its use, "dependence of the employee upon the employer is greatly increased. It is much more difficult for today's employee, trained in only one particular function, to find reemployment than it was for his predecessor, a many-sided, well-instructed business man, able and fitted to fill a variety of positions."[16]

A similar view is advanced in the more recent studies of industrial organization in Yankee City, which were made by W. L. Warner and J. O. Low. "While machine processes were adopted by shoe factories primarily to reduce costs and to speed the processing, the machine has other great advantages over the human worker from the managerial point of view," comment Warner and Low.

> Control problems are simplified . . . on two counts through mechanization: (1) machines are easier to control than human beings, and (2) mechanization tends to disrupt the social solidarity of the workers, who thereby become easier to control than they would if they were able to maintain close social relations during working hours . . . these factors tend to increase the subordination of the individual worker to management; from the management's viewpoint they are valuable means of social control over workers. . . . The routinization of jobs also simplifies control of workers in another way. The individual operative today does not have the feeling of security that the oldtime craftsman derived from his special technical abilities. In most cases, today's operative is aware that only a comparatively brief training period protects him in his job from a large number of untrained individuals. The members of the supervisory hierarchy are also well aware of this fact. The psychological effect of this result of the division of labor is to intensify the subordinate position of the individual operative and to make him submit the more readily to the limitations on his behavior required by the supervisory group.[17]

It is unnecessary for our purpose here to resolve this disparity between Warner and Dreyfuss, on the one hand, and Parsons, on the other. What may be suggested, however, is that there is considerable reason for holding Parsons' position to be both logically and empirically inadequate and to recognize that it has, without compelling scientific warrant, accommodated itself to the metaphysical pathos of organizational theory, which sees no escape from bureaucracy.

[15] *Ibid.*, p. 75.
[16] *Ibid.*, p. 77.
[17] W. Lloyd Warner and J. O. Low, *The Social System of the Modern Factory* (New Haven, 1947), pp. 78, 80, 174.

III. The Tradition of Michels

There is another offshoot among the structural-functionalists which is distinguished by its concern for the problems bequeathed by Robert Michels and, as such, it is even more morosely pessimistic than others in the school. Michels, it will be remembered, focused his empirical studies on the Social Democratic parties of pre-World War I Europe. He chose these, quite deliberately, because he wanted to see whether groups which stood for greater freedom and democracy, and were hostile to authoritarianism, were not themselves afflicted by the very organizational deformity to which they were opposed.

Michel's conclusions were, of course, formulated in his "iron law of oligarchy," in which he maintained that always and everywhere a "system of leadership is incompatible with the most essential postulates of democracy."[18] Oligarchy, said Michels, "derives from the tactical and technical necessities which result from the consolidation of every disciplined political aggregate. . . ."[19] It is the outcome of organic necessity, and consequently affects every organization, be it socialist or even anarchist."[20]

In concluding his study, Michels remarks with a flourish of defensive pathos, ". . . it seemed necessary to lay considerable stress upon the pessimist aspect of democracy which is forced upon us by historical study. . . ."[21] "The democratic currents of history resemble successive waves. They break ever on the same shoals. . . . It is probable that this cruel game will continue without end."[22]

Focusing, as Michels did, on an apparently democratic group, Philip Selznick examined the TVA, which many Americans had long believed to be an advanced expression of democratic values. Like Michels, Selznick assumes that "wherever there is organization, whether formally democratic or not, there is a split between the leader and the led, between the agent and the initiator. The phenomenon of abdication to bureaucratic directives in corporations, in trade unions, in parties, and in cooperatives is so widespread that it indicates a fundamental weakness of democracy."[23]

[18] Robert Michels, *Political Parties* (Glencoe, Ill., 1949), p. 400. Michel's work was first published in 1915.

[19] *Ibid.*, p. 401.

[20] *Ibid.*, p. 402.

[21] *Ibid.*, p. 405.

[22] *Ibid.*, p. 408.

[23] Philip Selznick, *TVA and the Grass Roots* (Berkeley and Los Angeles, 1949), p. 9.

Selznick's study concludes that the TVA's emphasis on "decentralization" is to be best understood as a result of that agency's needs to adapt to suspicious local communities and to survive in competition with older government agencies based in Washington. "Decentralization" is viewed as a "halo that becomes especially useful in countries which prize the symbols of democracy."[24] In its turn, the TVA's emphasis on "participation" is explained as a catchword, satisfying the agency's needs to transform "an unorganized citizenry into a reliable instrument for the achievement of administrative goals. . . ."[25]

Selznick, like Michels, is impressed with the similarity in the organizational devices employed by different groups, whether they are democratic or authoritarian in ideology. He asserts, ". . . there seems to be a continuum between the voluntary associations set up by the democratic (mass) state—such as committees of farmers to boost or control agricultural production—and the citizens' associations of the totalitarian (mass) state. Indeed the devices of corporatism emerge as relatively effective responses to the need to deal with the mass, and in time of war the administrative techniques of avowedly democratic countries and avowedly totalitarian countries tend to converge."[26]

In Selznick's analysis human action involves a commitment to two sets of interests: first to the *goals* intended, and second to the organizational *instruments* through which these goals are pursued. These tools are, however, recalcitrant; they generate "needs" which cannot be neglected. Hence if men persist in their ends, they are forced to satisfy the needs of their organizational instruments. They are, therefore, as much committed to their tools as to their ends, and "these commitments may lead to unanticipated consequences resulting in a deflection of original ends."[27]

For these reasons, organizational behavior must be interpreted not so much in terms of the *ends* that administrators deliberately seek, as in terms of the organizational "needs" which their pursuit engenders. "The needs in question are organizational, not individual, and include: the security of the organization as a whole in relation to social forces in its environment; the stability of the lines of authority and communication; the stability of informal relations within the organization; the continuity of policy and of the sources

[24] *Ibid.*, p. 220.
[25] *Loc. cit.*
[26] *Loc. cit.*
[27] *Ibid.*, p. 259.

of its determination; a homogeneity of outlook with respect to the means and role of the organization."[28]

"In general," writes Selznick, "we have been concerned to formulate some of the underlying tendencies which are likely to inhibit the democratic process. Like all conservative or pessimistic criticism, such a statement of inherent problems seems to cast doubt upon the possibility of complete democratic achievement. It does cast such a doubt. The alternative, however, is the transformation of democracy into a utopian notion which, unaware of its internal dangers, is unarmed to meet them."[29] This, however, is an argument that rests upon assumptions which are not transparently self-evident and are acceptable without dispute only by those who are susceptible to its metaphysical pathos. Despite demagogic appeals to democratic symbols, there seem to be few places in either the Eastern or Western worlds in which there is a real and present danger of the "transformation of democracy into a utopian notion." Surely this is not to be expected among the class-conscious working classes of Europe, the laborite masses of England, the untutored peasants of China, or among the confused and often apathetic American electorate to whom politics is something of a dirty game, to be periodically enlivened with scandals and investigations. And if this appraisal is correct, then just who is there to be "armed" with this knowledge of the internal dangers of democracy?

For some reason Selznick has chosen—and this was not forced upon him by the data—to focus on the things which harry and impede democratic aspirations, rather than on those which strengthen and energize it. It is for this reason perhaps that he is led to reiterate Michel apologia: "Attention being focused on the structural conditions which influence behavior, we are directed to emphasize constraints, the limitation of alternatives imposed by the system upon its participants. This will tend to give pessimistic overtones to the analysis, since such factors as good will and intelligence will be de-emphasized."[30]

Selznick chose to focus on those social constraints that *thwart* democratic aspirations, but neglected to consider the constraints that enable them to be *realized*, and that foster and encourage "good will" and "intelligence." Are these, however, random occurrences, mere historic butterflies which flit through events with only ephemeral beauty? Or are they, as much as anything else,

[28] *Ibid.*, p. 252.
[29] *Ibid.*, p. 265.
[30] *Ibid.*, p. 252.

often the unanticipated products of our "commitments"? Why is it that "unanticipated consequences" are always tacitly assumed to be destructive of democratic values and "bad"; why can't they sometimes be "good"? Are there no constraints which *force* men to adhere valorously to their democratic beliefs, which *compel* them to be intelligent rather than blind, which leave them *no choice* but to be men of good will rather than predators? The neglect of these possibilities suggests the presence of a distorting pathos.

It is the pathos of pessimism, rather than the compulsions of rigorous analysis, that lead to the assumption that organizational constraints have stacked the deck against democracy. For on the face of it there is every reason to assume that "the underlying tendencies which are likely to inhibit the democratic process" are just as likely to impair authoritarian rule. It is only in the light of such a pessimistic pathos that the defeat of democratic values can be assumed to be probable, while their victory is seen as a slender thing, delicately constituted and precariously balanced.

When, for example, Michels spoke of the "iron law of oligarchy," he attended solely to the ways in which organizational needs inhibit democratic possibilities. But the very same evidence to which he called attention could enable us to formulate the very opposite theorem—the "iron law of democracy." Even as Michels himself saw, if oligarchical waves repeatedly wash away the bridges of democracy, this eternal recurrence can happen only because men doggedly rebuild them after each inundation. Michels chose to dwell on only one aspect of this process, neglecting to consider this other side. There cannot be an iron law of oligarchy, however, unless there is an iron law of democracy.

Much the same may be said for Selznick. He posits certain organizational needs: a need for the *security* of the organization, for *stable* lines of authority and communication, for *stable* informal relationships. But for each of the organizational needs which Selznick postulates, a set of contrary needs can also be posited, and the satisfaction of these would seem to be just as necessary for the survival of an organization. If, as Selznick says, an organization must have security in its environment, then certainly Toynbee's observations that too much security can be stultifying and corrosive is at least as well taken. To Selznick's security need, a Toynbee might counterpose a need for a moderate *challenge* or *threat*.

A similar analysis might also be made of Selznick's postulated need for homogeneity of outlook concerning the means and role of the organization. For unless there is some *heterogeneity* of outlook, then where is an organization to find the tools and flexibility to cope with changes in its environment? Underlying Selznick's need for homogeneity in outlook, is there not another "need," *a need that consent of the governed be given—at least in some measure—to their governors?* Indeed, this would seem to be at the very core of Selznick's empirical analysis, though it is obscured in his high-level theoretical statement of the needs of organizations. And if all organizations must adjust to such a need for consent, is there not built into the very marrow of organization a large element of what we mean by democracy? This would appear to be an organizational constraint that makes oligarchies, and all separation of leaders from those led, no less inherently unstable than democratic organization.[31]

These contrary needs are just as real and just as consequential for organizational behavior as those proposed by Selznick. But they point in a different direction. They are oriented to problems of change, of growth, of challenging contingencies, of provoking and unsettling encounters. Selznick's analysis seems almost to imply that survival is possible only in an icy stasis, in which "security," "continuity," and "stability" are the key terms. If anything, the opposite seems more likely to be true, and organizational survival is impossible in such a state.

Wrapping themselves in the shrouds of nineteenth-century political economy, some social scientists appear to be bent on resurrecting a dismal science. For the iron law of wages, which maintained that workers could never improve their material standards of life, some sociologists have substituted the iron law of oligarchy, which declares that men cannot improve their political standards of life. Woven to a great extent out of theoretical whole cloth, much of the discussion of bureaucracy and of organizational needs seems to have provided a screen onto which some intellectuals have projected their own despair and pessimism, reinforcing the despair of others.

Perhaps the situation can be illuminated with an analogy. For many years now, infantile paralysis has killed and maimed scores

---

[31] See Arthur Schweitzer, "Ideological Groups," *American Sociological Review*, Vol. 9 (Aug. 1944), pp. 415–27, particularly his discussion of factors inhibiting oligarchy. For example, "A leadership concentrating all power in its hands creates indifference among the functionaries and sympathizers as well as decline in membership of the organization. This process of shrinkage, endangering the position of the leaders, is the best protection against the supposedly inevitable iron law of oligarchy" (p. 419). Much of the research deriving from the Lewinian tradition would seem to lend credence to this inference.

of people. For many years also doctors, biologists, and chemists have been searching for the causes and cure of this disease. Consider the public reaction if, instead of reporting on their newest vaccines, these scientists had issued the following announcement: "We have not reached any conclusions concerning the causes of the disease, nor has our research investigated defenses against it. The public seems to have perfectionist aspirations of flawless health, they have 'utopian' illusions concerning the possibilities of immortality and it is this—not the disease—that is the danger against which the public needs to be armed. We must remember that the human animal is not immortal and that for definite reasons his lifespan is finite." It is likely, of course, that such scientists would be castigated for having usurped the prerogatives and functions of clergymen.

This, however, seems to parallel the way in which some social scientists have approached the study of organizational pathology. Instead of telling men how bureaucracy might be mitigated, they insist that it is inevitable. Instead of explaining how democratic patterns may, to some extent, be fortified and extended, they warn us that democracy cannot be perfect. Instead of controlling the disease, they suggest that we are deluded, or more politely, incurably romantic, for hoping to control it. Instead of assuming responsibilities as realistic clinicians, striving to further democratic potentialities wherever they can, many social scientists have become morticians, all too eager to bury men's hopes.[32]

[32] We have sought to develop the positive implications of this approach to bureaucratic organization in *Patterns of Industrial Bureaucracy* (Glencoe, Ill., 1954).

16 ❧ THE INSUFFICIENCY OF ELITE COMPETITION

T. B. BOTTOMORE

The criticism of democratic theories of politics which Mosca and Pareto formulated in the theory of elites began with the observation that in every society there is a minority which effectively rules. This criticism could be met—as Mosca himself saw—while acknowledging the fact that a governing elite is necessary in every society, by arguing that the distinctive feature of democracy, as a form of government, is that it permits elites to form freely, and establishes a regulated competition between elites for the positions of power. This conception of democracy as a political system in which political parties compete for the votes of a mass electorate implies further that the elites are relatively "open" and are recruited on the basis of merit (*i.e.*, there is presumed to be a continuous and extensive circulation of elites), and that the mass of the population is able to participate in ruling society at least in the sense that it can exercise a choice between the rival elites. Karl Mannheim . . . had originally connected elite theories with Fascism and with anti-intellectualist doctrines of "direct action," but came later to hold a view of this kind: ". . . the actual shaping of policy is in the hands of elites; but this does not mean that the society is not democratic. For it is sufficient for democracy that the individual citizens, though prevented from taking a direct part in government all the time, have at least the *possibility* of making their aspirations felt at certain intervals . . . Pareto is right in stressing that political power is always exercised by minorities (elites), and we may also accept Robert Michels' law of the trend toward oligarchic rule in party organizations. Nevertheless, it would be wrong to overestimate the stability of such elites in democratic societies, or their ability to wield power in arbitrary ways. In a democracy, the governed can always act to remove their leaders or to force them to take decisions in the interests of the many."[1] Mannheim also emphasized the importance of selection by merit, and of the reduced distance between elites and masses in creating a compatibility between elite rule and democratic govern-

FROM "Democracy and the Plurality of Elites," Chap. VI of *Elites and Society,* by T. B. Bottomore. Copyright © T. B. Bottomore, 1964. Reprinted by permission of C. A. Watts & Co., Ltd.

[1] Karl Mannheim, *Essays on the Sociology of Culture*, p. 179.

ment: "We assume that democracy is characterized, not by the absence of all elite strata, but rather by a new mode of elite selection and a new self-interpretation of the elite . . . What changes most of all in the course of democratization is the distance between the elite and the rank-and-file. The democratic elite has a mass background; this is why it can mean something for the mass."[2]

The reconciliation between the idea of elites and the idea of democratic government has proceeded apace during the twentieth century, as Mannheim's own work bears witness, and it has been assisted by a number of favorable circumstances. One of these is the general enhancement of the importance of leadership which has resulted from large-scale warfare, from international rivalry in economic growth and from the rise and development of new nations; all of which has turned men's thoughts away from the dangers of elite rule toward the need for efficient and enterprising elites. Another circumstance which has lent support to the competition model of democracy is the contrast between the consequences of elite rule in one-party states, and the experiences of those democratic societies in which there is competition for power among several political parties, none of which aims to bring about a radical change in the social structure. Furthermore, this model has also a scientific appeal, by reason of the analogy which it presents to the model of economic behavior in a free enterprise system, and of the promise which it thus holds out of an analysis of political behavior as exact and rigorous, if also as limited, as economic analysis. The analogy was stated plainly by Schumpeter,[3] who also went on to argue, more generally, that modern democracy arose with the capitalist economic system and is causally connected with it.[4] The view is conveyed succinctly in the remark made by a successful politician, which Schumpeter quotes: "What businessmen do not understand is that exactly as they are dealing in oil so I am dealing in votes."[5] More recently, this conception of democracy as a competition for votes between political parties has been presented in more elaborate forms, as for example in the "economic theory of democracy" of A. Downs, who summarizes his theory in the following terms: "Our main thesis is that parties in democratic politics are analogous to entrepreneurs in a

---

[2] *Ibid.*, p. 200.

[3] In *Capitalism, Socialism and Democracy*, Chap. XXII, "Another Theory of Democracy." See also above, p. 10.

[4] *Ibid.*, pp. 296–7.

[5] *Ibid.*, p. 285.

profit-seeking economy. So as to attain their private ends, they formulate whatever policies they believe will gain the most votes, just as entrepreneurs produce whatever products they believe will gain the most profits for the same reasons."[6] Another example of the use of this model is to be found in the tentative efforts to apply the theory of games to political behavior, *i.e.*, to apply to the activities of political parties a mathematical scheme which is extensively used in analyzing the behavior of business enterprises.[7]

But it is not only the competition between political parties which serves to reconcile the existence of elites with democracy. The advocates of this view discover a more general system of checks and balances in the plurality of elites which characterizes democratic societies. Raymond Aron has presented the case in a cogent and revealing manner:

Although there are everywhere business managers, government officials, trade union secretaries and ministers, they are not everywhere recruited in the same way and they may either form one coherent whole or remain comparatively distinct from one another. The fundamental difference between a society of the Soviet type and one of the Western type is that the former has a unified elite and the latter a divided elite. In the USSR the trade union secretaries, the business managers and the higher officials generally belong to the Communist party . . . On the other hand, democratic societies, which I would rather call pluralistic societies, are full of the noise of public strife between the owners of the means of production, trade union leaders and politicians. As all are entitled to form associations, professional and political organizations abound, each one defending its members' interests with passionate ardour. Government becomes a business of compromises. Those in power are well aware of their precarious position. They are considerate of the opposition because they themselves have been, and will one day again be, in opposition.[8]

The definition of democracy as competition between elites may be criticized on various grounds—that it is excessively arbitrary and leaves out of account generally recognized characteristics of the phenomenon which it defines, or that the theory in which it

[6] A. Downs, *An Economic Theory of Democracy*, pp. 295–6.

[7] Up to the present, however, the theory of games has been used most extensively in the study of international conflicts, notably in the currently fashionable "war games." Its uses in this field are critically examined in Raymond Aron, *Paix et Guerre entre les nations*, Note finale, "Stratégie rationnelle et politique raisonnable," pp. 751–70.

[8] Raymond Aron, "Social Structure and the Ruling Class," *British Journal of Sociology*, I (1), p. 10.

is used is inadequate or untrue, or that it proceeds from a set of value judgments to which other value judgments can be opposed. Modern democracy has most often, and by most political thinkers, been defined as the participation of the mass of the people in government, and one of its classical formulations is that of Lincoln's Gettysburg Address: "government of the people, by the people, for the people." All elite theories deny that there can be, in any real sense, government *by* the people.[9] The denial may be founded, as in the case of Pareto and Mosca, upon the somewhat trivial observation that in most known societies of the past there has been a clear distinction between the rulers and the ruled, or it may rest upon a more theoretical analysis, as in the writings of Michels, Mannheim, and Aron, which seeks to show that in any large and complex society (and in large and complex organizations within society) democracy can only be *representative,* not direct, and that the representatives are a minority who clearly possess greater political power than those whom they represent, since the influence of the latter is confined to passing judgment, at fairly long intervals, upon the activities of the minority. But several objections can be brought against this analysis. In the first place, according to the view of democracy which we are now considering, the system of government by representation is quite clearly regarded as an imperfect realization of democracy, insofar as it does permanently exclude the many from any experience of government. The undemocratic character of representative government becomes most apparent when the representative principle is applied in a system of indirect election, whereby an elected elite itself elects a second elite which is endowed with equal or superior political power. This device has often been resorted to by the opponents of popular rule—a recent example is to be found in the constitution of the Fifth Republic in France under the leadership of de Gaulle—and de Tocqueville, among others, saw in it an effective means of restricting democracy. Even when the defenders of the idea of democracy as competition between elites do not propound it deliberately as a defense against democracy in its other sense—against that incursion of the masses into politics which de Tocqueville, Pareto, Mosca, and Ortega y Gasset unite in deploring—they are still inclined to take representative government as the ideal, instead of measuring it against the ideal of direct participa-

[9] Raymond Aron, in the article quoted above, says that "it is quite impossible for the government of a society to be in the hands of any but a few . . . there is government *for* the people; there is no government *by* the people."

tion by the people in legislation and administration and looking about for means by which this end might be more closely approached.

This argument suggests a second objection to the analysis of democracy, which Schumpeter, Aron, and others provide. According to their accounts democracy is to be conceived as something accomplished and complete, which can be contrasted straightforwardly with other types of political system. On the other hand, in the conception of democracy as government *by* the people which prevailed during most of the nineteenth century, democracy was conceived as a continuing process in which political rights, the power to influence decisions on social policy, were progressively extended to groups in the population which had formerly been deprived of them. This implies two things: first, that democracy appeared primarily as a doctrine and political movement of the lower classes of society against the dominance of the aristocratic and wealthy classes (and this is, of course, one of the main causes which provoked the response of the elite theories); and second, that it was regarded as a movement toward an ideal condition of society in which men would be fully self-governing, which might never be completely achieved, but which democrats ought to strive for. It would not have occurred to most of the democratic political thinkers of the nineteenth century to regard universal suffrage, competition between several political parties, and representative government, however valuable by contrast with the institutions of other political regimes, as the ultimate point of democratic progress beyond which it was impossible to venture.

The reasons for the emergence, in the twentieth century, of a static conception of democracy in which elite rule is sanctioned by periodic elections have to be sought in the political circumstances of this century. It was the establishment of one-party states, in a fascist form in Germany and Italy, and in a communist form in the USSR, which gave point and credibility to the identification of democracy with a multiparty, representative system. The passage which I quoted earlier from Raymond Aron, in which the unified elite in Soviet-type societies is contrasted with the plurality of elites in Western-type societies, makes this perfectly clear. We may, however, question whether organized political parties—and more broadly, organized elite groups—are necessary or sufficient for the existence of a democratic system of government. It has often been held that they are not necessary, and that, for example, in a more decentralized type of political system than those which now exist in most nations, the selection of the political leaders for the time being might be accomplished through the activities of associations which would be less highly organized, less bureaucratic and less permanent than the present-day political parties. To this should be added that in a society from which social classes had been eliminated (which many thinkers have envisaged as a consequence of the growth of democracy) the most important single basis for the formation of parties would likewise have disappeared; and although it is not impossible to think of other social distinctions which might engender political parties, it is difficult to conceive that such parties would have the same scope and influence in political life as those with which we are familiar now. This argument refers, it will be noted, to a political system without any political parties, and not to a one-party regime. The latter is not democratic at all, for it deprives the individual, confronted by the ruling party, of any real possibility of expressing or giving effect to his disagreement with important social decisions, since he lacks any forum in which to expound his own opinions or to discover the opinions of his fellows, in the shape of an autonomous and powerful association. It may well be that in periods of popular enthusiasm a single party does express the purpose of the great majority of a nation, and succeeds in drawing large numbers of people, without compulsion, into the activities of legislation and administration; but in that case there can be no need for it to suppress such other political parties as still survive. It may also be that the rule of a single party can be justified by the necessities of war, of rapid industrialization, or of the creation of a new nation out of a former colonial territory, but that does not make the political regime in which it functions a democratic one. If the necessity can be demonstrated, the ruling party may be regarded as governing *for* the people, but it is not the case that the people govern themselves.

A discussion of whether political parties are *necessary* to a democratic system of government must remain unavoidably speculative, and it is both easier and more practical to consider whether the competition between parties and elites is *sufficient* to ensure democracy. There are many liberal thinkers today who would assert that it is sufficient, or who would at least regard the competition between elites as being so important as to absolve them from further inquiry into the conditions of democracy. They would have the support of Karl Mannheim, who, as we have seen, claimed that what made a society democratic was simply that individual citizens should have "at least the *possibility* of making their aspirations felt at certain intervals."[10] On the other hand, Schumpeter and Aron both pay much attention to other influences upon the political system. Schumpeter sets out explicitly what he terms "conditions for the success of the democratic method," which he classifies under four headings: (i) that the human material of politics (*i.e.*, the elites) should be of sufficiently high quality; (ii) that the effective range of political decision should not be extended too far; (iii) that the government should be able to command the services of a well-trained bureaucracy of good standing and tradition; and (iv) that there should be democratic self-control, *i.e.*, that the competing elites should tolerate each other's rule and should resist the offerings of crooks and cranks, while the electorate, having made its choice, should refrain from interfering incessantly in the political actions of its representatives. Similarly, Aron, in the article cited earlier, states three conditions for the success of the contemporary pluralistic democracies: (i) the restoration of government authority capable of settling the disputes between groups and enforcing the decisions necessary in the community's joint interest; (ii) an efficient economic administration which will preserve mobility and revive incentives; and (iii) a limitation of the influence of those individuals and groups which want to change the whole framework of society. It is obvious, however, that these accounts remain within the scheme of ideas which sees democracy as competition between elites, and explore its further implications while they neglect many other factors which influence the success or failure, and the extent, of democracy in a larger sense. I shall examine first some of the other political influences. It has been very generally assumed—it is assumed, for example, by Mannheim, although this does not accord well with his other pronouncements on the conditions for democracy—that the development of a democratic polity requires, in addition to the competition between elites, changes in the structure and composition of elites, in their self-conceptions, and in their relations with the rest of the population. Briefly, it seems to be assumed that in a democracy there will be a more rapid and extensive movement of individuals into and out of the elites, that there will be an increasing number of elite positions in relation to the population as a whole, that the elites will develop a less "aristocratic" outlook and will regard themselves as being closely linked with the masses, and that, in consequence

[10] Although he went on, somewhat inconsistently, to discuss the growth of equality and the reduction in the distance between elites and masses as factors in the development of modern democracy.

of various leveling influences they will actually be closer to the masses in their style of life. The first two of these conditions would bring about a situation in which a far greater number of individuals had the experience of ruling as well as of being ruled, while the other conditions would change the character of political rule in some measure, making it less remote, authoritarian, majestic, and irresistible. If we now look at the Western democracies of the present day we shall see that, while they conform well with the competition model of democracy, they are deficient in respect of these other conditions: there is not a rapid circulation of the personnel of the elites, which are still recruited predominantly from the upper class in society;[11] the outlook of the elites has changed only slowly and the old aristocratic view of their functions is kept alive by their recruitment from the upper class, by the elite theories themselves, and by the prevailing social doctrines of "getting on" and reaching "the top"; and lastly, the "leveling" of conditions in Western societies has gone on so slowly that the rulers are still very sharply distinguished, economically and socially, from the ruled. It should be noted, too, that the political parties which stand at the center of the competition between elites have themselves lost something of their democratic character with their transformation into mass parties. They may not have become, in most cases, quite the oligarchic organizations which Michels foresaw,[12] but they are more easily dominated by their officials, and it is correspondingly more difficult for the rank-and-file members to have an effective influence in the shaping of policy.

Besides these political factors, we should also consider whether there are not more general social conditions which are essential to the life and growth of a democratic system of government. It is a notable feature of the recent elite theories that, having defined democracy as simply a *form of government of a whole society,* and thus excluded from the definition any nonpolitical factors such as appear, for example, in the notions of "social democracy" or "industrial democracy," they go on to eliminate so far as possible even a consideration of the influence which factors of this kind may have upon the form of government itself. But this is to overlook or reject a fundamental idea of sociology—namely, that the

[11] See above, Chap. III. See also W. L. Guttsman, *The British Political Elite*, Chap. XI, where it is shown how few individuals are enabled to take part in the formulation of national policies. In Britain there is a small group of "the good and the great"—at most a few thousand people, drawn predominantly from the upper class in society—who participate in the work of advisory committees, Royal Commissions, and similar public bodies.

[12] Robert Michels, *Political Parties*

institutions which exist in the different spheres of society are not merely co-existent but are connected with each other by relations of concordance or contradiction and mutually affect each other— which was admirably formulated by Marx, in his criticism of the political philosophers of his day, when he argued that it was a profound error to separate man as a citizen (*i.e.,* as an individual with political rights) completely from man as a member of civil society (*i.e.,* as an individual engaged in family life and in economic production).[13] Are we to suppose, for instance, that the modern democratic family in Western societies, which has been exhaustively described by many sociologists, and in which the relations between the members are, generally speaking, more co-operative and less authoritarian than was the case in the nineteenth century, has come into being unaffected by democratic ideas of government; or that once it exists it has no significance for the maintenance and extension of democratic attitudes and practices in the sphere of government? Can we accept that democratic government, which requires of the individual independent judgment and active participation in deciding important social issues, will flourish when in one of the most important spheres of life—that of work and economic production—the great majority of individuals are denied the opportunity to take an effective part in reaching the decisions which vitally affect their lives? It does not seem to me that a man can live in a condition of complete and unalterable subordination during much of his life, and yet acquire the habits of responsible choice and self-government which political democracy calls for. It is true that in the Western societies the subordination of the individual at work is less onerous than it used to be in some respects; the individual worker has some influence upon his working conditions through his trade union and through institutions of joint consultation which have developed in a rudimentary fashion, while the substantial increase in leisure time has enlarged the sphere in which he is able to decide things for himself. On the other hand, much industrial work has become more subdivided and repetitive in modern times, with the result that the worker, even if he is not subjected to the old type of authoritarian control by his employer, still finds less and less opportunity to exercise judgment, imagination, or skill in the performance of his task.[14]

There are other circumstances, more frequently discussed,

[13] Karl Marx, *On the Jewish Question.*
[14] See, on these questions, Georges Friedmann, *The Anatomy of Work.*

which affect the practice of democratic government. Great inequalities of wealth and income plainly influence the extent to which individuals can participate in the activities of ruling the community. A rich man may have difficulty in entering the kingdom of heaven, but he will find it relatively easy to get into the higher councils of a political party, or into some branch of government. He can also exert an influence on political life in other ways: by controlling media of communication, by making acquaintances in the higher circles of politics, by taking a prominent part in the activities of pressure groups and advisory bodies of one kind or another. A poor man has none of these advantages: he has no relationships with influential people, he has little time or energy to devote to political activity, and little opportunity to acquire a thorough knowledge of political ideas or facts. The differences which originate in economic inequalities are enhanced by educational differences. In most of the Western democracies the kind of education provided for those classes which mainly provide the rulers of the community is sharply differentiated from that which is provided for the more numerous class of those who are ruled.[15] The educational system in most Western societies does not only consolidate the distinction between rulers and ruled; it keeps alive and flourishing the whole ideology of elite rule insofar as it emphasizes the selection of exceptional individuals for elite positions, and the rewards in income or status of scholastic achievement, rather than the raising of the general level of education throughout the community and the contribution which this might make to increasing the participation of the mass of citizens in government. The differences of wealth and education which I have mentioned are aspects of the division of society into classes;

[15] In Britain, the typical careers of upper-class and working-class children may be described as follows: children of the upper class are educated in the major public schools and at the universities of Oxford and Cambridge, whence they proceed into business, politics, the administrative class of the civil service, or the older professions; working-class children are educated in state schools, for the most part secondary modern schools, from which they go at the age of fifteen into manual jobs in industry or into minor clerical jobs, though some (a higher proportion today than twenty-five years ago) attend grammar schools and may go onto higher education in a provincial university or college of technology. Some children in each class may escape their fate, but the proportion who do so is too small to affect the general picture. The educational situation in the USA differs radically from that in Britain and other European countries, although the change is comparatively recent; there, a very high proportion (some 90 percent) of the relevant age group in all classes receives secondary education up to the age of seventeen and a still considerable proportion (about 35 percent) goes on to take a university course.

and it is this fundamental division which has often been regarded, in the theories of "social democracy" for example, as incompatible with democratic government. . . .

The objections which I have so far presented to the elite theories of democracy are based upon an alternative conception of democracy as "government by the people"; but there are other objections which arise from inconsistencies within the elite theories themselves. First, there is the question as to whether any form of government could survive for long if there were permanent opposition and conflict between elites, and an incessant circulation of their personnel. Mannheim, writing on the problems of political democracy in terms of the German situation of the early 1930s, observed that the growth of democracy means a loss of homogeneity in the governing elite and went on to say: "Modern democracy often breaks down because it is burdened with far more complex decision problems than those facing early democratic (or pre-democratic) societies with their more homogeneous ruling groups."[16] T. S. Eliot, in *Notes Towards the Definition of Culture*, has argued in a similar fashion that elites, which require a regular circulation of their personnel are unable to ensure social continuity in the way that the ruling classes of earlier times could do.[17] However, both writers exaggerate the dangers arising from these sources, for there is not at the present time any substantial circulation of individuals between the elites and the rest of the population, and the elites are not as a rule engaged in serious conflict with each other. As Aron says, in discussing the present situation of the Western societies: "The composition of the governing elite may be progressively altered, the relative importance of the various groups in the elite may be changed, but a society can only survive and prosper if there is true collaboration between those groups. In one way or another there must be unity of opinion and action on essential

[16] Karl Mannheim, *Essays on the Sociology of Culture*.

[17] T. S. Eliot, *Notes Towards the Definition of Culture*. Eliot criticizes Mannheim's view that elites in modern societies can perform adequately the functions of earlier ruling classes without noticing that Mannheim himself had already formulated the criticism. In fact, Mannheim seems never to have reached a settled view of the place of elites in modern society. Sometimes he argues in favor of the competition between elites as a safeguard of democracy; at other times he advocates rule by a single elite composed of the intellectuals; and finally he suggests that no elite, or group of elites, can ensure political stability unless it takes on the characteristics of a ruling class, possibly by association with an existing upper class, and becomes a hereditary and property-owning group. The only conception which Mannheim consistently excludes is that of a classless, egalitarian society.

points in the elite."[18] In fact, this unity of opinion and action—
and the social continuity which Eliot desires—is largely assured in
the Western societies by the recruitment of elites from the upper
class of society, and by the ideological support of the theory of
elites itself. It is still true that "from the hour of their birth some
are marked out for subjection and some for command."[19] In the
Western societies the elites stand, for the most part, on one side of
the great barrier constituted by class divisions; and so an entirely
misleading view of political life is created if we concentrate our
attention upon the competition between elites, and fail to examine
the conflicts between classes and the ways in which elites are
connected with the various social classes.

It is one of the political myths of our age that democracy is
protected and sustained principally or solely by the competition
between elites, which balance and limit each other's power. When
we look at the arguments of the elite theorists in favor of this thesis
we find a second inconsistency, which consists in moving, at
different stages of the argument, from the concept of a plurality of
elites to the quite different concept of a multiplicity of voluntary
associations. Mosca, for example, referred to the possibility, in a
democratic system, for many different "social forces" (not elites)
to take part in political life and to limit the power of other social
forces, and especially bureaucracy. Similarly, Aron, when he urges
the importance of the diffusion of power in the pluralistic democracies does not invoke only the principal elites which he has
distinguished, but speaks of the great variety of professional and
political organizations which are to be found in such societies, and
which set bounds to the power of the rulers. But this advocacy of
flourishing voluntary associations as a vital condition for effective
democracy does not lend support to the elite theories. For what is
being asserted, when the importance of vigorous local government,
professional associations, and other voluntary and autonomous
bodies is given such prominence, is not that those organizations
are elites which are engaged in major struggles for political power,
but that they provide so many occasions and opportunities for
ordinary men and women to learn and practice the business of
self-government. They are means through which government *by*
the people is made more real and practical in a large, complex
society.

[18] Raymond Aron, "Social Structure and the Ruling Class," *British
Journal of Sociology*, I (2), p. 129.
[19] Aristotle, *Politics*.

Thus we are led by this path also to the view expressed earlier, that the preservation, and especially the development and improvement, of a democratic system of government does not depend primarily upon fostering the competition between small elite groups whose activities are carried on in realms far removed from the observation or control of ordinary citizens, but upon creating and establishing the conditions in which a large majority of citizens, if not all citizens, can take part in deciding those social issues which vitally affect their individual lives—at work, in the local community, and in the nation—and in which the distinction between elites and masses is reduced to the smallest possible degree. Such a view implies, first, that opportunities to extend the scope of self-government should be assiduously sought, especially in the sphere of economic production, where some modern experiments such as the workers' councils in Yugoslavia and the community development projects in India, for all the difficulties that they encounter, deserve serious attention; and second, that the present hindrances to full participation in the government of voluntary associations, which arise in the main from differences of social class, and are apparent in the predominance of upper-class and middle-class individuals as officials of such organizations, should in some way be overcome.

17 THE PLURALIST NORM

HENRY S. KARIEL

Social scientists themselves [have been] caught up in the current of American pluralism. Despite their frequently professed desire to remain purely analytical or hypothetical, an appreciable number of them have in fact helped give theoretical stability and respectability to a technologically harnessed pluralism. How, it is worth inquiring, have they reinforced pluralist institutions, grant-

FROM Henry S. Kariel, *The Decline of American Pluralism*, pp. 113–137, with the permission of the publishers, Stanford University Press. Copyright © 1961 by the Board of Trustees of Leland Stanford Junior University.

ing them, so to speak, a patent? How have their abstract projections made clear what our concrete institutions have so far left in an undeveloped stage?

Ostensibly objective students of society and politics, they have accepted an undiscussed frame of reference which has the unsought effect of exalting the autonomous group, the functional community, and what is recently going under the name of the homeostatic system. By committing themselves to an analytical model suitable for understanding the behavior of small groups, they have kept themselves from enlarging the scope of their science. Failing to go beyond an attractive image of pluralism, they have treated large groups as if they were small and have, in effect, protected from professional scrutiny a newer, barely understood economic and industrial order. Moreover, insofar as the model which orients their work defines a set of prevailing social relationships as natural, they have unintentionally provided what is nothing less than a criterion for alternative public reforms.

Although we are not compelled to accept the offered analytical model, we are made aware of the cost of ignoring it. To ignore it, we have been told, is to exchange a functional system for one fundamentally incoherent and anarchical. We are free to make our choice. But from a scientific point of view, in any case, the most efficient system is the comprehensively organized one—society defined in terms of the ties between its constituents. These ties give the system unity. Their presence makes it; their absence breaks it. Although the knowledge of social science can be used to plan for play and freedom, to achieve nonconservative ends disrupting the existing social scheme, this cannot be certified as sound by social scientists when they believe that deeply embedded within our social world there is a functional structure, a closed, boundary-maintaining, internally harmonious whole, an ideal—strikingly like the America we know—that lies deeper than mere appearances.

To the extent that the social scientist identifies his search for knowledge with the gradual realization of an ideal deemed immanent in reality, he participates in patterning seemingly random behavior. Of course, his approach may remain purely formal and analytical. When engaged in purely relativistic, comparative analysis, he leaves unsettled what factors specifically impede the attainment of the ideal. Indeed, he will be careful not to offer ideals, acknowledging that what is marginal in one case might well be central in another—depending always on ultimate social purposes. Thereby he leaves open any public discussion about ideals. But the moment he extracts a *substantive* definition of a disequilibrium from the American experience and quietly incorporates it in his analytical scheme, he shuts off discussion—or assumes that the last word has already been said. What constitutes an equilibrium in particular cases is then believed to be settled. Everyone will then simply know what is meant by the characterization of behavior as a departure from "the system in homeostasis." The phrase will be vacuous only to the uninitiated, to those not altogether at home in America and its halls of higher learning.

It would be tedious to show with what readiness deviations from the "homeostatic model" or "the going society" or "the American system" are being identified. They are widely seen as the conflicts and displacements which have been generated by a complex industrial society. Only a deeply prejudiced person, it is made to appear, could fail to see that, whatever our twentieth-century opportunities and goods, the present is really a painful era of individual neuroses, community disruption, complicated politics, and endless factional crises. This "condition" makes the application of social skills, of knowledge about human relations, mandatory. And such knowledge, at its finest, is the product of an instrumental social science.

There being little disagreement about what constitutes the substantive nature of social delinquencies, pathological conditions may be objectively defined, and social science may rightly apply its knowledge and methods to the task of discovering how individuals may be moved with speed and efficiency toward the healthy goal.[1] It becomes credible to argue that psychologists should "seek to provide a basic science of human thinking, character, skill learning, motives, conduct, etc., which will serve all the sciences of man (e.g., anthropology, sociology, economics, government, education, medicine, etc.) in much the same way and to the same extent that biology now serves the agricultural and medical sciences."[2] So fixed are the ends of government that the social scientist can go to work furnishing the means. "In much the same way" as agronomists and physicians apply the laws of biology to assure productivity and

[1] According to one writer, three "aspects of definition" have been approximately agreed on: (1) "the internal inconsistencies of the [social] unit, as a result of which common objectives are relatively lacking"; (2) "*anomie*, or lack of internal organization, and conflicting social organizations within the units"; and (3) "conflicting rules of behavior" and "conflicts of values." (Edwin H. Sutherland, "Social Pathology," *American Journal of Sociology*, 50 [May 1945], 429–35, 431.)

[2] Harvard University Commission to Advise on the Future of Psychology at Harvard, Alan Gregg, chairman, *The Place of Psychology in an Ideal University* (Cambridge: Harvard University Press, 1947), p. 2.

longevity, social scientists might apply those of psychology. The "theorizing" they engage in will be the theorizing not about ends but about means. As Dwight Waldo observed in a 1956 survey, "American political science has not been characterized by works seeking either to justify or to controvert the political order. Rather, the political order has been 'accepted,' and distinctive American 'political theory' has tended to be concerned with means and methodology."[3]

Knowing the common good, seeing it manifest in America, social scientists are prepared and subsidized to perfect the devices for gaining consensus on it—if need be, by encouraging the influential to promote the practices of social engineering. Understanding their own functions, social therapists or policy scientists are not only studying society in a scientific manner, but are also seeking to make politics itself increasingly scientific. Politics will become infused by science as they will show, in the language of Harold D. Lasswell, "a lively concern . . . for the problem of overcoming the divisive tendencies of modern life and of bringing into existence a more thorough integration of the goals and methods of public and private action."[4] As Hobbes had hoped long ago when he wished his speculations to fall into the hands of a sovereign, social theory and social action can at last coalesce. Without putting its assumptions into question, social science can specify the ties which provide, in practice, for America's unity.

The task of social research is easily defined: it is to identify the social structure and determine what is functional in it. It is, moreover, to gain knowledge of the factors which cause the idle to be engaged, the distracted to be attracted, the weary to be enlisted. It is to search for the conditions of instability, the prerequisites for stability. It is to restore upset balances, resolve conflicts, heal sore spots, facilitate assimilation, and, most important, remove the innumerable blocks to understanding. It can be peremp-

---

[3] Dwight Waldo, *Political Science in the United States: A Trend Report* (Paris: UNESCO, 1956), p. 17. He also noted that "however great the heat engendered by professional disputes, the range of opinion has on the whole and in the larger perspective of all political thought been remarkably small. The very fact that there could be widespread agreement on the possibility and desirability of reducing the study of politics to the single level of a 'science' signifies a large amount of basic agreement as to political ends." See also C. Wright Mills, *The Sociological Imagination* (New York: Oxford, 1959) and Bernard Crick, *The American Science of Politics* (Berkeley: University of California Press, 1959).

[4] "The Policy Orientation," in Daniel Lerner and Harold D. Lasswell, eds., *The Policy Sciences: Recent Developments in Science and Method* (Stanford: Stanford University Press, 1951), pp. 3–15, 3.

torily concerned with the reduction of discord, the relief of tension, the softening of competition. Even where this view is opposed, the organization man is expected not to constitutionalize or break up the corporate unit but somehow, while preserving his individuality, to adapt to it. About the prevalent research orientation, the testimony of Robert A. Nisbet is especially instructive because it is offered with genuine sympathy for the work described:

Research projects tend to center increasingly on problems of individual assimilation within groups, classes, and cultures. The astonishing spread of the study of group structure, group dynamics, interpersonal relations, and of associative components in economic and political behavior bears rich testimony to the change that has taken place in recent decades in the type of problem regarded as significant. . . . The social group has replaced the individual as the key concept . . . and it is almost as apt to observe that social *order* has replaced social change as the key problem. Beyond count are the present speculations, theories, and projects focused on the mechanics of group cohesion, structure, function, and the varied processes of assimilation and adjustment. . . .

[This] is now a conservative revolt and is to be seen in those approaches to the study of man where the individual has been replaced by the social group as the central unit of theoretical inquiry and ameliorative action; where organicism and its offspring, functionalism, hold sway in the interpretation of behavior and belief; where there is a dominant interest in themes and patterns of cultural integration, in ritual, role, and tradition, and in the whole range of problems connected with social position and social role.

While the objectives of this "conservative revolt" are analytical, Nisbet concedes that they nevertheless "reflect a set of deep moral urgencies" insofar as they are "given meaning and drive by moral aspirations toward community."[5]

The specific problems which beset the community of men, men whose discomforts have in the past inspired the politician's calling, are to be attacked by what in the broadest sense is a science of public administration, personnel management, or human relations. A "preventive politics" closely allied with "general medicine, psychopathology, physiological psychology, and related disciplines" is to be created. In 1930, Lasswell saw that

the time has come to abandon the assumption that the problem of politics is the problem of promoting discussion among all the interests concerned in a given problem. Discussion frequently complicates social difficulties, for the discussion by far-flung interests arouses a psychol-

5 *Quest for Community* (New York: Oxford, 1953), pp. 28–29.

ogy of conflict which produces obstructive, fictitious and irrelevant values. The problem of politics is less to solve conflicts than to prevent them; less to serve as a safety valve for social protest than to apply social energy to the abolition of recurrent sources of strain in society.[6]

A "unified natural science of human life" may well help channel social energy so as to diminish existing strains or demolish their recurrent sources.[7] The late Kurt Lewin, according to one social scientist who has sympathetically commemorated his work, seems to have grasped what is required:

He felt that, if we could but correctly conceptualize the a-historical, situational factors determinative of behavior, then we could manipulate these contemporaneous situational factors and produce the sort of behavior which all persons of good will would desire. If we can but discover the "systematic laws," the laws of the "pure case," *i.e.*, those laws whereby a given "life-space" inevitably produces a given behavior, then we can know how to change persons and groups to remake their behavior according to our heart's desires.[8]

Effective action must spring from a comprehensive view of the social system. Thanks especially to the pioneer work of Mary Parker Follett and Elton Mayo in the areas of private administration, it has become clear that behavior remains inexplicable until an administrative or industrial organization is seen not as a formal, authoritarian unit within which commands pass rationally from top to bottom but as a more amorphous social system of uncharted groups. Because these informal groups manifestly exist, the duly functioning manager must understand them. What must be understood, most specifically, is the extent of irrationality characterizing the behavior of those within the informal subgroupings. The system maintains itself precisely because its components, individual workers, are moved by nonrational impulses. Since their action is primarily emotional reaction, it can be regulated by appropriately touching their emotions, and for this it is essential for the mana-

---

[6] *Psychopathology and Politics* (Chicago: University of Chicago Press, 1930), pp. 203, 196–97.

[7] The phrase is Conrad Arensberg's ("Behavior and Organization," in John H. Rohrer and Muzafer Sherif, eds., *Social Psychology at the Crossroads* [New York: Harper, 1951], pp. 324–52, 352).

[8] Edward C. Tolman, "Kurt Lewin—1890–1947," *Journal of Social Issues*, VI, Suppl. ser. No. 1 (Fall 1948), 22–26, 23. "In short," Tolman adds, "it was his humanity, I believe, which would not allow him to dwell for long on any considerations other than those of the manipulable present." Thus Lewin's interest in manipulation would seem to have grown out of his desire to do good; and in America, at least, the nature of the good appeared sufficiently obvious to "all persons of good will."

gers to understand the feelings and sentiments of the rank and file at the bottom.[9] The rational, logical table of organization hides what right-minded management must take into account: the irrational bonds between men which bring order to their relations. These ties—sentiments, customs, social codes—guarantee stability.[10] Never recorded (except by anthropologists studying the factory subculture), they are transmitted orally from worker to worker. They are implicitly understood and acted upon. They are the folk mind discerned by the well-trained leader.

Once accepted, this view makes considerations of power or authority superfluous. To maintain the industrial state, what is significant is not any specific allocation of power but instead the prevailing harmony of relations, the efficiency of communications, the cordiality of intercourse. Hence it is far less important to worry about the distribution of power and influence than to perfect the devices by which good feelings can be improved. "Whether or not a group functions in an atmosphere that is hostile or congenial, or whether the production is high or low, depends upon the amount of genuine cooperative participation entirely apart from the parity of power."[11] Since the good manager does not govern, at least not in the scientifically governed state, there can be no justification for checking, opposing, or resenting him. He will have been informed by empirical science that an efficient productive unit can be maintained "only by working through the informal organization. It is only in this area that it is possible to manipulate the mental and emotional processes of people so as to build a harmonious organization. . . . The successful executive therefore cannot rely simply upon his 'power' to get orders carried out. To carry his organization along with him he also needs understanding, skill, and personal influence."[12] Put differently, "the administrator is the guardian or preserver of morale through the function of maintaining a condition of equilibrium which will preserve the

[9] F. J. Roethlisberger, *Management and Morale* (Cambridge: Harvard University Press, 1950), pp. 192–93, 63; see also p. 111. While management, having "economic objectives," communicates with the managed "in terms of the logical jargon and cold discriminations of the technical specialist . . . the bottom . . . is trying to communicate with the top through its own peculiar language of social sentiments and feelings."

[10] See T. N. Whitehead, *The Industrial Worker*, 2 vols. (Cambridge: Harvard University Press, 1938), I, 248.

[11] Alfred Marrow, "Conflict and Cooperation in Industry," in Schuyler Dean Hoslett, ed., *Human Factors in Management* (New York: Harper, 1946), pp. 172–208, 204.

[12] William Foote Whyte, ed., *Industry and Society* (New York: McGraw-Hill, 1946), p. 192.

social values existing in the cooperative system. Only in this sense does he have 'authority.' "[13]

"In spite of the power of his position," it has been affirmed, "the top executive cannot decide arbitrarily what the organization will be like and how it will function. . . . The skilled executive can, however, use his knowledge of the organization and of his position in it to *permit* the development of an effective whole."[14] What he permits, they want to do anyway—provided they understand. "The essence of democratic leadership," another writer has explained, "is the capacity to influence people to act in ways that they come to realize are good for them."[15] The "central problem of leadership," as the authors of a textbook on American public administration have noted, is the gaining of acceptance of the leader's objectives.[16] "By what means can he persuade his employees to *want* to do what he wants to do?" "How can employees be stimulated to put loyalty to the company above their own self-interest?"

The problem, at least for Americans, is one of means. "By developing an atmosphere in which changes and improvements can be generated from within the organization rather than imposed from above, the skilled executive can eliminate much of the organization's resistance to change without forfeiting any of its stability."[17] Applied science has pointed the way, so that it has in fact become reasonable to conclude from experiments resting on Kurt Lewin's studies that "the more 'democratic' the procedures, the less resistance there is to change, and the greater the productivity."[18] As a result of an experiment conducted in a Virginia

[13] Roethlisberger, *Management and Morale*, p. 193.

[14] Burleigh B. Gardner, *Human Relations in Industry* (Chicago: Irwin, 1945), p. 292; the emphasis is Gardner's.

[15] Ordway Tead, *New Adventures in Democracy* (New York: McGraw-Hill, 1939), p. 137.

[16] Marshall Edward Dimock and Gladys Ogden Dimock, *Public Administration* (New York: Rinehart, 1953), p. 237.

[17] Gardner, *Human Relations in Industry*, p. 216.

[18] Otto Klineberg, *Social Psychology* (New York: Holt, 1954), p. 462. There is no reason to doubt the words of Herbert A. Simon: "We now have a considerable body of evidence on the participation hypothesis—the hypothesis that significant changes in human behavior can be brought about rapidly only if the persons *who are expected to change* participate in deciding what the changes shall be and how it shall be made." (In Stephen K. Bailey *et al.*, *Research Frontiers in Politics and Government* [Washington, D.C.: The Brookings Institution, 1955], pp. 28–29; the emphasis is supplied.) Perhaps Stuart Chase's *Roads to Agreement: Successful Methods in the Science of Human Relations* (1951) is the most readable exposition, almost wholly sympathetic, of semantic reconciliations, group dynamics, Quaker

pajama-manufacturing plant, to cite but one example, it proved possible to overcome worker opposition to changes in production methods "by the use of group meetings for which management effectively communicates the need for [predetermined] change and stimulates group participation in planning the changes."[19] Management expectations are fulfilled "democratically," according to Morris S. Viteles, because the group dynamics work of Lewin and his followers had shown how to

produce not only direct benefits in the form of better results in influencing attitudes, but a feeling of participation on the part of employees in planning programs which can, in itself, contribute to successful achievement in moulding and modifying attitudes and in improving motivation and morale.

Such feelings can be evoked by providing for employee participation in decision making. Their cooperation "becomes an effective device for lowering resistance to change, and aiding production by lowering the resistance of barriers to the 'goal' of higher output." Of course, undisguised coercion can also produce change. But, says Viteles,

the use of group participation permits smoother "locomotion" to the same "goal" without the creation of "tensions" which may lead to industrial strife. Participation in decision-making in industry is generally viewed as an experience wherein attitudes favorable to change are taken on by the workers. . . .
    The potential for industrial strife is lowered, since the change in group perception associated with group participation tends to bring the production "goal" closer to the standard desired by management. Furthermore, "emotionality" is lowered since workers playing the "role" of planners tend to keep discussion at a relatively depersonalized level.[20]

In practice, getting consensus on goals calls for an emphasis not on the mechanism of politics, not on specific institutions or procedures for compromising competing interests, but, far more broadly, on morale, on the "style of living," the "social climate," the spirit pervading the dynamic field. Lewin and his associates provided a concise demonstration of this in an experiment during the Second World War. They tried to discover how best to moti-

---

meetings, group writing, role playing, and gripe weeks as techniques for overcoming intragroup hostility.
    [19] Lester Coch and John R. P. French, Jr., "Overcoming Resistance to Change," in Hoslett, ed., *Human Factors in Management*, pp. 242–68, 268.
    [20] Morris S. Viteles, *Motivation and Morale in Industry* (New York: Norton, 1953), pp. 436, 118.

vate the students who were using eight of the dining rooms at the State University of Iowa to choose and then eat whole-wheat bread. Lewin verified that in the dining rooms where consumers were *lectured* about the desirability of switching from white to whole-wheat bread and could privately weigh their interests, it was more difficult to induce the change than in the rooms where the leadership "permitted" them to make the change by "voluntary group decision," the leaders and the led assuming, of course, that the overriding wartime goal—a healthy, viable nation—was beyond the scope of any "voluntary" decision.[21]

When there is no doubt about the meaning of the general will, when morale within the field is good, anything within wide biological limits is indeed possible and acceptable. Within the group that gives behavior what is defined as its true socio-psychological meaning, the most painful or unpleasant action can be made palatable. "Under ordinary circumstances," Lewin has pointed out, "an individual will strongly resist an order . . . to eat three dozen unsalted soda crackers. As 'subjects' in an experiment, on the other hand, individuals were found ready to 'take it' without either hesitation or resistance." Enlightened and therefore enthusiastic about the ultimate end, the individual, like the victim of disease who desires life above all, will subordinate all diverting interests. "In the role of patient, for example, the individual permits as 'treatment' by the doctor what would otherwise be vigorously resisted because of bodily pain or social unpleasantness."[22] To break human resistance and smooth man's way, the overriding good must be clarified. To improve the tone of society, men must be moved not to misconstrue their genuine interests. Gardner Murphy has seen fit to observe:

Human relations will almost automatically be bettered if new ways of perceiving one's situation can be made available, not too solemnly, but with zest and humor, through stories, skits, movies, or better still, actual games, parties, work-projects. As the therapist might state the matter, the person must be assisted in a friendly manner to see himself and his associates in an accepting way, parking his defenses and especially his sense of guilt outside the gate. . . .[23]

[21] See Kurt Lewin, *Resolving Social Conflicts* (New York: Harper 1948), pp. 80, 82; Lewin, "Forces Behind Food Habits and Methods of Change," in National Research Council, Committee on Food Habits, *The Problem of Changing Food Habits* (Washington, D.C.: National Research Council, 1943), pp. 36–65.
[22] Kurt Lewin, "Time Perspective and Morale," in Goodwin Watson, ed., *Civilian Morale* (New York: Houghton Mifflin, 1942), pp. 48–70, 51–52.
[23] Gardner Murphy, "The Role of Psychologists in the Establishment

Such careful assistance will bring the final goal into precise focus, eventually making it possible to rule out all conflicting subjective visions, all conscientious objections. The "facts" will simply be accepted. To lead the good life will be to embrace and be loyal to those identified ultimate objectives which are self-evidently right. When the good life is finally led within the right order, the problems that once terrified men will dissolve, their apparent actuality having been due to misguided imagination and extraneous works. Within the "democratic" group, choices between alternatives will no longer create anxiety, since all alternatives but the fixed goal can be shown to be opposed to the publicly validated common interest.

Once it becomes coordinated, the healthy social organism will move steadily and easily, each of its parts adjusted to every other. It will be free to operate as each member performs its function. The freedom of the parts is assured by the freedom of the whole. When the whole is functioning efficiently, when it is maintaining its poise and integrity, the parts will experience satisfaction. After all, we are told, "freedom is only possible for an individual in so far as he genuinely identifies his own satisfaction with the general well-being."[24] It becomes legitimate to counsel, therefore, that "the whole personality must be involved in such a complete way as to make future conduct a spontaneous expression of that involvement."[25] Such involvement is the cornerstone of a wholesome, democratic regime. Democracy will grow naturally from the interpersonal relations experienced in tolerant and generous community living. More specifically, in a community thus prepared to experience democracy, economic leadership will not be irresponsible, as heretofore. The new economic leader, as Gardner Murphy has sketched him, will "understand the democratic process as well as the economic reality"; he will be able to "take hold of his corporation, his board of directors, his stockholders, his workers, his consumers, his public as a wise political leader would take hold, revolutionizing the guidance of his enterprise from within and without. Many of those who talk of the partnership of business and government vaguely grope toward some such conceptions." Perhaps through plebiscites, referendums, and public-

of Better Human Relations," in Lyman Bryson et al., eds., Perspectives on a Troubled Decade (New York: Harper, 1950), pp. 1–11, 2–3.

[24] T. N. Whitehead, Leadership in a Free Society (Cambridge: Harvard University Press, 1936), p. 255.

[25] Hoslett, Human Factors in Management, p. 105.

opinion polls, everyone will get a due sense of participation and make democracy work.[26]

Man will find his bearings in social action. Integrated, he will achieve fulfillment; enclosed, he will find his freedom. Absorbed and liberated, he will be able to look down on the pathological society which still accommodates conflicts of interests by deliberately leaving a margin for the unadjusted, the disoriented, and the apathetic.

It has been contended here that the proponents of at least one research approach celebrate a specific political order by constructing a formal framework which absorbs alternatives. Their formalism, it has been suggested, is easily come by, for there is widespread agreement on what in fact constitutes a social equilibrium. If these observations are accurate, it would seem that a radically restrictive, illiberal impetus lies at the very center of a considerable part of current social science. To be sure, there is a wholesome diversity of research interests. No single ideal, after all, has been consistently operative to guide all current social science—nor even all the works of the authors mentioned. Highlighting the area in which innumerable projects intersect has meant not being fully appreciative of the various motives and hopes of professional social scientists. This needs all the more emphasis because there has literally been no meeting ground for them: no single headquarters, organization, or journal. There is in fact little convergence, little interdisciplinary work, whatever the long-run tendency. Thus it cannot be validly maintained that the bulk of American social scientists are consciously aiming to construct some specific social order and fit men into it. They would definitely deny favoring the normative pattern which supports a good part of their activities. Indeed, they prefer, probably without exception, a pattern altogether contrary to the one which gives meaning to their work. Surely Lasswell speaks not only for himself when he proclaims his conviction that in America the main accent of the social sciences "will be upon the development of knowledge pertinent to the fuller realization of human dignity."[27] The belief that it is necessary to serve only the cause of the individual is often

[26] Gardner Murphy, in Murphy, *Human Nature and Enduring Peace* (Boston: Houghton Mifflin, 1945), pp. 298–99; Jerome S. Bruner, pp. 372–84; Ronald Lippit and Charles Henry, pp. 313, 315–18. See also the discussion in "Citizen Participation in World Affairs: Problems and Possibilities," *Journal of Social Issues*, 4 (Winter 1948), 21–61.

[27] Lasswell, "The Policy Orientation," *loc. cit.*, p. 10.

voiced and always implied. American social scientists, in short, are liberals.

Yet it should be apparent that this liberalism is not relevant to the perspective which gives status and coherence to all of the scientific operations actually proposed or executed during office or laboratory hours. The postulates which provide the basis for a portion of the work in human relations institutes, in research centers, or in the field remain incompatible with or divorced from the ardently expressed interest and worthy motives of social scientists. By consistently adhering to their postulates rather than to their liberal sentiments, they should be able to construct and test an abstract behavioral system of functional, neutral terms which would potentially provide an exhaustive relation of variables. Assuming social forces to be in a state of natural balance, they should have a norm by which to put existing social orders to the test. Contributing to a unified science of means, they should be able to determine how variables might be economically moved toward the norm.

The proper approach to social reality, they assume, will disclose man's most elemental bonds; it will dissolve all peculiarities by revealing them to be harmonious universals. When suitably embraced, what appears as incongruous will disclose itself as congruent. By the familiar procedure of diligent scientific probing, it will be possible to approximate the natural, right, and necessary order of man and his society. Once established and refined, a full set of generalizations will make the real organization of the facts of social and political life intelligible. Constructed according to an adequate theory, man's history will be understood in all its contingencies. Any diversity of circumstances still perceived will then be misperception, a resultant of ignorance, sentiment, or willfulness.

Within the total field, nothing can be exempt from the reach of a naturalistic social science. To produce social change—which is assumed to be the only way to gain social knowledge—the social scientist must rigorously exclude any possible ties with an order presumed to transcend the field he desires to affect. To grant the possibility of autonomy to such a link between the factual and the normative would spoil the integrity of his final position. Of course, individual action is not ignored; it is treated as a significant, because efficacious, function of the all-determinate group structure. Thereby made scientifically commensurable, it cannot threaten to make the state of affairs with which the social scientist is experimentally concerned unmanageable or unpredictable.

This applies even to the social scientist's own prejudices and sentiments. He is called to approach society with sensitivity and self-restraint, to handle the social field with a delicate touch, with his off-duty interests and impulses under control because objectives finding their source somewhere beyond the field would cause the object under investigation to become disturbed. What is required of him is a purgation of preconceptions which check his empathy. Only when he acts free from those ever-diverting ends which transcend the field can the final revelation—the law which does and should order man's behavior—be his; only at this timeless moment when the truth is formulated can he join the stream of humanity and can humanity once again join nature. His finished theory would at last make it possible for him to understand and control every baffling idiosyncrasy, to know that nothing is really detached and unnatural because all the things that matter are buried here and now, concealed more or less deeply in the present state of man's development. The true nature of things is immanent within experience. Nothing stands outside it; no autonomous vagrant spoils its integrity; no independent purpose governs it. Hence a humanistic concern with transhistorical objectives is irresponsible, a distraction from the scientific need to develop timeless hypotheses for the analysis of factual, aimless flux, of motion without beginning or end. Thus, as the future is held to inhere in the past, the ideal blends into the real.

The vision of the well-functioning community in which all is motion and behavior may be a most shadowy one. Yet even those who have not beheld it in its fullness work as if it were the basis of their faith. Not having in fact encountered the immanent harmonious order, they labor as if determined to achieve its incarnation, as if aspiring to give birth to that very state which, though far from realized, is woven into the nature of society and constitutes a system of relations among the perceived disparities. They may proceed to engineer harmony in a given industrial or administrative unit in response to "the mood of the times" or the call issued by those in positions of power. Alternatively, they may insist that some intuited or provided definition of harmony sets up tensions and is therefore not sufficiently inclusive. In any case, if social scientists are not atempting to resolve some practical problem by activating what appears sluggish and by integrating what appears fickle, they are seeking to draft a framework which will ideally encompass all variable, unstable, and disturbing forces— including those embodied in some particular government of the moment.

That analytical research, even when pointedly empirical, should ultimately be forced to employ such a total view for its orientation is actually not surprising, given its initial understanding of social units as self-sufficient wholes. As it feels compelled by sensed conflicts to step back from the minute particulars and enlarge its field of vision, it comes to see that the "real" system must be larger than had originally been suspected. There is always an impinging environment. The specific organization, it becomes evident, must be seen in a progressively broader context. For those few whose vision penetrates all boundaries, there is finally nothing but an undifferentiated whole, the wonderful unity of nineteenth-century German idealism and romanticism. The plurality of previously esteemed parts fades entirely. No valid theory can reveal their distinctiveness, and it becomes unnecessary to consider the possibility of conflict between them. On the contrary, the very institutions—such as parliamentary procedures—which might mediate such conflict must at last be recognized as unscientific expedients, superfluous in the healthy system, obscuring the reality of the underlying order.

Thus whether the research is applied or pure, the assumption of an underlying harmony of parts is placed beyond challenge, and social scientists are steadily led toward a theoretical scheme, a constitutive order, which will finally synthesize all conflicting social units. Their frameworks for political inquiry (to borrow the subtitle of a work by Harold D. Lasswell and Abraham Kaplan) are such as to establish a position from which it appears to be altogether self-evident and unarguable how "expensive" it is to society when variables remain unintegrated, when seemingly novel, unique, idle features are not adjusted, when the individual is not granted due status, or at least the entrancing belief in status. Noting this expense from their special point of vantage, pained by society's inefficient, uneconomical, dysfunctional forces, they delineate or hope for a scientifically objective and morally satisfying theory arranging for individual freedom within a state indulgent toward its constituents. Their manifold models, still incomplete and tentative, imply that man's social order merits allegiance when it fulfills the individual, and hence at once liberates and stabilizes him, by representing his diverse interests. Holding in esteem precisely that communal pattern which manifests the general will, they are consistent in assigning both a scientific and a normative plus to the socialized individual, to man as a selfless, political animal. Paralleling Rousseau's famous plea for "some form of association . . . as a result of which the whole strength of the community will be enlisted for the protection of the person and property of each constituent member, in such a way that each, when united to his fellows, renders obedience to his own will, and remains as free as he was before," reinforcing this ideal, they have come to assume that attributing primacy to the all-embracing social system accords with the very structure of social reality.

Using an approach which values above all its freedom from values, its absolute objectivity, the social scientist can legitimately set up as well as move society. His knowledge lies in his action. As he arranges his state so as to strip it of data—more accurately, pseudo-data—not amenable to incorporation in the body of scientific knowledge, he becomes, to the extent that he is permitted to be successful, its founding father.[28] And since he feels justified in claiming empirically confirmed objectivity for it—for he has, indeed, confirmed it by making it—he may go to work in the public arena, in the legislature and the market place, on the basis of decisive assumptions to which those whose interests and goods are affected by his action have not had to consent—however readily they may in fact acquiesce. He is, after all, fulfilling their inherent will, helping an ideal to realization.

As academic research gives aid to this immanent ideal, adopting it as final norm, converting its hypothesis into positive knowledge, its model into dogma, it implicitly identifies *its* ideal with man's ideal. It offers not an approach but a norm, not a tool for analysis but a theory justifying an existing state of affairs. It offers a system of values which, when all is said and done, vindicates the previously discussed American pluralist experience. More interestingly, it points up conclusions of which there have so far been only faint intimations.

That a good deal of American social science research has the effect of unwittingly condoning a closed order should not surprise those familiar with the longing of the European founders of sociology for the feudal system. Their bias, too, was antipolitical. They, too, hoped to take things "out of politics." Their quest for reintegration, it will be remembered, had been provoked by the dissolution of the social units associated with the *Ancien Régime* and the atomization of society brought about by the Industrial Revolution. Beginning with Fourier and Comte, their concern was to find clear echoes in the works of all those continental

---

[28] Note Leo Strauss's analysis of Machiavelli's method (*Natural Right and History* [Chicago: University of Chicago Press, 1953], pp. 177–80).

Europeans whose distaste for the politics of liberalism, for civil negotiation between conflicting interests, makes their ultimate conservatism intelligible: Tarde, LeBon, Lombroso, Durkheim, Pareto, and Freud. In the United States—where Burke and Locke could flourish side by side and where it was possible to speak of conserving liberalism—those students of man and society reacting against the French and Industrial Revolutions did not, however, have to search for institutional arrangements modeled on the pre-revolutionary social scheme. Nor was any theoretical defense of conservatism forced into existence. Tocqueville rightly anticipated that all advocacy of feudalism, of the hierarchical community, and of a consistent federalism, would remain qualified, inconclusive, and ambiguous—at least to the extent that it would be persuasive. In a country pervaded by a sweeping, frequently infuriating, all-corrosive liberalism, no creed frankly espousing the establishment or the conservation of a status society was able to take hold. In fact, some of the very students of society who have come closest to embracing a neo-feudalism—Elton Mayo, Mary Parker Follett, and Erich Fromm among others—have all taken pains to repudiate the feudal past. Yet if a frankly conservative rhetoric had to be rejected, a conservative ideology did not. Schemes defeated at the polls, blocked by the legislative process, or blown up by civil war could complacently find their way into the undiscussed premises of social analysis. Having nowhere else to become lodged, they could become the hidden foundation of research. The premises of pluralism, in brief, could become the premises of social science.

It is possible for this to happen only when social scientists are impatient and prematurely conclusive, when they build their conclusions into their initial assumptions. There is nothing inherent in the methods of social science which compels a conservative stand.[29] On the contrary, sound scientific analysis remains forever negative, comparative, relative, and even ironical. It must challenge all settlements, both practical and theoretical. But social analysis betrays a loyalty to an unamendable theory, an ideological commitment, the moment its hypothetical character is neglected, the moment its approach—elevated to become an end itself—is assumed to be embedded in the very nature of social reality or of human history. The orientation for the study of social, political, and economic phenomena then becomes identified with "the

[29] See Bernard Barber, "Structural-Functional Analysis," *American Sociological Review*, 21 (April 1956), 129–35.

real state of affairs."[30] A pattern of constructs becomes synonymous with the very structure of society.

When social scientists identify their analytical models with significant reality, they make it appear credible to hold that certain social arrangements are objectively inefficient. Having converted hypothetical presuppositions into dogmas, degrading other possible perspectives and settling for one as final, they make their empirical science the autonomous warrant for reform, authenticating the credentials of science as it is made to work. Their work thus has the effect of securing agreement on the substance of goals not by the method of politics, but by what wrongly seems to be the method of science. Their dogma, of course, remains concealed, forced into the interstices of methodology rather than into the frame of systematic argument. There is an inevitable loss when this happens, for the merits of alternative social orders are not so much undisputed as made the subject of methodological disputes. And because participation in debates about methodological matters is restricted to initiated and accredited professionals—whose language is not common speech—potentially concerned interests are excluded. The perspective by which reality is approached thus tends to settle what, from another point of view, may well be a subject still open to debate. The perspective, in short, becomes doctrinaire.

Such a doctrine may be detected in one significant part of current American academic practice—the part which has found it easy to accommodate itself to an institutional pluralism. It can be shown to be both didactic and doctrinaire when it embodies any one of three postulates: (1) that the mechanics of social change are completely determined by interacting groups; (2) that government is nothing but a responsive instrument for stabilizing an equilibrium of competing interests; and (3) that public policy is exclusively a group product. Where it has uncritically reflected an ideology of pluralism, it has accepted it interchangeably as a norm of social health, a model for analysis, and an ideal immanent in reality.

---

[30] Studies by American anthropologists are not, it seems, immune to this critique, as David Bidney has shown in his review of their analytical schemes. How these carry the stamp of a characteristically American pluralism is made evident by his discussion of the culturalistic fallacy, that is, the conversion of "an epistemic or methodological abstraction into a distinct ontological entity. . . ." According to Bidney, they make culture "represent an autonomous, superorganic level of reality subject to its own laws and stage of evolution"; and they hold cultural phenomena to be a self-explanatory, closed, homogeneous system. (*Theoretical Anthropology* [New York: Columbia University Press, 1953], pp. 51, 73–74, 77.)

Close to the turn of the century an appreciable number of American political scientists, reacting against philosophical idealism, had hoped to find a more solid comprehension of the political scene than had their legalistic and formalistic predecessors. They sought to deal with observable and preferably countable facts. Their quest took the form of studies of constitutional conventions, city governments, and the private governments of corporations, interest groups, labor unions, and trade associations. Their studies purported to provide unsentimental reports of what is "really" happening, at least insofar as the stuff of reality was susceptible to what seemed a straightforward positivist approach. In detail, frequently with statistics and charts, they described not the statics but the fascinating and often muddy flow and counterflow of politics. Having shown up statics as fiction, they became progressively more concerned with the dynamic process of politics. While they did not deny the reality of human ideals—surely they were keenly aware of their own—they permitted their studies to circumscribe them. They reduced purposes to the only thing which could count: their measurable impact. Students of political groups therefore tended to treat ideas of justice as potent myths, as efficacious means.[31] And they concerned themselves precisely with the nature of these means, the nature of all means, the nature of power. Assuming power to be the unifying key to politics, they could properly make it the focal point of their work. In the name of realism, they proceeded from the baseline drawn by Arthur F. Bentley's influential *Process of Government* (1908).[32] With Bentley, they could not accept "brain-spooks" or "mind-stuff" as the determinants of political action. They held that the state might at last be really understood by the investigation of palpable activity, by getting the feel of an endless stream of decisions. "Mind-stuff" could still play a role, but only in relation to a continuum of behavior, only as a manifestation of the autonomous, genuinely operative substruc-

[31] The work of Karl Mannheim testifies, of course, that this type of propaganda analysis does not merely arise in an American context. But it should be noted that only Mannheim's faith in the benign working out of historical forces, only his ultimately conservative assumption that all is right in the world, could sustain his analytical activity. Systematic debunking, it must have seemed to him, would surely not despoil a reality worthy of vindication. Not until the rise of Hitler, not until a substantive transformation in a political regime had taken place, did Mannheim have those misgivings about inevitable progress which Americans could escape experiencing at home.

[32] *The Process of Government: A Study of Social Pressures* (Chicago: University of Chicago Press, 1908); the volume has been twice republished, most recently by Principia Press (Bloomington, Indiana) in 1949.

ture of politics. Thus Charles A. Beard in his study of the basis of politics perceived a substructure of economic groups; Charles E. Merriam embraced an undifferentiated concept of power; and Harold D. Lasswell posited psychological foundations.

This search for the simplest effective foundation of the field of politics, for the most durable constellation of atoms, led readily enough to the employment of the old and fruitful hypothesis of the group nature of society. Social theory had of course always taken cognizance of groups, realizing that to postulate an associational disposition in man explains a great deal of politics and suggests otherwise hidden relationships. A thoroughgoing application of the hypothesis was therefore perfectly natural. Indeed, ever since the appearance of Bentley's pioneer work, as Earl Latham has shown, "American writers have increasingly accepted the view that the group is the basic political form."[33] This has made it possible for social scientists to approach man and his ideas as functions of the group, to see him in relation to a total configuration of social forces, to "understand" him by understanding his group, and ultimately to reach and activate him by reaching and activating his group. In the field of social psychology it has become possible to conclude empirically that the individual knows the world and acts within it primarily through his associations, that his associations produce those patterns of knowledge which regulate his behavior.[34] "These patterns," David B. Truman has written, "are, or are rapidly becoming, the primary data of the social scientist. To identify and interpret these uniformities . . . is the most effective approach to understanding a society—or a segment of it such as its political institutions."[35] Such understanding, it is affirmed, need not depend on any knowledge of a common good or a public interest independent of a compromise of group interests. The governmental process can be seen simply as group warfare. Governmental phenomena are a function of groups freely interacting.[36]

The belief that society and politics are best understood by taking

33 The Group Basis of Politics: A Study in Basing-Point Legislation (Ithaca, N.Y.: Cornell University Press, 1952), p. 10.

34 See especially the writings of Muzafer Sherif, Kurt Lewin, Nelson N. Foote, Jerome S. Bruner, Hadley Cantril, Gardner Murphy, Dorwin Cartwright, and Theodore M. Newcomb.

35 The Governmental Process (New York: Knopf, 1951), p. 21.

36 See especially the work of Arthur F. Bentley (The Process of Government, p. 269, and his Behavior, Knowledge, Fact [Bloomington, Indiana: Principia Press, 1935], p. 29) and David B. Truman (The Governmental Process, p. 31). The limitations of Truman's approach are fully discussed in Stanley Rothman, "Systematic Political Theory: Observations on the Group Approach," American Political Science Review, 54 (March 1960), 15–33.

full account of man's affiliations has been entertained so broadly, fervently, and uncritically that, in application, its instrumental nature has not always remained clear.[37] The casual facility with which the group hypothesis has come to be handled has made it easy to see politics as substantially nothing more than a process of interacting power blocs. As the political process has thereby been identified with an equilibrium of competing forces, a final ground for analysis is reached. To fully comprehend the very substance of politics and policy, we learn, is to accept the world of men, at least the world of Americans, for what it has presumably been right along: a polity in which groups struggle to gain or maintain power over one another. This polity is the only polity. Nothing more profound or less formalistic "really" exists or goes on. Whatever else may be part of American life, it is private, not part of public politics, not to be caught in the net woven by the practitioners of group analysis.

As this view becomes the only meaningful one, pluralism is in effect hypostatized. And as the immutable nature of political reality is presumed to be clear, all that remains necessary for its assessment is to extend and deepen one's knowledge of America by the rigorous application of that ultimate conceptual framework which allows one to behold a vibrant pluralism. To know America is to know it as a community within which those who care will struggle fraternally for public power. To have knowledge of America's political process is coincidentally to have knowledge of America's substantive goals as well. What had once been dealt with by an inexact political philosophy concerned with eliciting, juxtaposing, and sifting common opinions—a philosophy aspiring to discriminate between right and wrong conduct—is to become an amoral, natural science of human behavior.

Although the need for such a science has for long been proclaimed in America, with Henry Adams the first to do so systematically, there has until recently been little interest in integrating the overwhelming variety of group studies. Only as innumerable uncoordinated and sometimes intensely personal projects have begun to reveal how colorful and complex our behavior really is has it come to appear imperative to discipline the study of society and politics. This new concern with the unification of research (a concern always meticulously qualified by the caveat that integra-

[37] See especially the descriptive and critical accounts of William G. Carleton, "Political Science and the Group Process," *South Atlantic Quarterly*, 54 (July 1955), 340–50; W. J. M. Mackenzie, "Pressure Groups: The 'Conceptual Framework,'" *Political Studies*, 3 (October 1955), 247–55; Bernard Crick, *The American Science of Politics*, Ch. 7.

tion should never be "premature") has resulted in a dogged quest for a theoretical system of human behavior, for something like Boyle's general theory of gases. Despite the questions raised about the feasibility or desirability of the integration of techniques, and despite the warnings about a new scholasticism, the interest in developing an architectonic science of human behavior remains undiminished.[38]

It is now hoped (and not for the first time in the history of ideas) to find a substitute for the traditional, and so far always inconclusive, effort of social science to distinguish between the degrees of excellence of social institutions, historical regimes, public policies, or individual doctrines. This allegedly dated emphasis on examining the relative wisdom of alternatives is to be replaced by a stress on the building of a general descriptive theory of social behavior. In line with this, consideration is to be given to the purification of methods and the definition of operational models. Identified by an array of vague labels which significantly suggest the convergence of various disciplines—labels such as functionalism, sociometry, operationalism, equilibrium analysis, topological psychology, social field theory, social geometry, homeostatic model construction, or even socio-psychobiology—truly synthetic knowledge is to be earnestly pursued and, so it would appear, respectably endowed. And because the skeleton of the new science is believed to be embedded in all sound research, whatever is being produced in the social sciences may be confidently drawn on and integrated. Empirical research which happens to be centered on specific problems is to be reviewed for its contributions to a systematic theory.

38 See C. B. MacPherson, "World Trends in Political Science Research," *American Political Science Review*, 48 (June 1954), 427–49, 430–37; Bernard Barber, *Science and the Social Order* (Glencoe, Illinois: The Free Press, 1952), p. 244; Stephen K. Bailey et al., *Research Frontiers in Politics and Government* (Washington, D.C.: The Brookings Institution, 1955); Harold D. Lasswell and Abraham Kaplan, *Power and Society: A Framework for Political Inquiry* (New Haven: Yale University Press, 1950); Roy R. Grinker, ed., *Toward a Unified Theory of Human Behavior* (New York: Basic Books, 1956); John Gillin, ed., *For a Science of Social Man: Convergences in Anthropology, Psychology and Sociology* (New York: Macmillan, 1954); James G. Miller, "Toward a General Theory for the Behavioral Sciences," in Leonard D. White, ed., *The State of the Social Sciences* (Chicago: University of Chicago Press, 1956), pp. 29–65; and Roland Young, ed., *Approaches to the Study of Politics* (Evanston, Illinois: Northwestern University Press, 1958), *passim*. For some attempts to put new models to work, see Stuart C. Dodd, *Dimensions of Society: Quantitative Systematics for the Social Sciences* (New York: Macmillan, 1942); Nicolas Rashevsky, *Mathematical Biology of Social Behavior* (Chicago: University of Chicago Press, 1951); Marion J. Levy, *The Structure of Society* (Princeton: Princeton University Press, 1952); Morton A. Kaplan, *System and Process in International Politics* (New York: Wiley, 1957).

Thus inductive and deductive thought are to merge so that out of variety it may be possible to forge unity.

Such a body of united knowledge, at once empirical and rational, is to give formal expression to relationships between observed phenomena. These phenomena, it is hoped, will be unambiguously linked by a network of logical or quantitative notations. The links, expressing the functions of the data they connect, are to be set forth in functional terms, the only terms able to signify relations. There can be no escape, in fact, from mathematical terminology, for only mathematics is able to designate the relationships between "things" devoid of qualities other than such relationships.

Genuine social knowledge will therefore consist of a framework of unequivocal connections between data. Because terms of "intrinsic" meaning cannot validly become the object of discourse, whatever may appear to be intrinsic must be eliminated. It is necessary to escape the prison of a language which incorporates values, to cease using quality-ascribing adjectives which intriguingly hint at the existence of essentials, to center instead on dynamic processes, on potencies and actualities. As long as ambiguities slip into the framework, as long as dramatic or partially subjective symbols remain potent, the conditions for a natural science of society—one which might make it at last possible to predict the probable results of any variation of data—must be unsatisfied. "One of the great tasks of the value sciences (social sciences) in our day," Harold D. Lasswell and Abraham Kaplan have written, "is to develop a naturalistic treatment of the distinctively human values potential in the social process."[39] To fulfill this task it becomes mandatory to convert subjective value standards into precise indices, to attack all random terms, to eliminate concepts which happen to embody more than the concrete field or laboratory operation for which they stand, and, in short, to make discourse operational. This requires attempting what is never fully possible to achieve: tying language to action in every particular. Symbols useful when the channels of communications are not clear—when redundancies are required to catch our attention or to overcome troublesome noises on the line—must be extinguished. Freed of emotive terms, a satisfactory language will refer to nothing but those social and political arrangements which have objective existence in what scientific convention defines as the world of real experience. Since every possible condition which surrounds the data-connecting terms will be actually included in the scheme of

[39] *Power and Society*, p. xxiv.

descriptive statements, all metaphysical assertions subversively hinting at the existence of a realm other than the "operative" will be eliminated. At their best, social scientists will manage to design a thoroughly refined theory untarnished by moral consideration, subjectively felt data, and historical bias—a theory enabling us to grasp the nature of social and political reality in what is presumably the only meaningful way possible.

Recognizing the unrewarding nature of so much of what is being published in the academic journals, discussed by convention panels, and nourished by philanthropic foundations, and recognizing a failure to illuminate the human condition under nonutopian circumstances, some writers have been tempted to characterize social science research at mid-century as compulsive, uncritical, or cynical.[40] Nevertheless, if in the efforts to construct a social and political form there has indeed been a shying away from substance, might this not be due to the belief that concern with substance is irrelevant? Conceivably, the offered work is not anemic and barren, as some of the critics have said, but inconsequential. What keeps it alive is a deeply felt (though innocent) consensus on the "real problems" which makes bother with anything but methods and appearances seem irresponsible. There is tacit agreement on what is substantively economical, functional, progressive, healthy—and therefore just.

It may be precisely this agreement which invites the preoccupation with abstract form, the appreciation and perception of a static order underlying the fluctuations of history. The abstract form, in other words, may be widely identified with what good fortune has granted: the American system. Thus, without further consideration of what it substantively entails, an existing, well-institutionalized pluralism may be equated with a value-neutral science. The social facts unearthed by the appropriate method will happen to coincide with a particular ethic, the one Americans are believed to have cherished right along. Thanks to this most fortunate of coincidences, scientific knowledge of natural facts will reinforce what is indubitably the great American cause. It will consider as irreducible, as beyond analysis and critique, an esteem for the individual, for his material and spiritual goods, and, furthermore, for the institutional order which has traditionally facilitated "self-realization."

[40] See, for examples, Pitirim Sorokin, *Fads and Foibles in Modern Sociology and Related Sciences* (Chicago: Regnery, 1956); Mills, *The Sociological Imagination;* Crick, *The American Science of Politics.*

Thereby the progressive realization of the scientific ideal will have the effect of approximating what is unarguably the American one as well. If this is the case, there is no lamentable shying away from matters of substance on the part of social science. On the contrary. The substance—vulgarly called "Americanism"—is simply known and accepted. American ideals and American institutions are thus made exempt from that type of analysis which shows other ideals and institutions to be mere rationalizations or weapons. American ideals and institutions have a different status. They are not façades. They, and they alone, are not to be correlated with the power struggle all others disguise.

If social scientists think ideals to be mere functions of an underlying pluralistic order but do not hold that this applies to their own, does not at least one set of ideals, namely theirs, gain the status of objectivity? If values generally are to be subsumed under the new science of society but the specific value system of pluralism is somehow preserved exempt from reduction (as it is when used as final ground for explanation) is this not due to a belief in the *natural* rightness of a pervasive pluralism? The tenet of a normative pluralism, the identification of the common good with the struggle of groups for power, becomes consequently something more than subjective preference. The notion that men find fulfillment in "congenial and creative interpersonal relations" will be viewed interchangeably as natural fact and normative judgment. What is more, the tenet of pluralism will be confidently embraced as an objective good. Whatever situation it happens to describe may then be rightly desired without further reliance on an action-confounding metaphysics. Whatever threatens such a situation will necessarily be objectively undesirable. It will be understood as diseased, regressive, dysfunctional, uneconomical—and therefor unjust. To see this requires no further debate.

CHRISTIAN BAY[1]

A curious state of affairs has developed within the academic
discipline that bravely calls itself Political Science—the discipline
that in a much-quoted phrase has been called "a device, invented
by university teachers, for avoiding that dangerous subject politics,
without achieving science."[2] A growing and now indeed a predominant proportion of leading American political scientists, the behavioralists, have become determined to achieve science. Yet in
the process many of them remain open to the charge of strenuously
avoiding that dangerous subject, politics.

Consider a recent essay on the behavioral persuasion in politics.
The conclusion stresses the purpose of political inquiry: "The Goal
is Man." There is to be a commitment to some humane purpose
after all. But what kind of man? A democratic kind of man, a just
man, or perhaps a power-seeking man? The answer follows:
"These are philosophical questions better left to the philosophers."[3]
Behavioral students of politics should, as scientists, engage in no
value judgments concerning the kind of man or society their researches ought to serve. This is the general inference to be drawn,
not only from this particular essay, but from much of the contemporary literature on political behavior.

As Heinz Eulau, the author, points out in the same essay, the
area of behavioral political science includes a particular domain
called policy science, in which empirical inquiry is geared to explicitly stated goal formulations; within *this* domain "political science, as all science, should be put in the service of whatever goals
men pursue in politics." *Any* goals? Not quite; in this context Eulau
points out that the choice of what goals to serve is a matter of per-

FROM Christian Bay, "Politics and Pseudopolitics," *American Political
Science Review*, 59 (March 1965), 39–51. Reprinted with permission.
1 I am indebted to my friend Herbert H. Hyman, who has been generous
with advice for improvements on an earlier draft. It should not be inferred
that he is in agreement with opinions expressed in this paper, or that he
might not once again find much to criticize in it. At a later stage I have
received helpful suggestions also from Sidney Verba and Andrew Hacker.
2 Alfred Cobban, "The Decline of Political Theory," *Political Science
Quarterly*, Vol. 48 (1953), p. 335.
3 Heinz Eulau, *The Behavioral Persuasion in Politics* (New York, 1963),
p. 133 and pp. 133–37.

sonal ethics, and incidentally reminds us that behavioral research can be readily utilized also for purposes conflicting with the original ones. "In this sense, at least, science is value-free. I don't think the scientist can escape this dilemma of having his work misused without giving up his calling." And the author concludes with these words: "Only if he places himself at the service of those whose values he disagrees with does he commit intellectual treason."

In these pages I am concerned with sins less serious than intellectual treason; perhaps intellectual indolence is a more accurate term. My argument will be that much of the current work on political behavior generally fails to articulate its very real value biases, and that the political impact of this supposedly neutral literature is generally conservative and in a special sense anti-political. In conclusion I propose to develop a perspective on political inquiry that would relate it more meaningfully to problems of human needs and values; in that context I will suggest some important but neglected problems lending themselves to empirical research.

I am not about to argue that our investments in political behavior research have been too large; on the contrary, we need much more work in this area. But my principal concern is to argue for a more pressing need: an intellectually more defensible and a politically more responsible theoretical framework for guiding and interpreting our empirical work; a theory that would give more meaning to our research, even at the expense of reducing its conceptual and operational neatness.

I

It is necessary first to clarify some basic terms in which my concern is stated.

The prevailing concepts of "politics" in the literature under consideration are surely an important source of the difficulty. Definitions gravitate toward the most conspicuous *facts* and shy away from all reference to more norm-laden and less easily measurable aspects of social life. For the sake of brevity, let us consider only the most recent formulation by one of the unquestionably most influential political scientists of the present generation: "A political system is any persistent pattern of human relationships that involves, to a significant extent, power, rule, or authority."[4]

[4] Robert Dahl, *Modern Political Analysis* (Englewood Cliffs, 1963), p. 6.

My objection is not primarily to the extension of the reference of "political" to private as well as to public associations, and even to clans and families as well; rather, it is to the absence of any reference to a public purpose. Research work on power, rule, or authority can contribute significantly to our political knowledge, even if the data come from contexts not ordinarily thought of as political. But its significance must be gauged in relation to some criteria; until these are articulated and justified, or at any rate chosen, we can only intuit whether our researches on, say, power behavior are tackling significant or trivial issues.

"Politics" should refer to power, but the term should also refer to some conception of human welfare or the public good. The achievement of Plato and Aristotle is in part a result of their starting out by asking some of the right questions; above all, what is politics *for*? Their limitations were logical and methodological or, if you prefer, conceptual: they had not learned to distinguish between verifiable *descriptive* statements, statements of *normative* positions, and (empirically empty and normatively neutral) *analytical* statements, including definitions and other equations.

Once these distinctions had been developed, a process that began with David Hume, it became easy and fashionable to expose fallacies in Plato and Aristotle; but instead of attacking the ancient and perennial problems of politics with our new and sharper conceptual tools, recent generations of political scientists appear to have sought safety in seeking to exclude the normative realm altogether from the scope of their scientific inquiry. "Politics" has consequently been defined in a simple institutional or behavioral manner, unrelated to normative conceptions of any sort. Ironically, most modern behavioralists are back with the Greeks again in their assumption that political inquiry can be pursued by much the same methods as natural science inquiry; they have adjusted to David Hume and the modern logical positivists by the neat device of definitions that limit the scope of their inquiry to observable behavior.

This surely is a stance of premature closure. The alternative proposed here is to insist on the need for a political theory that deals with *basic human needs* as well as overt desires and other observable aspects of behavior. The task of improving concepts and methods toward establishing a stricter science of politics is formidable; but let us avoid establishing an orthodoxy that would have the whole profession contract for a fainthearted purchase of rigor at the price of excluding much of the meat and spirit of politics.

As a modest and fragmentary beginning toward a more appropriate theory, let me suggest a distinction between "politics" and "pseudopolitics." I would define as *political* all activity aimed at improving or protecting conditions for the satisfaction of human needs and demands in a given society or community, according to some universalistic scheme of priorities, implicit or explicit.[5] *Pseudopolitical* in this paper refers to activity that resembles political activity but is exclusively concerned with either the alleviation of personal neuroses or with promoting private or private interest-group advantage, deterred by no articulate or disinterested conception of what would be just or fair to other groups.

Pseudopolitics is the counterfeit of politics. The relative prevalence of the counterfeit variety of democratic politics presumably depends on many ascertainable factors, including a society's degree of commercialization and the degree of socioeconomic mobility (or the size of the stakes in the competitive struggle); on the other hand, the proportion of pseudopolitical activity would correlate negatively with the amount of psychological security, the amount of social welfare-type security, and the amount of political education effectively taught.

For present purposes it is not necessary to demonstrate in detail how the distinction between politics in the narrower sense and pseudopolitics can be made operationally useful. Suffice it to say that only a saint is pure from the taint of pseudopolitics and that hardly any pseudopolitician would be *wholly* without concern for the public welfare; mixed motives, in proportions varying from one person to the next and from one situation to the next, pervade all actions. It is a difficult but surely not an impossible task to develop indices for assessing the relative prevalence of political versus pseudopolitical incentives in voters and other political actors; the only essential prerequisite is to decide that the task must be tackled.

Without attempting to make this kind of distinction, untidy as it may at first appear to many a behavioralist, I don't see how we can begin to approach a condition of tidiness in our discussions of the *political significance* of research, or of the *political responsibility* of political scientists. But what should we mean by these two highly eulogistic terms; might we not be better advised to shun them altogether? The bulk of this paper seeks to demonstrate

[5] "Priorities" here refers to norms for guiding the choice among conflicting needs and demands. Political ideals and visions of the good life enter in here, and would do so even if our knowledge of needs and of human nature were as extensive as our knowledge of demands and of social determinants of "public opinion."

some sorry consequences of the later course. We cannot avoid the realm of normative issues unless we really wish to disclaim all political significance for our work. Probably very few in our profession would adopt this position.

Although explicit cognizance of normative assumptions in his theoretical frame of reference is likely to entail some inconvenience for the researcher, he will by no means be blocked from continuing much of his present work. It should be clear that all competent research on pseudopolitical behavior illuminates political behavior as well, as the relative presence of one signals the relative absence of the other. In the real world the two aspects of behavior always coexist. My quarrel is not with research on pseudopolitics *per se*, but with the way findings are usually reported and interpreted. I object to the tendency in much of the behavior literature to deal with the pseudopolitical aspects of behavior almost exclusively, and to imply that the prevalence of pseudopolitics is and always will be the natural or even the desirable state of affairs in a democracy. Consequently, I object also to the absence of interest in research that could reveal some of the determinants of the relative prevalence of pseudopolitical behavior on our political arena, by which we might learn more about how we may advance toward a more strictly political consciousness, in the sense of concern for the public interest and for the future, in our population.

Now, how should we define political significance and political responsibility? In my conceptual world the two terms are tied together; I would judge degrees of political significance of research studies in the same way that I would judge degrees of political responsibility of political scientists (in the role of theorist-researcher, as distinct from the role of citizen). A research report is politically significant to the extent that it contributes to the kinds of knowledge most needed by politically responsible political scientists.

"Political responsibility" in this paper refers to the extent to which the social scientist observes the canons of rationality on two levels which I shall call formal and substantive.[6] Formal rationality refers to the familiar notion of clarifying the objectives first and then paying heed to the best available knowledge when seeking ways and means to implement them. Competent behavioral research in political science is highly rational in this formal sense; this is what the extensive work in theory and methodology is *for*.

---

[6] Karl Mannheim employs a similar dichotomy of terms, though with different concepts, in his *Man and Society in an Age of Reconstruction* (New York, 1954), pp. 51–60.

The lack of political responsibility that I ascribe to much political behavior literature relates to the other level of rationality, the substantive level, which involves articulate attention to questions of fundamental commitment in social and political research literature. Problems of human welfare (including justice, liberty, security, etc.), the objects of political research and of politics, can be adequately studied, and dealt with, only if their *ought*-side is investigated as carefully as their *is*-side. Ought-side inquiry must pertain to wants (or desires or, if insisted on, demands) as well as needs. Political communication must be analyzed carefully so that we may learn what aspects of *wants* are most salient and could be frustrated only at the cost of resentment, alienation, or upheaval. Yet, only analysis of data on wants in terms of a theory of *needs* will permit us to evaluate wants and aspects of wants with a view to longer-term consequences of their relative satisfaction or frustration.

There will be more to say about wants and needs in the concluding section. At this point it should only be added that the student of politics, once he has adopted a conception of human needs, should proceed from there to make explicit his inferences about political objectives and his choice of commitments with the utmost care. If this kind of inquiry is neglected, as it certainly is in the political science curricula in most of our universities, the danger is that the political scientist unwittingly becomes the tool of other people's commitments. And *theirs* may be even less responsibly arrived at; conceivably, the expertise of the political scientist may come to serve the irrational purposes of genteel bigotry in domestic policies or of paranoid jingoism and reckless gambling with our chances of survival in foreign policies. If advice-giving social scientists don't feel called on to invest their best intellectual energies in studying the ultimate ends of our national policies, it is unlikely that anyone else of influence will; most active politicians have, after all, more immediately pressing worries, and these are anyway the kinds of concerns they are best trained to handle.

Intellectual treason, to return to Eulau's phrase, is probably a remote hazard in our profession. For, rather than placing himself in the service "of those whose values he disagrees with," the political scientist usually will by natural, uninvestigated processes come to agree with the prevailing values of his profession, of the major foundations and of his government, at least on the more basic public policy objectives and assumptions. His training and career incentives focus on formal rationality. It is fortunate that many social scientists for other reasons tend to be humane and liberal individuals. We will be far better off, however, if we can make it respectable or even mandatory for many more of our researchers to be guided in their choice of theory and problems by their own articulated values, instead of acting willy-nilly on the supposedly neutral values impressed on them by the conventional wisdom of their profession.

II

In the contemporary political science literature it is by no means unusual to see the articulation of political norms begin and end with a commitment to "democracy" in some unspecified sense. Fifteen years ago a respected political scientist suggested a more critical orientation: "The democratic myth is that the people are inherently wise and just, and that they are the real rulers of the republic. These propositions do have meaning; but if they become, as they do even among scholars, matters of faith, then scientific progress has been sacrificed in the interest of a morally satisfying demagogy."[7] This advice has not been generally heeded. Even today many political scientists are writing as if democracy unquestionably is a good thing, from which unquestionably good things will flow, while at the same time they profess a disinterest in settling value issues. "The only cure for the ills of democracy is more democracy," is still the implicit slogan of quite a few social scientists, who seem unaware of even the *conceptual* difficulties involved in developing generally useful criteria, let alone a rationale, for "more democracy." To put it bluntly, it appears that a good number of otherwise able political scientists confuse a vaguely stated conventional "democratism"[8] with scientific objectivity.

That behavioral research not explicitly related to problems of democracy tends to be vague in its implications for normative democratic theory is perhaps to be expected. It is paradoxical that some of the leading behavioral writers *on democracy* continue to write as if they want to have it both ways: to be rigorously value-neutral and at the same time be impeccable champions of conventional pluralist democracy. To straddle on a sharp issue would not be comfortable; if we want to write as good democrats and as logical positivists, too, it is perhaps necessary to be obtuse on issues

[7] Gabriel A. Almond, *The American People and Foreign Policy* (New York, 1950), p. 4.

[8] The term is from Leo Strauss. See his "Epilogue" in Herbert J. Storing, ed., *Essays on the Scientific Study of Politics* (New York, 1962), p. 326.

like "Why democracy?" or "What is democracy for?" and, indeed, "What is democracy?"

For a first example, take the late V. O. Key's most recent book on *Public Opinion and American Democracy*.[9] Here we are presented with an admirably organized survey of what is now known of the characteristics of contemporary public opinion and of the extent of its bearing on American governmental decision processes. Yet for all these facts about public opinion, there is hardly a hint of their implications, in the author's judgment, for any of the relevant normative issues of democracy; what little is said on this score is uninformative indeed. For example, the point is made toward the end that political deviants "play a critical role in the preservation of the vitality of a democratic order as they urge alterations and modifications better to achieve the aspirations of men. Hence the fundamental significance of freedom of speech and agitation" (p. 555). There is no elaboration of this point, which one might take to be an important issue, considering the book's title and general subject. And there is no other discussion of what purpose all this political knowledge should serve. Is it the "preservation of the vitality of a democratic order" as far as we can articulate the criteria for the best possible government, or for trends in the best direction? What does "vitality" mean here, and what aspects of our democracy are most in need of it? Is free speech valuable solely as a means to this rather obscurely conceived end?

Or take the volume on *Voting*, by a team of top-notch political sociologists.[10] One of the book's two themes, we are told (p. x), is the social problem of how political preferences are formed, while the "confrontation of democratic theory with democratic practice is the second implied theme that runs throughout the book." There is much about certain kinds of practices, yes; but democratic theory is limited to a few examples of "impossible" demands of "traditional normative theory" on the role of the citizen: that he should be politically interested, knowledgeable and rational. These investigators find that most voters are indeed politically apathetic, ignorant and far from rational in their political behavior.

Given the second theme one might have expected the authors to raise some pertinent questions concerning the sense, if any, in which we nevertheless do have a democracy, or possibly the sense in which we nevertheless *ought* to be able to have a democracy, if

[9] New York, 1961.
[10] Bernard R. Berelson, Paul F. Lazarsfeld and William N. McPhee, *Voting: A Study of Opinion Formation in a Presidential Campaign* (Chicago, University of Chicago Press, 1954).

what we have now does not fit this concept. Or perhaps an attempt toward reformulating democratic norms in better accord with political realities, if the term "democracy" should be saved for new uses.

Nothing of the sort happens. Instead, the authors make the happy discovery that the *system of democracy* that we have "does meet certain requirements for a going political organization"; indeed, as it is said just before, "it often works with distinction" (p. 312). What is good and bad about the system is left in the dark, as is the question of criteria for "distinction." Instead, we are given a list of dimensions of citizen behavior, and are told that the fact that individuals differ on these various dimensions (*e.g.*, involvement—indifference) somehow is exactly what the modern democratic system requires. It all ends well, then; and in parting the authors leave us with this comforting if question-begging assurance: "Twentieth-century political theory—both analytic and *normative*—will arise *only* from hard and long observation of the actual world of politics, closely identified with the deeper problems of practical politics" (p. 323; italics supplied). *Only*?

Turn now to a widely and deservedly praised book with the promising title, *A Preface to Democratic Theory*. Robert Dahl explains his choice of title by asserting that "there is no democratic theory—only democratic theories. This fact suggests that we had better proceed by considering some representative theories in order to discover what kinds of problems they raise . . ."[11] And in the landscape of behavioral literature this work does stand out as an impressive exercise in logical analysis. Excellent critical evaluations of the Madisonian and the populist-type democratic theories are offered; but subsequently Dahl changes his tack to what he calls (p. 63) the descriptive method: under "polyarchal democracy" he seeks to develop empirical criteria for a concept of democracy based on our knowledge of existing species. As we would expect of a competent behavioralist, the author develops some enlightening perspectives on how "the American hybrid" in fact appears to be functioning.

Penetrating as this account of the basic operating procedures of the American democracy is, the author's criteria for evaluating the result are surprisingly inarticulate and *ad hoc*. He will *not* try to determine whether it is a desirable system of government, he assures us toward the end of the book; and then proceeds to do just that, but vaguely:

---

[11] Chicago, University of Chicago Press, 1956, p. 1.

It appears to be a relatively efficient system for reinforcing agreement, encouraging moderation, and maintaining social peace in a restless and immoderate people operating a gigantic, powerful, diversified, and incredibly complex society. This is no negligible contribution, then, that Americans have made to the arts of government—and to that branch, which of all the arts of politics is the most difficult, the art of democratic government.

These are Dahl's parting words.

Having subjected the assumptions, hypotheses, implied definitions, and even the presumed value axioms of two theories of democracy to painstaking analysis, the author's ambition not to discuss the desirability of the American system of government would be difficult to understand for someone unacquainted with the currently prevailing fashions among behavioralists. To study the definitional characteristics of this hybrid species of government and of the genus, "polyarchal democracy," is a worthwhile endeavor, to be sure, but would in my opinion assume far greater significance if pursued within a framework of value assumptions, however tentatively presented, from which could be derived operational criteria for judging what aspects of a functioning democracy ought to be valued and strengthened, as against other aspects that should be deplored and, if possible, counteracted. Why does the author never say clearly whether in *his* view democracy is something to be valued in itself, and maximized (as he takes Madisonian theory to assert), or as valuable for some specified ends (for example, for maximizing political equality, after the fashion of populists)?

In a Preface to democratic theory, and one which demonstrates a high order of rigor in analyzing other theories of democracy, the author's reluctance even to begin to develop operating criteria toward making meaningful the present system, or to provide pointers toward its more meaningful further development, is as astounding as it is disappointing. Reluctantly one concludes that Dahl in this particular context behaves like most political behavioralists: he feels he can permit himself to write normatively about political purposes, it would seem, only if they are stated in terms of "democracy" and are reasonably indeterminate, lest the suspicion should arise that he is pleading for some politically partisan position. Thus, a demeanor of scientific objectivity is maintained, and so is a persistently implied commitment to a certain political bias, which favors democracy roughly as it now exists in the West, or in this country.

III

Leo Strauss charges the behavioralists with a bias toward liberal democracy, and rightly so, in comparison to his position. Yet in some respects the bias of much behavioralist political literature is profoundly conservative, although this is a species of conservatism rather different from Strauss'. Philosophically speaking, this behaviorally oriented conservatism frequently includes an *antipolitical* dimension which is not found in Strauss' work.[12] What is antipolitical is the assumption, explicit or implicit, that politics, or at any rate American politics, is and must always remain primarily a system of rules for peaceful battles between competing private interests, and not an arena for the struggle toward a more humane and more rationally organized society.

Consider S. M. Lipset's recent suggestion that the age-old search for the good society can be terminated, for we have got it now. Democracy as we know it "is the good society itself in operation." Not that our democracy cannot still be improved upon, but roughly speaking, it appears, "the give-and-take of a free society's internal struggles" is the best that men can hope for. Our society is so good that Lipset welcomes, at least for the West, what he sees as a trend toward replacing political ideology with sociological analysis.[13]

This is an extreme statement, although by a leading and deservedly famous political sociologist. We cannot saddle behavioralists in general with responsibility for such phrasing. But in substance, as we shall see, the same tendency toward affirming the *status quo* and, what is worse, toward disclaiming the importance and even the legitimacy of political ideology, and ideals, is discernible in other leading behaviorally oriented works as well.

Let us note incidentally that all the behavioral works referred to so far wind up affirming that American democracy on the whole works well, while failing to articulate the criteria on which this

[12] This is not to deny that the Straussian position is more authoritarian and far less respectful of the right to radical dissent, as is to be expected when a corner on objective truth is being claimed. *Cf.* especially Leo Strauss, *What Is Political Philosophy and Other Studies* (Glencoe, 1959); and his "Epilogue" in Herbert J. Storing, ed., *op. cit.* See also Walter Berns, "The Behavioral Sciences and the Study of Political Things: The Case of Christian Bay's *The Structure of Freedom*," *American Political Science Review*, Vol. 55 (1961), pp. 550–59.

[13] Seymour Martin Lipset, *Political Man: The Social Bases of Politics* (Garden City, 1960), esp. pp. 403 and 415.

judgment is based.[14] In fairness it should be added that probably all these writers would make an exception for the place of the Negro and certain other underprivileged groups or categories for whom our democracy admittedly does not work so well; there are flaws, then, but fundamentally all is well or else will become well without any basic changes.

What is more troublesome than this somewhat conservative commitment to a somewhat liberal conception of democracy[15]— whether acknowledged or surreptitious—is the antipolitical orientation referred to a moment ago; the failure to see politics as potentially, at least, an instrument of reason, legitimately dedicated to the improvement of social conditions.

Within a brief space that allows no extensive documentation perhaps the next best thing to do is to consider for a moment a recent example of a behavioralist approach in which, for a change, the underlying assumptions are spelled out with commendable clarity, and then let the reader judge to what extent other literature referred to above may not implicitly rest on similar starkly antipolitical premises.

James M. Buchanan and Gordon Tullock have called their book *The Calculus of Consent,* with subtitle *Logical Foundations of Constitutional Democracy.*[16] The task set for the book, we are told in the Preface, is "to analyze the calculus of the rational individual when he is faced with questions of constitutional choice"; the authors, both of whom have most of their training in economics, intend to develop what they take to be the rationale for group action in the public sector in a free society—*i.e.,* for political action.

[14] An interesting attempt to evaluate the 1952 Presidential election in terms of five criteria of democratic consent (as opposed to non-rational responses to manipulated processes) is reported in Morris Janowitz and Dwaine Marvick, *Competitive Pressure and Democratic Consent* (Ann Arbor, Bureau of Government, University of Michigan, 1956). The five criteria are chosen somewhat haphazardly, but they are carefully and ingeniously operationalized and brought to bear on available data. The study shows what could just as well be done, in years to come, within a more carefully and systematically stated framework of political objectives and norms.

[15] Though perhaps paradoxical, the statement is not self-contradictory. A democracy that guarantees many liberties to people of most persuasions, and in theory to everybody, may well be considered a liberal democracy. Freedom of speech and related freedoms have a strong appeal to most intellectuals, many of whom may become staunch conservatives *because* they believe in preserving their liberal democracy. Some, indeed, will become fixated on the need for defense of the social order to the point of ignoring the plight of poverty-stricken fellow-citizens whose formal liberty may seem worthless to themselves.

[16] Ann Arbor, University of Michigan Press, 1962.

The authors take pains to assert the value-free nature of their approach to the science of politics. True, they choose to go along with "the Western philosophical tradition" insofar as they consider the human individual "the primary philosophical entity" (p. 11). From here on, supposedly, we are dealing with the political processes that flow from the desire of all individuals to try to maximize whatever they may value. "The grail-like search for some 'public interest' apart from, and independent of, the separate interests of the individual participants in social choice" (p. 12) is not the concern of *these* authors.

Only in one limited sense do the authors recognize a sort of collective interest in a free society: "it is rational to *have a constitution*" (p. 21), or a set of rules for deciding how decisions in the public sector are to be arrived at; *constitutional* issues are in principle to be settled by unanimity, while *operational* issues—all other political issues—must be settled according to constitutional provisions. The authors see no rationale for majoritarianism as a way of deciding, unless a constitution happens to require it in given contexts; consequently, constitutions can be changed only by unanimity, according to this "individualistic theory of political process," as one of the authors has lately named the theory.[17]

In his more recent statement, Buchanan recognizes as an "entirely reasonable interpretation" (p. 7) that this approach to political processes can be seen as a model for the defense of the *status quo*. His most important rejoinder is that "analysis must start from somewhere, and the existing set of rules and institutions is the only place from which it is possible to start" (p. 7).

The previously cited writings of leading behavioralists have been less explicit and also less bold in showing the way from assertedly value-free premises toward a conservative and in my sense antipolitical orientation. Yet, in all the works given critical attention above, there are normative ambiguities wide enough to make room for a theory such as the one offered by Buchanan and Tullock. This is not to say that Eulau, Key, Berelson *et al.*, Dahl, or Lipset would concur with Buchanan and Tullock in their normative position. But their approach to politics is philosophically similar in its emphasis on prevailing behavior patterns here and now as the thing to study and in its rejection of the legitimacy of normative positions as frameworks for research (except in a normatively *ad hoc* policy science context). Buchanan and Tullock

---

[17] James M. Buchanan, "An Individualistic Theory of Political Process." Paper prepared for delivery at the 1963 Annual Meeting of the American Political Science Association in Commodore Hotel, New York City.

have been able to explicate in considerable detail *one* rationale for an implicit stance that appears to be widely shared by students of politics today.

If a similar orientation were to be adopted in medical literature, its scope would in the main be confined to studying how patients choose to cope or at any rate do cope with their pathologies, while omitting or neglecting fundamental study of conditions for possible treatment and prevention.

IV

Unlike other behavioral literature, modern works in comparative politics almost always focus on real political problems; when political institutions are compared cross-nationally or cross-culturally, pseudopolitical behavior can more readily be seen as dysfunctional in terms of some conception or other of the public good; usually such conceptions are couched in terms of "modernization" or "development," at least if comparisons are cross-cultural as well as cross-national. The point is that developmental perspectives and therefore political purposes are ever-present in this literature, even if they are not often well articulated. Yet, what is particularly impressive in some of this literature is its conceptual and theoretical scope, including the stress on psychological as well as social component explanations of political behavior, and on the need for integrating micro-analyses of personalities and small groups with macro-analyses of large collectivities.[18]

Concerned as the modern students of comparative politics have been with substantive problems, they have resisted temptations to pursue their inquiries according to immediately practical considerations such as the availability of operational indices and techniques of measurement.[19] On the contrary, insistent efforts

[18] Some of the milestones in this literature are Gabriel A. Almond, "Comparative Political Systems," *Journal of Politics*, Vol. 18 (1956), pp. 391–409; Almond and James S. Coleman, eds., *The Politics of the Developing Areas* (Princeton, Princeton University Press, 1960); Almond and Sidney Verba, *The Civic Culture* (Princeton, Princeton University Press, 1963).

[19] For contrast, consider this statement on the ways of other behavioralists: "The focus of the political behaviorist, however, does not seem to be a result of the state of political theory. Elections have been intensively studied because they lend themselves to the methodology of empirical research into politics." Morris Janowitz, Deil Wright, and William Delany, *Public Administration and the Public—Perspectives Toward Government in a Metropolitan Community* (Ann Arbor, Bureau of Government, University of Michigan, 1958), p. 2.

have been made to innovate concepts that would take account of variables which are not as yet accessible to observation and quantification—concepts such as political culture, political socialization, political identity, and political style, for example. The long-term strategy appears to be to start out with concepts broad enough to encompass all significant aspects of political reality, and then work toward parceling out component concepts which come closer to corresponding to variables that can be observed, perhaps indirectly and by tentative indices at first. Thus the theoretical working hypotheses can gradually, it is hoped, be subjected to increasingly direct and stringent tests. This is a far cry from the piecemeal approach to political (or pseudopolitical) reality in many other works, which almost exclusively pays attention to disparate empirical relationships while neglecting to consider the possible systematic-theoretical reasons we might have for taking an interest in them.

There is also this to be said about the modern comparative politics literature, however, that its conceptual and theoretical innovations have as yet failed to make a significant dent in the same democratic myth that Almond himself—the leader in this field—has warned us against years ago. The dilemma already discussed, of desiring to support democracy and adopt a stance of value neutrality, too, has not as yet been satisfactorily resolved in this literature either. And this failure is paradoxical in this particular context, in part because the ostensible chief concern is with "development" or "modernization" as the dependent variable, so that the question of development toward *what* immediately suggests itself. The failure is paradoxical also because these scholars have coined bold new concepts on the independent side of the ledger, and some have written extensively about concepts as far removed from realms of observation as "political culture" and "political identity."[20] Yet a concept such as "human need" has not been touched, and discussions of key terms like "political development" or "modernization" have been hampered, it would seem, by an unwillingness to question whether democratic ways or what kinds of democratic ways are most conducive to satisfying human needs.[21]

[20] *Cf.* Almond and Verba, *op. cit.*, and Lucian W. Pye, *Politics, Personality, and Nation Building: Burma's Search for Identity* (New Haven, Yale University Press, 1962).

[21] Concepts of modernization or development are discussed by James S. Coleman in Almond and Coleman, eds., *op. cit.*, pp. 532–36; by Lucian W. Pye, ed., *Communication and Political Development* (Princeton, Princeton University Press, 1963), pp. 14–20; and by Joseph La Palombara (ed.) in his

In the most extensive recent discussion of these concepts La Palombara begins well with a warning that what many scholars appear to have in mind "when they speak of a modern or developed system is one that approximates the institutional and structural configuration that we associate with the Anglo-American (in any event, the Western) democratic systems" (p. 10). He calls this conceptualization culture-bound; yet in the same and the following chapter he goes to considerable lengths himself in arguing for the use of the same kinds of culture-bound criteria to evaluate development or modernity abroad. While he contributes a useful discussion of different dimensions along which political change can be measured, he never inquires whether in other countries there might be other criteria of development of equal or greater significance than his own essentially Anglo-Saxon criteria. "One of the great dilemmas of many of the developing countries," he writes, "is that they seem to want economic development more than freedom" (p. 41), and the last term he takes as a matter of course to refer to pluralist institutions. "Why should it not be possible to raise a belief in and desire for democracy to the same level?" (p. 58). And in conclusion La Palombara asserts that we Americans must expand our efforts to export not only technical know-how "but our political ideology and reasonable facsimiles of our political institutions and practices as well." Without such an effort, he adds, he is reasonably confident that "the probability of attaining democratic configuration in most of the newer states is very low indeed" (pp. 60–61).

The main difficulty with this reasoning is that men are motivated, also politically, by their immediate needs and wants, and not by foreign orthodoxies. La Palombara speculates "whether it would not be possible to manipulate demands so that goals of political development enjoy a status equal to that of economic change" (p. 30), and suggests the encouragement of private as against collectively oriented enterprise for this end. The answer is surely a flat no: it is *not* possible, in most countries in which most people are economically underprivileged, to create a broad popular interest in pluralist democratic institutions. "Acceptance of the norms of democracy requires a high level of sophistication and ego security," writes Lipset, on the basis of a variety of loosely connected empirical data.[22] An active concern for the public welfare presupposes a liberation both from anxiety neuroses and from

---

Bureaucracy and Political Development (Princeton University Press, 1963), chs. 1 and 2.

[22] *Political Man, op. cit.*, p. 115 and ch. 4.

realistic fears concerning one's own and one's family's physical sustenance, welfare and security. To put it more succinctly, needs for food and safety take precedence over political interest; no amount of political manipulation could be expected to alter such priorities.

To be sure, individuals can be lured into "the game of politics" as advantageous careers under the right circumstances; but is this the kind of political development that the West should desire? If budding Western-democracy-type pluralist institutions turn out to benefit only the middle and upper classes—as in many Latin American countries—then we should not be surprised if idealistic students and others with a passion for social justice, or for politics as distinct from pseudopolitics, may become disposed to reject the forms of pluralist democracy altogether.[23]

Nevertheless, the trend among political behavioralists, including students of comparative politics, appears to be toward a clean break not only with Plato's concern with justice as something above democracy, for the true philosopher; also, it seems that the classical conception of democracy as a system of rational deliberation for settling issues of justice and welfare is on its way out, *even as a political ideal.* Reference has been made to the *ad hoc* attempts of Berelson *et al.* to bring the norms of democracy in better accord with the facts of what I have termed pseudopolitical behavior. In *The Civic Culture* Almond and Verba present and discuss a variety of usefully differentiated survey data collected in five countries (United States, Britain, West Germany, Italy and Mexico). "What we have done in this book," they conclude, "is to spell out methodically the mixture of attitudes that support a democratic system. If it can create a more sober and informed appreciation of the nature and complexity of the problems of democratization, it will have served its purpose."[24] But what kind of democracy? The theoretical point of departure is neither in a conception of human needs nor in the classical theories of democracy, but in such literature as has been discussed above—notably Dahl's *Preface to Democratic Theory* and the last chapter in Berelson's *Voting.* In fact, Almond and Verba emphatically reject the classical "rationality-activist" ideal of democratic citizenship in favor of a more balanced "parochial-subject-participant" orientation; in a healthy, stable democracy as they conceive it (and American political culture comes close even though it does not quite embody

---

[23] Fidel Castro's wide following in Latin America can be plausibly explained in these terms.

[24] *Op. cit.,* p. 505 and ch. 15.

this ideal), "the democratic citizen is called on to pursue contradictory goals; he must be active, yet passive; involved, yet not too involved; influential, yet deferential."[25]

Perhaps so, if the ultimate goal is democratic stability. And there is no denying, from my normative position, that democratic stability is valuable, and that many nations ought to have more of it. But is it the most important goal for political development; is it the goal that should serve as the basis for evaluating all other goals (whether wholly, in terms of instrumentality, or partially, in terms of compatibility)? Should we not instead hold, in Eulau's phrase, that "The Goal is Man"?

V

In the study of political behavior, "analysis must start from somewhere, and the existing set of rules and institutions is the only place from which it is possible to start," according to Buchanan. Students of comparative politics have nevertheless demonstrated the feasibility of analyzing political developments in some countries in terms of valuable outcomes achieved in others.[26] It remains to be shown that political behavior and institutions can be analyzed also in terms of normative assumptions to the effect that the purpose of politics is to meet human needs and facilitate human development.

Contrary to an apparently prevailing assumption among political behavioralists, psychological phenomena are just as *real* as economic and voting behavior phenomena, even though admittedly less accessible to observation and measurement. Some more of the same conceptual boldness displayed in the recent literature on comparative politics is required if political inquiry is to become related to important human wants and needs. For one thing, we need to distinguish more clearly between pseudo-political and more strictly political behavior, if we want to learn how to encourage the latter at the expense of the former.[27]

A major conceptual and theoretical task is to develop a satisfactory theory of human needs and of the relationships between

[25] *Ibid.*, pp. 478–79 and 440–41.
[26] See especially Robert E. Ward and Dankwart A. Rustow, *The Political Modernization of Japan and Turkey* (Princeton University Press, 1964).
[27] However, we should not assume without inquiry that *all* pseudopolitical behavior is dysfunctional for all high-priority human wants and needs; not, of course, that all varieties of political behavior are to be preferred to pseudopolitical self-seeking or neurotic striving.

needs and *wants*—here referring to perceived or felt needs. Wants (or, synonymously, desires) and demands can be observed and measured by way of asking people or observing their behavior. Needs, on the other hand, can only be inferred from their hypothetical consequences for behavior or, more manifestly, from the actual consequences of their frustration. Whenever superficial wants are fulfilled but underlying needs remain frustrated, pathological behavior is likely to ensue.

Prior to the development of a viable theory of political development is at least a beginning toward a theory of individual human development. Such a beginning exists in psychological literature, but it has so far been inadequately drawn on by students of political behavior. Let me very briefly suggest the direction of this theorizing, and some of its implications for the study of political behavior.

Basic human needs are characteristics of the human organism, and they are presumably less subject to change than the social or even the physical conditions under which men live. Wants are sometimes manifestations of real needs but, as Plato and many other wise men since have insisted, we cannot always infer the existence of needs from wants. Wants are often artificially induced by outside manipulation, or they may be neurotically based desires whose satisfaction fails to satisfy needs, or both. Emphasis on a civic-culture type of democracy as the goal for political development may well perpetuate a state of affairs in which human needs as seen by the political-minded (in my strict sense of "political") will remain in the shadow of much-advertised human wants as promoted by pseudopoliticians and other enterprisers whose horizons do not extend beyond their own occupational or career interests and status anxieties.[28]

I say *may*, for I am raising a question rather than adopting a position. In order to investigate the relationship between needs and wants as they pertain to political functions we must start out with a tentative conception of priorities among human needs. The best available point of departure, in my opinion, is in A. H. Maslow's theory of a hierarchy of human needs; this theorizing ought

[28] Joseph Tussman also stresses the danger of destroying the integrity of political communication when the modern bargaining approach to politics enters the "forum or tribunal" that a democratic electorate ought to constitute, according to classical theories of democracy. "We teach men to compete and bargain. Are we to be surprised, then, at the corruption of the tribunal into its marketplace parody?" *Obligation and the Body Politic* (New York, Oxford University Press, 1960), p. 109 and pp. 104–21.

to be drawn on until a more plausible and useful theory becomes available.

Maslow lists five categories of needs in the order of their assumed priority: (1) physical needs (air, water, food, etc.); (2) safety needs (assurance of survival and of continuing satisfaction of basic needs); (3) needs to love and be loved; (4) need for esteem (by self and others); and (5) need for self-actualization and growth. This list presents a hierarchy, according to Maslow, in the sense that the "less prepotent needs are minimized, even forgotten or denied. But when a need is fairly well satisfied, the next prepotent ('higher') need emerges, in turn to dominate the conscious life and to serve as the center of organization of behavior, since gratified needs are not active motivators.[29] Note, however, that whenever in the course of a human life the "higher" needs have become activated, they are not necessarily extinguished as a result of later deprivation of "lower" or more basic needs. For example, some individuals, provided they have once known physical safety, will unhesitatingly sacrifice all of it for love, or for standards of right conduct tied in with their self-esteem, etc.

In a recent volume, James C. Davies has suggested the utility of Maslow's theory as a generator of propositions regarding political behavior, and he illustrates the plausibility (without demonstrating the validity) of such propositions with a wealth of historical and contemporary political behavior data. For example, according to Davies' theorizing it is impractical to suggest, with La Palombara, that it might be "possible to manipulate demands" in economically underdeveloped countries so that widespread loyalties to democratic institutions could emerge: "Long before there can be responsible or irresponsible popular government, long before the question of dictatorship or democracy can be taken up, the problem of survival must be solved so that a political community itself can develop, so that people can direct some of their attention to politics."[30] In another context he says, "Propaganda cannot paint a picture which conflicts with reality as it is seen by individuals in the light of their basic needs" (p. 134); the picture can be painted all right, but it will be a wasted effort. And Davies quotes Kwame Nkrumah, whose implicit rejoinder to La Palombara's

[29] Abraham H. Maslow, "A Theory of Human Motivation," *Psychological Review*, Vol. 50 (1943), p. 394 and pp. 370–96. See also his *Motivation and Personality* (New York, 1954).

[30] *Human Nature in Politics* (New York, 1963), p. 28. Davies does not refer to La Palombara.

argument is hard to improve on: "We cannot tell our people that material benefits in growth and modern progress are not for them. If we do, they will throw us out and seek other leaders who promise more . . . We have to modernize. Either we shall do so with the interest and support of the West or we shall be compelled to turn elsewhere. This is not a warning or a threat, but a straight statement of political reality" (p. 135).

One shortcoming in Davies' as well as Maslow's work, in my judgment, is that both authors seek to relate events and behavior directly to the elusive concept of "need," without the use of an intermediate and more manageable concept such as "want." Both concepts are badly needed, and their interrelations and their application in hypotheses must be developed if we want to move toward a more adequate knowledge of political behavior. It must be granted that manifest wants are important aspects of our political reality, especially in democracies; what matters is that we also keep remembering, unlike many behavioralists, that there also are genuine needs to worry about, elusive though they may be to the researcher's conventional tools. The volume of competing loudspeakers, if I may use a metaphor, is in a pluralist democracy perhaps more likely to depend on the power of the purse than on the urgency of the need. Even the most democratic governments are likely to come to a bad end—to say nothing of the individuals living under them—unless they learn to become at least as responsive to the basic needs of all their citizens as they are to the most insistent wants of the various articulate and influential interest groups and parties.

Most of Maslow's as well as Davies' discussion is highly speculative; only a beginning has been made. But their theory does lend itself to the production of testable hypotheses. For example, Almond's theory of political "input functions" (political socialization and recruitment; interest articulation; interest aggregation; political communication) and "output functions" (rule making; rule application; rule adjudication),[31] would seem to provide a fertile field for exploring what the participation in or other ego-involvement with each type of function can mean, in satisfying individual personality needs as well as wants. Moving in this direction we can perhaps get away from the customary clichés about the value of democracy, toward research-based knowledge on what (aspects of) democratic institutions have what kinds of value for human development.

I have argued elsewhere that the human goals of politics should

[31] *Cf.* his introduction to Almond and Coleman, eds., *op. cit.*

be conceived in terms of maximizing individual freedom—psychological, social, and potential.[32] Democracy and indeed every law
and constitutional clause should be judged as a means to this end.
A comprehensive treatment of norms of liberty with interrela-
tionships and empirical consequences is necessary for this purpose, and so is a theory of human needs such as Maslow's, which
in effect predicts that with increasing satisfaction of sustenance
and security needs men's tendency will be to become less anti-
social, more capable of respecting and eventually perhaps insisting
on respect for the basic needs and liberties of others.

The normative research[33] to be recommended can be done with
far more precision than was attempted or achieved in the work on
freedom just referred to. Perhaps philosophers working with political scientists can be expected to be active on this research frontier
in future years. One good example of normative research of this
kind, even though its reference to empirical data is for purposes
of normative interpretation only, is Naess's study of Gandhi's
ethics of conflict resolution.[34]

The burden of this paper, then, is to plead for an expansion and
a more systematic articulation of the psychological and the normative perspectives of political behavior research. I propose as a
normative basis the proposition that politics exists for the purpose
of progressively removing the most stultifying obstacles to a free
human development, with priority for the worst obstacles, whether
they hit many or few—in other words, with priority for those
individuals who are most severely oppressed; as Harrington points
out with respect to the poverty-stricken in the United States, they
are also the least articulate, and the least likely to achieve redress
by way of the ordinary democratic processes.[35] It is argued in this

[32] *The Structure of Freedom* (Stanford, Stanford University Press, 1958,
and New York, 1965).

[33] The term "normative research" may be puzzling to some, who think
of research exclusively as systematically repeated search for empirical
data, in the real world or in contrived experimental worlds. And "research"
has been one of the empirical social scientist's proud banners in his uphill
fight against the sometime supremacy of armchair speculators. In our
time a less parochial use of "research" is called for, as a way of recognizing
the close interplay between the empirical, normative and logical aspects of
inquiry that, as the present paper argues, is necessary for the further development of our knowledge of political as of other human behavior.

[34] Arne Naess, "A Systematization of Gandhian Ethics of Conflict Resolution," *Journal of Conflict Resolution*, Vol. 2 (1958), pp. 140–55; and also
Johan Galtung and Arne Naess, *Gandhis politiske etikk* (Oslo, Tanum,
1955).

[35] Michael Harrington, *The Other America: Poverty in the United States*
(Baltimore, Penguin Books, 1963; New York, 1962).

paper that the current preoccupation with pseudopolitical behavior carries conservative and antipolitical implications, and that
the best hope for a more politically useful reorientation of behavioral research—in addition to and beyond the comparative
politics perspective—is to study how the various functions of
government bear, and could bear, on the satisfaction of basic needs
as well as conscious wants.

Among the questions to ask are these: What kinds of enduring
satisfactions tend to be associated, for example, with particular
participant and subject roles established by alternate forms of
centralized or decentralized decision processes? Under what sociocultural and socioeconomic circumstances are majoritarian decision processes, of given types, likely to produce substantive
satisfaction of the basic needs of, in Harrington's phrase, society's
"rejects"?

As so often in our human condition, the dimensions of our
ignorance appear to grow larger the closer we come to the most
enduringly important issues of our social life. Much conceptual
as well as basic psychological work remains to be done before our
technical proficiency in the study of the relation of political forms
to basic needs and to liberty can come to match the current work
on analysis of voting patterns. But in this work political scientists
should participate; our stakes in its progress are as high as anyone
else's.

One particular type of research that should be pushed, as a
much needed complement to the large supply of data on pseudopolitical behavior, is work that would focus on just how some
citizens "graduate" from the role of pseudopolitical actor to that
of political actor. Or, more accurately—for surely there are more
pseudopolitical actors in the older age groups, "hardened in the
school of life"—how it is that some categories of individuals (or
individuals in some categories of situations) manage to remain
concerned with ideals and with politics, i.e., with the welfare of
their fellowmen, all their lives?

A theory of human development is implied in the research approaches here recommended. It asserts that man is likely to become
increasingly capable of being rational, or intellectual,"[36] to the
extent that he no longer needs the services of his beliefs and attitudes for the purpose of keeping his various anxieties in check.
Deep-seated neurotic anxieties about one's worth as a human

---

[36] Cf. my "A Social Theory of Intellectual Development," in Nevitt San-
ford, ed., The American College (New York, 1961), pp. 972–1005, esp. pp.
978 and 1000–1005.

being predispose to right-wing or occasionally left-wing extremism, with glorification of ingroups or individuals, living or dead, along with hatreds against outgroups and deviants. Neurotic status anxieties predispose to eager adherence to whatever views appear expected in one's reference groups. Realistic fears about employment or future career prospects predispose against maintaining the luxury of political opinions at all, unless they are "safe." Only for individuals whose main anxiety problems have been faced and in some way resolved is it generally possible to think of and care about problems of politics in terms of standards of justice or the public interest, independently of personal worries.

The development of strictly political incentives in the individual, then, depends on a gradual process of liberation from a preoccupation with personal anxieties and worries. Stages in this process can be identified by research, although our concepts and instruments need some improvement before we can with confidence relate specific categories of political irrationality to (repressed or acknowledged) anxieties associated with specific levels in a hierarchy of human needs. Human nature being complex, so is the task of fully comprehending the dynamics of political behavior. My essential argument here is that we must face up to but not complacently accept, as the pseudopolitical outlook does, the fact that most of our citizens live too harassed lives or lack the education or opportunities for reflection to permit them the real satisfactions and the full dignity of democratic citizenship. We must pose the empirical problem of how the more stultifying pressures on adults and preadults can be reduced. A premature ruling out of the classic democratic citizenship ideal, with its stress on reason as a crucial factor in politics, would seem particularly inappropriate in our age of rapid technological change; never was the need for politics in the strict sense greater.

It is conceivable that our prospects for developing much larger proportions of political-minded citizens will improve substantially if or when the "cybernetics revolution" does away with our omnipresent worries about making a living. On the other hand, unless educational and cultural resources can be expanded as rapidly, so that more people may be enabled to base their sense of identity and self-esteem on their own attributes or ideals rather than on their occupational roles, status anxieties and despair about lack of purpose in life might remain at present levels, and become aggravated for some. But the overall prospects surely would be brighter, to the extent that more of the principal *real* worries on which our current anxieties feed were removed.

In any event, let us not as political scientists rule out the possibility that a real *polity* may emerge eventually—a community of people capable of giving some of their energies to political as distinct from pseudopolitical reflection and activity. A less utopian first step that may be hoped for is that many more political scientists will adopt a more political (or a less pseudopolitical) perspective in their theorizing and research. As the horizons of behavior research expand to encompass latent need-behavior as well as manifest want-behavior, our political science will not only produce a new order of intellectual challenge; it may also become a potent instrument for promoting political development in the service of human development.

19 🐟 DEMOCRACY RESTATED

GRAEME DUNCAN AND STEVEN LUKES

One of the most salutary results of this vast accumulation of data on politics has been to discredit the older speculative theorists and utopia-makers.

CHARLES BEARD, 1908

The fact that traditional political theory has been held recently in low esteem can be traced in part to the extension of scientific methods to the study of society. At times this has led to a wholesale rejection of the older subject as value-laden and unscientific.[1]

FROM Graeme Duncan and Steven Lukes, "The New Democracy," *Political Studies*, 11 (1963), 156–177. Reprinted by permission of Clarendon Press, Oxford.

[1] The general position was well put by Charles Merriam: "Politics, in short, faces the common problem of passing from rule of thumb to more precise measurement, from the art to the science," quoted in Eulau, Eldersveld, and Janowitz (ed.), *Political Behavior, A Reader in Theory and Research* (The Free Press, Glencoe, 1956), p. 274. This view is evident throughout this work. For discussion of it, see B. Crick, *The American Science of Politics* (Routledge, London, 1959). Some writers have a practical and

But a number of more sophisticated political scientists have seen some value in the work of speculative political theorists and have condemned, not political theory as such, but a philosophical approach to questions which they thought could best be answered in a more scientific manner. After paying some homage to the older theory, they have argued that its abstract notions and principles misdescribe the ways in which men behave and societies function. As a result, attempts have been made to confront certain traditional theories with the facts of political life, and to carry through a substantial revision of these theories. Nowhere has this confrontation and revision advanced further than in the field of democratic theory, which has been examined from the new perspective afforded by research into voting behavior. Armed with material from the voting studies, Bernard Berelson and others have hastened to declare that past democratic theory is in many respects patently unrealistic and have tried therefore to produce a new and more adequate theory of democracy.[2]

Berelson, probably the most influential of these writers, has sought explicitly to confront normative theory with empirical research, to their mutual advantage. He suggests in particular that political theorists

---

simple view of political theory, as in this statement from William A. Glazer: "Many of the problems now besetting the world arise from the fact that physicists and engineers know how to combine theory and fact more efficiently than do political scientists and policy makers," "The Types and Uses of Political Theory," *Social Research*, Autumn 1955, p. 292. The general methodological questions raised by these views and by some of the claims of the voting-behavior researchers, *e.g.*, Lazarsfeld, are not, however, the subject of this paper.

[2] We are mainly concerned with those who give detailed consideration to empirical findings in reformulating democratic theory. The main references are: Berelson, Lazarsfeld, and McPhee, *Voting* (University of Chicago Press, 1954), especially chapter 14 (hereafter referred to as Berelson (1)); B. Berelson, "Democratic Theory and Public Opinion," *Public Opinion Quarterly*, vol. 16, Autumn 1952, and reprinted in Eulau *et al.*, *op. cit.* pp. 107–15 (hereafter, Berelson (2)); Milne and Mackenzie, *Marginal Seat, 1955* (The Hansard Society for Parliamentary Government, 1958), chapter 13; S. M. Lipset, *Political Man* (Heinemann, London, 1960), *passim;* and R. A. Dahl, "Hierarchy, Democracy and Bargaining in Politics and Economics," reprinted in Eulau *et al.*, *op. cit.*, pp. 83–90. See also: Talcott Parsons, "Voting and the Equilibrium of the American Political System," and Eugene Burdick, "Political Theory and the Voting Studies," in *American Voting Behaviour*, ed. Burdick and Brodbeck (The Free Press, Glencoe, 1960), chapters 4 and 6; J. A. Schumpeter, *Capitalism, Socialism and Democracy* (Allen & Unwin, 1950) 3rd ed., part iv; J. P. Plamenatz, "Electoral Studies and Democratic Theory," *Political Studies*, vol. vi, 1958, pp. 1–9; and W. H. Morris-Jones, "In Defence of Apathy," *Political Studies*, vol. ii, 1954, pp. 25–37.

might explore the relevance, the implications, and the meaning of such empirical facts as are contained in this and similar studies. Political theory written with reference to practice has the advantage that its categories are the categories in which political life really occurs . . . empirical research can help to clarify the standards and correct the empirical presuppositions of normative theory.[3]

Such an aim sounds unexceptionable and, if fulfilled, might be expected to increase men's understanding of society. It is not our intention to deny that voting-behavior research can be useful in this respect, although its results do seem to have been disappointingly meager. But we do wish to argue that the actual revision of democratic theory that has been attempted has considerably less justification than Berelson's general statement might suggest. In the first place, the writers with whom we are concerned misunderstand the nature of eighteenth- and nineteenth-century democratic theories,[4] which were not, nor did they purport to be, descriptions of the way in which people actually behaved. Moreover, the older theories are not usually considered in sufficient detail to show which theorists are being subjected to criticism. In the second place, the new theory of democracy, which seems to be founded upon facts, has serious though hidden shortcomings. It is, as we hope to show in the second part, loosely formulated and sometimes superficial, and it rests upon a vague notion of equilibrium and *a priori* assumptions about the self-adjusting powers of the "system." In the face of the failure of men to meet the classical norms, it provides a new set of norms, the chief among them apathy, which are much closer to realization in present-day America and Britain. Those whom we describe as theorists of the new democracy are not all equally inadequate and complacent, but they use similar arguments and the general direction of their thought is toward an easy acceptance of the existing order. This, as we will suggest in the final section, is partly due to their fear of ideology and resulting preoccupation with the supposed conditions of a stable and nontotalitarian political system, which leads them to reject outright the old democratic vision of a community of participating members, in its various forms. Not only are the stated reasons for such a rejection inadequate; it can still reason-

---

[3] Berelson (1), *op. cit.*, p. 306.
[4] There are, of course, dangers in generalizing in this way, and we hope to bring out some of the differences as our argument develops. The main works considered are Rousseau's *Social Contract*, James Mill's *Essay on Government* and J. S. Mill's *Representative Government*.

ably be argued that the realization of this vision, in one form or another, remains a desirable goal of social and political activity.

1

There are a number of different strands in classical democratic theory and it cannot therefore be characterized simply. Its major exponents differ over both the institutional requirements for democracy and the arguments which can best be urged in its favor. It is true to say, however, that in general a democratic society is treated as one in which all the citizens (the people) continuously and actively participate in the various community affairs.[5] A democratic society, whether conceived on the Greek model, as by Rousseau, or on a national basis, as by John Stuart Mill, is pre-eminently a society marked by wide discussion and consultation, so that the whole people know the reasons for political decisions through taking part directly or indirectly in their formulation. J. S. Mill, whom we choose as the central democratic theorist because of his concern with representative government, as well as for his clarity, put the argument for widespread participation clearly. He wrote that

the only government which can fully satisfy all the exigencies of the social state is one in which the whole people participate; that any participation, even in the smallest public function, is useful; that the participation should everywhere be as great as the general degree of improvement of the community will allow, and that nothing less can be ultimately desirable than the admission of all to a share in the sovereign power of the state.[6]

Mill proclaimed the need for general participation in a wide variety of affairs, not all of which were specifically political, and related this to his ideal of self-development.

The extension of the franchise and frequent elections, which have been central demands at least in English and American democratic theory, were supported for a number of reasons: that only the vote can reveal the general interest of the community; that it is a natural right, or a right deriving from the rendering of

[5] Participation was not always limited to specifically political activities. Mill, in particular, wrote in *The Political Economy* that "all classes of the community, down to the very lowest, should have much to do for themselves and should be encouraged to manage as many as possible of their joint concerns by voluntary co-operation."

[6] *Representative Government* (Everyman), p. 217.

services; that powerful groups or interests must be absorbed into society rather than driven into violent action against established institutions; that the vote is necessary for self-protection; and that it, along with other forms of participation in the life of the nation, elevates those who possess it.[7] The most important for the purposes of our analysis are the last two, which are also those least objectionable to modern democratic thinkers.[8]

The utilitarians, disturbed at the ease with which governments became the property of "sinister interests," developed one of the characteristic democratic arguments. The most difficult problem for government (which arises naturally from their psychological premises) is that of "restraining those in whose hands are lodged the powers necessary for the protection of all, from making a bad use of it."[9] Assuming that self-preference is unrestrained by social feelings, the only means of bringing about a rough identity between the interests of community and ruler are "artificial"—widening the electorate and limiting the duration of governmental power by frequent elections. J. S. Mill, who believed like his father in the natural tendency of rulers to misuse their power, traced this tendency to a deficiency of understanding rather than to mere ill-will and selfishness. Rulers are less ill-disposed than ignorant. Only the man himself can adequately judge and safeguard his own interests—"in the absence of its natural defenders, the interest of the excluded is always in danger of being overlooked."[10] Constant vigilance and general participation ensure that all interests will be considered and thus that greater justice will prevail in the settlement of claims.

For the younger Mill, however, the franchise was more than a weapon against arbitrary power and a means whereby each group could ensure that its claims were adequately considered. Although he feared that an enfranchised working class would misuse its

[7] This is not an exhaustive list of the arguments which have been urged in support of democracy. Others might be added: *e.g.,* that the vote is a good means of informing the government of specific areas of dissatisfaction, that the expertise of administrators can be controlled by the wisdom of the plain man, that the election allows the government to calculate the limits to its possible activity, and so on.

[8] Political sociology has not eliminated the tendency to argue the case for democracy in the old terms, though some space may be given to elite theorists, *e.g.,* Mosca and Pareto, in passing. *Cf.* J. H. Hallowell, *The Moral Foundation of Democracy* (University of Chicago Press, 1954); N. Micklem, *The Idea of Liberal Democracy* (London, 1957); A. Ross, *Why Democracy?* (Massachusetts, 1952), for a restatement of some of the traditional arguments. Christian beliefs are important in the first two of these.

[9] James Mill, *Essay on Government* (Cambridge, 1937), p. 6.

[10] *Representative Government*, p. 209.

powers and suggested certain safeguards to secure the authority of the enlightened, he had great faith in the civilizing effects of political participation itself. He described the franchise as "a potent instrument of mental improvement" and followed Tocqueville in explaining the conscientious citizenship of the Americans by their democratic institutions. Self-government is in this sense self-sustaining: through the possession of legal rights men become capable of properly exercising them and thus they approach that moral autonomy which is the true end of life.

Those who have, like Mill and Rousseau, gone beyond self-protection and the possibility of peaceful change as the chief advantages of the democratic form of government have tended to speak in terms of man's realization of some characteristic excellence. The democratic society is the good society, bringing out the best in men; democracy, as Lindsay said, is a theory of society as well as a theory of government. Rousseau, who idealizes only direct or "populistic" democracy, eliminates conflict, since when men rationally seek the common good, which is ascertainable, there are no possible grounds for disagreement between them; whereas Mill pictures a community of critical, restless, dissatisfied individuals, constantly questioning one another's principles in the pursuit of truth and the general happiness. They evaluate differently "long debates, discussion and tumult."

Voting, as the chief institutional means of participation, becomes of crucial importance. It is conceived, not as a spasmodic or casual act, but as one in which rationality and disinterestedness are manifest. Rousseau wrote that when the people are called to vote upon a law, what "it" is asked "is not exactly whether it approves or rejects the proposal, but whether it is in conformity with the general will, which is their will. Each man in giving his vote states his opinion on that point, and the general will is found by counting the votes."[11] Mill had a similarly high conception of the act of voting, though it is not linked so strongly with the notion of an ascertainable common good. In his words, "The voter is under an absolute moral obligation to consider the interests of the public, not his private, advantage and to give his vote, to the best of his judgment, exactly as he would be bound to do if he were the sole voter and the election depended upon him alone."[12]

To the eighteenth- and nineteenth-century democratic theorists, voting was perhaps the citizen's most important act, in which the people as a whole were to reveal their political energy and virtue.

[11] *The Social Contract* (Everyman), p. 88.
[12] *Representative Government*, p. 300.

It was to be the culmination of long, thoughtful, and fair consideration of the relevant issues. But these writers never claimed to be
simply describing existing reality, for they were elaborating, at
least in part, a set of ideals for a democratic society, which were
also meant to be operative ideals for their own times. They have
been taken to task, however, for "utopianism" and for making demands on the ordinary man that are impossible and indeed undesirable. Research into voting behavior—Who votes, how, and
why? Who does not vote and why not?—would seem to have confirmed abundantly the old impressionistic conservative arguments
about the "bovine stupidity" and the "heavy, lumpish acquiescence"
of the mass electorate and to have shown the democratic hope to
be a mere delusion, based on false intellectualist assumptions
about human nature.

The voting studies[13] generally agree in showing that the voters
fail to satisfy most of the traditional requirements of democracy.
This is, perhaps, not too surprising, but detailed documentation of
voting behavior by panel study is certainly of value in confirming
suspicions. Berelson gives a composite list of the qualities demanded by the older democratic theorists and confronts them with
the actual qualities as revealed in the opinion surveys. Involvement, participation, and the sharing of responsibility were held to
be virtues; disinterest and apathy were not approved. In fact, the
evidence, says Berelson, shows that less than one-third of the
electorate is really interested in politics, many vote without real
involvement, open discussion and motives for participation are
almost nonexistent. Secondly, knowledge and information are inadequate. "One persistent conclusion is that the public is not
particularly well-informed about the specific issues of the day."[14]
Even when voters are well-informed, their knowledge reinforces
inclinations more than it contributes to a "free" decision. Nor do
voters seem to vote on principles, of whatever kind, which they
have considered carefully, and the standards which they do use
are often irrelevant to "the major problems of the age." Finally,
voters do not seem to decide rationally, in any of the traditional

[13] See especially Lazarsfeld, Berelson, and Gaudet, *The People's Choice*
(Duell, Sloan and Pearce, New York, 1944); Berelson (1), *op. cit.*; Campbell,
Gurin, and Miller, *The Voter Decides* (Row, Peterson & Co., Evanston, 1954);
Campbell *et al., The American Voter* (Wiley & Sons, Michigan, 1960); Milne
and Mackenzie, *op. cit.;* Benney, Gray, and Pear, *How People Vote* (Rout-
ledge & Kegan Paul, 1956). For a convenient survey of the findings, see
Lipset, *op. cit.*, though this tends to be somewhat cavalier in interpretation
and generalization.

[14] Berelson (2), p. 109.

senses of that porous term. The studies have noted the prevalence of selective perception and the way in which the campaign reinforces the influence of a whole set of environmental factors, so that in the end its function seems to be largely that of "activating latent predispositions." Furthermore, the voters showing the greatest degree of "open-mindedness," that is, the changers or floaters, are, in some of the studies at least, shown to be the most cross-pressured, the least interested, and the least politically capable.[15] In brief, the voter is shown to be deficient in most of the ideal qualities of traditional democratic theory.

Before detailed research into voting behavior had ever taken place, several writers (for instance, Lord Bryce and Graham Wallas) had rejected much of the old and largely *a priori* account of the rational democratic citizen as a description applicable to the bulk of their fellow citizens, yet they did not feel it necessary on this account to undertake a complete revision of democratic theory, as is now demanded.[16] Some more recent writers have, on the other hand, held on to the notion of the rational citizen as applicable, despite the evidence of the voting surveys. The impact of these has been lessened by the claim that the short-term questionnaire method is too clumsy to elicit the important truths about the voter.[17] Schumpeter suggests a distinction between rationality in thought and rationality in action. The latter "may be present without any conscious deliberation and irrespective of any ability to formulate the rationale of one's action correctly. The observer, particularly the observer who uses interview and questionnaire methods, often overlooks this and hence acquires an exaggerated idea of the importance of irrationality in behavior."[18] Plamenatz[19] draws a similar distinction between what men do and their awareness of the significance of their actions. He suggests that voters may be condemned by inarticulateness or private language to seem less reasonable than they in fact are, at least in the present state of interview techniques. It is true that men's ability to put thoughts into words and describe actions differs, and that there may be good

[15] However, for an elaborate critique of the Anglo-American treatment of this problem see H. Daudt, *Floating Voters and the Floating Vote* (Stenfert Kroese, Leiden, 1961).

[16] Schumpeter attacks Wallas on precisely these grounds, see Schumpeter, *op. cit.*, p. 256, n. 7. He declares that Wallas's analysis should have led to a more drastic revision of the classical doctrine than it in fact did.

[17] This point is made by Key, "The Politically Relevant in Surveys," *Public Opinion Quarterly* (1960).

[18] Schumpeter, *op. cit.*, p. 259, n. 11.

[19] *Op. cit.*

reasons, of which the agent is unaware, for his doing what he does (for instance, many traditional forms of behavior). It is almost certain that the survey methods used do give a distorted picture of the complex reality that they seek to describe. But, as so far stated, these objections can serve only as a general warning and, if pressed, may easily develop into a mystical faith in the good sense of the common man. This criticism of the panel surveys is not, in any case, central to our purposes. The authors with whom we are mainly concerned accept the soundness of the survey findings and demand in consequence a substantial revision of classical democratic theory.

Berelson writes: "Perhaps the main impact of realistic research on contemporary politics has been to temper some of the requirements set by our traditional normative theory for the typical citizen."[20] The clearest statement of the nature of the revision comes, however, from Robert Dahl. He writes:

> We must conclude that the classic assumptions about the need for citizen participation in democracy were, at the very least, inadequate. If one regards political equality in the making of decisions as a kind of limit to be achieved, then it is axiomatic that this limit could only be arrived at with the complete participation of every adult citizen. Nevertheless, *what we call "democracy"*—that is, a system of decision-making in which the leaders are more or less responsive to the preferences of non-leaders—does seem to operate with a relatively low level of citizen participation. Hence it is inaccurate to say that one of the necessary conditions for "democracy" is extensive citizen participation.[21]

Not only is Dahl's definition of democracy extremely loose (in what political system are leaders not more or less responsive to nonleaders?) but the rejection of the classical requirement of participation rests upon an obvious redefinition of democracy, in which what are taken for present-day facts supplant the ideal. Dahl's conclusion is an obvious *non sequitur*, involving a slide from "what we call 'democracy'" to "democracy." He suspects that it may have represented a "kind of ideal limit," but in restating the requirements of the system he ignores this central element of the old democracy, which was defined and justified as a system in which all participate. Without further argument it is misleading to claim that facts can simply refute ideals and demand changes in the essential requirements of a normative theory, or to reject (for

[20] Berelson (1), *op. cit.*, p. 306.
[21] Dahl, *op. cit.*, p. 87 (our emphasis).

example) Mill's democracy by means of a tacit redefinition of the notion. It needs, moreover, to be established that the new democracy, "what we call 'democracy'" is democratic in a sense acceptable to traditional theory.

This brings us to the central point in the first part of our analysis: that although what may now be called "democracies" may function with little rationality, interest, or participation on the part of the majority of citizens, this cannot count simply as a refutation of largely normative theories, which were centrally concerned with the quality of men's social life and not only with the functioning of a "political system." Dahl again provides the most explicit statement:

One of the most interesting developments of the past century is the full-blown contrast that has arisen between the assumptions of many of the older democratic theorists and what now appear to be the actual facts of political life. *Yet if classical theory is demonstrably invalid in some crucial respects,* it is not so clear how we are to go about constructing theoretical models to replace the older ones.[22]

To claim that sociological findings can show these older political theories to be demonstrably invalid is seriously to misunderstand the most basic features of much political theory, which often touches reality only at the edges, and is only at that point open to empirical refutation. "Political theory" is a general term which covers different types of statements and theories which yield conclusions of different sorts in different ways, and are therefore open to objection in different ways.[23]

In this connection, a familiar distinction can be made at the most general level between "normative" theories, which present and elaborate goals and ideals, and "empirical" theories, which describe and explain political reality. A theory of the first kind involves some vision of the Good Life and the Good Society, resting ultimately on a view of human nature and on assumptions about human needs and potentialities; two obvious examples are Plato's republic and Rousseau's ideal community. These ideals almost al-

[22] *Ibid.*, p. 86 (our emphasis). Dahl's *A Preface to Democratic Theory* (Chicago, 1956) is, however, a more sophisticated formulation.

[23] ". . . Any clear-headed theory of politics requires discrimination between states of fact, causal connections, formal implications, and the values or ends that a policy is designed to achieve. In any political philosophy all these factors are combined, but no combination can alter the fact that they are logically different and that conclusions about them are differently warranted." G. H. Sabine, *A History of Political Theory* (Holt, New York, 2nd ed., 1950), p. ix.

ways conflict with existing realities, though they need not do so (cf. the later Hegel). Empirical theories, however, start from a set of explanatory concepts and classifications, which are then employed, in a number of markedly different ways, in describing and explaining political reality. They are descriptions, concerned with given societies, and they are not primarily moral critiques of them.

This general distinction is, of course, a formal one: these kinds of theory are often intimately connected, with each closely dependent on the other. Few empirical theories avoid value judgments, whether or not they are explicit, and the vision of a normative theory generally rests upon a particular assessment of the present and past. The ideal may involve a moral estimate of the explanatory concepts, particularly if the ideal is of a kind that is supposedly being progressively realized in history, while empirical study may put ideals in a new light, as when the discovery of trends or movements in existing societies curbs the utopian fancy.

Most of the traditional theories of democracy were largely, if not primarily, normative, and critical of the societies in which they were conceived. They were essentially concerned with the achievement in society of what were regarded as various desirable human ends—liberty, good government, responsibility, moral autonomy, self-realization, and so on—and with the means, including the franchise and general participation in politics, but also education and wise leadership, which could best contribute to these ends. Rousseau and J. S. Mill had serious doubts about the feasibility of their ideals, because of the corruptibility of the multitude, or the power of vested interests, or the sheer extent of societies. Mill had some sympathy with those reformers who favored despotism because of "the impediments imposed to the most salutary public improvements by the ignorance, the indifference, the intractableness, the perverse obstinacy of a people, and the corrupt combinations of selfish private interests armed with the powerful weapons afforded by free institutions."[24] He feared that the extension of democracy would endanger good government and relied upon a variety of institutional devices to secure a privileged position for the educated, hoping, like his father, that the influence of the wise would spread to the community as a whole. Rousseau, similarly,

[24] *Representative Government*, p. 206. Mill devoted a great deal of attention to the possible dangers to good government resulting from the extension of the franchise to the working class, *e.g.*, in "Democracy in America" in *Dissertations and Discussions*, vol. II, pp. 1–83 *passim*. He wrote that a laboring class prematurely given political power might easily interfere with contracts, introducing "unenlightened legislation for the supposed interests of the many; laws founded on mistakes in political economy." *Ibid.*, p. 37.

had a long list of the conditions for the realization of his ideal community, and he was very pessimistic about most of the societies of his time. In choosing democracy the classical theorists were in general aware of the ease with which it could be forestalled and perverted, though they were not without illusions; and they were aware, too, of the capacity of undemocratic societies to survive. Their theories are a critique of reality in terms of a vision of human nature and possibilities, and for this reason cannot simply be re-futed on the grounds that people do not satisfy the required standards and that *soi-disant* "democracies" nonetheless survive. Their ideals can logically contrast with the facts without being invalidated by empirical research, which does not in any *obvious* way call for their general revision. The term "democracy" may perhaps legitimately be used to describe political systems like that of the contemporary United States, but it is wrong to assume that the validity of that theory of democracy in which general par-ticipation is central to the very notion itself is thereby destroyed.

All this is not, however, to say that evidence can never force changes or modifications in theories which are largely normative.[25] If such a theory seems intolerably remote from reality, it may be charged with utopianism. It is an endemic danger of normative political theory that it will maintain what Dewey called "an im-mune and monastic impeccability." A particular ideal or set of ideals may, in the Marxist sense, be condemned by historical forces to sterility; it might be shown that it is realizable, but only at the cost of further consequences which violate it; it might itself be shown to be incompatible with other important values; it might be shown that the conditions of realization of an ideal are too vast or unexpected for men to endure; or else it may be shown to be literally impossible to effect the changes demanded. All these means of casting doubt on the feasibility of ideals are legitimate weapons to be used by skeptics; the effectiveness of each is clearly open to dispute, particularly in the case of the last two. For men may disagree about the degree to which social circumstances affect attitudes and behavior and thus about the extent to which any given traits are alterable. (To what extent, for example, is the lack of a sense of responsibility a function of a social situation?) Never-theless, the use of any of these forms of objection needs to be fully and extensively pursued, and it needs to be shown exactly how and

[25] For a very illuminating discussion of this problem and with particular reference to our concerns see W. G. Runciman, "Sociological Evidence and Political Theory" in *Philosophy, Politics and Society: Second Series*, ed. Laslett and Runciman (Blackwell, Oxford, 1962).

why the ideal is rendered improbable or impossible of attainment. This has nowhere been done. Thus, when it is stated baldly that the old theory made impossible demands, this is more like the recognition of a complacent or despairing abandonment of an ideal than the proof that that ideal must needs be abandoned. And it should be realized that, unless one takes a crude historicist position, this proof could only be really convincing if one could show that traditional democratic theory made demands which men are by nature unable to satisfy. Only then would the ideal be literally *invalidated*, for it would have been shown that the obstacles to its realization are irremovable. Such a demonstration would presumably come from social psychology, but it has certainly not been achieved, nor is it likely to be even possible until that study is very much further advanced. Only then could the facts (about human nature) even in principle serve to invalidate the old theories of democracy. Otherwise, one can certainly argue over its *feasibility* in the light of case studies—from Michels onward. Even so, it seems that very little has been done to show that the classical democratic ideals are manifestly utopian. It is not, to repeat, our point that normative political theory is simply independent of sociological evidence; obviously, any theory of democracy must take into account the main features of actual societies. It is simply that empirical study and analysis can only in certain specified cases actually compel us to abandon the ideal or transform it out of all recognition.

Finally, it ought to be added that research into voting behavior has performed the valuable service of destroying some popular myths about the actual functioning of elections—myths which exist at the level of public rhetoric rather than that of political theory. The "mandate" theory, for example, has been damaged beyond repair by the voting studies (though by much else besides): as the authors of *The American Voter* put it, "The thinness of the electorate's understanding of concrete policy alternatives— its inability to respond to government and politics at this level— helps explain why it is that efforts to interpret a national election in terms of a policy mandate are speculative, contradictory and inconclusive."[26] Similarly, many of the studies have thrown into question the notion of the independent or floating voter, a kind of rational jellyfish, preferably of the middle class, floating one way or the other to decide the issue. At these and probably other points the election studies have refuted or at least modified some simple and widely believed theories about what happens in elections: the

[26] *Op. cit.*, p. 544.

"business vocabulary" for describing actual elections has at least been purged. But these low-level and noncritical theories are open to support and objection in this simple way, whereas the old ideal of democratic man is not.

II

It has been generally agreed that the theory of the whole electorate as politically competent and interested, expressing these qualities in democratic elections, has not proved suitable as a basis for empirical analysis. The lack of realism in many of the older descriptive accounts of elections has led a number of political scientists to work with the so-called "competitive theory of democracy." Joseph Schumpeter, one of the leading exponents of this theory, has defined the "democratic method" as "that institutional arrangement for arriving at political decisions in which individuals acquire the power to decide by means of a competitive struggle for the people's vote."[27] Voting, which provides the electors with the opportunity to change their leaders, and competition between candidates for office are here the key institutional devices of democracy. If "democracy" is taken to be a political system defined institutionally in this way, empirical analysis then concentrates on the conditions for its successful operation, while the chief problem of policy becomes that of ensuring that these conditions in fact exist. The main requirement seems to be effective competition between leaders: this, in Plamenatz's view, ensures that the electorate is not "manipulated" by the active ruling élite. (This view that freedom is guaranteed by free competition between élites derives ultimately from Mosca.) When there is no effective competition, the system ceases to be one in which the leaders are responsive to the independent wishes of nonleaders. Thus Dahl, for example, sees the main problem of democracy as that of regulating the "great political oligopolies"—which is much as it seemed to the early utilitarians.

This "competitive model" is adopted with variations by the writers with whom we are concerned. It is a general model useful as a point of departure in the description of existing democracies. The general picture is one of energetic and competing minorities at the top and a relatively apathetic majority, whose role is essentially that of exercising a very generalized control during the

[27] Schumpeter, *op. cit.*, p. 269.

election, which is seen as a process of selecting and rejecting candidates in competition for public office. It should be seen clearly that such a model is not necessarily inconsistent with most traditional theories of democracy (except Rousseau's), for it clearly recognizes that an election in a large society can only produce clear-cut and satisfactory results in this sort of way. As Schumpeter writes:

Even if the opinions and desires of individual citizens were perfectly definite and independent data for the democratic process to work with, and even if everyone acted on them with rationality and promptitude, it would not necessarily follow that the political decisions produced by that process from the raw material of those individual volitions would represent anything that could in any convincing sense be called the will of the people.[28]

The competitive model need not be incompatible with traditional notions of democracy, and it is just because classical democracy was *not* defined institutionally as a "system of decision making" that this is so. For, as we have seen, democracy in the traditional sense involves a great deal more than the correspondence of individual wills and collective decisions; it involves, for example, political equality, active consent about the form of government and the "rules of the game," widespread discussion and participation, political and otherwise, through all kinds of activities and channels. To take a particular and relevant example, a study by Janowitz and Marvick,[29] which explicitly uses this competitive model, attempts to distinguish between a process of genuine consent and manipulation. The authors emphasize the importance of the quality of the voting decision, pointing out that high turnout does not necessarily reflect the process of consent. They write, in words of which John Stuart Mill would have approved:

The underlying belief in a democracy that everyone ought to vote is indeed such a deep-seated belief that it must be regarded as a utopian goal. Reforms have been suggested . . . that are designed to enhance the quality of the vote by modification of the social structure. Yet in terms of practical political reform, the crucial problem is to improve the quality of competing political leaders and to increase voter competence.[30]

The theorists of the new democracy, however, are less concerned to make the competitive "democratic system" more demo-

---

[28] Schumpeter, *op. cit.*, p. 254.

[29] "Competitive Pressure and Democratic Consent" in Eulau *et al.*, *op. cit.*, pp. 275–85, which is based on a larger study with the same title (Institute of Public Administration, Michigan, 1956).

[30] *Ibid.*, p. 280.

cratic in the traditional sense than to justify it as an efficient and stable system, depending on compromise, "pluralism," and a general background of apathy and political incompetence. In fact, their theory, which is intended to explain the "democratic system," becomes in the end the new normative theory of democracy. We are driven to this conclusion by the form of their arguments. The question arises: What implications have election studies for democratic theory? The conclusion is that that theory must be made more "realistic." The confrontation of classical democratic ideals with actual "democratic systems" ("what we call democracy") has no other result than the acceptance of the actual systems and their assumed conditions as entirely desirable. Electoral apathy, incompetence, and so on, which exist in most stable "modern democracies" are now considered to be conditions of their successful functioning and are therefore taken to be the new democratic norms.

There are, of course, differences between the writers under consideration. The sociologists, *e.g.*, Dahl and Parsons, are more concerned to produce a scientific theory of the system, whereas others, *e.g.*, Plamenatz and Schumpeter, are much less ambitious, which is not to say that their caution is misplaced. The system is justified on a number of different grounds, and doubtless there are a number of important internal disagreements between these different writers. We can only examine a number of the most common arguments and assumptions, which may not be shared in detail by all of them.

The most notable feature of this recent democratic theory is the shift in emphasis from the needs and potentialities of the individual citizen to the requirements of the system. Despite inadequacies in individuals, the system works. In Berelson's vague words, "The *system of democracy* does meet certain requirements of a going political organization. The individuals may not meet all the standards, but the whole nevertheless survives and grows. This suggests that where the classical theory is defective is in its concentration on the *individual citizen*."[31] And again, in more exalted vein, "Where the rational citizen seems to abdicate, nevertheless angels seem to tread."[32]

It may be useful to look in some detail at Berelson's own account of the democratic system. He sees it pre-eminently as a system in equilibrium and he is followed in this by Talcott Parsons in an essay entitled "Voting and the Equilibrium of the American Politi-

[31] Berelson (1), *op. cit.*, p. 312.
[32] *Ibid.*, p. 311.

cal System." (Parsons in fact attempts to integrate Berelson's picture into his own "general theory of social systems.") Berelson describes the system mainly in terms of "balances" and the distribution of qualities in various dimensions. For political democracy to survive, the elements of the system must be distributed and related in a certain way. "What seems to be required of the electorate as a whole is a distribution of qualities along important dimensions. We need some people who are active in a certain respect, others in the middle and still others passive."[33] And, "happily for the system," the voters are distributed along a smooth continuum. There must be a "balance" between "involvement and indifference," "stability and flexibility," "progress and conservatism," "consensus and cleavage," and, finally, "individualism and collectivism." Low interest provides "maneuvering room" ("only the doctrinaire would deprecate the moderate indifference that facilitates compromise") and heterogeneity produces a balance between strongly and weakly motivated actions. Also, apart from the many factors making for social stability, "voters carry to each new election remnants of issues raised in previous elections—and so there is always an overlapping of old and new decisions that gives a cohesion in time to the political system."[34] On the other hand, the least partisan are also functional to the system, making for "flexibility"—"for those who change political preferences most readily are those who are least interested, who are subject to conflicting social pressures, who have inconsistent beliefs and erratic voting histories. Without them . . . the system might prove too rigid to adapt to changing domestic and international conditions."[35] There is, says Berelson, "stability on both sides and flexibility in the middle" and once again "an individual 'inadequacy' provides a positive service for the society." Finally, there is the essential requirement of "pluralism," which "makes for enough consensus to hold the system together and enough cleavage to make it move." This social heterogeneity produces a "cross-cutting and harmonious community interest" with a "balance between total political war between segments of the society and total political indifference to group interests of that society."[36]

There are a number of important objections to Berelson's account. To begin with, the description of the conditions claimed to be necessary and functional to the system all embody the basic

[33] Berelson (1), *op. cit.*, p. 314.
[34] *Ibid.*, p. 316.
[35] *Ibid.*, p. 316.
[36] *Ibid.*, p. 320.

assumption of a system in equilibrium. The use, explicit or otherwise, of equilibrium concepts in the social sciences is often open
to serious methodological criticisms[37] and leaves its practitioners
subject to the suspicion of having based conservatism upon a
pseudoscientific foundation. More specifically, the application of
an equilibrium model to actual social situations does require either
careful quantification of the relevant variables (ordinally or
cardinally) or else a situation where an equilibrium situation is
directly visible (although, of course, the use of such a model may
always lead to fruitful questions). Otherwise little specific sense
can be made of the idea of "balance" between elements. Yet Berelson speaks quite glibly of the balance between his various "qualities," where neither of these conditions is fulfilled. Parsons, following Berelson, seems to accept these "balances," translating them
into his own terms as "functional requirements." He writes that,
within a broad framework, "if the political system is, in the relation
between leadership and support, to be a relatively stable one that
can integrate multifarious pluralistic interests and yet adapt to
changing conditions, it must, *within broadly specifiable limits*,
have certain characteristics."[38] What we dispute is that any precise
characterization has been given of these "broadly specifiable
limits" (by Berelson or by Parsons) such that we must accept their
account of an equilibrium system with "checks and balances" and
the capacity for self-adjustment afforded by heterogeneity and
apathy within the electorate. There is, in other words, no reason
to agree that the "democratic system" is in smoothly functioning
equilibrium; and if we look hard at the assumptions behind this
theory, we tend to be left with vague and questionable assertions
about social harmony.

In the second place, the supposed requirements of the system
are presented in an obviously value-laden and tendentious way.
Berelson claims, in a rather obscure passage, that "it turns out that
this distribution itself, with its internal checks and balances, can
perform the functions and incorporate the same values ascribed
by some theorists to each individual in the systems, as well as to
the constitutive political institutions"![39] Berelson here seems to be
trying to have the best of both worlds. Not only is his theory of

[37] See in this connection an interesting paper by David Easton called
"Limits of the Equilibrium Model in Social Research," *Chicago Behavioral
Sciences Publications*, No. 1 (1953), reprinted in Eulau *et al., op. cit.*

[38] Parsons, *op. cit.*, p. 114 (our emphasis). For general criticism of Parsons' functional theories see Dahrendorf, "Out of Utopia," *American Journal
of Sociology* (1958), pp. 115–27.

[39] Berelson (1), *op. cit.*, p. 323.

democracy realistic, describing actual societies, but the old individual values are somehow incorporated in it. Apart from the
verbal peculiarity (how can a distribution of qualities incorporate
the values ascribed to individuals?) the claim seems hardly to have
been sustained in any detail. Both he and Parsons try to show that
the *system* is rational—that is, its parts are coordinated and it
develops smoothly—but this is not rationality in any of the senses
normally ascribed to individuals. Some people are active, interested, and competent; others are not. Does the distribution itself,
rather than any individual, incorporate these values? If this is
what Berelson means, it is a roundabout and deceptive way of
putting the view that, though Americans as a whole are not ideal
democratic citizens, a few people do possess the required qualities
and, moreover, the political system does not disintegrate.

Thirdly, the system's supposed requirements are stated very
loosely—often too loosely for the validity of the account to be
assessed—and sometimes tautologously, with little descriptive
content. What, for example, does the requirement that there
should be a "nice balance" between consensus and cleavage, reflecting the "health of a democratic order," really amount to? It is
true but uninformative to say that if there is *too much* cleavage a
democratic system—or any other system—will disintegrate: one
can scarcely disagree with Berelson when he writes, "Political
parties in a democracy should disagree—but not too much, too
sharply, nor too fundamentally." Yet how can one measure these
qualities to find out whether they are in balance (and what is so
sacrosanct about this notional equilibrium point in any case)?
This is not to say that the ideas of consensus and conflict are
analytically useless; it is simply that here they are being misused,
for, given that there is a measure of basic or "higher order" consensus, there is room for wide dispute over the nature and degree
of cleavage that is tolerable or desirable (and, as Lipset shows,
cleavage may itself be a factor making for consensus). And it
does not help to speak of "pluralism" as a "kind of glue" which
holds the system together when threatened by cleavage. Does this
mean anything precise? What, for instance, is one to make of the
following obscure passage from Berelson: "The multiplicity and
the heterogeneity of identifications and associations in the great
society develop an overlapping, pluralistic social organization
which both sharpens and softens the impact and the consequences
of political activity."[40]

Finally, there is no warrant for saying that the features isolated

[40] Berelson (2), *op. cit.*, p. 114.

are requirements of the system—unless, of course, they are included definitionally as parts of it. The clearest and most important instance is that of apathy. Apathy serves, says Berelson, as a " 'cushion' to absorb the intense action of highly-motivated partisans." Apathy, it is claimed, helps the democratic system to function smoothly by facilitating change and reducing the impact of fanaticism thus guarding against the danger of "total politics." Also, in Parsons' words, there is the "indifference reaction" among the apathetic and incompetent floaters, which is the "element of flexibility necessary to allow sufficient shift of votes to permit a two-party system to function effectively without introducing unduly disruptive elements into the system."[41] Yet what is the basis for this claim that apathy must exist to hold the system together and give it flexibility, while cushioning the shock of disagreement and change? The theoretical framework seems hardly adequate to allow the role of apathy as an element of the system to be described in this way. That is to say, arguments about the necessity of apathy may always be confronted with the suggestion that any given society with democratic institutions or a democratic temper can in certain conditions tolerate an appreciably higher degree of participation than these theorists allow. The evidence, such as it is, does not in any way prove or even confirm the theory of the necessity of apathy to the survival of democracy.

Yet many of the writers under discussion support this theory, either on the basis of the equilibrium model criticized above or more generally on the basis of the evidence of scattered historical cases of differing degrees of participation. For example, Tingsten[42] makes the point, on the basis of interwar election figures in Austria and Germany, that "an exceptionally high voting frequency may indicate an intensification of political controversy which may involve a danger to the democratic system." His conclusion is that high political participation *may* not be a sign of the health of a democracy, but he also points out that it is misleading to speak of participation as though it were one thing whatever the community or circumstances: in other countries "a high degree of participation cannot be judged in the same manner."[43] Moreover, in the cases mentioned, high participation seems less a cause than a consequence of deeper-rooted social conflicts—high participation may mark some periods of crisis but it does not explain their origins.

[41] Parsons, *op. cit.*, p. 114.
[42] Herbert Tingsten, *Political Behaviour* (P. S. King & Son, London, 1937).
[43] *Ibid.*, p. 226.

All that the evidence shows is that a high degree of electoral participation has sometimes been a symptom of crises in democracy and not even, as Lipset says, misinterpreting Tingsten's point, that "political apathy may reflect the health of a democracy.[44] The historical examples need careful handling—one might well argue, for instance, that the Weimar Republic fell chiefly because of apathy about the regime. In any case, neither apathy nor participation can profitably be considered in abstraction from historical contexts: apathy in the Weimar Republic can scarcely be identified with that of the affluent society of contemporary America, while increased participation, if it means a sudden "intrusion of the masses into politics" in an artificial way, is hardly equivalent to the classical prescriptions for heightened general participation in the political and other activities in the life of the community. In brief, it has nowhere been shown that apathy is either necessary or functional to democracy.

To sum up, our conclusion is that no adequate empirical theory, still less a "scientific" theory, of institutional "democracy" has been provided. Apart from incidental insights, the notion of a stable equilibrium system is misleading as an account of "what we call democracy" and is deceptively presented as a development of traditional theories of democracy. Furthermore, the "requirements" of the "democratic system"—in particular, apathy—have certainly not been proved to be necessary to the survival of a democratic society.

III

It is evident that the theorists of the new democracy share a number of contemporary preoccupations which have blinded them both to the possible development and to the possible diversity of democratic societies and have led them to describe apathy as a central requirement of the functioning of such societies. Essentially, these preoccupations center on a basic distinction between totalitarianism and liberal democracy which underlies a great deal of recent sociological and political writing. This dichotomy, his-

[44] Lipset, op. cit., p. 32, n. 20. Lipset claims on the same page that "the belief that a very high level of participation is always good for democracy is not valid." This statement is true but misleading. In supporting participation the classical democrats were thinking mainly in terms of a stable, liberal society, in which people accepted the good faith of their opponents and were prepared to work within the system.

torically explicable though it is, has, in our view, distorted much recent thinking about politics among Western intellectuals. It has led to an exaggerated fear of "ideology" and the celebration of its supposed end in the modern affluent Western society, and, in addition, the familiar "argument from the concentration camp" has often been used to condemn traditionally democratic and radical ideas which really have no necessary connection with totalitarianism. In general, this argument takes the form of isolating a particular idea or policy from its context, either theoretical or historical, and then indicating its putative affinity with totalitarian ideas and practices. One may well question not only the specific interpretations, but also the belief that political ideas can, in any case, be more or less clearly divided into the liberal-democratic and totalitarian categories. In times of great uncertainty conservatism has a natural appeal and the advantages of stable societies are apt to be greatly exaggerated. The political system is seen as an exquisitely fragile mechanism and all possible dangers to its stability are jealously guarded against. Hence the general contemporary concern with the conditions of a stable, nontotalitarian political system and the resulting desire to avoid anything which might lead to a dangerous involvement of the masses in politics. Such a development, it is claimed, would threaten both the smooth functioning of the system and the freedom and privacy of the individual.

This background helps to explain the new directions of democratic theory. The early democratic theorists, hating the tyranny of the old regime of monarchs and aristocrats, stressed the role of vigilance and participation in protecting hard-won rights against predatory "sinister interests." Political participation especially was to safeguard society, protect individuals and groups, and develop individual qualities as well as men's control over their social lives. The theorists of the new democracy tend to see widespread participation, interest, and conflict as substantial dangers to democracy and like to refer to the fraudulent claims of those totalitarians who see themselves as the real practitioners of democracy and the true representatives of the people. There are thus these twin dangers of "total politics," which may disrupt the system, and totalitarian politics, which may eliminate freedom and privacy. This explains their eagerness to define the new political role of democratic man very narrowly. Meanwhile all the more radical features of the democratic tradition are abandoned in favor of a timid conservatism.

A characteristic piece of writing in this connection is W. H. Morris-Jones's article, "In Defence of Apathy,"[45] which is often referred to in the literature and has had some measure of influence. The explicit purpose of this article is "to suggest that many of the ideas connected with the general theme of a duty to vote belong properly to the totalitarian camp and are out of place in the vocabulary of liberal democracy."[46] But the discussion proceeds less by detailed argument than by a process of contamination: from ideas which are part of the liberal-democratic tradition the slide is made to allegedly connected notions which are clearly totalitarian. "Political interestedness," says Morris-Jones, is the "mark of the elect" and the obligation to vote is a dangerous idea, for "it needs no demonstration that a totalitarian view of life easily involves an obligation not only to vote, but to do much more—and to do it, moreover, in the right direction."[47] The trick is transparent. There is really no connection between the obligation to vote and the obligation to act in the right direction; any idea can be simply contaminated in this way by detaching it from the theory within which it was advanced and then showing that some people have held it alongside genuinely nasty views. Apart from this, Morris-Jones advances the positive argument that parliamentary democracy should be seen less as a "system of government resting primarily on participation and consent" but rather as "a manner of dealing with business, a way of going about things." In this case, the presence of the apathetic is a "sign of understanding and tolerance of human variety" and has a "beneficial effect on the tone of political life [being] a more or less effective counterforce to those fanatics who constitute the real danger to political democracy."[48] The implication is obvious: to advocate widespread and general political participation is to advocate the development of intolerance and doctrinaire fanaticism.

This inference is frequently drawn in contemporary political theory and it is usually carried further, to the totalitarian conclusion that men are to be made purely political, privacy and liberty are to be invaded, and all the good things of civilized life destroyed. Examples of this kind of argument are to be found in Morris-Jones's article, in Hogan's book on *Election and Representation*,[49]

[45] *Political Studies*, vol. ii., 1954, pp. 25–37.
[46] *Op. cit.*, p. 25.
[47] *Ibid.*, p. 36.
[48] *Ibid.*, p. 37.
[49] D. N. Hogan, *Election and Representation* (Cork University Press and Blackwell, Oxford, 1945).

in Talmon's critique of Rousseau,[50] and in Berlin's *Two Concepts of Liberty*.[51] On the one hand, the connection is claimed to be established between the desire to participate and the totalitarian result. Berlin, for example, writes:

The desire to be governed by myself, or at any rate to participate in the process by which my life is to be controlled, may be as deep a wish as that for a free area for action, and perhaps historically older. But it is not a desire for the same thing. So different is it, indeed, as to have led in the end to the great clash of ideologies that dominates our world.[52]

On the other hand, apathy is held to be valuable because it shows the "limitations of politics," that men are more than political creatures and can if they wish ignore politics entirely. In Hogan's words, "Viewed in this light, the apathy and caprice for which political democracy has been blamed is seen to be rather to its credit than otherwise. It means at any rate that people are free to interest themselves or to disinterest themselves as they please in political affairs."[53] This argument in terms of an ideal of freedom is deeply misleading. What is in question is not the right of men to be apathetic (and thus the enforcement of a duty to vote) but whether a society in which men concern themselves with political matters, as well as with many other matters, is likely to be more desirable than one marked by widespread apathy. If the vast majority of men were quite uninterested in politics and full general participation were demanded of everybody immediately, it is perhaps natural to infer that only constant coercion could achieve the desired result—and even more so if the desired result were unanimity. But it should hardly need saying that the ideal of general political participation is quite compatible with liberal safeguards and the rejection of coercion for partisan political goals, for instance, "voting in the right direction." It may be urged, with no totalitarian overtones whatsoever, that men ought to play some part in politics for their own good and for the good of society. The old democratic ideal sees apathy as dangerous because men cannot rely on others to protect

[50] J. L. Talmon, *The Origins of Totalitarian Democracy* (Mercury Books, 1961). See especially pp. 46–47.

[51] Sir I. Berlin, *Two Concepts of Liberty* (Oxford University Press, 1958).

[52] *Ibid.*, pp. 15–16. Berlin, however, does not support the view that apathy preserves democracy and liberty. His position is that positive liberty can lead to totalitarian consequences when the meaning of the word "self" is extended.

[53] Hogan, *op. cit.*, p. 276.

their own interests and because the holders of power are likely to exercise it with too little concern for the general body of the people and for minority interests. It also considers politics to be a proper concern of the citizen and one of the fields of human excellence. In doing this, the classical theorists were very far indeed from urging constant and active participation at the behest of totalitarian masters; Stalinist Russia is as far removed from their ideals as it is from those of these modern antitotalitarians.

As for coercion, this was the very thing that the classical theorists of democracy were concerned at all costs to avoid. The new theorists may argue that the old ideals must lead to this result, but we see no compelling reason to believe them. The now familiar dichotomies between totalitarianism and liberal democracy, between positive and negative liberty, between "utopianism" and piecemeal pragmatism, have achieved something like a stranglehold over political theorizing. No middle way is conceded between the concentration camp and a cautious conservatism. Talmon remarks characteristically of the "early totalitarians" that they refused "to take the people as it was for granted; the people, that is to say the sum total of the given generation, the good and the bad, the advanced and the backward, with their wishes, enlightened or otherwise."[54] The implicit bias of this kind of view is obvious: we must accept the existing situation in its entirety, so that the only political issue left is that of making the "system" work more efficiently. Yet the refusal simply to accept the existing situation by no means implies the acceptance of coercion and minority domination, shaping the fabric of an existing society in the image of a utopia.

The voices of sanity and reason sound above all in times of crisis and rapid change, and their conservative tone is familiar. Edmund Burke similarly appealed to the proved virtues of stable societies against the widespread criticism of established institutions at the time of the French Revolution. The arguments of the writers we have discussed bear witness to a worthy concern with avoiding the real dangers of totalitarian politics, dangers which no one should minimize; but they have gone too far in the opposite direction. Preoccupied with stability and protecting the system against too much participation, they have in reality abandoned, without realizing it, a whole tradition of political thinking—a tradition which they claim to be developing and revising. Their arguments are, in any case, too loose to convince and too complacent to excite. This is not to say that the older democratic theories are not in need of any revision. But they have survived these particular attacks and re-

54 Talmon, *op. cit.*, p. 232.

tain their central interest and value. In particular, general political participation has not been destroyed as a desirable goal for democratic societies, nor are the new ideals that have been offered to us imposed upon us by the facts of contemporary political life.

20 🙐 THE COST OF THE NEW REALISM

LANE DAVIS

During the last thirty years, there have been a number of efforts to restate democratic political theory in terms which would be more satisfactory to the needs of the present day. This reconsideration of the theory of democracy extends to writers of many diverse points of view responding, as one might expect, to the challenges raised by alternatives to political democracy and to problems internal to democratic societies.

The weaknesses which these restatements seek to remedy are various and resistant to any neat summary. They range from the philosophical foundations of democratic values through conventional notions about conditions conducive to the success of a democratic polity or particular democratic institutions. From this broad range of possibilities, this essay will consider those recent statements which exhibit a particular concern for the descriptive accuracy of democratic political theory.[1]

FROM Lane Davis, "The Cost of Realism: Contemporary Restatements of Democracy," *Western Political Quarterly*, 17 (1964), 37–46. Reprinted by permission of the University of Utah, copyright owners.

[1] The classic expression of this point of view is found in Joseph Schumpeter, *Capitalism, Socialism and Democracy* (2nd ed.; New York and London: Harper, 1942), Part IV: it is still the clearest and best. For recent and explicitly theoretical statements see, among others, Bernard Berelson *et al.*, *Voting* (Chicago: University of Chicago Press, 1954), chap. 14; Samuel H. Beer, "New Structures of Democracy: Britain and America," and Louis Hartz, "Democracy: Image and Reality," in W. N. Chambers and R. H. Salisbury (eds.), *Democracy in Mid-20th Century* (St. Louis: Washington University Press, 1960); Walter Lippmann, *The Public Philosophy* (New York: New American Library, 1956); S. M. Lipset, *Political Man* (Garden

These contemporary writers seek to delineate the descriptive weaknesses of existing democratic political theory and to present an amended theory of political democracy more in line with contemporary knowledge of empirical political reality. It is the argument of this essay that the effort to make democratic theory more realistic has brought many other changes with it; that the effect of these restatements goes considerably further than just improved descriptive realism. The values and expectations which justified political democracy have been changed. The rationale for popular political activity which is at the very center of much democratic theory has been rejected. In short, the cost of realism has been the practical abandonment of what has been the distinctive moral function of democratic politics and government.

I

The object of criticism and restatement by this group of contemporary democrats is the so-called "classical" theory of political democracy which prescribes popular rule after the model of the New England town meeting or the seventeenth-century nonconformist church congregation. This theory posits the existence of rational and active citizens who seek to realize a generally recognized common good through the collective initiation, discussion, and decision of policy questions concerning public affairs, and who delegate authority to agents (elected government officials) to carry through the broad decisions reached by the people through majority vote.[2]

City: Doubleday, 1960); Henry Mayo, *An Introduction to Democratic Theory* (New York: Oxford University Press, 1960). Mayo is particularly useful as a relatively complete statement of this position. This point of view informs many recent studies of American politics. See James Q. Wilson, *The Amateur Democrat* (Chicago: University of Chicago Press, 1962), for a persuasive defense of this position and an excellent brief account (pp. 341 ff.) of how it finds expression in the literature of American political parties. In the discussion which follows, I will use the relatively neutral label of *contemporary* to refer to this particular conception of democracy and those who espouse it.

[2] Classical political democracy refers to the mainstream of the democratic intellectual tradition which includes such diverse figures as the seventeenth-century Levellers, Jean Jacques Rousseau, Jeremy Bentham, James Mill, and the Jacksonian democrats. Among its many twentieth-century spokesmen may be mentioned Ernest Barker, John Dewey, A. D. Lindsay and Roland Pennock. Two recent statements which agree on classical democracy, though perhaps little else, are Joseph Tussman, *Obligation and the Body Politic* (New York: Oxford University Press, 1960), and Raymond Williams, *The Long Revolution* (New York: Columbia University Press, 1961).

The indictment brought against this version of political democracy is a sweeping one. The theory has been asserted to be logically unsatisfactory. It fails to provide clear definitions of such terms as "rule" and "people" which are obviously central to a conception of government by rule of the people. It posits a substantive common good as "the beacon light of policy" but fails to develop a consistent explanation of the nature of such a common good or how men may come to recognize it.[3] It lacks a satisfactory treatment of the problems raised by the simultaneous affirmation of majority rule and minority rights.[4] Finally, the theory defines democracy in ideal terms rather than by reference to existing political reality. The effect of this "is to rob the theory of all operational and empirical content," destroy its utility for description or explanation, and make communication about it "virtually impossible."[5]

The departures of classical theory from reality also have been pointed out in detail. Classical democracy, it is asserted, rests on untenable or radically incomplete conceptions of man and politics. Democratic man is neither as rational, as disinterested, as informed, nor as active in public affairs as he is assumed to be. The roles of organized groups, leadership, and emotion in political affairs are either ignored, underplayed, or simply condemned. The highly technical and complex process of policy making is oversimplified and misunderstood.[6]

Sloughing off these asserted errors of logic and fact, contemporary democratic theorists propose a conception of political democracy based on a realistic description of the political systems through which existing states have sought to realize popular rule.[7]

[3] The phrase and the argument belong to Schumpeter. See Schumpeter, op. cit., pp. 250 ff.

[4] An excellent discussion of these problems is found in R. A. Dahl, A Preface to Democratic Theory (Chicago: University of Chicago Press, 1956). See also H. S. Commager, Majority Rule and Minority Rights (New York: Oxford University Press, 1943); Willmore Kendall, John Locke and the Doctrine of Majority Rule (Urbana: University of Illinois Press, 1941); and Willmore Kendall and Austin Ranney, Democracy and the American Party System (New York: Harcourt, Brace, 1956), Part I, for further discussions.

[5] Mayo, op. cit., p. 31.

[6] This paragraph is a summary of criticisms found in the contemporary democrats mentioned above. In particular: on the political nature of man see Berelson, op. cit., pp. 306–11; on the role of leadership, Schumpeter, op. cit., p. 270; on the roles of emotion and organized groups, Hartz, op. cit., pp. 13–25; on the misunderstanding of the policy-making process, Lippmann, op. cit., pp. 30–50.

[7] We have made the Enlightenment work in spite of itself, and surely it is time we ceased to be frightened of the mechanisms we have devised to do so. We have implemented popular government, democratic judgment and the

The heart of this contemporary restatement was summed up by Joseph Schumpeter. "The democratic method is that institutional arrangement for arriving at political decisions in which individuals acquire the power to decide by means of a competitive struggle for the people's vote."[8]

The essential role of the public in democratic political rule is thus defined as the choice of key governmental policy makers. Popular control of government is limited to after-the-fact decisions on this question alone. The function of the electorate is to legitimate governmental authority. It is not to initiate or decide issues of public policy.[9]

Such a conception of political democracy sharply reduces the extent and the intensity of necessary individual participation in democratic politics. This permits the abandonment of the classical notion that general attainment of the ideal of rational, active, and informed democratic man is essential to the realization of genuine political democracy. Political democracy is now considered to be a complex system within which apathy and ignorance as well as activity and informed reason have a part to play.[10] Thus, the reality of irrational mass emotion, self-interest, group egoism, and the prevalence of oligarchic and hierarchical social and economic organizations need no longer be denied in the name of democratic values. The way is cleared for recognition of, and scientific inquiry into, the workings of democratic political systems as they actually exist.

II

In considering the indictment brought against classical democratic theory, the charge that it fails as a descriptive and explanatory tool can only be met by a plea of *nolo contendere*. The theory was not created to describe any existing democratic polity of any considerable size employing representative institutions. It grew from many sources as an essay in prescription. As such, it contains

---

equal state on a scale that is remarkable by any earthly standard." Hartz, *op. cit.*, p. 29. See also Mayo, *op. cit.*, pp. 55–61.

[8] Schumpeter, *op. cit.*, p. 269.

[9] Mayo, *op. cit.*, pp. 85–87.

[10] "What seems to be required of the electorate as a whole is a distribution of qualities along important dimensions. We need some people who are active in a certain respect, others in the middle, and still others passive." Berelson, *op. cit.*, p. 314.

a prescription for a worthwhile polity which should be sought after. Perhaps the American Progressives, so far as they were concerned with increasing the amount of direct popular participation in policy making, represent the clearest example in recent American experience of an organized movement which took this goal seriously. The Progressives, however, have not been alone in their aspirations. For many others, classical democracy has been—and still is—used as a point of departure for criticism of existing politics and society.

The classical theory represents an effort, however inadequate it might be, to construct a practical political theory for democracy. Not practical in the sense of containing a realistic description of existing society, but practical in the sense of providing guide lines for those who seek to transcend existing political reality for something better: a polity which would realize among its citizens generally, "the 'dignity' which is found in sharing the collegial life of the rulers of the human city."[11]

The immediate objective of classical democracy has always been to extend the opportunity for individuals to take an equal and an effective part in the management of public affairs. Through this opportunity, it was believed, the horizons of the participating individual would be widened, his knowledge extended, his sympathies made less parochial, his practical intelligence developed. Participation in the management of public affairs would serve as a vital means of intellectual, emotional, and moral education leading toward the full development of the capacities of individual human beings. Participation in politics would provide men with opportunities to take part in making significant decisions and to transcend the narrow bounds of their private affairs. It would build and consolidate a sense of genuine community that would serve as a solid foundation for government. It would provide a strenuous and rewarding field of endeavor by extending opportunities for free activity and self-government beyond the frequently petty sphere of private life into the realm of the public domain which had hitherto been largely beyond the control, or the hope of control, of ordinary men.

This opportunity for education in public responsibility is the peculiar and distinguishing contribution which classical democracy makes to the ideal of human dignity and development. Of course it is possible for a democratic regime to do more than provide the opportunity for participation in government. The mere

[11] Tussman, *op. cit.*, p. 121.

provision of peace and order, which is scarcely a unique contribution of democratic government, is necessary for the development of human personality. And the protection of certain individual rights, the provision of various services, are also important. There are good reasons for thinking that democratic government may perform these essential functions more fully and more reliably than other kinds of government. This provides additional grounds for preferring it. But the heart of the matter is the value which is attached to individual participation in making decisions about public affairs.

To speak precisely, it is not the substantive choices which are made in various policy decisions which are crucial for *this* justification of democracy—though they are important—but the *human* results which accrue to those who take part in this method of managing public affairs.[12] In shorthand fashion, one may speak of the method of political democracy as valuable in itself regardless of results which it produces. In this way, one avoids the confusion of distinguishing between different sorts of results of the process; that is, between what might be called "policy results"—for example, the stringent regulation of private business or the legal prohibition of certain forms of racial segregation—and other results, "human results"—the growing practical capacities of those who take part in the process. So long as one keeps in mind that speaking of the method as an end in itself—at least in the context of classical democracy—is only a convenient eliptical expression, no confusion results.

It follows from what has been said that classical democratic theory is informed by an exceedingly ambitious purpose: the education of an entire people to the point where their intellectual, emotional, and moral capacities have reached their full potential and they are joined, freely and actively, in a genuine community. Beyond this magnificent general purpose, classical democratic theory also embodies one great strategy for the pursuit of this goal: the use of political activity and government for the purposes of public education. Governance is to be a continued effort in mass education. The key to the realization of human potentialities and creation of genuine community becomes the pursuit of the common good through political activity.

This strategy need not involve any denigration of the realm of private activity. Private life—family, friends, work, and religion—

---

[12] Ernest Barker, *Reflections on Government* (New York: Oxford University Press, 1942), pp. 35 ff.

are part of the necessary social foundation upon which the citizen builds his concern with, and his participation in, public affairs.[13] Nevertheless, the conclusion cannot be avoided that, for the classical democrat, private life is not enough. The road to intellectual and moral growth must lead to participation in the practical problems of public affairs. Full moral development for most men is only to be attained by taking part in, and accepting some responsibility for, the realization of a common good. The ancient Greek ideal, trimmed to the dimensions of modern society with its recognized spheres of human activity, is with us still. Man will attain his natural state only through the practical responsibilities of political action.

When we press classical democracy beyond this point, the unfinished business of democratic theory becomes increasingly evident. This is not a matter of patching up utopian holes in the structure of classical theory. Rather it is the elaboration of plans of action and specific prescriptions which offer hope of progress toward a genuinely democratic polity; detailed prescriptions which bring the general strategy of classical democracy down to earth in the varied contexts of contemporary states of all kinds.

Such prescriptions cannot be constructed only of aspiration and imagination, yet both are vitally necessary. Empirical research in politics and a variety of related fields is also necessary to provide more satisfactory explanations of the gaps which exist between political reality and the polity to which the classical democrats aspire. Such research requires "realistic" conceptual schemes which will permit the identification of phenomena which are relevant to the purpose at hand. But in the context of classical democracy, another purpose lies behind the effort to describe and explain. Description and explanation are only a means to facilitate democratic strategy, not a criterion of judgment. Hopefully, research may lead to the determination of an increasing number of reasonably well-validated hypotheses concerning the way people behave in politics and political institutions work in contemporary societies. These hypotheses may suggest limits on what can be done and how it can be done most efficiently—given the goal which the democrat seeks. Generalizations based on reliable knowledge of past and present reality are good bases for educated guessing

[13] "The development of man thus expresses itself not only in the State, but also in the social group which constitutes the substance of society." Barker, op. cit., p. 22. See also Barker, Principles of Social and Political Theory (New York: Oxford University Press, 1951), pp. 42–43 and 123–35.

about the future and may shorten the inevitable process of trial and error.[14]

By providing more accurate understanding of present political reality, explanatory theories furnish a basis from which the classical democrat can estimate where he stands in relation to the goal he seeks. They also provide a roster of various possibilities which he can exploit in order to move closer to his goal. The study of American politics and the models which grow out of this study have a good deal to say about the multiform ways in which influence is exercised on the formation of public policy. Presumably, some of these forms contain more possibilities for advancing the political capacities of individuals than others. Such information as this will further the task of those who would develop prescriptive democratic theory.[15]

By knowing where he stands in relation to his goal, by knowing what probably can be done in the near future and what probably cannot, the classical democrat is better prepared to amend and elaborate the prescriptions of classical democratic theory. Yet, if explanation is valuable, it is valuable as an aid to prescription. It is not a substitute for it. To assume that the task of democratic political theory is description, and that an accurate account of what is provides us with a statement of what ought to be, is to take issue with a good deal more than merely the descriptive accuracy of classical democratic theory.[16] Such an assumption rejects the elements of aspiration and imagination which make the grand strategy of classical democracy and the prescriptions which follow from it relevant to the affairs of everyday life.

---

[14] There is, however, a compelling practical consideration for much caution when making predictions about the limits of the possible. Unlike predictions about what may happen and what may work, predictions about what may not are likely to foreclose the continued persistent efforts which may eventually succeed in achieving the "impossible." One might even suggest that authoritative predictions of the highly unlikely will only receive a thoroughgoing test from the dedicated or the ignorant—or from those who are both. Those best qualified by training and knowledge are likely to be diverted into more "practical" lines of endeavor. Thus a prediction that some state of affairs such as greatly increased popular political activity is probably unattainable is likely to be a self-fulfilling prophecy.

[15] For an example of this, see Roland Pennock, "Democracy and Leadership," in Chambers and Salisbury, op. cit., pp. 95–125.

[16] In some cases, the task of democratic theory is simply descriptive accuracy. See Schumpeter, op. cit., chap. xxii. In other cases, the second part of the assumption is quite explicit. For example: "We can then tentatively agree to call a democratic political system one which has characteristic principles of operation both descriptive and normative, and a complete theory of democracy will be one which lays bare and justifies the separate principles of both kinds, and the system as a whole." Mayo, op. cit., p. 33.

III

It would be an exceedingly hard statement to say that those contemporary democrats who aspire to greater political realism have entirely rejected the value of individual human development. Yet it seems clear that contemporary democrats are more concerned with democracy as a functioning system of government than with its direct or indirect effects on the individual.[17] As a consequence, they are inclined to stress characteristics of the system as a whole as the criteria for the evaluation of politics.[18]

So far as human development serves these writers as a justifying value, its relevance rests primarily on the proposition that the probable *policy* results of a democratic government will be more conducive to human development than the probable *policy* results which can be expected from other kinds of government. Democratic government is defined as that in which the governed choose key government officials in periodic free elections. Such a government, being ultimately answerable to the governed, may be more responsible to their needs and wishes. It can be expected to provide better protection for individual rights, more adequate social services, better control of would-be exploiters, a more just system of taxation, and greater freedom for individuals and groups to express their interests and desires concerning public policy.

Popular participation is reduced to the manageable task of periodic choices in elections. This kind of participation is, at best, a pale and rather pathetic version of the responsible and active participation which was the aspiration of classical democracy. It is hard to see this sort of thing, intermittent in time and marginal in importance for an overwhelming majority of the public, as the central means to educate the intellectual, emotional, and moral capacities of the citizen. Such an argument provides a very feeble justification for the contemporary version of democratic government. If active and responsible participation in collective activity is necessary for individual human development, the contribution

[17] Berelson, *op. cit.*, pp. 312–13, is most explicit on this point.

[18] For example, these remarks of Samuel Beer: ". . . by what criteria shall we judge that a system governs well or ill. . . . If one word were to be chosen that suggests them, it would be *efficiency*. . . . (1) the capacity to produce policies that are coherent within each field and over the whole area of governing; and (2) the capacity to identify new problems and make such innovations as may be called for." Samuel H. Beer, "New Structures of Democracy: Britain and America," in Chambers and Salisbury, *op. cit.*, pp. 55–57.

of contemporary democracy must be chiefly one of removing obstacles to free and responsible activity in *other* areas of human
life *outside* of politics.

Such a position has certain advantages which may recommend
it to the political theorist. It permits him, if he wishes, to justify
existing democratic systems through an argument to their probable
policy results. It relieves him of the obligation to chart the road beyond the present, and frees him to concern himself with the description of existing democratic politics or past political ideas.
Modestly curbing his aspirations and imagination, the contemporary democrat can remind us that democratic government can only
do so much. Political democracy—as he defines the term—prescribes no single highroad to the goods of human life. Politics is
only a method for managing public affairs. The goal of full human
development must be sought in many ways, and a democratic society provides for responsible activity in many nonpolitical spheres
of human life. Political activity can only be directly important for
a few. For the rest, government can best serve as an expert and
beneficent steward who clears away obstacles, manages the vital
necessities, and submits his accounts—simplified to his master's
level of understanding—for periodic review.

IV

In the face of such a position, exhibiting the virtues of realism
and moderation and cast in the fashionable terms of pluralism, it
is necessary to emphasize what has been changed. Contemporary
democracy is much more (or much less) than simply a more realistic statement of classical democracy which "salvages much of
what sponsors of the [classical] democratic method really mean by
this term."[19]

In the first place, although the purpose of both kinds of theory
is to prescribe, their approach and emphasis is strikingly different.
The heart of classical democracy is moral purpose. It prescribes
this purpose, then a general strategy for its fulfillment, and finally
various institutions through which this strategy may be carried
into operation. Contemporary democracy, on the other hand,
begins with institutions—that set of institutions which realistically
describe the essential features of existing democratic political
systems. It moves from institutions to values, taking as democratic

[19] Schumpeter, *op. cit.*, p. 269.

those values which are inherent in, or can be accommodated to, the given political institutions.

The assumptions of fact and value which underlie the prescriptive contents of the two theories are quite distinct, and the differences between them fall into a familiar pattern. Contemporary democracy may be considered less a restatement of classical democracy than a twentieth-century manifestation of the sober, cautious, Whig pluralism which, though often expressing itself politically in aristocratic terms, has been accounted a part of the democratic tradition since the seventeenth century. As with the earlier Whigs, these men "tend to accept existing society as a datum, susceptible to minor modifications, but always within a frame of reference supplied by the status quo."[20] As with the earlier Whigs, these men are dubious of notions of common good and social harmony and inclined to see politics in terms of the conflict of private interests. As with the earlier Whigs, these men are respectful of the limits of human reason and well aware of the irrational elements in human behavior. For both, this leads toward reliance on the political talents of an active elite. For earlier Whig and contemporary democrat, the basis of knowledge is empirical reality. For both, a clear understanding of empirical reality is necessary for men to measure the natural limits of their power and to exploit effectively what freedom of action they do possess. A realistic understanding of present circumstances is a compelling necessity. Both seem less concerned with change than with reasonable stability; less concerned with progress than with the virtues of the present. By limiting the moral possibilities of political activity, contemporary democrats reflect something of earlier Whig suspicions of political power. Politics serves, it does not create. As political power facilitated the enjoyment of natural rights for Locke, so political power may facilitate the pursuit of human fulfillment outside of politics for contemporary democracy.

Contemporary democracy changes the means and the locus of the contribution of government to human development, although the ideal itself is not necessarily rejected. Politics may still play a part in the pursuit of the ideal, but it no longer has the paramount role which it had before. The most significant realms for responsible personal activity now lie beyond the limits of politics— in economics, education, religion, art, social life, and even rec-

[20] Sheldon Wolin, *Politics and Vision* (Boston: Little, Brown, 1960), p. 298. On the general point discussed in this paragraph, see Wolin, Chap. 9, and G. H. Sabine, "The Two Democratic Traditions," *Philosophical Review*, (1952), 451–74.

reation. Without denying traditional democratic hopes for moral progress and social regeneration, contemporary democratic theory carefully excludes them from the list of essential features which define democracy. It is, at the very most, noncommital as to the possibilities which active political participation offer as a means to such ends. The best chance lies in the policy results of responsible popular government.

Although both theories of democracy prescribe a system of responsible popular government, the words have different meanings in the two theories. Popular government or popular rule means, in the case of classical democracy, the active participation of most adult citizens in the determination of public policies. In contemporary democracy, as its exponents have been at great pains to make clear, popular rule means only the popular choice at periodic elections of governors who make policy decisions. The extent of popular participation which is *essential* to political democracy is no more than that. Though popular participation may often go well beyond this minimum, this is, strictly speaking, a matter of indifference to the theory.[21]

It follows from this that although both theories prescribe responsible government, the conception of responsibility to which they give effect is not the same. The strategy of classical democracy requires the active and creative participation of the citizen in collective self-government and the pursuit of the common good. Popular responsibility arises from the role of the citizens as the active creators of public policy, from their engagement with public questions and their commitment to the search for a common good. Responsibility is conceived in active terms. The citizen is responsible because he is an active creator; the primary meaning of popular responsibility is that the citizens are responsible to themselves for what they have done. The responsibility of government is a secondary and derivative responsibility. Government is responsible to its citizens for the way in which it has carried out *their* directions.

In contemporary democracy, the active role of the citizen as a

---

21 "The popular influence upon policies, as distinct from control over policy-making, goes on all the time and may take many institutionalized and legitimate forms. The extent of such influence, however, cannot be reduced to any public test which can be incorporated at the present time into a general theory. The reason is that popular influence and consultation take such an infinity of forms—of which interest or pressure groups are perhaps the best known—that hardly any general principle can as yet be enunciated." Mayo, *op. cit.*, p. 62.

defining feature of democratic government is limited to the periodic choice of governors. Responsible government refers primarily to the accountability of a creative and active governing elite to those who have been the objects of its policies. The citizen has only a minimal involvement as a creative actor in what he judges. He must necessarily judge governors, their records and their promises, largely as a passive object of the actions of others. To the extent that this notion of responsibility is accepted and the citizens are considered primarily as objects rather than as creative actors, they must be considered as essentially irresponsible. They are to judge a world they never made, and thus to become a genteel counterpart of the mobs which sporadically unseated aristocratic governments in eighteenth- and nineteenth-century Europe. If a high degree of social solidarity and sense of community are necessary for the effective functioning of any sort of democratic government, it must come largely from some other source than the political activities of the citizen. Contemporary democracy is, in fact, a theory dependent on the prior existence of an established community, to the development of which it makes little, if any, contribution.[22]

Given the uncompromising demands of its ideal and its strategy, classical democracy is almost necessarily radical in relation to any existing political system. At their best, the realities of democratic politics are but a poor copy of what they should be, and classical democracy assumes that this is an undesirable but *not* unalterable state of affairs. Recognition of the gap between ideal and present reality and the difficulties of doing anything about it may create anxiety and gloom on the part of some who cherish the ideal.[23] This may lead to an effort to reject politics or to paper over the gap with a mythical view of present political reality. To assuage anxiety and avoid its possible consequences, the contemporary democrat proposes to reduce the tension between ideal and reality by changing the ideal to correspond—or nearly cor-

[22] Schumpeter saw this clearly. In discussing conditions for the success of the democratic method—as he defined it—he said: "Every system can stand deviating practices to a certain extent. But even the necessary minimum of democratic self-control evidently requires a national character and national habits of a certain type which have not everywhere had the opportunity to evolve and which the democratic method cannot be relied upon to produce." Schumpeter, *op. cit.*, p. 295. See also Tussman, *op. cit.*, p. 60. On the relation between community and active responsibility see W. E. Olson, "Responsibility: An Escape and an Approach," *Bulletin of the Atomic Scientists*, 19 (March 1963), 2–6.

[23] Hartz, *op. cit.*, pp. 13–29.

respond—to reality. For those who find anything more than minor adjustments in the status quo unacceptable, this remedy makes sense. For others, I suggest, it is very doubtful.

It may be, of course, that even a fair approximation of the ideal of classical democracy really is unattainable. The failure of a substantial majority of men to participate consistently or intelligently in existing democratic politics may be rooted in the nature of things. Plato may already have said the last word. This is possible, but enough changes have taken place in the last century or so in the political behavior of men to make it seem rather unlikely.

Assuming that change is possible, classical democracy suggests that even in the most advanced and successful countries far-reaching innovations are desirable—not only in the political systems but also in the social, economic, and cultural milieux associated with them.[24] While this tension between ideal and reality may lead to political neurosis in some, it can provide others with practical guidance for both theoretical and practical activity that is not tied down by commitments to the status quo. Classical democracy calls into question the failures of politics, which are an integral part of contemporary political reality, and suggests that we direct our energies toward dealing with them. It suggests inquiries and actions which lead out from politics to other aspects of human life in search for explanations and remedies. From this point of view, the significant problems are determined by their relevance to the future pursuit of the democratic ideal, not by their convenience for compiling descriptive data as a preliminary to a general explanatory theory of politics or by reference to the needs of the existing powers that be.

The institutional ideal of contemporary democracy necessarily lacks the radical bite of classical theory. It is bound in time and space by its realistic description of political reality. In a world inundated by change and rebellion against the past, this is scarcely an advantage. Contemporary democracy is less a guide to future action than a codification of past accomplishments. By translating the descriptive principles of present democratic reality into prescriptive terms, it vindicates the main features of the status quo and provides a model for tidying up loose ends. Democracy becomes a system to be preserved, not an end to be sought. Those who wish a guide to the future must look elsewhere.

---

[24] See Williams, *op. cit.*, pp. 306–16, for a statement of classical democracy that is an integral part of a thoroughgoing economic and social radicalism.

21 ❧ NORMATIVE CONSEQUENCES OF "DEMOCRATIC" THEORY

JACK L. WALKER

During the last thirty years, there have been numerous attempts to revise or reconstitute the "classical" theory of democracy: the familiar doctrine of popular rule, patterned after the New England town meeting, which asserts that public policy should result from extensive, informed discussion and debate.[1] By extending general participation in decision making the classical theorists hoped to increase the citizen's awareness of his moral and social responsibilities, reduce the danger of tyranny, and improve the quality of government. Public officials, acting as agents of the public at large, would then carry out the broad policies decided upon by majority vote in popular assemblies.

Although it is seldom made clear just which of the classical democratic theorists is being referred to, contemporary criticism has focused primarily on the descriptive elements of the theory, on its basic conceptions of citizenship, representation and decision making.[2] The concept of an active, informed, democratic citizenry, the most distinctive feature of the traditional theory, is the principal object of attack. On empirical grounds it is argued that very few such people can be found in Western societies. Public policy is not the expression of the common good as conceived of by the

FROM Jack L. Walker, "A Critique of the Elitist Theory of Democracy," *American Political Science Review*, 60 (June 1966), 285–295, 391–392.

[1] For discussions of the meaning of the classical theory of democracy see: George Sabine, "The Two Democratic Traditions," *The Philosophical Review*, 61 (1952), 451–474; and his *A History of Political Theory* (New York, 1958), especially Chs. 31 and 32. Also see J. Roland Pennock, *Liberal Democracy: Its Merits and Prospects* (New York, 1950); and Sheldon Wolin, *Politics and Vision* (Boston, 1960), especially Chs. 9 and 10.

[2] Criticism of the descriptive accuracy of the classical theory has been widespread in recent years. The best statement of the basic objections usually made is Joseph Schumpeter, *Capitalism, Socialism and Democracy* (New York, 1942), Part IV. See also Bernard Berelson *et al.*, *Voting* (Chicago, 1954), Chapter 14; articles by Louis Hartz and Samuel Beer in W. N. Chambers and R. H. Salisbury (eds.), *Democracy in the Mid-20th Century* (St. Louis, 1960); Seymour Martin Lipset, *Political Man* (New York, 1960); Robert Dahl, *A Preface to Democratic Theory* (Chicago, 1956), and *Who Governs?* (New Haven, 1961), especially pp. 223–325; V. O. Key, *Public Opinion and American Democracy* (New York, 1961), especially Part VI; Lester W. Milbrath, *Political Participation* (Chicago, 1965), especially Chapter VI; and for a general summary of the position: Henry Mayo, *An Introduction to Democratic Theory* (New York, 1960).

citizenry after widespread discussion and compromise. This description of policy making is held to be dangerously naïve because it overlooks the role of demagogic leadership, mass psychology, group coercion, and the influence of those who control concentrated economic power. In short, classical democratic theory is held to be unrealistic; first because it employs conceptions of the nature of man and the operation of society which are utopian, and second because it does not provide adequate, operational definition of its key concepts.

Since contemporary scholars have found the classical theory of democracy inadequate, a "revisionist" movement has developed, much as it has among contemporary Marxists, seeking to reconstitute the theory and bring it into closer correspondence with the latest findings of empirical research. One major restatement, called the "elitist theory of democracy" by Seymour Martin Lipset,[3] is now employed in many contemporary books and articles on American politics and political behavior and is fast becoming part of the conventional wisdom of political science.

The adequacy of the elitist theory of democracy, both as a set of political norms and as a guide to empirical research, is open to serious question. It has two major shortcomings: first, in their quest for realism, the revisionists have fundamentally changed the normative significance of democracy, rendering it a more conservative doctrine in the process; second, the general acceptance of the elitist theory by contemporary political scientists has led them to neglect almost completely some profoundly important developments in American society.

I. Normative Implications of the Elitist Theory

At the heart of the elitist theory is a clear presumption of the average citizen's inadequacies. As a consequence, democratic systems must rely on the wisdom, loyalty, and skill of their political leaders, not on the population at large. The political system is divided into two groups: the *elite,* or the "political entrepreneurs,"[4] who possess ideological commitments and manipulative skills; and the *citizens at large,* the masses, or the "apolitical clay"[5] of the system, a much larger class of passive, inert followers who have

[3] Introduction by Lipset to the Collier Books paperback edition of Robert Michels' *Political Parties* (New York, 1962), p. 33.
[4] The phrase is Dahl's in *Who Governs?*, p. 227.
[5] *Ibid.*, p. 225.

little knowledge of public affairs and even less interest. The factor that distinguishes democratic and authoritarian systems, according to this view, is the provision for limited, peaceful competition among members of the elite for the formal positions of leadership within the system. As Joseph Schumpeter summarized the theory: "The democratic method is that institutional arrangement for arriving at political decisions in which individuals acquire the power to decide by means of a competitive struggle for the people's vote."[6]

Democracy is thus conceived primarily in procedural terms; it is seen as a method of making decisions which ensures efficiency in administration and policy making and yet requires some measure of responsiveness to popular opinion on the part of the ruling elites. The average citizen still has some measure of effective political power under this system, even though he does not initiate policy, because of his right to vote (if he chooses) in regularly scheduled elections. The political leaders, in an effort to gain support at the polls, will shape public policy to fit the citizen's desires. By anticipating public reaction the elite grants the citizenry a form of indirect access to public policy making, without the creation of any kind of formal institutions and even in the absence of any direct communication. "A few citizens who are non-voters, and who for some reason have no influential contact with voters, have no indirect influence. Most citizens, however, possess a moderate degree of indirect influence, for elected officials keep the real or imagined preferences of constituents constantly in mind in deciding what policies to adopt or reject."[7] An ambiguity is created here because obviously leaders sometimes create opinions as well as respond to them, but since the leaders are constantly being challenged by rivals seeking to gain the allegiance of the masses it is assumed that the individual citizen will receive information from several conflicting sources, making it extremely difficult for any one group to "engineer consent" by manipulating public opinion. As Lipset puts it: "Representation is neither simply a means of political adjustment to social pressures nor an instrument of manipulation. It involves both functions, since the purpose of representation is to locate the combinations of relationships between parties and social bases which make possible the operation of efficient government."[8]

There has been extensive research and speculation about the

[6] Schumpeter, *op. cit.*, p. 269.
[7] Dahl, *Who Governs?*, p. 164.
[8] Lipset, Introduction to Michels, *op. cit.*, p. 34.

prerequisites for a democratic system of this kind. There is general agreement that a well-developed social pluralism and an extensive system of voluntary groups or associations is needed, along with a prevailing sense of psychological security, widespread education, and limited disparities of wealth. There must be no arbitrary barriers to political participation, and "enough people must participate in the governmental process so that political leaders compete for the support of a large and more or less representative cross section of the population."[9]

Elitist theory departs markedly from the classical tradition at this point. Traditionally it was assumed that the most important prerequisite for a stable democracy was general agreement among the politically active (those who vote) on certain fundamental policies and basic values, and widespread acceptance of democratic procedures and restraints on political activity. Political leaders would not violate the basic consensus, or "democratic mold," if they wished to be successful in gaining their objectives, because once these fundamental restraints were broken the otherwise passive public would become aroused and would organize against the offending leaders. Elitist theorists argue instead that agreement on democratic values among the "intervening structure of elites," the very elements which had been seen earlier as potential threats to democracy, is the main bulwark against a breakdown in constitutionalism. Writing in 1959 David Truman discards his notion of "potential groups," a variation of the traditional doctrine of consensus, and calls instead for a "consensus of elites," a determination on the part of the leaders of political parties, labor unions, trade associations, and other voluntary associations to defend the fundamental procedures of democracy in order to protect their own positions and the basic structure of society itself from the threat of an irresponsible demagogue.[10] V. O. Key, in his *Public Opinion and the American Democracy*, concludes that "the critical element for the health of a democratic order consists in the beliefs, standards, and competence of those who constitute the influentials, the opinion-leaders, the political activists in the order."[11] Similarly, Robert Dahl concludes in his study of New Haven that the

[9] Robert Dahl and Charles Lindblom, *Politics, Economics and Welfare* (New York, 1953), p. 309.
[10] David Truman, "The American System in Crisis," *Political Science Quarterly* (December, 1959), pp. 481–497. See also a perceptive critique of Truman's change of attitude in Peter Bachrach, "Elite Consensus and Democracy," *The Journal of Politics*, 24 (1962), 439–452.
[11] Key, *op. cit.*, p. 558. See also Key's "Public Opinion and the Decay of Democracy," *The Virginia Quarterly Review*, 37 (1961), 481–494.

skillful, active political leaders in the system are the true democratic "legitimists."[12] Since democratic procedures regulate their conflicts and protect their privileged positions in the system the leaders can be counted on to defend the democratic creed even if a majority of the voters might prefer some other set of procedures.[13]

It has also been suggested by several elitist theorists that democracies have good reason to fear increased political participation. They argue that a successful (that is, stable) democratic system depends on widespread apathy and general political incompetence.[14] The ideal of democratic participation is thus transformed into a "noble lie" designed chiefly to ensure a sense of responsibility among political leaders. As Lester Milbrath puts it:

. . . it is important to continue moral admonishment for citizens to become active in politics, not because we want or expect great masses of them to become active, but rather because the admonishment helps keep the system open and sustains a belief in the right of all to participate, which is an important norm governing the behavior of political elites.[15]

If the uninformed masses participate in large numbers, democratic self-restraint will break down and peaceful competition among the

[12] Dahl's position on this issue seems to have undergone a transformation somewhat similar to Truman's. Compare Dahl and Lindblom, *op. cit.*, Chapter 11 with Dahl, *Who Governs?*, Books IV, V, VI.

[13] Dahl, *Who Governs?*, pp. 311–325. It is important to note that these conclusions about the crucial function of an elite consensus in democracy were based on little empirical evidence. Truman, Key and Dahl seem to rely most heavily on Samuel Stouffer, *Communism, Conformity, and Civil Liberties* (New York, 1955), a study based on national opinion surveys which was concerned with only one issue (McCarthyism) and did not investigate the relationship between the expressed opinions of its subjects and their behavior under stress; and James Prothro and Charles Grigg, "Fundamental Principles of Democracy: Bases of Agreement and Disagreement," *Journal of Politics*, 22 (1960), 276–294, a study of attitudes in two small cities. More recently, however, Herbert McClosky has produced more convincing data in his "Consensus and Ideology in American Politics," *American Political Science Review*, 58 (1964), 361–382. On page 377 McClosky concludes that widespread agreement on procedural norms is not a prerequisite to the success of a democratic system: "Consensus may strengthen democratic viability, but its absence in an otherwise stable society need not be fatal, or even particularly damaging." McClosky's conclusions are called into question by data presented by Samuel Eldersveld, *Political Parties: A Behavioral Analysis* (Chicago, 1964), pp. 183–219; and Edmond Constantini, "Intraparty Attitude Conflict: Democratic Party Leadership in California," *Western Political Quarterly*, 16 (1963), 956–972.

[14] See Bernard Berelson, *et al.*, *op. cit.*, Chapter 14; Lipset, *op. cit.*, pp. 14–16; W. H. Morris-Jones, "In Defense of Apathy," *Political Studies*, II (1954), 25–37.

[15] Milbrath, *op. cit.*, p. 152.

elites, the central element in the elitist theory, will become impossible.

The principal aim of the critics whose views we are examining has been to make the theory of democracy more realistic, to bring it into closer correspondence with empirical reality. They are convinced that the classical theory does not account for "much of the real machinery"[16] by which the system operates, and they have expressed concern about the possible spread among Americans of either unwarranted anxiety or cynical disillusionment over the condition of democracy. But it is difficult to transform a utopian theory into a realistic account of political behavior without changing the theory's normative foundations. By revising the theory to bring it into closer correspondence with reality, the elitist theorists have transformed democracy from a radical into a conservative political doctrine, stripping away its distinctive emphasis on popular political activity so that it no longer serves as a set of ideals toward which society ought to be striving.[17]

The most distinctive feature, and the principal orienting value, of classical democratic theory was its emphasis on individual participation in the development of public policy. By taking part in the affairs of his society the citizen would gain in knowledge and understanding, develop a deeper sense of social responsibility, and broaden his perspective beyond the narrow confines of his private life. Although the classical theorists accepted the basic framework of Lockean democracy, with its emphasis on limited government, they were *not* primarily concerned with the *policies* which might be produced in a democracy; above all else they were concerned

[16] Louis Hartz, "Democracy: Image and Reality," in Chambers and Salisbury (eds.), *op. cit.*, p. 26.

[17] Several articles have recently appeared which attack the elitist theory on normative grounds. The best and most insightful is Lane Davis, "The Cost of Realism: Contemporary Restatements of Democracy," *Western Political Quarterly*, 17 (1964), 37–46. Also see: Graeme Duncan and Steven Lukes, "The New Democracy," *Political Studies*, 11 (1963), 156–177; Steven W. Rousseas and James Farganis, "American Politics and the End of Ideology," *British Journal of Sociology*, 14 (1963) 347–360; and Christian Bay, "Politics and Pseudopolitics," *American Political Science Review*, 59 (1965), 39–51. The subject is also treated in: Henry Kariel, *The Decline of American Pluralism* (Stanford, 1961), Chapters 9 and 11; T. B. Bottomore, *Elites and Society* (London, 1964), 108–110; Robert Presthus, *Men at the Top* (New York, 1964), 3–47; and Robert Agger, Daniel Goldrich, and Bert Swanson, *The Rulers and the Ruled* (New York, 1964), 93–99, 524–532. For an insightful critique of the work of Dahl and Mills, conceived of as opposing ideological positions see: William E. Connolly, *Responsible Political Ideology: Implications of the Sociology of Knowledge for Political Inquiry* (unpublished doctoral dissertation, University of Michigan, 1965), pp. 18–39. This section of this article depends heavily on Lane Davis' analysis.

with *human development*, the opportunities which existed in political activity to realize the untapped potentials of men and to create the foundations of a genuine human community. In the words of John Stuart Mill:

... the most important point of excellence which any form of government can possess is to promote the virtue and intelligence of the people themselves. The first question in respect to any political institutions is how far they tend to foster in the members of the community the various desirable qualities ... moral, intellectual, and active.[18]

In the elitist version of the theory, however, emphasis has shifted to the needs and functions of the system as a whole; there is no longer a direct concern with human development. The central question is not how to design a political system which stimulates greater individual participation and enhances the moral development of its citizens, but how "to combine a substantial degree of popular participation with a system of power capable of governing *effectively* and *coherently*."[19]

The elitist theory allows the citizen only a passive role as an object of political activity; he exerts influence on policy making only by rendering judgments after the fact in national elections. The safety of contemporary democracy lies in the high-minded sense of responsibility of its leaders, the only elements of society who are actively striving to discover and implement the common good. The citizens are left to "judge a world they never made, and thus to become a genteel counter-part of the mobs which sporadically unseated aristocratic governments in eighteenth- and nineteenth-century Europe."[20]

The contemporary version of democratic theory has, it seems, lost much of the vital force, the radical thrust of the classical theory. The elitist theorists, in trying to develop a theory which takes account of the way the political system actually operates, have changed the principal orienting values of democracy. The heart of the classical theory was its justification of broad participation in the public affairs of the community; the aim was the production of citizens who were capable enough and responsible enough to play this role. The classical theory was not meant to describe any existing system of government; it was an outline, a set of prescriptions for the ideal polity which men should strive

[18] John Stuart Mill, *Considerations on Representative Government* (New York, 1862), pp. 39–40.
[19] Samuel Beer, "New Structures of Democracy: Britain and America," in Chambers and Salisbury (eds.), *op. cit.*, p. 46.
[20] Davis, *op. cit.*, p. 45.

to create. The elitist theorists, in their quest for realism, have changed this distinctive prescriptive element in democratic theory; they have substituted stability and efficiency as the prime goals of democracy. If these revisions are accepted, the danger arises that in striving to develop more reliable explanations of political behavior, political scientists will also become sophisticated apologists for the existing political order. Robert Lane, in concluding his study of the political ideologies of fifteen "common men" in an Eastern city, observes that they lack a utopian vision, a well-defined sense of social justice that would allow them to stand in judgment on their society and its institutions.[21] To some degree, the "men of Eastport" share this disability with much of the American academic elite.

II. The Elitist Theory as a Guide For Research

The shortcomings of the elitist theory are not confined to its normative implications. Serious questions also arise concerning its descriptive accuracy and its utility as a guide to empirical research. The most unsatisfactory element in the theory is its concept of the passive, apolitical, common man who pays allegiance to his governors and to the sideshow of politics while remaining primarily concerned with his private life, evenings of television with his family, or the demands of his job. Occasionally, when the average citizen finds his primary goals threatened by the actions or inactions of government, he may strive vigorously to influence the course of public policy, but "Homo Civicus" as Dahl calls him, "is not, by nature, a political animal."[22]

It was the acceptance of this concept that led the elitist theorists to reject the traditional notion of consensus. It became implausible to argue that the citizenry is watchful and jealous of the great democratic values while at the same time suggesting that they are uninvolved, uninformed, and apathetic. Widespread apathy also is said to contribute to democratic stability by ensuring that the disagreements that arise during campaigns and elections will not

[21] Robert Lane, *Political Ideology* (New York, 1962), p. 475. See also Donald Stokes' comments on the same topic in "Popular Evaluations of Government: An Empirical Assessment," in Harlan Cleveland and Harold Lasswell (eds.), *Ethics and Bigness* (Published by the Conference on Science, Philosophy and Religion in their relation to the Democratic Way of Life, 1962), p. 72.
[22] Dahl, *Who Governs?*, p. 225.

involve large numbers of people or plunge the society into violent disorders or civil war.

No one can deny that there is widespread political apathy among many sectors of the American public. But it is important to ask why this is so and not simply to explain how this phenomenon contributes to the smooth functioning of the system. Of course, the citizens' passivity might stem from their satisfaction with the operation of the political system, and thus they would naturally become aroused only if they perceived a threat to the system. Dahl, for one, argues that the political system operates largely through "inertia," tradition, or habitual responses. It remains stable because only a few "key" issues are the objects of controversy at any one time, the rest of public policy having been settled and established in past controversies which are now all but forgotten. Similarly, Nelson Polsby argues that it is fallacious to assume that the quiescent citizens in a community, especially those in the lower income groups, have grievances unless they actually express them. To do so is to arbitrarily assign "upper- and middle-class values to all actors in the community."[23]

But it is hard to believe, in these days of protest demonstrations, of Black Muslims and the Deacons of Defense and Justice, that the mood of cynical apathy toward politics which affects so many American Negroes is an indication of their satisfaction with the political system, and with the weak, essentially meaningless alternatives it usually presents to them. To assume that apathy is a sign of satisfaction in this case is to overlook the tragic history of the Negroes in America and the system of violent repression long used to deny them any entrance into the regular channels of democratic decision making.

Students of race relations have concluded that hostile attitudes toward a racial group do not necessarily lead to hostile actions, and amicable feelings do not ensure amicable actions. Instead, "it is the social demands of the situation, particularly when supported by accepted authority figures, which are the effective determinants of individual action. . . ."[24] This insight might apply to other areas

[23] Nelson Polsby, *Community Power and Political Theory* (New Haven, 1963), p. 117.

[24] Herbert Blumer, "Recent research [on race relations in the] United States of America," *International Social Science Bulletin* (UNESCO), 10 (1958), p. 432. Similar arguments concerning the relationship of beliefs and action can be found in J. D. Lohman and D. C. Reitzes, "Deliberately Organized Groups and Racial Behavior," *American Sociological Review*, 19 (1954), 342–344; and in Earl Raab (ed.), *American Race Relations Today* (Garden City, 1962).

besides race relations. It suggests that a society's political culture, the general perceptions about the nature of authority and the prevailing expectations of significant reference groups, might be a major influence on the political behavior of the average citizen regardless of his own feelings of satisfaction or hostility. There have been sizable shifts in rates of political participation throughout American history which suggests that these rates are not rigidly determined. A recent analysis indicates that rates of voter participation are now *lower* than they were in the nineteenth century even though the population is now much better educated and the facilities for communication much better developed.[25] Other studies indicate that there are marked differences in the political milieu of towns and cities which lead citizens of one area to exhibit much more cynicism and distrust of the political system than others.[26] Although the studies showed no corresponding changes in feelings of political competence, cynical attitudes might inhibit many forms of participation and thus induce apathy.

Political apathy obviously has many sources. It may stem from feelings of personal inadequacy, from a fear of endangering important personal relationships, or from a lack of interest in the issues; but it may also have its roots in the society's institutional structure, in the weakness or absence of group stimulation or support, in the positive opposition of elements within the political system to wider participation; in the absence, in other words, of appropriate spurs to action, or the presence of tangible deterrents.[27] Before the causes of apathy can be established with confidence much more attention must be directed to the role of the mass media. How are the perceptions of individual citizens affected by the version of reality they receive, either directly or indirectly, from television, the national wire services, and the public schools[28]— and how do these perceptions affect their motivations? Political

[25] Walter Dean Burnham, "The Changing Shape of the American Political Universe," *American Political Science Review*, 59 (1965), 7–28.

[26] Robert Agger, Marshall Goldstein and Stanley Pearl, "Political Cynicism: Measurement and Meaning," *The Journal of Politics*, 23 (1961), 477–506; and Edgar Litt, "Political Cynicism and Political Futility," *The Journal of Politics*, 25 (1963) 312–323.

[27] For a brief survey of findings on this subject, see Milbrath, *op. cit.;* and for a clear, brief summary, see: Morris Rosenburg, "Some Determinants of Political Apathy," *Public Opinion Quarterly*, 18 (1954–55), 349–366. Also see David Apter (ed.), *Ideology and Discontent* (New York, 1964), especially chapters by Converse and Wolfinger, *et al.*

[28] A major study of the influence of secondary schools on political attitudes is underway at the University of Michigan under the direction of M. Kent Jennings.

scientists have also largely neglected to study the use of both legitimate and illegitimate sanctions and private intimidation to gain political ends. How do the activities of the police,[29] social workers, or elements of organized crime affect the desires and the opportunities available for individual political participation?

Certainly the apparent calm of American politics is not matched by our general social life, which is marked by high crime rates, numerous fads and crazes, and much intergroup tension.[30] One recent study showed that during the civil rights protests in Atlanta, Georgia, and Cambridge, Maryland, crime rates in the Negro communities dropped substantially.[31] A finding of this kind suggests that there is some connection between these two realms of social conflict and that both may serve as outlets for individual distress and frustration. High crime (or suicide) rates and low rates of voting may very well be related; the former may represent "leakage" from the political system.[32]

Once we admit that the society is not based on a widespread consensus, we must look at our loosely organized, decentralized political parties in a different light. It may be that the parties have developed in this way precisely because no broad consensus exists. In a fragmented society which contains numerous geographic, religious, and racial conflicts, the successful politician has been the man adept at negotiation and bargaining, the man best able to play these numerous animosities off against each other, and thereby build *ad hoc* coalitions of support for specific programs. Success at this delicate business of coalition building depends on achieving some basis for communication among the leaders of otherwise antagonistic groups and finding a formula for compromise. To create these circumstances sharp conflicts must be avoided; highly controversial, potentially explosive issues shunned. Controversy is shifted to other issues or the public authorities

[29] An extensive investigation of the role of the police and the courts in city politics is being conducted at Harvard University by James Q. Wilson.

[30] It is very difficult to compare crime rates or other indications of social disorganization in the United States with those in other countries. For a discussion of some of the difficulties see: UNESCO 1963 *Report on the World Social Situation* (New York, 1963).

[31] Fredric Solomon, Walter L. Walker, Garrett O'Connor, and Jacob Fishman, "Civil Rights Activity and Reduction of Crime Among Negroes," *Archives of General Psychiatry*, 12 (March, 1965), 227–236.

[32] For an excellent study of the Black Muslims which portrays the movement as a nonpolitical outlet for the frustration and bitterness felt by many American Negroes see the study by an African scholar: E. V. Essien-Udom, *Black Nationalism: A Search for an Identity in America* (Chicago, 1962).

simply refuse to deal with the question, claiming that they have no legitimate jurisdiction in the case or burying it quietly in some committee room or bureaucratic pigeonhole.[33]

In other words, one of the chief characteristics of our political system has been its success in suppressing and controlling internal conflict. But the avoidance of conflict, the suppression of strife, is *not* necessarily the creation of satisfaction or consensus. The citizens may remain quiescent, the political system might retain its stability, but significant differences of opinion remain, numerous conflicts are unresolved, and many desires go unfulfilled. The frustrations resulting from such deprivations can create conflict in other, nonpolitical realms. Fads, religious revivals, or wild, anomic riots such as those which occurred in the Negro ghettos of several large American cities during the summers of 1964 and 1965, phenomena not directly related to the achievement of any clearly conceived political goals, may be touched off by unresolved tensions left untended by the society's political leaders.

The American political system is highly complex, with conflicting jurisdictions and numerous checks and balances. A large commitment in time and energy must be made, even by a well-educated citizen, to keep informed of the issues and personalities in all levels of government. Most citizens are not able or willing to pay this kind of cost to gain the information necessary for effective political participation. This may be especially true in a political system in which weak or unclear alternatives are usually presented to the electorate. For most citizens the world of politics is remote, bewildering, and meaningless, having no direct relation to daily concerns about jobs or family life. Many citizens have desires or frustrations with which public agencies might be expected to deal, but they usually remain unaware of possible solutions to their problems in the public sphere. This group within our political system are citizens only from the legal point of view. If a high degree of social solidarity and sense of community are necessary for true democratic participation, then these marginal men are not

33 Herbert Agar makes a similar analysis and argues for the retention of the system in *The Price of Union* (Boston, 1950). On page 689 he states: "The lesson which Americans learned [from the Civil War] was useful: in a large federal nation, when a problem is passionately felt, and is discussed in terms of morals, each party may divide within itself, against itself. And if the parties divide, the nation may divide; for the parties, with their enjoyable pursuit of power, are a unifying influence. Wise men, therefore, may seek to dodge such problems as long as possible. And the easiest way to dodge them is for both parties to take both sides."

really citizens of the state. The polity has not been extended to include them.[34]

For the elitist theorist widespread apathy is merely a fact of political life, something to be anticipated, a prerequisite for democratic stability. But for the classical democrat political apathy is an object of intense concern because the overriding moral purpose of the classical theory is to expand the boundaries of the political community and build the foundations for human understanding through participation by the citizens in the affairs of their government.

III. Leaders and Followers

While most elitist theorists are agreed in conceiving of the average citizen as politically passive and uncreative, there seems to be a difference of opinion (or at least of emphasis) over the likelihood of some irrational, antidemocratic outburst from the society's common men. Dahl does not dwell on this possibility. He seemingly conceives of *homo civicus*, the average citizen, as a man who consciously chooses to avoid politics and to devote himself to the pleasures and problems of his job and family:

Typically, as a source of direct gratifications political activity will appear to *homo civicus* as less attractive than a host of other activities; and, as a strategy to achieve his gratifications indirectly political action will seem considerably less efficient than working at his job, earning more money, taking out insurance, joining a club, planning a vacation, moving to another neighborhood or city, or coping with an uncertain future in manifold other ways.[35]

Lipset, on the other hand, seems much more concerned with the danger that the common man might suddenly enter the political system, smashing democratic institutions in the process, as part of an irrational, authoritarian political force. He sees "profoundly anti-democratic tendencies in lower class groups,"[36] and he has been frequently concerned in his work with Hitler, McCarthy, and

[34] For a study of several important factors affecting the degree of participation in American politics see: E. E. Schattschneider, *The Semi-Sovereign People* (New York, 1960), especially Chs. 5 and 6.

[35] Dahl, *Who Governs?*, p. 224.

[36] Lipset, *op. cit.*, p. 121.

other demagogic leaders who have led antidemocratic mass movements.

Although there are obviously some important differences of opinion and emphasis concerning the political capacities of average citizens and the relative security of democratic institutions, the elitist theorists agree on the crucial importance of leadership in ensuring both the safety and viability of representative government. This set of basic assumptions serves as a foundation for their explanation of change and innovation in American politics, a process in which they feel creative leadership plays the central role.

Running throughout the work of these writers is a vision of the "professional" politician as hero, much as he is pictured in Max Weber's essay "Politics as a Vocation." Dahl's Mayor Lee, Edward Banfield's Mayor Daley, Richard Neustadt's ideal occupant of the White House all possess great skill and drive, and are engaged in the delicate art of persuasion and coalition building. They are actively moving the society forward toward their own goals, according to their own special vision. All of them possess the preeminent qualities of Weber's ideal-type politician: "passion, a feeling of responsibility, and a sense of proportion."[37] As in Schumpeter's analysis of capitalism, the primary source of change and innovation in the political system is the "political entrepreneur"; only such a leader can break through the inherent conservatism of organizations and shake the masses from their habitual passivity.

It is obvious that political leaders (especially chief executives) have played a very important role in American politics, but it is also clear that the American system's large degree of internal bargaining, the lack of many strong hierarchical controls, and its numerous checks and balances, both constitutional and political, place powerful constraints on the behavior of political executives. American presidents, governors, and mayors usually find themselves caught in a web of cross pressures which prevent them from making bold departures in policy or firmly attaching themselves to either side of a controversy. The agenda of controversy, the list of questions which are recognized by the active participants in politics as legitimate subjects of attention and concern, is very hard to change.

Just as it can be argued that the common citizens have a form of indirect influence, so it can also be argued that the top leaders of other institutions in the society, such as the business community,

[37] Hans Gerth and C. Wright Mills (eds.), *From Max Weber: Essays in Sociology* (New York, 1946), p. 115.

possess indirect influence as well. As Banfield suggests in his study of Chicago, the top business leaders have great potential power: "If the twenty or thirty wealthiest men in Chicago acted as one and put all their wealth into the fight, they could easily destroy or capture the machine."[38] The skillful politician, following Carl Friedrich's "rule of anticipated reactions,"[39] is unlikely to make proposals which would unite the business community against him. The aspiring politician learns early in his career, by absorbing the folklore which circulates among the politically active, which issues can and cannot be exploited successfully. It is this constellation of influences and anticipated reactions, "the peculiar mobilization of bias" in the community, fortified by a general consensus of elites, that determines the agenda of controversy.[40] The American political system, above all others, seems to be especially designed to frustrate the creative leader.

But as rigid and inflexible as it is, the political system does produce new policies; new programs and schemes are approved; even basic procedural changes are made from time to time. Of course, each major shift in public policy has a great many causes. The elitist theory of democracy looks for the principal source of innovation in the competition among rival leaders and the clever maneuvering of political entrepreneurs, which is, in its view, the most distinctive aspect of a democratic system. Because so many political scientists have worn the theoretical blinders of the elitist theory, however, we have overlooked the importance of broadly based social movements, arising from the public at large, as powerful agents of innovation and change.

The primary concerns of the elitist theorists have been the maintenance of democratic stability, the preservation of democratic procedures, and the creation of machinery which would produce efficient administration and coherent public policies. With these goals in mind, social movements (if they have been studied at all) have usually been pictured as threats to democracy, as manifestations of "political extremism." Lipset asserts that such movements typically appeal to the "disgruntled and the psychologically home-

[38] Edward Banfield, *Political Influence* (New York, 1961), p. 290.

[39] Carl Friedrich, *Constitutional Government and Politics* (New York, 1939), pp. 17–18.

[40] This point is made persuasively by Peter Bachrach and Morton Baratz, "The Two Faces of Power," *American Political Science Review*, 56 (1962), 947–952. Also see their "Decisions and Nondecisions: An Analytical Framework," *American Political Science Review*, 57 (1963), 632–642; and Thomas J. Anton, "Power, Pluralism and Local Politics," *Administrative Quarterly*, 7 (1963), 425–457.

less, to the personal failures, the socially isolated, the economically insecure, the uneducated, unsophisticated, and authoritarian persons at every level of the society."[41] Movements of this kind throw the political system out of gear and disrupt the mechanisms designed to maintain due process; if the elites were overwhelmed by such forces, democracy would be destroyed. This narrow, antagonistic view of social movements stems from the elitist theorists' suspicion of the political capacities of the common citizens,[42] their fear of instability and their failure to recognize the elements of rigidity and constraint existing in the political system. But if one holds that view and at the same time recognizes the tendency of the prevailing political system to frustrate strong leaders, it becomes difficult to explain how significant innovations in public policy, such as the social security system, the Wagner Act, the Subversive Activities Control Act of 1950, or the Civil Rights Bill of 1964, ever came about.

During the last century American society has spawned numerous social movements, some of which have made extensive demands on the political system, while others have been highly esoteric, mystical, and apolitical. These movements arise because some form of social dislocation or widespread sense of frustration exists within the society. But dissatisfaction alone is not a sufficient cause; it must be coupled with the necessary resources and the existence of potential leadership which can motivate a group to take action designed to change the offending circumstances.[43]

[41] Lipset, op. cit., p. 178.

[42] Ruth Searles and J. Allen Williams, in a study of Negro students who took part in the sit-in demonstrations, found no evidence that they were authoritarian or posed threats to democracy. "Far from being alienated, the students appear to be committed to the society and its middle class leaders": "Negro College Students' Participation in Sit-ins," Social Forces, 40 (1962), p. 219. For other studies of this particular social movement see: Robert Coles, "Social Struggle and Weariness," Psychiatry, 27 (1964), 305–315; and three articles by Fredric Solomon and Jacob Fishman: "Perspectives on Student Sit-in Movement," American Journal of Ortho-psychiatry, 33 (1963), 872–882; "Action and Identity Formation in First Student Sit-in Demonstration," Journal of Social Issues, 20 (1964), 36–45; and "Psychosocial Meaning of Nonviolence in Student Civil Rights Activities," Psychiatry, 27 (1964) 91–99. Also see the October 1964 issue of The Journal of Social Issues, entitled "Youth and Social Action," edited by Fredric Solomon and Jacob Fishman; and Jack L. Walker, "Protest and Negotiation: A Case Study of Negro Leaders in Atlanta, Georgia," Midwest Journal of Political Science, 7 (1963), 99–124.

[43] Sociologists usually study social movements under the rubric of collective behavior. For general treatments see: Herbert Blumer, "Collective Behavior" in J. B. Gittler (ed.), Review of Sociology (New York, 1957); Rudolph Heberle, Social Movements (New York, 1951); Lewis Killian,

Often such movements erupt along the margins of the political system, and they sometimes serve the purpose of encouraging political and social mobilization, of widening the boundaries of the polity.[44] Through movements such as the Negroes' drive for civil rights, or the Midwestern farmers' crusade for fair prices in the 1890s, the Ku Klux Klan, or the "radical right" movements of the 1960s, *pre-political* people who have not yet found, or only begun to find, a specific language in which to express their aspirations about the world"[45] are given new orientation, confidence, knowledge, sources of information, and leadership.

Social movements also serve, in Rudolf Heberle's words, as the "creators and carriers of public opinion."[46] By confronting the political authorities, or by locking themselves in peaceful—or violent[47]—conflict with some other element of the society, social movements provoke trials of strength between contending forces or ideas. Those trials of economic, political, or moral strength take place in the court of public opinion and sometimes place enormous strain on democratic institutions and even the social fabric itself. But through such trials, as tumultuous as they may sometimes be, the agenda of controversy, the list of acceptable, "key" issues may be changed. In an effort to conciliate and mediate, the political

---

"Social Movements," in Robert Faris (ed.), *Handbook of Modern Sociology* (Chicago, 1964); Charles King, *Social Movements in the United States* (New York, 1956); Karl Lang and Gladys Lang, *Collective Dynamics* (New York, 1961); Neil Smelser, *Theory of Collective Behavior* (New York, 1963); Ralph Turner and Lewis Killian, *Collective Behavior* (Englewood Cliffs, N.J., 1957). For a brief historical sketch of some American social movements see: Thomas Greer, *American Social Reform Movements: Their Pattern Since 1865* (Englewood Cliffs, N.J., 1946).

[44] For a book which investigates social movements which have served this function among Italian peasants see: E. J. Hobsbawn, *Primitive Rebels* (Manchester, 1959). See also: Vittorio Lanternari, *The Religions of the Oppressed* (New York, 1963) for a study of the relationship of messianic cults and revolutionary movements on five continents; and George Rude, *The Crowd in History* (New York, 1964) for a study of popular uprisings in England and France from 1730–1848.

[45] Hobsbawn, *op. cit.*, p. 2.

[46] Heberle, *op. cit.*, pp. 417–418.

[47] American political scientists have not been sufficiently concerned with the role of violence in the governmental process. Among all the articles published in *The American Political Science Review* between 1906 and 1963, there was only one whose title contained the word "violence," only one with the word "coercive" (it concerned India), and none with the word "force." During the same period there were forty-nine articles on governmental reorganization and twenty-four on civil service reform. See Kenneth Janda (ed.), *Cumulative Index to The American Political Science Review* (Evanston, 1964). Efforts to retrieve this situation have begun in Harry Eckstein (ed.), *Internal War* (New York, 1964).

leaders fashion new legislation, create unique regulatory bodies, and strive to establish channels of communication and accommodation among the combatants.

Of course, members of the political elite may respond to the movement by resisting it, driving it underground, or destroying it; they may try to co-opt the movement's leaders by granting them privileges or by accepting parts of its program, or even by making the leaders part of the established elite; they may surrender to the movement, losing control of their offices in the political system in the process. The nature of the political leader's response is probably a prime determinant of the tactics the movement will adopt, the kind of leadership that arises within it, and the ideological appeals it develops. Other factors might determine the response of the leadership, such as the existence of competing social movements with conflicting demands, the resources available to the political leaders to satisfy the demands of the movement, the social status of the participants in the movement, the presence of competing sets of leaders claiming to represent the same movement, and many other elements peculiar to each particular situation. In this process social movements may be highly disruptive and some institutions may be completely destroyed; the story does not always have a happy ending. But one major consequence (function, if you will) of social movements is to break society's log jams, to prevent ossification in the political system, to prompt and justify major innovations in social policy and economic organization.[48]

This relationship of challenge and response between the established political system and social movements has gone without much systematic study by political scientists. Sociologists have been concerned with social movements, but they have directed most of their attention to the causes of the movements, their "natural history," and the relationship between leaders and followers within them.[49] Historians have produced many case studies of social movements but little in the way of systematic explana-

[48] Lewis Coser has discussed the role of conflict in provoking social change in his The Functions of Social Conflict (Glencoe, 1956); and in his "Social Conflict and the Theory of Social Change," British Journal of Sociology, 9 (1957) 197–207. See also Irving Louis Horowitz, "Consensus, Conflict and Cooperation: A Sociological Inventory," Social Forces, 41 (1962), 177–188.

[49] For an insightful and stimulating example, see Joseph Gusfield, Symbolic Crusade (Urbana, 1963), which makes an excellent analysis of the causes of the Temperance movement and changes in its leadership but makes only brief mention of the movement's impact on the government and the responses of political leaders to its efforts.

tion.[50] This would seem to be a fruitful area for investigation by political scientists. But this research is not likely to appear unless we revise our concept of the masses as politically inert, apathetic, and bound by habitual responses. We must also shift our emphasis from theories which conceive of the "social structure in terms of a functionally integrated system held in equilibrium by certain patterned and recurrent processes," to theories which place greater emphasis on the role of coercion and constraint in the political system and which concentrate on the influences within society which produce "the forces that maintain it in an unending process of change."[51] The greatest contribution of Marx to the understanding of society was his realization that internal conflict is a major source of change and innovation. One need not accept his metaphysical assumptions to appreciate this important insight.

IV. Conclusion

In a society undergoing massive social change, fresh theoretical perspectives are essential. Political theorists are charged with the responsibility of constantly reformulating the dogmas of the past so that democratic theory remains relevant to the stormy realities of twentieth-century American society with its sprawling urban centers, its innumerable social conflicts, and its enormous bureaucratic hierarchies.

In restating the classical theory, however, contemporary political scientists have stripped democracy of much of its radical *élan* and have diluted its utopian vision, thus rendering it inadequate as a guide to the future. The elitist theorists generally accept the prevailing distribution of status in the society (with exceptions usually made for the American Negro), and find it "not only compatible with political freedom but even . . . a condition of it."[52] They place great emphasis on the limitations of the average citizen and are suspicious of schemes which might encourage greater participation in public affairs. Accordingly, they put their trust in the wisdom and energy of an active, responsible elite.

[50] John Higham is somewhat of an exception of this generalization. See his *Strangers in the Land: Patterns of American Nativism 1860–1925* (New York, 1963). Also see his "Another Look at Nativism," *Catholic Historical Review*, 44 (1958), 147–158; and his "The Cult of the 'American Consensus': Homogenizing Our History," *Commentary* (February 1959), p. 159.

[51] Ralf Dahrendorf, *Class and Class Conflict in Industrial Society* (Stanford, 1959), p. 159.

[52] Sabine, "The Two Democratic Traditions," *op. cit.*, p. 459.

Besides these normative shortcomings the elitist theory has served as an inadequate guide to empirical research, providing an unconvincing explanation of widespread political apathy in American society and leading political scientists to ignore manifestations of discontent not directly related to the political system. Few studies have been conducted of the use of force, or informal, illegitimate coercion in the American political system, and little attention has been directed to the great social movements which have marked American society in the last one hundred years.

If political science is to be relevant to society's pressing needs and urgent problems, professional students of politics must broaden their perspectives and become aware of new problems which are in need of scientific investigation. They must examine the norms that guide their efforts and guard against the danger of uncritically accepting the values of the going system in the name of scientific objectivity. Political scientists must strive for heightened awareness and self-knowledge; they must avoid rigid presumptions which diminish their vision, destroy their capacities for criticism, and blind them to some of the most significant social and political developments of our time.

A Postscript[53]

I am convinced that it was a mistake to use the label "The Elitist Theory of Democracy" (even though it came directly from Lipset) to describe the doctrines with which I tried to deal. The word "theory" gives a false precision to what would be more properly identified as a prevailing attitude toward the American political process. The word "elitist" apparently carries, at least in Dahl's view, some objectionable antidemocratic connotations. My intent was not to question Dahl's, or anyone else's democratic *bona fides*. My article was intended as a critique of the prescriptive implications of a set of ideas concerning democratic political systems which can be found, in varying degrees of prominence, in the writings of many contemporary students of politics—Dahl among them.

The doctrines with which I was concerned were: (1) the belief that the political inactivity of the average citizen is a more or less permanent aspect of his behavior, not an artifact of the social and

53 [This postscript is part of Jack L. Walker's response to an article by Robert A. Dahl criticizing Walker. Both the article and the response appeared in the *American Political Science Review*, June 1966.]

political systems; (2) the related belief that political inactivity is a sign of satisfaction with the operation of the political system, a form of passive consent; (3) the belief that political apathy is not seriously dysfunctional in a democratic system and, on the part of some writers, the belief that widespread apathy may be a prerequisite for the successful functioning of the system; (4) the belief that agreement on democratic norms among political leaders is more important than consensus among the common citizens for achieving political stability; and (5) an overriding concern with maintaining the stability of democratic systems. I meant to analyze this set of ideas and its consequences; I did not set out to write a comprehensive appraisal of the political theory of Professor Dahl, or any other single writer. . . .

Ideas and beliefs have manifold consequences, some intended and others wholly unexpected; writings meant by their author to be purely descriptive may still lead their readers to draw normative conclusions, and it is quite possible to study these conclusions without violating the logical distinction between descriptive and prescriptive statements. It would be extremely difficult, perhaps impossible, for any single writer to describe every aspect of the American political system. Each writer must choose among innumerable phenomena which could conceivably be studied. Regardless of the writer's intention, I would argue that the facts he presents and the explanations he proposes may prompt his readers to make certain normative inferences. In the case of the beliefs I considered in my article, the normative impact has been to reduce the urgency of the need to extend the limits of the active political community; and as I argued further, this has tended to divert the attention of political scientists from such phenomena as social movements which appear on the periphery of the organized political system. . . .

ROBERT E. AGGER, DANIEL GOLDRICH,
AND BERT E. SWANSON

The Scope of Government: The Core of Politics

. . . A government may be viewed at a moment in time as being
more or less involved in people's lives. We may picture two opposite
ideal states: one where there is no governmental functioning and
one where governmental functioning is ever-present or total. In
the one case private institutions meet all citizen needs; in the other
a total—totalitarian—government is the sole value-producing, dis-
tributing, and consuming institution. The first would best characterize a prepolitical society or community; the latter a postpolitical
one. Both societies or communities would actually be apolitical. In
order to evaluate the analysis that follows, it is essential to understand the rationale for the seeming paradox that these two opposites represent a single condition: the absence of politics.

. . . Political history may be viewed as a series of large or small
movements of government along a continuum of expansion and
contraction. Governments may move in one or the other direction
or they may alternate, making little net progress in either direction. The extremes of this continuum are situations in which
(1) there is no government activity and consequently no governmental intervention in the other institutions of organized life, and
(2) government is total. In the second case, government is so pervasive in the organized life of the community that its activities
cannot be distinguished from nongovernmental activities. At either
extreme, then, it would presumably be impossible, theoretically or
empirically, to characterize a functionally distinct government.

There are thus two ways to attain such an apolitical condition.
One is to reduce the functions of government; the other is to extend
them. The former alternative is preferred by some people who are
called reactionaries: they want to return to a previous era or to a
state of nature where government is minimal.[1] Most "romantic"
philosophical anarchists consider this the preferable path to a
society without government. Point *A* in Figure 1.1 represents this

FROM Robert Agger, Daniel Goldrich, and Bert E. Swanson, *The Rulers
and the Ruled* (New York: John Wiley & Sons, 1964), pp. 6–13, 93–98.

[1] A modern reactionary in this sense is Friedrich A. Hayek; see *The
Road to Serfdom* (Chicago: University of Chicago Press, 1944).

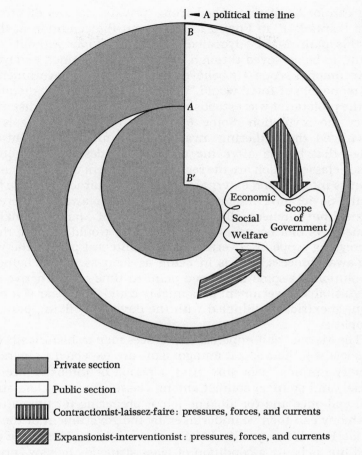

| ← A political time line

Private section

Public section

Contractionist-laissez-faire: pressures, forces, and currents

Expansionist-interventionist: pressures, forces, and currents

FIGURE 1.1   *Expansion-contraction Continuum of the*
Local Scope of Government

condition as a result of the contraction of the scope of local government.

If life in "nature" is not considered brutish, nasty, and short, if it is considered idyllic instead, the society is pictured as being cohesive and organic, without conflicting social divisions. Philosophical reactionaries may advocate doing away with social antagonisms by returning to the imagined social harmony of earlier epochs.

Other philosophical anarchists prefer the second path: the extension of the scope of government to the point where its functioning cannot be distinguished from "private" sectors of organized life. Points B–B' in Figure 1.1 represent the condition at the end of this path. Marx advocated a political utopia without government, to be achieved through a purposeful, planned extension of government's scope. He believed that the state or government with its monopoly of force would "wither away" when the dictatorship of the proletariat was established, rather than at some distant time after the revolution. Some Marxists, particularly Engels, have envisaged the withering away of government as an historical stage that begins after the dictatorship destroys economically based classes which are the reason government exists. Khrushchev blames internal and external capitalist conspiracies for the failure of the Soviet government to begin to wither away. A more paradoxical but intellectually consistent view of Marxist thinking, in some ways more consistent than Engels', would propose that the increasing scope of government is an integral part of the withering-away process, and is in being as soon as, if not before, the revolution. At some undefined point in time, a distinctive or distinguishable government presumably could disappear if it had become inextricably mingled with the day-to-day living patterns of people.

The Marxist philosophical school sees man as historically locked in social conflict. Social antagonisms are expected to increase as history unfolds; it is only after a period of intensive economic, social, and political conflict among classes that the class struggle will end once and for all. The job of preparing for utopian social harmony can then be undertaken by the government of the proletariat. Engels has qualified Marx's view of the beginnings of organized life as being a condition of class struggle: he saw "primeval communities" to be socially cohesive, cooperative, and harmonious.[2] The suggested model would be closer to Engels' than to Marx's view in that it indicates a return to a hypothetical earlier *agovernmental* condition by the juxtaposition or interpenetration of Points A and B–B' of Figure 1.1.

In order to understand national and international political movements in the nineteenth and twentieth centuries, this belief in the possibility of a withering-away of government by expanding

[2] Engels refers to the "natural simplicity" of such communities; he calls them "wonderful," "natural and spontaneous," and says they produce "splendid men and women." Frederick Engels, *The Origin of the Family, Private Property and the State* (Chicago: Charles H. Kerr & Co., Co-operative, 1902), pp. 117–119.

or contracting its net scope is of critical importance. Whether either alternative can be realized is irrelevant for the student of politics. But the existence of these as conceptual possibilities shapes the model of politics for the analyst of community, national, and international politics. Although it would be virtually impossible to reach either extreme, pressures for or actual movements in one direction or the other are possible; these pressures constitute part of the basic forces of politics, local or otherwise, whether or not so intended.

The analogue model of politics may be pictured in the following way. Local government, or any government, is considered to be located in a public space. The boundaries of this public space (curves A–B and A–B' on Figure 1.1) are represented by the extent to which government can actively function in the day-to-day lives of people. The activities of people may be viewed as a community space (the innermost and outermost circles). The private space is represented by the shaded portion of the total community space. In the public space are the currents, forces, or pressures directed toward moving government in the direction of expansion and intervention or that of contraction and laissez-faire, an increase or decrease in the scope of government. Movement in the former direction may result in a greater overlapping of the community space by the public space; movement in the latter direction may result in a relative decrease in the proportion of public to community space. This ratio of public to private space is what we mean by the words "net scope" of government.

The mixed public and private character of activities in which purposeful government regulation is a manifest factor makes any set of curves for such a model of the real world difficult to construct. Further conceptualization and research are needed to make such models more useful and to establish the character of general and particular social-psychological distinctions between governmental and private institutions, as well as the conditions under which such conceptions undergo various kinds of reorganization. It may or may not be that, in social-psychological terms, as government extends its programs into formerly nongovernmental areas and apparently moves toward points B–B', people extend their activities and, hence, community space, so that the ratio of public to private space remains relatively constant.

The action units in this model are people; it is the demands of people that constitute the pressures for a shift in government's scope. It is through the actions of government officials that shifts in local government's scope finally occur. A demand that government act in a particular way may be made by any unit or group of units—any private citizen or government official—in the political system.

Every demand that government act in one way rather than another, or that it function in some way different from the way it has in the past, is a pressure for a shift in government's scope. For example, people may demand a higher level of welfare services. This constitutes a pressure on government to expand. If such demands are made at a time when the level of government services has been declining, it is, nevertheless, a demand for a move back toward the expansionist pole. Suppose a person suggests that his street be paved and the community paves it instead of someone else's. This is not an increase in the net scope of government; the total street paving resources of government are held constant. But for the man whose street is paved, there has seemed to be an increase in government's scope. The scope actually has been balanced by a decrease for those others whose streets were not paved. The petitioner was, in effect, demanding an increased scope of government for himself, but the decisional outcome balanced this demand by reducing someone else's scope of government. Thus, the total or net scope of local government may remain the same, as a result of two, sometimes simultaneous, movements. Such decisional outcomes are regarded as changes in the scope of government wherein there is an *internal* although no *net* shift in scope.

Suppose a question arose as to whether local government ought to build a civic center. Those urging that this be done would be demanding an increased scope of government, whether it was a matter of replacing an existing facility that was in poor condition or in a poor location, or one of extending government's recreational functions. If the most appropriate location became a decisional question, the proponents of one or another site would be demanding that government increase its scope to satisfy *their* needs. In effect, they are saying that government will be serving them more fully by providing a convenient facility that will enable them to consume a greater amount of recreational resources than if the facility were located on some other site. If a proponent of one site asks that a civic center be built or moved there for aesthetic reasons or because it will take most people, but not himself, less time to reach the facility, his request is still a demand for an increased scope of government. Such a person would be urging government to expand its function to satisfy his aesthetic or altruistic need, needs as genuine as that for food.

Conflict may be generated by demands for an internal shift of government that would result in the deprivation of other citizens, or by demands that require a shift in the net scope of government. A demand for school desegregation is a case in point. Opposition to desegregation may be understood as opposition to the increased functioning of government to satisfy a multiplicity of needs of Negroes. Opponents of desegregation might cast the issue in terms of an undesirable increase in the net scope of government, or as a novel and unwarranted intervention of government in the social system. But since government has already exercised its authority to decide whose children should be educated, and how and where, these demands and counterdemands may be more appropriately viewed as involving a redistribution of government's need-satisfying functions, rather than a change in the ratio of public to private space. Only when there has been a change in the ratio of governmental to private satisfaction of human needs in the community has a net shift in scope occurred. If there is no such net shift, all other changes in the way government functions that result in the satisfaction of different needs of different people constitute internal shifts in the scope of local government.

What of demands to maintain the *status quo* rather than to expand or reduce the scope of government? Because of *status quo* demands, political decision making obviously may result in maintaining rather than changing the scope of government. Politics was broadly defined earlier as that aspect of life wherein certain people act to maintain or to shift what now may be referred to as the scope of government. If all demands were directed to the maintenance of an extant scope of government, this would presumably reflect a fundamental consensus. In this unlikely situation, politics would be present but it would be of a very special sort. Even in the absence of political decision making political demands can be made and political influence successfully exerted to maintain the scope of government. How long such a politics of consensus could endure in a modern, complex community is open to question.

The model of the political process encompasses demands for maintaining a given scope of government even though the demands may be outside a particular decision-making process; this may constitute an effective force for stasis in the body politic. Perhaps no broader definition of politics than that it is the web of political decision making is required to study the conditions that may result in decisional questions leading to conflict or triggering other decisional processes. However, to understand what conditions produce variations among or within communities in the content of decision making does require a broader definition. This definition includes action designed to increase or decrease general satisfaction with a current scope of government, even though no shifts in that scope have been or are currently being demanded. It is important that these definitions be clearly understood.

Some analysts of American politics view politics as the resolving of decisional issues or questions; others maintain that it encompasses the conditions that affect the raising of decisional issues and questions. Some analysts have maintained that American politics is characterized by a nearly unitary power structure wherein a relatively few like-minded men rule.[3] Others have countered by attempting to show that in the resolution of decisional controversies, the outcome is a function of compromise by numerous participants.[4] To some, the messages of the mass media and the propaganda of public relations specialists devoted to the glorification of the existing net scope of American government and the American way of life are the central facts of our politics. They presume that the exercise of political influence prevents demands for shifts in the scope of government and the appearance of radical alternatives. To others the influence of the media in particular decisional processes is relatively minor: they believe that the similarity in the various scopes of government that are subject to political decision making results from the character of modern industrial society and is not due to the manipulation of political consensus by a top power elite.

For example, the "ruling elite model" of American national and community politics offered by such analysts as C. Wright Mills and Floyd Hunter has been criticized by Robert Dahl on the ground that it has not been put to the test of empirical research. Dahl admits that the influence of a ruling elite over ideas, attitudes, and opinions can create "a kind of false consensus" and proposes that

[3] C. Wright Mills, *The Power Elite* (New York: Oxford University Press, 1956); Floyd Hunter, *Community Power Structure* (Chapel Hill: University of North Carolina Press, 1953); Andrew Hacker, "Liberal Democracy and Social Control," *The American Political Science Review*, Vol. LI, No. 4 (December 1957), pp. 1009–1025.

[4] Robert Dahl, "A Critique of the Ruling Elite Model," *The American Political Science Review*, Vol. LII, No. 2 (June 1958), pp. 463–469. See also David B. Truman, "The American System in Crisis," *Political Science Quarterly*, Vol. LXXIV, No. 4 (December 1959), 481–497.

this be tested in "a series of concrete cases where key decisions are made." Only in that way, he asserts, can it be determined whether one group initiates and vetoes while others merely respond to the leaders. However, he does not consider that political influence might be exercised so skillfully by the few that they succeed in averting demands for other scopes of government or in preventing such preferences from being pursued or strengthened to the point of becoming issues in "key decisions."

We would propose studies of influence relations in which it is recognized that the intentions of those attempting to influence others might be to prevent decisional questions from arising or to restrict the domain of decisional choices to a more or less acceptable few. The analyst should recognize that the absence of political decision making or the existence of a political decision-making process with one particular set of options rather than another might well be the result of political action on the part of a "ruling elite." Since the possibility of such situations may result from a variety of causes, including unintentional political consequences of non-political action, the problem of settling the question empirically is most complex. If we admit the possibility that political demands may be made to maintain a given scope of government and that the demands may not become part of a specific political decision-making process in the usual sense, the relative merits of pyramidal and pluralistic power structures become amenable to empirical tests.[5] Such issues are not likely to be resolved by empirical investigations unless and until a common definition of politics is agreed upon by those in dispute.

*　　*　　*

The Polyarchal Democracy

At this point, we must clarify the differences in orientation between the present study of democracy and the studies of pluralists. Important differences between their approach and ours may be misunderstood because of the many similarities in theoretical interests. We shall use the work of Robert Dahl, one of the most in-

[5] See Robert A. Dahl, *Who Governs?* (New Haven: Yale University Press, 1961), pp. 468–569. See also Robert Presthus, *Men at the Top: A Study in Community Power* (Oxford, Spring 1964); and Aaron Wildavsky, *Leadership in a Smalltown* (Bedminister Press, 1964).

fluential of that "school," to illustrate the difference in orientation.[6]

In constructing a theory of democracy, Dahl starts by treating

as a single class of phenomena all those nation states and social organizations that are commonly called democratic by political scientists, and by examining the members of this class to discover, first, the distinguishing characteristics they have in common, and, second, the necessary and sufficient conditions for social organizations possessing these characteristics.[7]

In dealing with all so-called democracies as actual democracies, Dahl and other pluralists run the risk of assuming that a characteristic common to all democracies is not shared by other political systems that are commonly thought to be oligarchies or dictatorships or to belong to a class of nondemocracies. Secondly, by putting all so-called democracies in a single class or category at the outset he creates a risk that those political systems or their subsystems—for example, communities with nation-states—will be thought to resemble each other more than they resemble purported nondemocracies. This may lead to a situation in which the degree to which they are democracies will be assumed without the necessary empirical study.

These considerations introduce the need for a comparison of those systems that political theorists have classified as democracies and those that have been called nondemocracies. It is useful to identify the similarities and differences between two such categories in order to derive and clarify criteria for classifying political systems, empirically and systematically, as democracies or nondemocracies. When these criteria have been established from the interplay of theoretical preferences and observations, they should be applied to determine the validity of the less systematic and more intuitive labeling that has already taken place. Then they can be used to classify polities that have not yet been labeled.

That pluralists sometimes do not systematize their criteria in this way can be illustrated by Dahl's discussion of Soviet and "Western" citizens.[8] Assuming that at least some Soviet citizens would prefer to vote against the ruling slate for a rival slate, they are said to be situated in a nondemocratic regime because a vote

---

[6] Dahl's major works in this connection include, with Charles A. Lindblom, *Politics, Economics, and Welfare,* his *A Preface to Democratic Theory,* and his *Who Governs?*

[7] Robert A. Dahl, *A Preface to Democratic Theory,* p. 63. Copyright 1956 by the University of Chicago.

[8] *Ibid.,* pp. 69–70.

against the ruling slate carries with it "living death in a concentration camp." In contrast, any American citizen "who perceives a set of alternatives, at least one of which he regards as preferable to any of the alternatives presently scheduled, can insert his preferred alternative(s) among those scheduled for voting," presumably without running such risks. The scheduling of such alternatives is regarded as one of the most important conditions of the type of democracy, termed "polyarchal" which describes the "normal American political process."

For the moment we can assume that in Dahl's view the probability that illegitimate sanctions will be applied is one of the criteria that differentiate democracies and oligarchies. He admits that no polity, including the United States, approaches the ideal; but he disposes of the problem that he notes is posed by the present situation of American Communists and by American Negroes "in the past" by defining American "polyarchal" democracy in a way that obscures the implied differences between the conditions of Soviet and American citizens.

Dahl defines the normal American political process, a polyarchal democracy, as "a political system in which all active and legitimate groups in the population can make themselves heard at some crucial stage in the process of decision."[9] Admitting that if a group is inactive it cannot be heard, Dahl maintains that there are still possibilities for that group to be represented in decision making. Active members may "include among their own goals the protection or advancement of inactive members"; active members may "expect that presently inactive members may become active in the future."[10] Thus, by the operation of what is termed "indirect influence" or, in our terms, the politically active according a positive political status to the inactive, the inactive may still get a hearing.

The inactivity of a group may be determined by "free choice, violence, intimidation, or law."[11] In the United States, Negroes in the past were, and Communists today are, presumably inactive not entirely out of free choice. Assuming that both legal prohibitions and informal intimidation operate to produce the inactivity, it is asserted that "Communists are not now a legitimate group." Their political activity is not "accepted as right and proper by a preponderant portion of the active." This does not violate democratic norms, it is contended, because such norms only hold for those

9 *Ibid.*, p. 137.
10 *Ibid.*, p. 138, fn. 15.
11 *Ibid.*, p. 138.

groups considered "legitimate"; even intimidated and outlawed groups such as Communists may become active by using or threatening "violence" or, in undefined ways, by "motivating the ingroups to incorporate the outgroup" and thus restore the legitimacy of the latter. Unfortunately, the same case may be made for the outgroups in the Soviet Union.[12]

What appeared to be a distinction between democracy and nondemocracy, based on the probability of whether the political leadership will use illegitimate sanctions or not, thus disappears. What was an attempt to argue that in a democracy there is no real danger of tyranny by majorities over minorities is disposed of by asserting that if the political activity of a minority is regarded as wrong and improper by a preponderant majority of the politically active, the minority does not possess minority rights in a democracy.

One of Dahl's key points is that in order to survive, such systems require an "underlying consensus on policy . . . among a predominant portion of the politically active members." Thus, although a minority rules in both a democracy and a dictatorship, "the characteristics of polyarchy greatly extend the number, size, and diversity of the minorities whose preferences will influence the outcome of governmental decisions." Dahl's argument that in polyarchal democracies "minorities" rule, even though these active groups must agree on some basic policy preferences, converts the problem of comparing polities on a democratic-dictatorial basis into an empirical question. He is aware of this when he recognizes that in some countries without a democratic electoral process the pre-electoral stage of decision making could be more democratic than that of the proverbial democracies, although he rejects the possibility on his assessment of the evidence.[13]

We are not suggesting that no important differences exist between the regimes in the United States and the Soviet Union. Compared to regimes in many other countries, all four of the present research communities are probably developed democracies, even though they seem to have very different types of regimes when compared only to one another. What needs to be understood is that if the dimensions used to classify regimes—such as whether citizen expectations that illegitimate sanctions will be used if they

[12] This is not to argue that the regimes in the United States and in the Soviet Union are equally democratic; rather it means that limiting the conception of democracy to "active and legitimate" groups begs rather than answers the question about the differences between such regimes.

[13] Dahl, *op. cit.*, pp. 66–67, fn. 2, and 132–133.

participate politically are valid or not—are assessed on the basis of the popular belief that a country or community is democratic or otherwise, empirical study becomes superfluous. If such dimensions are used initially to discriminate between types of regimes, but then regimes are classified in terms of power structures, it is impossible to empirically examine presumed relationships between regimes and power structures.[14]

Clearly, political status as it is accorded by political leaders—particularly elected officials—to active or inactive citizens is a most important variable in Dahl's conception of polyarchal democracy. A competitive electoral process in so-called democracies and its absence in so-called oligarchies or dictatorships makes such regime variables as the permeability or probability dimension seem relatively unimportant when Dahl discusses types of political systems. Nor should the end result of competition in polyarchy be minimized. According to Dahl, "continuous political competition among individuals, parties, or both" makes for the responsiveness of governmental leaders to nonleaders in such a way that "the distinction between democracy and dictatorship still makes sense."[15]

His basic argument that democracies are polities wherein active legitimate groups can make themselves "heard effectively at some crucial stage of decision" seems to rest on two lines of reasoning. First, even superficial observation suggests that in the United States "decisions are made by endless bargaining; perhaps in no other national political system in the world is bargaining so basic a component of the political process."[16] Secondly, the fact that there has been only one instance in which a minority felt itself so unheard and so disregarded by a majority—or by an authoritative minority—that it revolted leads to the assumption that, normally, minorities with intense feelings are heard. By "heard" Dahl means that "one or more officials are not only ready to listen to the noise, but expect to suffer in some significant way if they do not placate

---

[14] The authors feel that it is useful, for a variety of reasons, to distinguish between regimes and power structures until co-variations between and among them have been established empirically. We would call Dahl and Lindblom's characteristics #3 and #5 in their definition of polyarchy power-structure dimensions, and the other four characteristics regime dimensions. See *Politics, Economics, and Welfare*, p. 278.

[15] Robert A. Dahl, *A Preface to Democratic Theory*, p. 132. There is an important ambiguity in this stress on competition, given the stress on an underlying consensus on policy and an implied dislike of ideological competition on the part of pluralists generally.

[16] *Ibid.*, p. 150.

the group, its leaders, or its most vociferous members."[17] Thus, small groups are steadily "appeased." But at this point in Dahl's argument there is an important ambiguity. While Dahl states that a group may be satisfied by "expression of the appropriate emotions," his main argument seems to be that over a period of time it is probable that a group will receive some positive satisfactions through compromises and bargains over decisional outcomes. Such groups thus share in political power (our definition) and "minorities rule." If minorities do not exercise political influence effectively and acquire power by so doing, according to Dahl, they at least are accorded sufficient political status to prevent revolutions stemming from the disregard of their intense preferences by the majority.

The absence of revolution and the stability of the political system are high values to pluralist and to many nonpluralist democratic theorists, as well as to theorists of "dictatorship by the proletariat." They certainly are evidence that groups not heard do not revolt; but they are by no means evidence that groups necessarily are heard, in the sense apparently intended. Groups not only may be deactivated by illegitimate sanctions but they also may remain frustrated politically for very long periods of time. Groups that are so frustrated may even become apolitical; their intense preferences may become less intense as apathy sets in.[18] Although many pluralists, Dahl included, seem to take the position that minorities have a "right," natural or otherwise, to have their decisional preferences satisfied in a developed democracy, we do not assume this in our theoretical framework.[19] In the present study the degree to which minorities are heard, whether through the exercise of political influence or because of political status, is a political-system variable and needs to be investigated, even for developed democracies.[20] The absence of revolution does not indicate that

[17] *Ibid.*, p. 145.

[18] Robert C. Wood cites difficulties in maintaining competition and controversy in small towns as one of the reasons that democracy—as he and other pluralists define it—is difficult to develop or maintain there. See Wood, *Suburbia* (Boston: Houghton Mifflin, 1959).

[19] By limiting the term "democracy" to regimes, as defined, our theoretical framework in effect sets less stringent criteria for a developed democracy than do such analysts as Lasswell and Kaplan and Dahl and Lindblom.

[20] Although this is a difficult research problem, it is not the same as that raised by a number of political theorists when they talk of "individuality," "freedom," or "autonomy" as corollaries of democracy. Robert C. Wood, for example, in talking about the "quest for freedom," suggests that an important

broad policy consensus underlies minor differences in decisional preferences only in polyarchal democracies, in view of the absence of revolt in the Soviet Union. Not all minorities who feel deprived of their "natural rights" can or want to revolt. The possibility that, even in the absence of revolution, restricted or extensive policy consensus may exist should be explored in community studies in the United States. . . .

That groups are not heard directly, even in United States communities, may be inferred from various reports by journalists and social scientists. These journalists and social scientists have described some cities as "ruled by a small, entrenched economic-political oligarchy, which played rough with its foes and often winked at the trespasses and errors of its friends."[21] In this Texas city, now famous as the home of Billie Sol Estes, a person was reportedly fired from his job for his active opposition to the political leadership, while another was reportedly threatened that "the city administration [would] crack down on him on a flimsy ordinance-violation charge" unless he switched his advertising from an anti- to a pro-city-administration newspaper. In a California city in which one might not expect to find what some would dismiss as "Texas politics," a businessman reported that if he were quoted as saying anything against the man referred to by the writer as the community's "benevolent tyrant," he would probably lose his

───────────

ingredient of democracy is the ability of men to expand the number of alternative choices, to express and articulate individuality, and to engage in what might be called autonomous political action. Such political creativity or invention may be related to, but is something conceptually separate from, the matter of groups being "heard" or not in the formulation and communication of demands. These creative political acts should be explored to establish what kinds of political and nonpolitical individuality, freedom or autonomy are possible or are effected by different kinds of political regimes. To do this necessitates the creation of models of the individual participant as a potentially creative political person, but little has been done toward this end. A promising line of inquiry is the conceptualization of various politically relevant psychological traits of individuals, such as political efficacy, cynicism, alienation, authoritarianism, and the measurement thereof, with studies of the relationship between the frequency of such types of people or attributes and types of political systems. Perhaps it might be assumed that certain kinds of people (e.g., the highly inefficacious, etc.) are unlikely to engage in political creativity; but to assume that those more likely to create will do so under any political conditions is a matter that needs careful investigation. The often implicit assumption that democracies breed political creativity while nondemocracies breed political conformity would profit from such inquiry.

21 Fletcher Knebel, "The Predicament of Pecos, Texas," *Look Magazine,* July 31, 1962, pp. 76–78.

job the next day.[22] The Lynds reported in 1937 that in the mid-western city they call Middletown, there was probably some measure of truth in a businessman's statement: "If you don't join up with the inner ring, you can't work with them and you can't work against them, and you won't get the credit to run your business if they are not for you."[23] That "inner ring" did not refer to machine politicians, but to a family prominent in Middletown's business and social affairs. The Department of Justice in 1960 asked a federal court to grant an injunction against acts of "economic reprisal" by landowners, merchants, and bankers in one county of a Southern state against Negroes who had registered and voted in the November 1960 election. Among the acts intended to "threaten, intimidate, and coerce" Negro residents were:

Termination of leases or sharecrop arrangements; termination of employment of Negroes; refusals to sell necessities to them, even for cash; refusals to extend credit or lend them money; refusals to renew insurance policies; and circulating lists of Negro registrants to help merchants penalize them.

That such groups as American Negroes—and to some extent their primary antagonists, White Supremacists—still may not be "heard," even indirectly, is attested by the fact that in some communities they have resorted to civil disobedience, if not to revolution.[24] On occasion, groups may use abnormal channels of political participation, such as the sit-in, strike, and mass demonstration, to indicate that they feel they are not being heard adequately. Nor are these the only indications of a sense of low political status. Regardless of the trend wherein formerly outlawed groups have become more legitimized, communities in the United States may still differ considerably in the extent to which such groups are accorded political status and their political preferences taken into account, whether they are active or inactive.

[22] Time Magazine, November 17, 1961, pp. 40–41.
[23] R. S. and H. M. Lynd, Middletown in Transition (New York: Harcourt, Brace and Company, 1937), p. 79.
[24] For a description of illegitimate sanctions allegedly in use in Mississippi not so long ago, see Barbara Carter, "The Fifteenth Amendment Comes to Mississippi," The Reporter, January 17, 1963, pp. 20–24. Nor do we need to dwell on the murder of Medgar Evers and other Negro leaders and even Negro children.

23 ❧ TWO FACES OF POWER

PETER BACHRACH AND
MORTON S. BARATZ

The concept of power remains elusive despite the recent and prolific outpourings of case studies on community power. Its elusiveness is dramatically demonstrated by the regularity of disagreement as to the locus of community power between the sociologists and the political scientists. Sociologically oriented researchers have consistently found that power is highly centralized, while scholars trained in political science have just as regularly concluded that in "their" communities power is widely diffused.[1] Presumably, this explains why the latter group styles itself "pluralist," its counterpart "elitist."

There seems no room for doubt that the sharply divergent findings of the two groups are the product, not of sheer coincidence, but of fundamental differences in both their underlying assumptions and research methodology. The political scientists have contended that these differences in findings can be explained by the faulty approach and presuppositions of the sociologists. We contend in this paper that the pluralists themselves have not grasped the whole truth of the matter; that while their criticisms of the elitists are sound, they, like the elitists, utilize an approach and assumptions which predetermine their conclusions. Our argument is cast within the frame of our central thesis: that there are two faces of power, neither of which the sociologists see and only one of which the political scientists see.

From Peter Bachrach and Morton S. Baratz, "Two Faces of Power," *American Political Science Review*, 56 (December 1962), 947–952.

[1] Compare, for example, the sociological studies of Floyd Hunter, *Community Power Structure* (Chapel Hill, 1953); Roland Pellegrini and Charles H. Coates, "Absentee-Owned Corporations and Community Power Structure," *American Journal of Sociology*, Vol. 61 (March 1956), pp. 413–19; and Robert O. Schulze, "Economic Dominants and Community Power Structure," *American Sociological Review*, Vol. 23 (February 1958), pp. 3–9; with political science studies of Wallace S. Sayre and Herbert Kaufman, *Governing New York City* (New York, 1960); Robert A. Dahl, *Who Governs?* (New Haven, 1961); and Norton E. Long and George Belknap, "A Research Program on Leadership and Decision-Making in Metropolitan Areas" (New York, Governmental Affairs Institute, 1956). See also Nelson W. Polsby "How to Study Community Power: The Pluralist Alternative," *Journal of Politics*, Vol. 22 (August, 1960), pp. 474–84.

I

Against the elitist approach to power several criticisms may be, and have been leveled.[2] One has to do with its basic premise that in every human institution there is an ordered system of power, a "power structure" which is an integral part and the mirror image of the organization's stratification. This postulate the pluralists emphatically—and, to our mind, correctly—reject, on the ground that

nothing categorical can be assumed about power in any community. . . . If anything, there seems to be an unspoken notion among pluralist researchers that at bottom *nobody* dominates in a town, so that their first question is not likely to be, "Who runs this community?" but rather, "Does anyone at all run this community?" The first query is somewhat like, "Have you stopped beating your wife?" in that virtually any response short of total unwillingness to answer will supply the researchers with a "power elite" along the lines presupposed by the stratification theory.[3]

Equally objectionable to the pluralists—and to us—is the sociologists' hypothesis that the power structure tends to be stable over time.

Pluralists hold that power may be tied to issues, and issues can be fleeting or persistent, provoking coalitions among interested groups and citizens, ranging in their duration from momentary to semi-permanent. . . . To presume that the set of coalitions which exists in the community at any given time is a timelessly stable aspect of social structure is to introduce systematic inaccuracies into one's description of social reality.[4]

A third criticism of the elitist model is that it wrongly equates reputed with actual power:

If a man's major life work is banking, the pluralist presumes he will spend his time at the bank, and not in manipulating community decisions. This presumption holds until the banker's activities and participations indicate otherwise. . . . If we presume that the banker is "really" engaged in running the community, there is practically no way of disconfirming this notion, even if it is totally erroneous. On the other hand, it is easy to spot the banker who really *does* run community

---

[2] See especially N. W. Polsby, *op. cit.*, p. 475 f.
[3] *Ibid.*, p. 476.
[4] *Ibid.*, pp. 478–79.

affairs when we presume he does not, because his activities will make this fact apparent.[5]

This is not an exhaustive bill of particulars; there are flaws other than these in the sociological model and methodology[6]—including some which the pluralists themselves have not noticed. But to go into this would not materially serve our current purposes. Suffice it simply to observe that whatever the merits of their own approach to power, the pluralists have effectively exposed the main weaknesses of the elitist model.

As the foregoing quotations make clear, the pluralists concentrate their attention, not upon the sources of power, but its exercise. Power to them means "participation in decision-making"[7] and can be analyzed only after "careful examination of a series of concrete decisions."[8] As a result, the pluralist researcher is uninterested in the reputedly powerful. His concerns instead are to (a) select for study a number of "key" as opposed to "routine" political decisions, (b) identify the people who took an active part in the decision-making process, (c) obtain a full account of their actual behavior while the policy conflict was being resolved, and (d) determine and analyze the specific outcome of the conflict.

The advantages of this approach, relative to the elitist alternative, need no further exposition. The same may not be said, however, about its defects—two of which seem to us to be of fundamental importance. One is that the model takes no account of the fact that power may be, and often is, exercised by confining the scope of decision making to relatively "safe" issues. The other is that the model provides no *objective* criteria for distinguishing between "important" and "unimportant" issues arising in the political arena.

II

There is no gainsaying that an analysis grounded entirely upon what is specific and visible to the outside observer is more "scientific" than one based upon pure speculation. To put it another way:

[5] *Ibid.*, pp. 480–81.
[6] See especially Robert A. Dahl, "A Critique of the Ruling-Elite Model," *American Political Science Review*, Vol. 52 (June 1958), pp. 463–69; and Lawrence J. R. Herson, "In the Footsteps of Community Power," *American Political Science Review*, Vol. 55 (December 1961), pp. 817–31.
[7] This definition originated with Harold D. Lasswell and Abraham Kaplan, *Power and Society* (New Haven, 1950), p. 75.
[8] Robert A. Dahl, "A Critique of the Ruling-Elite Model," *loc. cit.*, p. 466.

If we can get our social life stated in terms of activity, and of nothing else, we have not indeed succeeded in measuring it, but we have at least reached a foundation upon which a coherent system of measurements can be built up. . . . We shall cease to be blocked by the intervention of unmeasurable elements, which claim to be themselves the real causes of all that is happening, and which by their spook-like arbitrariness make impossible any progress toward dependable knowledge.[9]

The question is, however, how can one be certain in any given situation that the "unmeasurable elements" are inconsequential, are not of decisive importance? Cast in slightly different terms, can a sound concept of power be predicated on the assumption that power is totally embodied and fully reflected in "concrete decisions" or in activity bearing directly upon their making?

We think not. Of course power is exercised when A participates in the making of decisions that affect B. But power is also exercised when A devotes his energies to creating or reinforcing social and political values and institutional practices that limit the scope of the political process to public consideration of only those issues which are comparatively innocuous to A. To the extent that A succeeds in doing this, B is prevented, for all practical purposes, from bringing to the fore any issues that might in their resolution be seriously detrimental to A's set of preferences.[10]

Situations of this kind are common. Consider, for example, the case—surely not unfamiliar to this audience—of the discontented faculty member in an academic institution headed by a tradition-bound executive. Aggrieved about a long-standing policy around which a strong vested interest has developed, the professor resolves in the privacy of his office to launch an attack upon the policy at the next faculty meeting. But, when the moment of truth is at hand, he sits frozen in silence. Why? Among the many possible reasons, one or more of these could have been of crucial im-

[9] Arthur Bentley, *The Process of Government* (Chicago, 1908), p. 202, quoted in Polsby, *op. cit.*, p. 481 n.

[10] As is perhaps self-evident, there are similarities in both faces of power. In each, A participates in decisions and thereby adversely affects B. But there is an important difference between the two: in the one case, A openly participates; in the other, he participates only in the sense that he works to sustain those values and rules of procedure that help him keep certain issues out of the public domain. True enough, participation of the second kind may at times be overt; that is the case, for instance, in cloture fights in the Congress. But the point is that it need not be. In fact, when the maneuver is most successfully executed, it neither involves nor can be identified with decisions arrived at on specific issues.

portance: (a) the professor was fearful that his intended action would be interpreted as an expression of his disloyalty to the institution; or (b) he decided that, given the beliefs and attitudes of his colleagues on the faculty, he would almost certainly constitute on this issue a minority of one; or (c) he concluded that, given the nature of the law-making process in the institution, his proposed remedies would be pigeonholed permanently. But whatever the case, the central point to be made is the same: to the extent that a person or group—consciously or unconsciously—creates or reinforces barriers to the public airing of policy conflicts, that person or group has power. Or, as Professor Schattschneider has so admirably put it:

All forms of political organization have a bias in favor of the exploitation of some kinds of conflict and the suppression of others because *organization is the mobilization of bias.* Some issues are organized into politics while others are organized out.[11]

Is such bias not relevant to the study of power? Should not the student be continuously alert to its possible existence in the human institution that he studies, and be ever prepared to examine the forces which brought it into being and sustain it? Can he safely ignore the possibility, for instance, that an individual or group in a community participates more vigorously in supporting the *non-decision-making* process than in participating in actual decisions within the process? Stated differently, can the researcher overlook the chance that some person or association could limit decision making to relatively noncontroversial matters, by influencing community values and political procedures and rituals, notwithstanding that there are in the community serious but latent power conflicts?[12] To do so is, in our judgment, to overlook the less apparent but nonetheless extremely important, face of power.

[11] E. E. Schattschneider, *The Semisovereign People* (New York, 1960), p. 71.

[12] Dahl *partially* concedes this point when he observes ("A Critique of the Ruling-Elite Model," pp. 468–69) that "one could argue that even in a society like ours a ruling elite might be so influential over ideas, attitudes, and opinions that a kind of false consensus will exist—not the phony consensus of a terroristic totalitarian dictatorship but the manipulated and superficially self-imposed adherence to the norms and goals of the elite by broad sections of a community. . . . This objection points to the need to be circumspect in interpreting the evidence." But that he largely misses our point is clear from the succeeding sentence: "Yet here, too, it seems to me that the hypothesis cannot be satisfactorily confirmed without something equivalent to the test I have proposed," and that is "by an examination of a series of concrete cases where key decisions are made. . . ."

III

In his critique of the "ruling-elite model," Professor Dahl argues that "the hypothesis of the existence of a ruling elite can be strictly tested only if . . . [t]here is a fair sample of cases involving key political decisions in which the preferences of the hypothetical ruling elite run counter to those of any other likely group that might be suggested."[13] With this assertion we have two complaints. One we have already discussed, *viz.*, in erroneously assuming that power is solely reflected in concrete decisions, Dahl thereby excludes the possibility that in the community in question there is a group capable of preventing contests from arising on issues of importance to it. Beyond that, however, by ignoring the less apparent face of power Dahl and those who accept his pluralist approach are unable adequately to differentiate between a "key" and a "routine" political decision.

Nelson Polsby, for example, proposes that "by pre-selecting as issues for study those which are generally agreed to be significant, pluralist researchers can test stratification theory."[14] He is silent, however, on how the researcher is to determine *what* issues are "generally agreed to be significant," and on how the researcher is to appraise the reliability of the agreement. In fact, Polsby is guilty here of the same fault he himself has found with elitist methodology: by presupposing that in any community there are significant issues in the political arena, he takes for granted the very question which is in doubt. He accepts as issues what are reputed to be issues. As a result, his findings are foreordained. For even if there is no "truly" significant issue in the community under study, there is every likelihood that Polsby (or any like-minded researcher) will find one or some and, after careful study, reach the appropriate pluralistic conclusions.[15]

Dahl's definition of "key political issues" in his essay on the ruling-elite model is open to the same criticism. He states that it is "a necessary although possibly not a sufficient condition that the [key] issue should involve actual disagreement in preferences among two or more groups."[16] In our view, this is an inadequate characterization of a "key political issue," simply because groups

[13] *Op. cit.*, p. 466.
[14] *Op. cit.*, p. 478.
[15] As he points out, the expectations of the pluralist researchers "have seldom been disappointed." (*Ibid.*, p. 477.)
[16] *Op. cit.*, p. 467.

can have disagreements in preferences on unimportant as well as on important issues. Elite preferences which border on the indifferent are certainly not significant in determining whether a monolithic or polylithic distribution of power prevails in a given community. Using Dahl's definition of "key political issues," the researcher would have little difficulty in finding such in practically any community; and it would not be surprising then if he ultimately concluded that power in the community was widely diffused.

The distinction between important and unimportant issues, we believe, cannot be made intelligently in the absence of an analysis of the "mobilization of bias" in the community; of the dominant values and the political myths, rituals, and institutions which tend to favor the vested interests of one or more groups, relative to others. Armed with this knowledge, one could conclude that any challenge to the predominant values or to the established "rules of the game" would constitute an "important" issue; all else, unimportant. To be sure, judgments of this kind cannot be entirely objective. But to avoid making them in a study of power is both to neglect a highly significant aspect of power and thereby to undermine the only sound basis for discriminating between "key" and "routine" decisions. In effect, we contend, the pluralists have made each of these mistakes; that is to say, they have done just that for which Kaufman and Jones so severely taxed Floyd Hunter: they have begun "their structure at the mezzanine without showing us a lobby or foundation,"[17] *i.e.*, they have begun by studying the issues rather than the values and biases that are built into the political system and that, for the student of power, give real meaning to those issues which do enter the political arena.

IV

There is no better fulcrum for our critique of the pluralist model than Dahl's recent study of power in New Haven.[18]

At the outset it may be observed that Dahl does not attempt in this work to define his concept, "key political decision." In asking whether the "Notables" of New Haven are "influential overtly or covertly in the making of government decisions," he simply states that he will examine "three different 'issue-areas' in which im-

[17] Herbert Kaufman and Victor Jones, "The Mystery of Power," *Public Administration Review*, Vol. 14 (Summer 1954), p. 207.
[18] Robert A. Dahl, *Who Governs?* (New Haven, 1961).

portant public decisions are made: nominations by the two political parties, urban redevelopment, and public education." These choices are justified on the grounds that "nominations determine which persons will hold public office. The New Haven redevelopment program measured by its cost—present and potential—is the largest in the country. Public education, aside from its intrinsic importance, is the costliest item in the city's budget." Therefore, Dahl concludes, "It is reasonable to expect . . . that the relative influence over public officials wielded by the . . . Notables would be revealed by an examination of their participation in these three areas of activity."[19]

The difficulty with this latter statement is that it is evident from Dahl's own account that the Notables are in fact uninterested in two of the three "key" decisions he has chosen. In regard to the public school issue, for example, Dahl points out that many of the Notables live in the suburbs and that those who do live in New Haven choose in the main to send their children to private schools. "As a consequence," he writes, "their interest in the public schools is ordinarily rather slight."[20] Nominations by the two political parties as an important "issue-area," is somewhat analogous to the public schools, in that the apparent lack of interest among the Notables in this issue is partially accounted for by their suburban residence—because of which they are disqualified from holding public office in New Haven. Indeed, Dahl himself concedes that with respect to both these issues the Notables are largely indifferent: "Business leaders might ignore the public schools or the political parties without any sharp awareness that their indifference would hurt their pocketbooks . . ." He goes on, however, to say that

the prospect of profound changes [as a result of the urban-redevelopment program] in ownership, physical layout, and usage of property in the downtown area and the effects of these changes on the commercial and industrial prosperity of New Haven were all related in an obvious way to the daily concerns of businessmen.[21]

Thus, if one believes—as Professor Dahl did when he wrote his critique of the ruling-elite model—that an issue, to be considered as important, "should involve actual disagreement in preferences among two or more groups,"[22] then clearly he has now for all practical purposes written off public education and party nominations

19 *Ibid.*, p. 64.
20 *Ibid.*, p. 70.
21 *Ibid.*, p. 74.
22 *Op. cit.*, p. 467.

as key "issue areas." But this point aside, it appears somewhat dubious at best that "the relative influence over public officials wielded by the Social Notables" can be revealed by an examination of their nonparticipation in areas in which they were not interested.

Furthermore, we would not rule out the possibility that even on those issues to which they appear indifferent, the Notables may have a significant degree of *indirect* influence. We would suggest, for example, that although they send their children to private schools, the Notables do recognize that public school expenditures have a direct bearing upon their own tax liabilities. This being so, and given their strong representation on the New Haven Board of Finance,[23] the expectation must be that it is in their direct interest to play an active role in fiscal policy making, in the establishment of the educational budget in particular. But as to this, Dahl is silent: he inquires not at all into either the decisions made by the Board of Finance with respect to education nor into their impact upon the public schools.[24] Let it be understood clearly that in making these points we are not attempting to refute Dahl's contention that the Notables lack power in New Haven. What we *are* saying, however, is that this conclusion is not adequately supported by his analysis of the "issue-areas" of public education and party nominations.

The same may not be said of redevelopment. This issue is by any reasonable standard important for purposes of determining whether New Haven is ruled by "the hidden hand of an economic elite."[25] For the Economic Notables have taken an active interest in the program and, beyond that, the socioeconomic implications of it are not necessarily in harmony with the basic interests and values of businesses and businessmen.

In an effort to ensure that the redevelopment program would be acceptable to what he dubbed "the biggest muscles" in New Haven,

[23] *Who Governs?*, p. 82. Dahl points out that "the main policy thrust of the Economic Notables is to oppose tax increases; this leads them to oppose expenditures for anything more than minimal traditional city services. In this effort their two most effective weapons ordinarily are the mayor and the Board of Finance. The policies of the Notables are most easily achieved under a strong mayor if his policies coincide with theirs or under a weak mayor if they have the support of the Board of Finance. . . . New Haven mayors have continued to find it expedient to create confidence in their financial policies among businessmen by appointing them to the Board" (pp. 81–82).

[24] Dahl does discuss in general terms (pp. 79–84) changes in the level of tax rates and assessments in past years, but not actual decisions of the Board of Finance or their effects on the public school system.

[25] *Ibid.*, p. 124.

Mayor Lee created the Citizens Action Commission (CAC) and appointed to it primarily representatives of the economic elite. It was given the function of overseeing the work of the mayor and other officials involved in redevelopment, and, as well, the responsibility for organizing and encouraging citizens' participation in the program through an extensive committee system.

In order to weigh the relative influence of the mayor, other key officials, and the members of the CAC, Dahl reconstructs "all the *important* decisions on redevelopment and renewal between 1950–58 . . . [to] determine which individuals most often initiated the proposals that were finally adopted or most often successfully vetoed the proposals of the others."[26] The results of this test indicate that the mayor and his development administrator were by far the most influential, and that the "muscles" on the commission, excepting in a few trivial instances, "never directly initiated, opposed, vetoed, or altered any proposal brought before them. . . ."[27]

This finding is, in our view, unreliable, not so much because Dahl was compelled to make a subjective selection of what constituted *important* decisions within what he felt to be an *important* "issue-area," as because the finding was based upon an excessively narrow test of influence. To measure relative influence solely in terms of the ability to initiate and veto proposals is to ignore the possible exercise of influence or power in limiting the scope of initiation. How, that is to say, can a judgment be made as to the relative influence of Mayor Lee and the CAC without knowing (through prior study of the political and social views of all concerned) the proposals that Lee did *not* make because he anticipated that they would provoke strenuous opposition and, perhaps, sanctions on the part of the CAC?[28]

[26] *Ibid.* "A rough test of a person's overt or covert influence," Dahl states in the first section of the book, "is the frequency with which he successfully initiates an important policy over the opposition of others, or vetoes policies initiated by others, or initiates a policy where no opposition appears" (*Ibid.*, p. 66).

[27] *Ibid.*, p. 131.

[28] Dahl is, of course, aware of the "law of anticipated reactions." In the case of the mayor's relationship with the CAC, Dahl notes that Lee was "particularly skillful in estimating what the CAC could be expected to support or reject" (p. 137). However, Dahl was not interested in analyzing or appraising to what extent the CAC limited Lee's freedom of action. Because of his restricted concept of power, Dahl did not consider that the CAC might in this respect have exercised power. That the CAC did not initiate or veto actual proposals by the mayor was to Dahl evidence enough that the CAC was virtually powerless; it might as plausibly be evidence that the CAC was (in itself or in what it represented) so powerful that Lee ventured nothing it would find worth quarreling with.

In sum, since he does not recognize *both* faces of power, Dahl is in no position to evaluate the relative influence of power of the initiator and decision maker, on the one hand, and of those persons, on the other, who may have been indirectly instrumental in preventing potentially dangerous issues from being raised.[29] As a result, he unduly emphasizes the importance of initiating, deciding, and vetoing, and in the process casts the pluralist conclusions of his study into serious doubt.

V

We have contended in this paper that a fresh approach to the study of power is called for, an approach based upon a recognition of the two faces of power. Under this approach the researcher would begin—not, as does the sociologist who asks, "Who rules?" nor as does the pluralist who asks, "Does anyone have power?"— but by investigating the particular "mobilization of bias" in the institution under scrutiny. Then, having analyzed the dominant values, the myths, and the established political procedures and rules of the game, he would make a careful inquiry into which persons or groups, if any, gain from the existing bias and which, if any, are handicapped by it. Next, he would investigate the dynamics of *nondecision making;* that is, he would examine the extent to which and the manner in which the *status quo* oriented persons and groups influence those community values and those political institutions (as, *e.g.,* the unanimity "rule" of New York City's Board of Estimate[30]) which tend to limit the scope of actual decision making to "safe" issues. Finally, using his knowledge of the restrictive face of power as a foundation for analysis and as a

[29] The fact that the initiator of decisions also refrains—because he anticipates adverse reactions—from initiating other proposals does not obviously lessen the power of the agent who limited his initiative powers. Dahl missed this point: "It is," he writes, "all the more improbable, then, that a secret cabal of Notables dominates the public life of New Haven through means so clandestine that not one of the fifty prominent citizens interviewed in the course of this study—citizens who had participated extensively in various decisions—hinted at the existence of such a cabal . . ." (p. 185).

In conceiving of elite domination exclusively in the form of a conscious cabal exercising the power of decision making and vetoing, he overlooks a more subtle form of domination; one in which those who actually dominate are not conscious of it themselves, simply because their position of dominance has never seriously been challenged.

[30] Sayre and Kaufman, *op. cit.,* p. 640. For perceptive study of the "mobilization of bias" in a rural American community, see Arthur Vidich and Joseph Bensman, *Small Town in Mass Society* (Princeton, 1958).

standard for distinguishing between "key" and "routine" political decisions, the researcher would, after the manner of the pluralists, analyze participation in decision making of concrete issues.

We reject in advance as unimpressive the possible criticism that this approach to the study of power is likely to prove fruitless because it goes beyond an investigation of what is objectively measurable. In reacting against the subjective aspects of the sociological model of power, the pluralists have, we believe, made the mistake of discarding "unmeasurable elements" as unreal. It is ironical that, by so doing, they have exposed themselves to the same fundamental criticism they have so forcefully leveled against the elitists: their approach to and assumptions about power predetermine their findings and conclusions.

24 🕊 THE PLURALIST FRAMEWORK

ROBERT PRESTHUS

Two questions dominate contemporary research on community power structure. One is the question of the meaning and the proper measurement of power. Ironically, empirical field research in this area has not been guided by any consistent conceptualization or theory about the nature of power. The second germinal question is the extent to which existing systems of community decision making approximate democratic values of pluralism, of widely shared power and participation in major community issues. . . .

Some Observations on Community Power

Theoretical conceptions of power are notoriously unsatisfactory. The concept of power is central to social analysis, yet it remains vague and abstract, with the result that empirical research has suffered from a lack of direction and agreement upon the nature of the phenomenon being studied. A good example of this is seen in the differing approaches of political scientists and sociologists to the question of power. As Dennis Wrong has noted, the latter tend to envisage power as an attribute of social or collective relationships, whereas the former tend to define it in highly individual terms, as if it were an absolute quality possessed by a leader with much less reference to the situation in which his power is brought to bear.[1]

These divergences result in a good deal of polemical talking-past-each-other, often seeking to justify one or another approach rather than moving toward more rigorous theoretical formulations that can provide better guides for empirical research. We hope to avoid this posture. Armed with the accumulated research of community power studies, with existing methodological experience, and realizing the need to get beyond data-free debate, we will try here to take a small step forward. Our first task is to set down a theoretical approach to community power . . .

Max Weber defined power as the chances of "a man or group of men to realize their own will," even against opposition.[2] He did not, it should be noted, include the capacity to gain one's ends all the time on every issue. Instead, he speaks of the "chance," the probability of such, thus avoiding what seems to be an unduly stringent requirement that even the most arbitrary and powerful elite could not meet. Weber's emphasis upon *opposition* is also a critical factor; it not only sharpens the test of power, but postulates an essential condition of pluralism, namely that opposition to an elite is the best test of the existence of competing centers of power.

However, one shortcoming of Weber's definition is that in focusing upon the individual aspects of power, it neglects, to some extent, its more important *social* dimensions. This is a crucial omission, for even though the power of individuals *qua* individuals can be empirically determined, such an emphasis overlooks two vital characteristics of power. One is that individual power is always worked out within some larger framework of institutional power. Even Robinson Crusoe's relations with Friday faced this

---

[1] Review of *Power and Democracy in America*, eds. W. V. D'Antonio and H. J. Ehrlich, 28 *American Sociological Review* (February, 1963), pp. 144–5; for attempts to conceptualize power systematically, see R. A. Dahl, "A Critique of the Ruling Elite Model," 52 *American Political Science Review* (June, 1958), pp. 463–9; and F. Oppenheim, "Degrees of Power and Freedom," 54 *American Political Science Review* (June, 1960), pp. 437–46.

[2] *From Max Weber: Essays in Sociology*, eds. H. H. Gerth and C. W. Mills (New York: Oxford University Press, 1946), p. 180.

imperative. Men are powerful *in relation* to other men. The other fact is that the power of any given individual is in large measure a result of his ability to manipulate this larger system.

. . . We shall conceptualize power as a system of social relationships. This presupposes in every community a certain ongoing network of fairly stable subsystems, activated by social, economic, ethnic, religious, and friendship ties and claims. Such systems of interest, values, and power have desirable consequences for their members to the extent that they satisfy various human needs. In a sense, however, such subsystems are suprahuman, in that they tend to persist indefinitely and, more important, that their members may change but the underlying network of interrelated interests and power relations continues. The United States Senate provides an example of such an institutional system. It is a body with venerable customs, traditions, expectations, and rules that provide a given structure *within which* its members must learn to act. If they achieve and retain power as individuals, they do so within and through this larger social apparatus. Without the ability to form coalitions with like-minded colleagues, to avoid fracturing the prestige aspirations, seniority-based assignments and prerogatives, as well as the latent political commitments of their fellow members, no individual Senator can become powerful. In a word, his own power and effectiveness are inherently bound up in a social interpersonal system, with its own complex rules and expectations.

In community political life it seems that a similar conception of power may help us give order and meaning to our mass of empirical data. We will look for discrete, yet overlapping, constellations of power, each with a major *raison d'être,* comprising individuals who share common social interests and attributes institutionalized in a given subsystem. We shall not, of course, find that such a subsystem is composed of homogeneous members fully committed to its norms, but rather that individuals have several overlapping group memberships, each of which tends to meet one or another of their varied interests—political, economic, ethnic, cultural, and so on. Simply put, individuals of similar interests combine to achieve their ends, and such combinations of interlaced values and interests form subsystems of power. The community is composed of a congeries of such subsystems, now cooperating, now competing, now engaged, now moribund, in terms of the rise and fall of local issues. Some subsystems are more powerful than others; some are transitory; others persist, one supposes, because the interests which they institutionalize are persistent.

Such a concept should help us understand why systems of power based upon mutual economic interests seem more durable than most, and hence have a greater power potentiality than purely "political" organizations, which are less likely to inspire the sustained interest and identification of their members. As political scientists, we would like to think that political issues and elections are equally compelling, but a review of the relative number of organizations, *i.e.*, subsystems of power, that serve the two interests suggest the futility of this preference.

The empirical implications of such a theory of community power include the need to redefine the meaning of the variables upon which research focuses. Thus the power disposed of by any given individual must be viewed less as an index of *personal* power than as an indicator of the existence of the social subsystems of power to which he belongs and from which, in some such manner as outlined above, he derives "his" power. As Hunter concludes, the "power of the individual must be structured into associations, cliques, or institutional patterns to be effective."[3] If individuals typically attribute great power to economic leaders in the community, we may assume that this is because such leaders personify an ongoing system of power and interest relationships that are vital in the total apparatus of community life. Today the *primary* factor in assigning class status is typically occupational role. Class status is not mainly differentiated according to individual attributes of age, charm, political values, or any of a battery of other conceivable indexes; but instead one's role in the occupational arena is critical.

Obviously, power is attributed to individuals in any community on other bases than economic or occupational role, but it is interesting to note how often the bases for such attributions are honorific legitimations of economic status. A nice continuity often exists between an individual's official role in service, welfare, school board, and hospital board organizations and his economic role in the community. Such continuities emphasize the centrality and durability of power based upon this sector of community social systems.

. . . We will try to point up the relevance of this essentially social

[3] Floyd Hunter, *Community Power Structure* (Chapel Hill: University of North Carolina Press, 1953), p. 6.

or institutional, as distinct from a purely individual, conception of community power. We shall probably find that individuals form coalitions with those of similar social and economic character and that the power of any given leader is in good part a function of the extent to which he is integrated into such coalitions. At the present time, the ability to command such resources often rests upon access and alliances that a local leader has with state and national systems of political and economic power. His "personal" resources, in this sense, become the commitments he can make of the economic, organizational, and prestige resources of one or another of such systems. His own power rests essentially upon his associations with various collective systems of power; without such alliances and reservoirs, he would not be deemed powerful.

In this context, we shall look for the social and economic bases upon which individual power rests. We will analyze community power through individuals, but we must go beyond this level of analysis to determine the larger, more permanent structure of *social* power within and outside the community. This should enable us to provide a more comprehensive explanation of power at the community level.

Community Power Structure and Pluralism

As noted earlier, community power-structure research has been characterized by opposing assumptions and findings. Whereas sociologists have usually found an "elitist" leadership structure, political scientists have often found a "pluralistic" system in which power is shared among several competing groups. Where the former have assumed and found that economic resources provide the critical basis of community power, the latter have assumed and found that power has many bases, each of which tends to be decisive in a given substantive area. In both cases, it seems, ideology is at work, with sociologists finding that political behavior often fails to conform to traditional social and political values, and political scientists supporting the view that mobility, equality, and pluralism are characteristic of current political systems. Both believe in democratic values and procedure per se, but they often differ as to the extent to which contemporary institutions honor them.

*   *   *

The small community is a useful point at which to test assumptions about the democratic political process.[4] Barriers of size, complexity, and organization that characterize state and national politics are largely absent, or are certainly less formidable. Here, at the "grass roots," meaningful participation would seem to have the best chance to occur. Indeed, the German sociologist Tönnies uses the very term "community," *Gemeinschaft*, to define a type of society based primarily upon the values of friendships, neighborliness, and blood relationships, all of which are ingredients of the "natural will" which he contrasts with the "rational will" found in *Gesellschaft*.[5] The latter is characteristic of modern bureaucratized societies, and there seems little doubt that Max Weber's later conceptions of "patrimonial," "patriarchal," and "bureaucratic" types of organization were inspired by Tönnie's dichotomy. In sum, the community level provides the most favorable environment for the realization of democratic values of participation and pluralism. The opposing ideology of elitism with its pessimistic themes of mass powerlessness and alienation has usually been an urban phenomenon. For elitism connotes huge size, impersonal relationships, and violent individualism, with every man seeking his own limited ends.

Democratic theory has always been concerned with these matters. From the time of the Greeks on, philosophers have set limits to the size of their ideal political communities. Aristotle insisted that "in order to do civic business properly, the citizens of a state should know one another personally."[6] Only then were a consensus and a constitution possible. Early critics of "mass democracy" rested their case in part upon the sheer size and numbers of modern society, and the consequent difficulty of achieving a feeling of community among its members. A similar concern persists in the United States today, symbolized by antitrust legislation and the ambivalence with which huge organizations are regarded.

[4] The "political process" is defined throughout to include *all* community decisions that involve the allocation of important resources. Thus the bringing in of a new industry, even though it primarily involves economic values, is viewed as a political transaction. We are concerned more with the *process* of negotiation, bargaining, compromise, and conflict whereby decisions are made than with their substantive content.

[5] F. Tönnies, *Community and Association*, trans. by C. P. Loomis (London: Routledge and Kegan Paul, Ltd., 1955), pp. 37-9.

[6] *Politics*, Chap. IV.

The Meaning of Pluralism

There has been a curious reluctance on the part of scholars precisely to define "pluralism." Perhaps it is one of those terms one takes for granted. It is defined here as a sociopolitical system in which the power of the state is shared with a large number of private groups, interest organizations, and individuals represented by such organizations. The ultimate philosophical justification for pluralism lies in natural law, in the belief that the individual's right of free association emanates from God. In brief, pluralism is a system in which political power is fragmented among the branches of government; it is moreover shared between the state and a multitude of private groups and individuals. "Elitism," which we may define as its antithesis, is a system in which disproportionate power rests in the hands of a minority of the community.[7] No invidious connotation need be attached to the term. As E. H. Carr has noted, elites are in part a product of full-blown democracy: "Mass democracy has, through its very nature, thrown up on all sides specialized groups of leaders—what are sometimes called elites. Everywhere, in government, in political parties, in trade unions, in co-operatives, these indispensable elites have taken shape with startling rapidity."[8] The traditional problem of controlling the power of such leaders in a *political* context has been magnified in modern society by this proliferation of power centers, which again makes clear why students of politics cannot confine themselves to "purely" political forms of power.

The more highly differentiated structure of modern society results in elites, which tend to become separated from the members of their various groups both by their interest in maintaining themselves in power and by the demands of technology and strategy which require secrecy, dispatch, flexibility, and skills generally not characteristic of mass behavior. Although the opposite is frequently implied, elitism is not limited to arbitrary forms of government or politically underdeveloped societies, but is more likely to occur under such conditions. As Pareto said, "Every people is

---

[7] Technically, the antithesis of pluralism is "monism," which from Aristotle to Bentham has meant that the state is the highest sovereign power, to which all its constituent associations are legally and ethically subordinate. For our purposes, however, it is more useful to use the term "elitist" since it relates less to the legal and institutional aspects of the state and more to the leadership processes by which it is governed. And, of course, it has become part of the vocabulary of community power research.

[8] *The New Society* (London: Macmillan and Co., Ltd., 1956), p. 77.

governed by an elite."[9] The crucial matter is the openness of the elite, the ends to which its power are devoted, the means used to achieve them, and the methods available to the mass for changing and controlling it. In this study, we shall conceptualize elites as minorities of specialized leaders who enjoy disproportionate amounts of power in community affairs.

At the outset, a brief definition of "participation" is also required. This concept means more than mere voting; it includes playing an active, though not necessarily direct, role in community decisions, some knowledge of local issues, attendance at public meetings, and related attempts to influence proposed measures through individual and group action. In research terms, "participation" is viewed here as an *indicator* of pluralism, as an instrument by which pluralism in a community may be measured, however roughly. Participation, in turn, is defined by several indicators, including voting, attending public meetings, and belonging to groups and committees.

Since the ideal and the reality of "pluralism" are our major concern, we must first trace its historical antecedents. We will find that the meaning of pluralism has changed over time and, indeed, that it is used in a somewhat traditional sense in this study which attempts to retain some of its historical emphasis upon the individual.

Modern democratic societies are generally believed to be pluralistic to the extent that governmental power and influence over important public decisions are broadly shared with a great number of private organizations. Many of these organizations are "extraofficial." They have neither legal nor constitutional status but instead exercise their influence on government informally. Using many paths of access, they apply pressure in an attempt to shape proposed actions to their own design. Obviously, no group succeeds in achieving its preferences all the time, nor are all groups equally concerned with all issues. Instead, each bargains and marshals its resources to do battle on those issues that impinge upon its own interests. A myriad of tactics is used in such struggles, including exchange, in which one group supports another on one issue, in return for which it receives support on another issue of vital importance to itself. We are told, for example, that in 1962 the American Medical Association offered its support to the National Chamber of Commerce against federal aid to education, in

9 V. Pareto, *Mind and Society* (New York: Harcourt, Brace, and Co., 1935), p. 246.

return for which the Chamber agreed to back the Association in its opposition to federal medical care legislation.

Such activities of voluntary organizations are widely viewed as the essence of democratic pluralism. Moreover, it is not only proper but *necessary* for private groups to influence public policy. As Durkheim maintains:

> Collective activity is always too complex to be able to be expressed through the single and unique organ of the state. Moreover, the state is too remote from individuals, its relations with them too external and intermittent to penetrate deeply within individual consciences and socialize them within. When the state is the only environment in which men can live communal lives, they inevitably lose contact, become detached and society disintegrates. A nation can be maintained only if, between the state and the individual, there is intercalated a whole series of secondary groups near enough to the individuals to attract them strongly in their sphere of action and drag them, in this way, into the general torrent of social life.[10]

Through their leaders, such groups mediate between individuals and all organized forms of power. In this way, government is kept close to the people, and decisions benefit from the skill and interest which such groups provide. The resulting atomization of governmental power is usually regarded with approval. It ensures the "representation" of affected interests, gives private citizens a voice in government, eases consensus, and so on. As Harold Laski, a sophisticated (although temporary) advocate of pluralism, said: "We have found that a state in which sovereignty is unified is morally inadequate and administratively inefficient."[11] The only remedy for this monistic state, which "results in apoplexy at the

---

[10] *The Division of Labor* (Glencoe: Free Press, 1947), p. 28; this conception of pluralism as a system in which membership in politically relevant subgroups is essential to the preservation of democratic processes, is central in a careful study of the typographers union. "Democratic rights have developed in societies largely through the struggles of various groups—class religious, sectional, economic, professional, and so on—against one another and against the group which controls the state. Each interest group may desire to carry out its own will, but if no one group is strong enough to gain complete power, the result is the development of tolerance." S. M. Lipset, M. Trow, J. Coleman, *Union Democracy* (New York: Doubleday and Co., 1962), pp. 15–16. A similarly positive conception of voluntary groups was expressed by A. F. Bentley in his early classic, *The Process of Government* (Chicago: University of Chicago Press, 1908). He believed that government represented "absent or quiescent" groups, and that the usurpation of "objectionable" power by any constellation of group interests brought the formation of new group interests to oppose them, pp. 454–5. This rationale is similar to the current "countervailing power" thesis.

[11] *Foundations of Sovereignty* (New Haven: Yale University Press, 1931), p. vi.

center and anaemia at the extremities," is widespread participation in governmental affairs by individuals and groups of many kinds regardless of their property interest. There must be competing organizations that challenge the power and authority which the modern Leviathan has gathered to itself. Pluralism is characterized by the changing alignments of such groups on changing issues. In effect, the constant structuring and restructuring of power ensure that the political process will be marked by considerable fluidity and variety.

Laski's views are based upon historical political theory, and particularly upon a well-known sixteenth-century tract, *Vindiciae Contra Tyrannos*. Perhaps the clearest expression of Laski's own views on pluralism is set down in his introduction to this noted work, which denied the omnipotence of the state and its rulers in order to make possible some measures of religious freedom for Huguenots in Catholic France.[12] From a modern perspective, the *Vindiciae Contra Tyrannos* appears aristocratic and quite unconcerned with individual rights, but it had wide contemporary repercussions on the Continent and in England as well. Although the author's main concern was for religious toleration, he made a case for the contract theory of government, which in turn was incorporated in the later writings of Rousseau and Locke, and through them, in the political values of those who wrote the American Constitution.

The origins of the pluralist rationale probably lie far back in history. Pluralism is inspired by the ancient fear of government, which results from impersonal, arbitrary rule, and by the reluctant conclusion that power corrupts in geometric progression as it grows. The possibility of curbing government's excessive demands by fragmenting its power was recognized as early as the Greek city-states. Aristotle, for example, believed that revolutions were caused by narrowing too much the circle of government; in effect, they followed when power and its prerequisites were limited to a single circle. He noted, too, that stability, the aim of every form of government, requires balance among its various parts.[13]

This fearful conception of governmental power which underlies pluralism is clear in our own Constitution and in the American tendency to interpret it *negatively,* as a limitation upon government rather than as an instrument which grants great power to it. The Founding Fathers' pervasive fear of government is explicit in

[12] S. J. Brutus (pseudonym), *A Defense of Liberty Against Tyrants,* Introduction by H. J. Laski (London: A. Bell and Sons, Ltd., 1924).
[13] *Politics,* 1306–13.

their efforts to limit its power. As a result, Madison, who was almost surely influenced by the *Vindiciae Contra Tyrannos*, set down a classic defense of pluralism in *The Federalist*, No. 10. The institutionalization of this view is seen in our "separation of powers" system and its checks and balances which doubly ensure that government can act expeditiously only in crises. Power is shared among the three great branches, each of which, in turn, exercises some portion of the specific power mainly allocated to the others.

Modern conceptions of pluralism, however, reflect the rise of industrial society, in which every other interest tends to be subordinate to *raisons d'état*. This rationale suggests that power is highly fragmented, that it is so amorphous, shifting, and tentative that few can be said to have more power than others over any period of time. Power is broadly shared among a congeries of competing public and private groups; those in high places may appear to have great power, but in reality they are only mediators among conflicting interests, for whose power and support they must continually bargain. Things get done by compromise; to get along, one goes along. Government and the bureaucracy may be viewed as disinterested umpires in the struggle among private groups for larger shares of desired values.

Normatively, such an interpretation meets the liberal belief that great concentrations of power are inherently evil. Since the Constitution says that power is separated and since it is clearly shared by a plethora of interest groups, our system is seen as one in which practically every interest can affect public decisions. Widespread group memberships, plus his vote, give every man the opportunity to make his will felt in the political and economic decisions that concern him. Certain paradoxes, compromises, and exceptions may apply to the generalization, but they do not vitiate the essentially pluralistic interpretation.

Another corollary holds that even if industrial and political integration and technological demands have made power more concentrated, the competition among fewer, but larger, interests results in a "countervailing" mechanism that works in the public interest. Happily, competition among big business, big labor, and big government keeps each interest from misusing its power. That the majority of citizens and consumers affected by these giants remains unorganized is not vital, since they too could organize if they had the will. Thus some 40,000,000 unorganized workers in retail trade and other marginal occupations, and 4,500,000 small-business enterprises have only themselves to blame if the CIO-AFL and the NAM dominate their respective fields. Inequities in power, education, skill, wealth, and other such resources are recognized, but, customarily, the mere fact that vast numbers of associations obviously do exist is accepted as conclusive evidence of pluralism. However, the uncomfortable question of the practical effects of serious power disequilibria among them is often avoided.

But it would be wrong to suggest that pluralism is interpreted only in this negative context, as a barrier to concentrated governmental power. Once again, necessity proves to be a virtue. The dominant conclusion is that pluralism ensures, for both groups and individuals, the access and participation that make democracy viable.[14] Pluralists insist that government is not merely the responsibility of politicians and officials, but that individuals and social groups of many kinds have their part to play and make their influence felt in indirect ways.

Ironies of Contemporary Pluralism

In order to bring pluralism into a modern context and suggest why its meaning has been modified somewhat to meet present social conditions, some criticisms of pluralism must be outlined. First, however, a brief note is required on its changing historical emphasis. Whereas historically the need and rationale for pluralism were largely of English or European origin, based upon conditions in which the supreme state was an actuality, the theory was apparently not really needed in America, where from the start the state has been a "broker of competing wills" rather than an idealized monolith.[15] Given these conditions, American pluralism tended to shift its emphasis toward ensuring the institutional means, through such devices as federalism and functionalism, for the "conditions of individuality." As Kariel concludes, "The principal driving impulse behind American pluralism has always been our commitment to uphold the dignity of the individual person."[16]

[14] Among others, D. Truman, *The Process of Government* (New York: A. Knopf, 1951); D. Boorstein, *The Genius of American Politics* (Chicago: University of Chicago Press, 1953). Obviously, pluralists recognize the costs and the limitations of popular participation, and the tendency for only the few to participate *directly* in political affairs. Nevertheless, their *conclusion*, on balance, is that our system remains a pluralistic one in which power is widely shared.

[15] H. Kariel, *The Decline of American Pluralism* (Stanford: Stanford University Press, 1961), pp. 146-7.

[16] *Ibid.*, p. 180.

Yet, by its emphasis upon group and corporate hegemony, the theory has contributed to the decline of individualism. "The demand of traditional pluralist theory for individual participation in the policy-forming process through primary voluntary groups has been made sentimental by modern organizational conditions."[17] This individualistic drift of pluralism underlies our focus on individual participation in community decisions as a test of pluralism. In order to accommodate the contemporary shift of pluralist attention to *group* behavior, without abandoning its historical emphasis on the individual, we have also included individual membership in groups (the major remaining means of individual influence) and group participation per se among our criteria of pluralism.

A critical assumption of pluralism is that it provides for the broadest possible representation of private interests vis-à-vis the state. But a problem arises in that such interests often achieve their ends at the expense of a broader, unorganized public, usually composed of individuals in their role as consumers. On any given social issue, the voice of this majority often goes unheard, while those with an immediate interest speak loudly. That the claims of the latter are usually rationalized in the "public interest" is of tactical interest, but hardly changes the essential dilemma. This inequality of bargaining power, which reflects the reality of inequitable access and power disequilibria between organized interests and the unorganized majority, may be recognized; it does not, it seems, vitiate the normative appeal and assumed consequences of pluralism.

A related question is how functional for democratic processes are the group divisions characteristic of pluralism? Can this system provide the commitment to the larger community interest that a democratic polity requires? V. O. Key, for example, asks "whether the conditions precedent to the existence of a pluralistic order may not include a relative absence or weakness of attachment among the mass of people to group causes."[18] Moreover, after a careful survey of the conditions of political consensus, and some sobering evidence on the limits of public knowledge, he concludes that the main requirement of our system is an interested, talented elite rather than consensus among the mass of citizens. "The critical element for the health of a democratic order consists in the beliefs, standards, and competence of those who constitute

17 *Ibid.,* p. 182.
18 *Public Opinion and American Democracy* (New York: A. Knopf, 1961), p. 530.

the influentials, the opinion-leaders, and the political activists."[19]

The pluralist case also rests on the argument that the essential thing is competition and participation among organized *groups,* not among individuals. That is, it may be argued that pluralism requires access and participation by *organizations,* which are necessarily directed by the few. One logical problem here is the organismic fallacy which imputes to organizations an existence apart from their members. Another assumption is that leaders do, indeed, represent their constituents and that merely by joining an organization, the individual makes his will felt. In the sense that group leaders derive their legitimacy and power from their role as representatives of large numbers of like-minded individuals, the extension of the pluralist rationale to include members of the organization as well as its elite may be valid.[20] I stress this point because in this study group membership per se is assumed to be a valid criterion for measuring pluralism. In the United States, where the separation-of-powers system gives private organizations an unusually broad degree of access and influence over the use of public power, and where those with political power tend to listen mainly to those who command organized power, it seems that individuals must belong to organizations if they are to gain the share of power promised them by pluralism.

An aspect of pluralism, which gives it a somewhat quaint character, is the changing popular attitude toward the modern state. On balance, and with many qualifications, what we have seen in the United States is the gradual erosion of the negative conception of the state, which is part of the classical pluralist view, in favor of a happier definition of its role. Today, the state is often seen as the only viable means of *ensuring* economic and civil liberty, as in the case of the Negro. This changing perspective may reflect a growing recognition that, among all social entities, the state alone possesses both ability to recognize and the resources to meet growing demands for security in industrial societies. As a result, many interests now look to the state for welfare bounties, subsidies, and the arbitration of competing group interests, rather than regarding

---

[19] *Ibid.,* p. 558.

[20] In congressional committee hearings, for example, one is impressed by the frequency with which the first question asked the witness is some variant of "What organization do you represent, and what is the size of your membership?" Congressmen, themselves, similarly reinforce their legitimacy and points of view vis-à-vis witnesses by noting that they represent the "people" of X state or district. In both cases, the representation of substantial numbers of organized individuals provides a normative basis for legitimacy, access, and influence.

it as a monolithic threat. In this normative sense, the pluralist conception of the state has been turned upside down.

Traditional conceptions of pluralism have changed in another way. Such reassessments may be based upon the changing nature of many groups which, instead of remaining *bona fide* instruments of pluralism, have become oligarchic and restrictive insofar as they monopolize access to governmental power and limit individual participation.[21] As one observer notes, "The voluntary organizations or associations which the early theorists of pluralism relied upon to sustain the individual against a unified omnipotent government have themselves become oligarchically governed hierarchies."[22] Such groups have so "collectivized" the individual member that, although he remains vital to the extent of providing the numerical base upon which the group's power rests, he has little influence on its policies. Often using democratic forms, its leaders maintain oligarchic control of the organization's resources. They *are* the organization, representing it before other publics, personifying its major values. A not too subtle rationalization follows whereby rank-and-file members are defined as somehow not true representatives of the group. Their role and judgments remain "unofficial." The effects on participation are generally restrictive, since the rank and file often accepts such limitations.

Viewed as independent systems, then, the private groups that give meaning to pluralism are rarely pluralistic, in the sense of having competing power centers *within* them. Such groups no longer meet traditional pluralist assumptions, because of the great inequality of bargaining power that characterizes them. The pluralism that exists is too often restricted to the few powerful organizations that monopolize most social areas. Producer groups, linked fundamentally by an economic interest, dominate, and the less disciplined voluntary associations rarely compete successfully with them in the struggle for access and influence.

Such developments underlie the changed conditions and meaning of pluralism, which continues nevertheless to be defined and defended in traditional terms. An example of recent efforts to accommodate pluralism to its new environment is seen in the area of community-power-structure research. *Its advocates now argue*

---

[21] It is interesting, for example, that despite the length of the 1963 New York City newspaper strike, with its economic losses and frustrations, it was difficult for anyone to adopt a punitive attitude or impugn the motives of the typographers union, mainly because this is one of the very few American unions which has maintained an ideal democratic system of internal government.

[22] Kariel, *op. cit.*, p. 2.

that pluralism exists if no single elite dominates decision making in every substantive area. In effect, if bargaining and opposition among three or four elite groups (who usually make up something less than 1 percent of the community) persist, pluralism remains viable. The existence of competition among elites, so to speak, has become the essential criterion. This is obviously a realistic theory in an age of superorganization, but whether by itself it provides a valid measure of "pluralism" remains questionable. Certainly this is a much more restricted definition than that traditionally associated with the concept.

Some Conditions of Pluralism

Such qualifications suggest that the concept of pluralism must be made more specific if it is to serve as a framework for systematic field research. Some necessary conditions of pluralism must be set down, against which research findings can be interpreted. Such conditions can provide empirically testable propositions which enable us to avoid a retreat into faith insofar as the documentation of the viability of pluralism is concerned. While the following propositions do not include every facet of pluralism, they do include several of its basic contemporary tenets:

1) *That competing centers and bases of power and influence exist within a political community.*

   To meet the pluralist standard, lively competition among several individuals, elites, or groups is required. Moreover, in a pluralistic community, the *bases* upon which power rests will be variable, *i.e.*, money power would be challenged by other bases of power, including class, expertise, access, and the control of the media of communication. To some extent, such power bases overlap; in a capitalistic society, for example, personal wealth and the control of the means of production often enable their possessors to co-opt several of the others. But viable competition among many elites possessing *different* bases of power is a critical factor in the pluralist equation, and it is related to the notion of "countervailing power," *i.e.*, the assumption that a built-in stabilizer exists whereby the rise of highly organized centers of power inspires opposing centers which tend to bring the system into equilibrium.

2) *That opportunity exists for individual and organizational access into the political system.*

Access is vital because it provides an instrument by which support and opposition toward a proposed measure may be expressed. Penetration of the formal political system must be possible if decisions are to be rational and equitable, *i.e.*, if they are to benefit from opposing points of view and to satisfy the demands of opposing interests. A panoply of constitutional and procedural guarantees makes such access possible. Yet, it remains necessary to determine empirically the extent of individual and group access by an analysis of specific decisions. It is important to note here that individual participation has been undercut by the complexity of issues and the growth of group representation as the typical means of political negotiation and influence. We shall, therefore, not expect to find very high levels of individual participation in the decisions analyzed here. Despite this, the amount of such participation provides a useful index of *comparative* levels of pluralism in the two communities analyzed in this study.

3) *That individuals actively participate in and make their will felt through organizations of many kinds.*

In this study, as noted earlier, the dichotomy between organizational leaders and their members is denied; unless groups are given some organic reality beyond that based upon their members, it seems that the group thesis must assume that individuals turn to collective action mainly to gain their individual desires. Certainly voting, the most characteristic form of political participation, is in the last analysis an eminently individual behavior. Not that the individual's political values and electoral preferences are not influenced by his group associations, but rather that the political parties must evoke his participation on an individual basis.

4) *That elections are a viable instrument of mass participation in political decisions, including those on specific issues.*

Two facets of this proposition are important. Not only do elections presumably provide a meaningful method of generalized mass influence over political leaders, but the assumption is that most adult citizens do, in fact, *use* their electoral power when referenda are available on specific issues. This assumption is especially vital because the electoral instrument is more accessible than other media of influence and access, such as legislative hearings, officeholding, organizational leadership, etc. In this sense, it is the most practical weapon in the pluralist armory.

5) *That a consensus exists on what may be called the "democratic creed."*

The importance of this consensus lies in the motivation to participate inspired by the belief that the democratic creed of the community is, in fact, operational. That is, voting, organizational membership, and other political activity are activated by an acceptance of the validity of the normative propositions underlying the social system. To some extent, these values provide the cement that holds society together. The absence of this consensus, which may culminate in alienation, seems to result either in a withdrawal from active participation or in somewhat indiscriminate efforts to defeat all community proposals.

These five propositions encompass several of the basic premises of pluralism; an attempt will be made to test them in following chapters.

Conditions of Elitism

We can now consider the nature of elitism. We shall use this term to define the condition that exists when the propositions above are not operational. Elitism is a pattern of decision making characterized by limited mass participation in community issues, and their domination by small groups of specialized or general leaders. This term suits the main drift of the analysis in the sense that it seems to define the conditions sometimes found in community-power-structure research; for example, the tendency for decisions to be initiated and directed by one or a few leadership groups. "Elitism" also enables us to speak of change, "competition among the few," and differential bases of power according to the substantive character of a decision. Elitism, in sum, connotes rule by the few, and when it occurs, we may assume that the five conditions of pluralism outlined above are rarely met.[23]

In a community context, we assume that a decision-making

[23] Here, it should be noted, we are specifically rejecting the revisionist notion that pluralism is adequately defined when competition or specialization exists among the elites participating in community decisions. Our definition, which we believe is more in keeping with the historical spirit and meaning of the concept, requires as necessary conditions some measure of "rank and file" and organizational participation in such decisions.

continuum exists, ranging from a high degree of pluralism at one end to a low degree (*i.e.*, elitism) at the other. Empirically, the position occupied by any given decision along this continuum will vary according to the combination of factors that characterize it, as well as according to the criteria used to define pluralism. This problem will be discussed below. For the moment, let us merely say that community decision making is viewed here as occurring along a *continuum*, and is characterized by varying degrees of rank-and-file participation in major decisions and competition among the elites who play a direct, *initiating* role in them. Elitism connotes domination of the decisional process by a single group or a few men, limited rank-and-file access, little or no opposition, and a failure on the part of most of the adult community to use their political resources to influence important decisions. It refers to the tendency of power, defined as the chances of a group to achieve its ends despite opposition, to rest in relatively few hands.

It is not assumed here that those who have power can achieve their ends all the time, or that they constitute a single, impenetrable, monolithic entity, or that the locus of power does not change historically (formal political power passed from Democratic to Republican hands in the two communities we studied during the time of our research), or that community power rests entirely upon the possession or control of economic resources. Such requirements, it seems, are a caricature of power relations, if not a mere straw man.

We do assume that a power elite, if found, will constitute a very small proportion of the community, and that it will not be representative in social terms of the larger community. It will be made up largely of middle- and upper-class people, who possess more of the skills and qualities required for leadership, and who tend to share certain values about politics, mobility, and requirements of leadership that differentiate them to some extent from others. However, the most critical basis of differentiation will probably be found in class status and leadership resources, rather than in attitudinal differences.

A corollary of these assumptions is that such elites are subject to relatively little influence from the rest of the community. Their power may rest upon expertise, class, status, or wealth, but its distinguishing feature is a decisive control of such resources. Elitism connotes limited numbers, limited consultation with affected groups, disproportionate control of scarce resources of money, skill, and information, and a certain continuity and commonality of interest. While political elites in Western society will typically operate through nominally "democratic" forms, *i.e.*, through public meetings, elections, referenda, and so on, these media are sometimes manipulated to achieve a democratic "consensus" that has little substance. For example, when presidential primary elections are made the target of vast and unequal expenditures of funds, organized like advertising campaigns, and carefully selected to ensure certain desired consequences, there is some doubt that the essentials of democratic participation have been met, even though technically its procedures have been followed. Elitism, as a political instrument, often rests upon similar highly differentiated and unequal access to valued resources.

A characteristic revealed in the community research of Hunter and the Lynds is the tendency for the power of a given elite to extend horizontally, as it were, across several decisional areas. That is, the elite's will may be decisive in economic, political, and social contexts; it cuts across various substantive areas of health, education, housing, urban redevelopment, tax policy, and recreation. It is sometimes argued that specialization of interest and knowledge makes such "cutting across" unlikely, but one explanation for this pattern of influence is that specialists are available as consultants or hired hands to those with economic and political power. Experts are aligned on either side of most technical issues, such as the effects of atomic radiation or the destructive capacity of 100-megaton bombs. The possibility of genuine disagreement among them, as well as the availability of some whose judgments nicely coincide with "official" policy, means that political leaders, allied with resourceful economic interests, may often make their will felt in several discrete and highly technical areas. . . .

. . . A theoretical framework for an empirical study of power and pluralism has been suggested. Power has been conceptualized as a social phenomenon, as distinguished from the primarily individualistic view of power as an absolute quality possessing comparable utility regardless of the situational context in which it is invoked. Instead, the power attributions of individual leaders are conceptualized as *indicators* of their role and status in one or more social subsystems. These subsystems, in effect, provide the bases of individual power, and the substantive issues to which they direct themselves provide the boundaries within which such power is effective. It is hypothesized that the centrality and continuity of *economically* oriented subsystems give their members an inside track in community power relationships. By contrast, *politically* oriented systems tend to provide relatively less viable bases of power, subject as they are to the ebb and flow of political fortune and changing electoral loyalties. In sum, we will try to look beneath individual attributions of power to their underlying social contexts.

Pluralism has been broadly defined as a sociopolitical system in which power and influence are widely dispersed and shared. Pluralism honors the fear of government and of all forms of power —a fear which motivated the Founding Fathers, as well as the English and French philosophers whose values they reflected. They reasoned that if power could not be eradicated, at least its bad effects could be eased by spreading it about.

A belief of pluralism is that most citizens are wise enough to make judgments about public affairs and to help manage them. Pluralism has meant more than the control of political affairs by organizational leaders. As Jackson maintained, the duties of public office are so simple that any man of ordinary intelligence can exercise them. This conception is important in the distinction made here between "pluralism" and "elitism." So defined, pluralism seems opposed to the belief that government works best when its leaders are selected from among the "elite," however this might be defined at a given time and place. It is opposed to this Burkian view in which parliaments are a necessary safeguard against the often ill-advised aims of the majority.

Nevertheless, sophisticated observers have concluded that some variant of elite rule by highly educated and interested groups is the essential requirement of our political system. Such assumptions are based upon research in public opinion and political behavior which indicates that apathy, ignorance of complex issues, and a certain alienation from "politics" are often characteristic of the "unpolitical man." The tension between "elitist" and "pluralist" conceptions of government has not been reduced. They remain as the visible manifestations of complex residual assumptions about man, society, and government.

Despite pluralist assumptions, the empirical question of the extent to which voluntary organizations participate in community decision making remains. It is important to determine whether such organizations are active, if they are really among the principal means by which individuals gain access to the political system. The answer to this question becomes critical in making judgments about the position of any community along the pluralist continuum.

Clearly, many private organizations compete and cooperate with government in determining the allocation of governmental largesse. Pluralists maintain that bargaining among such organizations culminates roughly in the "public interest." However, this rationale has one rather pressing shortcoming, namely, that all interests are not equally represented in the bargaining arena.[24] Real competition on any specific issue is limited to relatively few powerful groups. The weakness of the *consumer* interests is one glaring example of existing inequities in bargaining power. The organizations that have most influence vis-à-vis government are producer groups, galvanized into action by a focused and compelling economic interest.

These structural facets of contemporary pluralism mean that bargaining often proceeds among a presidium of elites, which disadvantages unorganized segments of society. This condition is reinforced in turn by organizational imperatives such as the demand for leadership, power, and dispatch which makes for a tendency toward oligarchy *within* organizations.

Given the challenge to pluralism brought by technological change and organizational necessity, perhaps one must shift the argument away from expectations of widespread participation toward some less sanguine but more reasonable criterion, such as the opportunity for those who *disagree* with the decisions of the governing minority to make their voice heard. If this were done, Michels' proposition, "He who says organization says oligarchy," might prove less disenchanting. Perhaps democracy could be made more viable by a more candid recognition of the limitations upon pluralism brought about by economic realities, apathy, and disparities in power among different elements of the community.

In sum, field studies of the political process at the community level are needed to test pluralist assumptions, for it is here that widespread participation has the best chance to occur. One would expect to find the closest approximation between pluralist ideals and the realities of social and political organization. Barriers of size, distance, and organization are minimal. Access to the politician, the press, and economic leaders is relatively open. The issues are neither so complex nor so far-removed that one feels ineffectual. Politics, and, hopefully, power, is less a mystery. . . .

[24] Among the few books by Americans which consider this unhappy theme are H. Kariel, *op. cit.;* C. Wright Mills, *The Power Elite* (New York: Oxford University Press, 1956); and K. Loewenstein, *Political Power and Governmental Process* (Chicago: University of Chicago Press, 1957).

Power Structure Analysis

While many community-power-structure studies have been made, mainly by sociologists, very few have been much concerned with the political institutions and processes that characterize American communities. As a group, sociologists have often been concerned with social and economic power, and those who have studied community power have tended, conceptually and ideologically, to operate in an elitist or Marxist context.[25] Politics has often been regarded as a mere handmaiden of economic and class interests. Political scientists, on the other hand, despite Charles Merriam's axiom that politics is the study of power in all its forms, have been reluctant to accept the notion of concentrated power which underlies the elitist point of view. They have often had a romantically pluralistic conception of American society, which has stressed equality, the fragmentation of power, and the role of public opinion and elections in influencing community leaders.[26] Although inequality of power may be subsumed under the pluralist rubric, there has been little concern with empirical tests of the extent to which the local political process approximates traditional values of pluralism and "grass roots" participation. Often this condition is assumed. We shall attempt in following chapters to analyze the extent of "pluralism" and "elitism" in community decision making, and to focus on both political and economic power.

This emphasis requires a note on the term "political." The term is used throughout in a broad sense to include what might sometimes be defined as "social" or "economic" factors or processes. This definition follows from a working conception of politics as the

[25] There is evidence that some sociologists now entertain a more positive view of contemporary society, as exemplified by one who remarked in a review of C. Wright Mills's work how "pitiful" it was that Mills criticized his own society! This reminds one of Freud's charge that Jung wanted to remove sexuality from psychoanalysis in order to make psychoanalysis more acceptable to the layman.

[26] For an analysis of the differing normative, theoretical, and methodological conceptions of sociologists and political scientists, see T. J. Anton, "Power, Pluralism, and Local Politics," 7 *Administrative Science Quarterly* (March, 1963), pp. 425–54; for a case study suggesting ways out of some existing methodological problems, see C. M. Bonjean, "Community Leadership: A Case Study and Conceptual Refinement," 48 *American Journal of Sociology* (May, 1963), pp. 672–81. For further specification of theoretical approaches and research problems in community-power-structure analysis, see the exchange between R. A. Dahl and T. J. Anton, 8 *Administrative Science Quarterly* (September, 1963), pp. 250–68.

study of power in all its contexts. We assume that values cannot be neatly divided into compartments, that our political and economic systems are inextricably bound together, and that the process by which each allocates desired values is essentially "political."

A survey of major community studies reveals that they have often regarded political power mainly as a by-product or a residual category of economic power.[27] This orientation marked the most famous of community studies, the *Middletown* research of sociologists Robert and Helen Lynd. It is important in evaluating this study to recall that it was written during the great depression, at a time when faith in liberal political and economic values and systems was tested as never before. Contemporary critics of the study, who are equally influenced it seems by current historical forces, including twenty-five years of prosperity and a threatening international milieu (both of which encourage rather more positive interpretations of our system), tend to overlook this point. Yet, when we abstract ourselves from contemporary influences, we must admit the relevance of such historical forces in shaping intellectual perspectives. Indeed, the truly seminal works have usually been those that interpret and give meaning to the major trends of an age. Adam Smith, Durkheim, Tönnies, Locke, Marx, Weber, and Veblen—all were inspired by existing economic and social systems, their transmutation into capitalism, and the resultant impact upon politics, community, religion, and other aspects of social life. To expect that the conceptual apparatus of the Lynds would not have included a somewhat pessimistic economic determinism seems as visionary as to expect that Marx would have drawn mainly upon precapitalistic data to sustain his thesis, or that Veblen would have turned to a subsistence agriculture to illustrate the triumph of the financiers.

The Lynds, accordingly, found an elitist system, in which the famous X family dominated social and economic life in Middletown. The depression made economic considerations larger than life since unemployment and attending dislocations were the

[27] This view of the political system was especially characteristic of Robert and Helen Lynd's *Middletown in Transition* (New York: Harcourt, Brace, 1937), p. 77. It should be noted, however, that the Lynds also specified two other conditions for the exercise of power: interest and identification with the community, and apprenticeship in political and service organizations. In this context, it is noteworthy that R. A. Dahl, a political scientist, concluded after a careful study of community power structure, that "in liberal societies, politics is a sideshow in the great circus of life," *Who Governs?: Democracy and Power in an American City* (New Haven: Yale University Press, 1961), p. 305.

dominant characteristics of the community and the times. Those who could ease these strains by providing jobs naturally enjoyed great influence. Noting that "the nucleus of business-class control is the X family,"[28] the Lynds found that education, religion, leisure, politics, philanthropy, and public opinion in the city were greatly influenced by this family's economic hegemony. Despite the fact that Middletown was not a "one industry" town (in 1925 Middletown had 100 manufacturing establishments; in 1933, 81), the apparent existence of a monolithic power structure is theoretically important in view of later attempts to fashion a typology of power structure in terms of economic domination of a city by a single large industry."[29]

Some of the community studies since *Middletown* have found a less rigidly elitist system in which competition exists between traditional economic elites long resident in the community and an "organization man" elite comprising executives of absentee-owned corporations. Competition between political and economic coalitions has also been found. The sociologist Robert Schulze, for example, discovered a bifurcation of economic and political power between local-firm economic dominants, the executives of national corporations located in Cibola, and a local "public leader" group which was found to be most widely perceived as being influential in community affairs. This latter group stood between the other two leadership groups in terms of age, education, vocational status, and social mobility.[30] The executives of absentee-owned corporations were found to be singularly uninterested in local affairs. The "local-firm economic dominants," children of men "who had once run Cibola," were also relatively inactive, although considerably less so than the executive group.[31] Others have found that political

[28] R. and H. Lynd, *op. cit.*, p. 77.

[29] C. Wright Mills and M. Ullmer, "Small Business and Civic Welfare. Report of the Smaller War Plants Corporation," U.S. Senate, Document No. 135, Washington, D.C., 1946; William H. Form and D. C. Miller, *Industry, Labor and Community* (New York: Harper & Bros., 1960); D. C. Miller, "Industry and Community Power Structure," 23 *American Sociological Review* (February, 1958), pp. 9–15; R. J. Pellegrin and C. H. Coats, "Absentee-Owned Corporations and Community Power Structure," 61 *American Journal of Sociology* (March, 1956), pp. 413–19. For a study suggesting that economic leaders, mainly because they now often represent nationally owned corporations, tend to *withdraw* from active participation in community affairs, see R. Schulze, "The Role of Economic Dominants in Community Power Structure," 23 *American Sociological Review* (February, 1958), pp. 3–9.

[30] "The Bifurcation of Power in a Satellite City," in M. Janowitz (ed.), *Community Political Systems* (New York: Free Press, 1960), pp. 19–80.

[31] *Ibid.*, pp. 42–3.

elites are less influential because increasing concentration of power in labor, business, and political affairs at the national level has made political decisions relatively less strategic in local economic and political matters.

The most influential of post-Lynd studies is undoubtedly Floyd Hunter's analysis of Atlanta.[32] Using mainly a "reputational" method of determining power, whereby a panel of knowledgeable heads of community organizations were asked to nominate leaders, who then ranked themselves, Hunter concluded that some forty "influentials," over half of whom were in business, finance, and industry, made the key decisions affecting the entire community. It is important to note that Hunter *began* his research by defining social power as being structured, the result of social and institutional alliances; his empirical findings indicated that this structure was activated by the forty influentials. By sociometric analysis, Hunter found that this group tended to interlock socially, culturally, and, to a lesser extent, economically. A nice distinction was found between this inner elite and its lieutenants, who in carrying out its policies tended to be viewed by the rank and file as the "real" holders of power. Defining power operationally as "the acts of men going about the business of moving other men to act in relation to themselves or in relation to organic and inorganic things,"[33] Hunter concluded that those who "really" have power possess financial resources and occupy or control the formal economic and governmental roles.

Sometimes forgetting Mr. Dooley's admonition, "you can't beat something with nothing," and, more important, forgetting that knowledge proceeds by accretion, some political scientists[34] have

[32] *Community Power Structure.*

[33] *Ibid.*, p. 44.

[34] For critiques of Hunter's work, see H. Kaufman and V. Jones, "The Mystery of Power," 14 *Public Administration Review* (Summer, 1953), pp. 205–12; the Lynds and Hunter have been assailed by R. A. Dahl, "A Critique of the Ruling Elite Model," 52 *American Political Science Review* (June, 1958), pp. 463–9; N. W. Polsby, "How to Study Community Power: The Pluralist Alternative," 22 *Journal of Politics* (August, 1960), pp. 474–84; and R. E. Wolfinger, "Reputation and Reality in the Study of 'Community Power,'" 25 *American Sociological Review* (October, 1960), pp. 636–44. It is interesting that some of Hunter's and Lynds' critics were apparently uninhibited by experience in systematic community-power-structure research. Some of them have remedied this shortcoming, but others continue to equate the elegance of abstract epistemology, grand language, and a purely logical rigor with the untidiness of field research. *Cf.* L. J. R. Herson, "In the Footsteps of Community Power," 55 *American Political Science Review* (December, 1961), pp. 817–30. For comments on this immaculate conception of the theory-research nexus, see J. Bensman and A. Vidich, "Social Theory in Field Research," 45 *American Journal of Sociology* (May, 1960), pp. 577–

criticized severely both Lynds' and Hunter's method and conclusions, particularly their elitist conception of power and their relegation of the political system to a mere artifact of the economic system. As a result, community-power-structure theory and analysis exhibit an intellectual and ideological schizophrenia. Beginning with an assumption that social power is structured, sociologists conclude, on the basis of considerable empirical research, that power is shared to some extent but that economic power is the dominant force in community affairs. Meanwhile, reasoning from a pluralist ideology, believing that power is highly diffused, and working from a rather limited amount of field research, many political scientists maintain that community power structure and decision making are characterized by widely shared power, made good by political ceremonials, and influenced by a public opinion expressed by an electorate highly organized into voluntary groups. One of the objectives of the current report is to throw some light on this interesting dichotomy. At the same time, it seems that such conceptions as Mannheim's concerning the "situational determinism" of social observation and interpretation may prove as relevant as field research in its resolution.

Political scientists have usually found pluralistic, specialized leadership structures. Robert Dahl, for example, concludes in his New Haven study that very little overlap exists among leaders, as measured by three key issue areas.[35] He did find, however, that the proportion of the total electorate playing an active role in each decision area was extremely small. Despite this, and despite the limited proportion of the electorate who voted in local elections in New Haven, he maintains that rank-and-file influence is greater than one might assume since those in positions of power are subjectively and objectively influenced by mass opinion as expressed through the vote, and by leaders' judgments about the assumed reactions of citizens to their policies.[36] This proposition may be valid, but no strong evidence is provided for it. Indeed, securing such evidence is among the most challenging of research enter-

---

84; and E. Shils, "Primordial, Personal, Sacred, and Civil Ties," 8 *British Journal of Sociology* (June, 1957), pp. 130–45.

[35] Dahl, *Who Governs?* p. 169.

[36] Related discussions of the method and pluralistic conclusions of Dahl's study include: D. Rogers (review), 48 *American Journal of Sociology* (September, 1962), pp. 271–2; A. H. Birch (review), 40 *Public Administration* (Autumn, 1962), pp. 341–2; P. Bachrach and M. Baratz, "Two Faces of Power," 51 *American Political Science Review* (December, 1962), pp. 947–52; M. Goldstein (review), 27 *American Sociological Review* (December, 1962), pp. 860–62; F. Hunter (review), 6 *Administrative Science Quarterly* (March, 1962), pp. 517–19.

prises. Whether generalized political preferences registered in periodic elections have much influence on specific political issues remains a moot point. Insofar as the "anticipated reaction" thesis—this holds that the assumed reaction of voters is an important factor in the decisional calculus of political leaders—is concerned, one is impressed by the professional politician's reliance upon the forgetfulness of the typical voter.[37]

In his study of Bennington, Vermont, Harry Scoble concluded similarly that "no single power structure existed in the city."[38] Only in the case of a hospital decision area did he find the "monolithic, flat-surfaced pyramid, with . . . a small number of power-holders, acting in predetermined concert, and with wealth as the dominant base . . ."[39]

Despite such findings, a by-product of post-Hunter research has been a modification of traditional pluralist assumptions concerning the extent of rank-and-file participation in community affairs. Essentially, it seems, pluralism has now been redefined to mean viable competition among elites and organized groups, whereas historically it included as a necessary condition active citizen participation in local and national affairs and a reasonable equity of bargaining power among interested groups. As noted earlier, we shall hold to this traditional conception of "pluralism" in this analysis. Researchers may, of course, define their terms as they will. However, not much is added to clarity if old words are given new connotations.

In sum, the historical conception of pluralism seems to have been constructed, if not redefined. As Dahl's conclusions indicate, a system may now be called pluralistic if there is competition among the leaders representing several substantive areas. *Within* each specialized group, decisions are dominated by the few: "In origins, conception, and execution, it is not too much to say that urban redevelopment has been the direct product of a small handful of leaders";[40] "The bulk of the voters had virtually no direct influence on the process of nomination";[41] "The number of citizens who participate directly in important decisions bearing on the pub-

[37] For evidence that voters neither know nor (apparently) care very much about their political representatives' voting record on programmatic issues, see D. Stokes and W. Miller, "Party Government and the Saliency of Congress," 26 *Public Opinion Quarterly* (Winter 1962), pp. 531–46.

[38] "Leadership Hierarchies and Political Issues in a New England Town," in M. Janowitz, *op. cit.*, p. 141.

[39] *Ibid.*

[40] Dahl, *op. cit.*, p. 115.

[41] *Ibid.*, p. 106.

lic schools is small . . .";[42] "A few people, the leaders, evidently exerted great direct influence on a series of decisions about teachers' salaries, appointments, appropriations, buildings."[43] Yet, because the *same* set of leaders does not exercise influence across all substantive areas and bcause of an unverified and perhaps unverifiable assumption that citizens exercise "very great" (p. 159) and "a good deal of" (p. 106) *indirect* influence on their political leaders, we are said to have a "pluralistic" system.

Although it is true that pluralism has traditionally meant the dispersal of power among many groups, it has surely meant more than bargaining and compromise among a few leaders. A fundamental problem of Dahl's analysis is that he demonstrates empirically that participation in political decision making is limited to a minority, but he is unable to demonstrate similarly the indirect "rank and file" influence which *is said to be exerted* through elections and the anticipated reaction mechanism which conditions leaders as they weigh decisional probabilities. Moreover, this concern with rank-and-file influence indicates that Dahl's conception of pluralism encompasses more than mere competition among elites. He is indeed concerned with demonstrating the influence of "followers," as expressed through "critical elections." The analysis does not always distinguish between empirical fact and value theory, between a careful methodological concern and judgments that seem to reflect the subjective preferences of most of us who received a traditional political science education.

Generally, then, on the theoretical and normative side community-power-structure research has been characterized by a discontinuity between sociological elitist assumptions and political scientist expectations of a pluralistic universe in which social power is elusive, atomized, transitory, and variegated. It seems fair to conclude that both the collection and the interpretation of empirical data have been influenced accordingly. . . .

The Future of Pluralism

Differences regarding the nature of the political system may lie in the interpretation of the data. To *some extent, where the sociologists found monopoly and called it elitism, political scientists*

---

[42] *Ibid.*, p. 151.
[43] *Ibid.*, p. 161; also, "Only a tiny group, the leaders, exerts great influence," p. 164.

found oligopoly but defined it in more honorific terms as pluralism. This conclusion, as we have tried to show, rests upon a restrictive, although eminently realistic, definition of pluralism, in which its historical emphasis upon individualism and a rough equality of bargaining power among groups has been subjugated to the assumption that pluralism exists if specialization and competition characterize groups of leaders who constitute some one-half of 1 percent of the community. Certainly this definition meets prevailing conditions of group organization and political access, but it seems to omit some of the conditions and normative by-products traditionally associated with pluralism.

Some of the implications of our power structure findings are disturbing. One of these is the paradox found in Edgewood and Riverview, where an inverse association exists between pluralism and participation. Riverview is a closer approximation to the traditional pluralist model. It has a more diversified socioeconomic structure; far more active political competition; its organizational membership rates are very similar to those of Edgewood; and participation in state and national elections is not greatly different from that in Edgewood, while in local elections it is higher. Yet, by the criteria of participation in the major decisions, there is less community interest and activism. Edgewood, on the other hand, is much more integrated socially and politically; its local political system was, until 1961, apparently nonpartisan. There is less controversy and sharp conflict on basic values within the community. Despite these conditions, which oppose those of traditional pluralism, with their assumed advantages, it has been somewhat more effective in meeting change and participation has been higher, as measured by the five major decisions.

Our results suggest that there may be some incompatibility between economic affluence and pluralist democracy, despite recent findings that democracy is associated with a high level of economic stability.[44] In Edgewood, industrial strength and major control of decisions by economic leaders make possible considerable self-reliance and effective decision making by those in its power structure; both its political and economic leaders tend to share dominant "free enterprise" values. They believe in doing things by themselves and for themselves, and even when government largesse is accepted, this fact is muted. But decisions are not the result of truly widespread participation (even though participation was more

[44] Among others, see J. Coleman and G. Almond, eds., *The Politics of Developing Areas* (Princeton, N.J.: Princeton University Press, 1960), and S. Lipset, *Political Man.*

"pluralistic" than in Riverview). There is instead a quiet consensus on most matters, with a belief that leaders know best and will work, as they do, in the community interest. All this results in effective, expeditious decision making, but it often occurs without the active citizen participation implied by pluralist theory.

The tendency for the major conditions of community decision making to be set down by higher levels of government and industry is another crucial finding. In this way the periphery of local autonomy is becoming more restricted. Our evidence indicates that participation both within the power structure and the community tends to be positively related to the degree to which decisions involve the use (as well as the rhetoric) of essentially local rather than "external" resources. In both communities, participation was highest in decisions such as schools, hospitals, and new industry, where a good proportion of the resources were of local origin. Essentially external, "political" decisions, such as Riverview's housing authority and the two flood control issues, evoked little participation. From this, we may hypothesize that if the trend toward reducing the scope of local decision making continues, pluralism at the community level will probably become even less likely. Since integration, easy access to the political apparatus, and "grass roots" democracy have been historically associated with small communities, it is ironic that the decline of pluralism seems to be occurring precisely at this level. The nation-wide centralization of both political and economic decisions on behalf of greater rationality and control probably includes such among its unanticipated consequences.

A final, somewhat disturbing continuity is that despite high levels of popular education, economic stability, a fair degree of social mobility, a marvelously efficient communication system, and related advantages usually assumed to provide sufficient conditions for democratic pluralism, the vast majority of citizens remains apathetic, uninterested, and inactive in political affairs at the community level. Most political scientists and sociologists who have analyzed community behavior accept this generalization. Some who believe in the cult of expertise or share a Burkian conception of political representation honor it. But whether this condition is attributed to majority apathy or to minority desires for power, status, and prestige, it remains an awkward reality for those who take democracy seriously.

25 ✿ THE EQUILIBRIUM RATIONALIZED

STEPHEN W. ROUSSEAS AND
JAMES FARGANIS

In a collection of essays written over a ten-year period, Daniel Bell[1] hails the end of ideology. In a similar volume of previously published essays, Seymour Martin Lipset[2] joins Bell in the apotheosis of a noncommitted scientism, or what amounts to pragmatism leached of all its passion for meaningful social reform. This growing litany in the United States, on the European Continent, and in England in praise of the status quo continues to remain, in its own image, inherently liberal. It is convinced that democracy today has solved all the major problems of industrial society, and that those which do remain are of a second-order magnitude involving merely technical adjustments within a now prevailing *consensus gentium*. If modern liberalism has thus been recast into a less critical mold, it is because of its conviction that modern democracy *is* the good society. Lipset makes this very clear in the epilogue to his book. "Democracy," he writes, "is not only or even primarily a means through which different groups can attain their ends or seek the good society; *it is the good society itself in operation*."[3]

More explicitly, we are told by Lipset that within the Western

From Stephen W. Rousseas and James Farganis, "American Politics and the End of Ideology," *British Journal of Sociology*, 14 (1963), 347–362.

[1] *The End of Ideology: On the Exhaustion of Political Ideas in the Fifties* (Collier Books, rev. ed., 1961).

[2] *Political Man* (Doubleday, 1960).

[3] Page 403, italics supplied. In response to criticisms of *Political Man*, Lipset has somewhat modified this statement and has sought to restate his liberalism ("My View From Our Left," *Columbia University Forum*, Fall, 1962). "Democracy," now, "is not simply a means to the end of the good society, it is itself the only society in which social tendencies which press man to exploit man may be restrained." This rather negative approach to democracy and the good society is further confirmed by his statement that his espousal of democracy "rests on the assumption that only a politically democratic society can reduce the pressures—endemic in social systems— to increase the punitive and discriminatory effects of stratification." For it is the democratic freedom of the underprivileged classes to organize which gives rise to an effective and leveling "counterpower" operating within the rules of the game of institutionalized conflict. The similarity of this to John Kenneth Galbraith's theory of "countervailing power" is obvious, and is subject to the same limitations. Lipset's ideal is the nonideological welfare state toward which, he believes, the United States is moving.

democracies "serious intellectual conflicts among groups representing different values have declined sharply"; that "the ideological issues dividing left and right [have] been reduced to a little more or a little less government ownership and economic planning"; and that it really makes little difference "which political party controls the domestic policies of individual nations." All this, according to Lipset, "reflects the fact that the fundamental political problems of the industrial revolution have been solved: the workers have achieved industrial and political citizenship; the conservatives have accepted the welfare state; and the democratic left has recognized that an increase in overall state power carries with it more dangers to freedom than solutions for economic problems,"[4]

In this milieu intellectuals functioning as critics of society have become disaffected, according to Lipset, because "domestic politics, even liberal or socialist politics, can no longer serve as the arena for serious criticism from the left" (p. 408). Disorganized, at a loss for a cause, and unable to fulfill their self-image, the liberal intellectuals "have turned from a basic concern with political and economic systems to criticism of other sections of the basic culture of society, particularly of elements which cannot be dealt with politically" (p. 409). Or, in Bell: "Some of the younger

[4] Pages 403–6. In addition Lipset cites, with apparent approval, a comment made to him by the editor of a leading Swedish newspaper: "Politics is now boring. The only issues are whether the metal workers should get a nickel more an hour, the price of milk should be raised, or old-age pensions extended." Similarly in Bell we have: "In the Western world . . . there is today a rough consensus among intellectuals on political issues: the acceptance of the Welfare State; the desirability of decentralized power; a system of mixed economy and of political pluralism . . . [And] the workers; whose grievances were once the driving energy for social change, are more satisfied with the society than the intellectuals" (pp. 397–9).

For other views reflecting the end of ideology the following recent works should be consulted: John Strachey, *Contemporary Capitalism* (Random House, 1956); C. A. R. Crosland, *The Future of Socialism* (Macmillan, 1957); John Kenneth Galbraith, *American Capitalism* (Houghton Mifflin, rev. ed., 1956), and *The Affluent Society* (Houghton Mifflin, 1958); Henry Wallich, *The Cost of Freedom* (Harper & Bros., 1960); and the debate going on in England between the neorevisionists and the fundamentalists in the pages of *Encounter, New Left Review*, and the *New Statesman*, particularly during 1960–1. Limitations of space preclude any examination of these various approaches. With the exception of the English "fundamentalists," they all reflect the view, in greater or lesser degree, that the major problems of industrial society have been solved and that the remaining problems are basically technical and easily within our grasp. Perhaps the most unabashed statement of this position is to be found in Arthur Schlesinger, Jr., "Where Does the Liberal Go From Here?" *New York Times Magazine*, August 4, 1957.

intellectuals have found an outlet in science or university pursuits, but often at the expense of narrowing their talent into mere technique" (p. 399).

II

The full import of the Bell-Lipset thesis can be derived principally from a misinterpretation of Max Weber; a misinterpretation which leads Bell to consider Machiavelli and Weber in the same light, and to quote them at the head of the two key chapters of his study.[5] In keeping with his own interpretation of Weber, Bell distinguishes between the normative "ought" and the empirical "is" of politics and the "ineluctable tension" between the two. Ethics is concerned with justice, whereas concrete politics involves "a power struggle between organized groups to determine the allocation of privilege" (p. 279). Concrete politics, in other words, is not concerned with the realization of an ideal, but, following Lord Acton, with the reaping of particular advantages within the limits of a given ethic—an ethic which sets out clearly the rules of the game governing the political jockeying for position and privilege. Thus, modern, mature democracies representing the end of ideology have, in effect, separated ethics from politics; and ideology, insofar as it continues to exist as a force in modern society, is nothing more than a cynical propaganda cover for the specific self-interest of competing groups. Modern politics, therefore, becomes amenable to analysis in terms of the mixed strategies of game theory (though neither Bell nor Lipset has done so). The game is to be played, however, according to the generally accepted constitutional limits of a Weberian "ethic of responsibility." It implies, above all, the flat rejection of the radical commitment required by an "ethic of conscience" which "creates 'true believers' who burn with pure, unquenchable flame and can accept no compromise with faith." The ethic of responsibility is, in sum, "the pragmatic view which seeks reconciliation as its goal" (pp. 279–80). Modern liberals, willing as they are to accept their progress piecemeal and within the rules of the game are, therefore, to be distinguished from genuine ideologues who are seemingly unaware that the good society has already been achieved.

[5] Ch. 12, and "The End of Ideology in the West: An Epilogue." The quotations used by Bell are: "He who seeks the salvation of souls, his own as well as others, should not seek it along the avenue of politics" (Weber); and "Men commit the error of not knowing when to limit their hopes" (Machiavelli).

The basic distinction between the modern liberal and the ideologue revolves around the notion of commitment. If the ideologue, in Bell's terms, is committed to the consequences of ideas and is governed by passion then, in contradistinction, the nonideological liberal is uncommitted and free of any chiliastic vision of the transforming moment. The ideologue seeks political success, according to Bell, by organizing and arousing the masses into a social movement, and the function of ideology, therefore, is to fuse the energies of the great unwashed and ignite their passions into a mighty river of fire. But in order to do so, ideology must "simplify ideas, establish a claim to truth, and, in the union of the two, demand a commitment to action" (p. 396).

The *end* of ideology is therefore linked to its inability nowadays to arouse the masses. And this inability, as we have seen, is the direct consequence of modern society's having solved the basic problems of the industrial order. In this kind of Panglossian society there is no room for ideologues who, standing on the upper rungs of the faith ladder, have become politically destabilizing factors. They are, if anything, a direct threat to the continuation of the good society. The modern politician qua politician is the man who understands how to manipulate and how to operate in a Machiavellian world which divorces ethics from politics. Modern democracy becomes, in this view, transformed into a system of technique *sans telos*. And democratic politics is reduced to a constellation of self-seeking pressure groups peaceably engaged in a power struggle to determine the allocation of privilege and particular advantage. Compromise and evolution are to be the means for achieving, in the context of this struggle, the few second-order social goals which continue to remain in an otherwise near perfect society. It is in this limited sense that the end of ideology clings desperately to its self-imposed label of enlightened, nonideological, noncommitted liberalism. And the status quo it defends in the name of democracy is a fundamental one—the already achieved good society.

All this is carefully nailed onto Max Weber's door by Bell. Had he, instead, opened the door and looked in, he would have found that Weber's primary concern was with the *fusion* of the "ethic of responsibility" and "the ethic of absolute ends." Contrary to Bell's easy interpretation, Weber was in no sense advocating a politics without passion. Passion without responsibility, and politics without commitment were equally unacceptable to Weber. "Passion," "a feeling of responsibility," and a "sense of proportion" were for Weber the three pre-eminent qualities which are decisive for the politician. For Weber, the problem was the forging of "a warm passion and a cool sense of proportion . . . in one and the same soul."[6] Insofar as the politician plays the game of politics without any sense of purpose, his actions are without meaning. In Weber's words, "The mere 'power politician' may get strong effects, but actually his work leads nowhere and is senseless."

In Weber, the "ethic of responsibility" and the "ethic of ultimate ends" were not to be regarded as absolute contrasts. They were, instead, to be thought of as supplements reinforcing each other within the mind of the true politician who was to act as the agent of social progress. In failing to take into account the consequences of his actions, and in refusing to admit the condition of human frailty, the chiliast was irresponsible and ineffective. But equally vacuous, in Weber's opinion, was the politician who sought to enhance his own power without any vision in mind. "Certainly all historical experience," wrote Weber, "confirms the truth—that man would not have attained the possible unless time and again he had reached out for the impossible."

III

Despite Bell's misinterpretation of Weber, there can be little doubt that his and Lipset's arguments on the decline, if not the end, of ideology as an operative force in the Western world are based largely on fact. But whether or not this represents a desirable state of affairs is quite another matter. The favorable interpretation given to this development by Bell and Lipset has been generally accepted, if not applauded, by most observers. Yet, there may be a great deal of potential confusion over the meaning of "ideology" and "ideological thought" if care is not taken to use these terms consistently. The most exhaustive analysis of the concept appears in Karl Mannheim's well-known *Ideology and Utopia*.[7] In Mannheim, *ideology* is taken to mean the ideas and thought patterns of the interest-bound ruling groups which explain, justify, and rationalize the status quo, while *utopia* is the intellectual stimulus provided by the oppressed groups who challenge the established order and seek to transform it into the good society. When Bell and Lipset speak of the "end of ideology," what they

[6] For Weber's position and the quotations used, see H. H. Gerth and C. Wright Mills, eds., *From Max Weber* (Oxford, 1946), pp. 115–16, 127–8.
[7] International Library of Psychology, Philosophy and Scientific Method, 1936. Reprinted as a paperback by Harcourt, Brace.

mean is the "end of utopian thought," for they are both clearly referring to the decline of socialist or Marxian ideas within the context of an affluent Western society. Lipset, however, pushes his argument further (and more explicitly than Bell) when he declares, contrary to the judgment of many of the most profound minds of Western political thought, that democracy "is the good society itself in operation." The classical distinction between "nature" and "convention" is thus obliterated, and the traditional role of the intellectual as social critic is no longer logically possible. For if "what ought to be" already is, then the intellectual has no other function than to describe and to celebrate the arrival of a utopia. Yet much of the intellectual output of today in film, on the stage, and in art reveals a profound discontent with things as they are. Lipset and Bell recognize this intellectual alienation but conclude that it is not political. It is only by narrowly defining politics as concerned with "voting behavior" or with "welfare measures" that they can come to such a conclusion. But if the traditional idea of political philosophy is maintained, there is yet some small contribution that intellectuals can make, which will be something other than a justification, tacit or overt, for whatever is.

"Liberals such as Lipset," writes one political scientist, "are proud of the progress which has been made in the Western world, but it is curious that they never acknowledge the fact that we have gotten as far as we have precisely because of the ideologies which stirred men to action." And if the end of ideology is, in fact, the case, "then we have the best explanation of why we in the West are standing still."[8]

But the most bitterly forceful comments have come from another source. C. Wright Mills and Bell-Lipset have been each other's severest critics[9] and C. Wright Mills, defining the end of ideology

[8] Andrew Hacker, in an otherwise favorable review of Lipset's book (*Commentary*, June 1961). A further criticism made by Hacker concerns the limitations of a purely empirical approach to the problems of modern society. If the myths of left-wing ideology have in fact declined, this does not necessarily imply that we have matured, politically, in the sense of being willing not only to face, but to live with the facts. In the words of Hacker: "Lipset hopes to supplant myth with fact. Empiricism, like it or not, forces one to concentrate on things as they are or as they have been. A description of how things *might be* were we to embark on changing the social order is bound to be speculative, not factual. . . . The visions of ideologues, then, coupled with their mythologies about the world of reality, should be evaluated not on empirical but on strategic grounds."

[9] To Bell and Lipset, C. Wright Mills was an annoying gadfly and a bad scholar. To many others he was, above all, a great social critic who, unlike most good scholars, had something meaningful to say. For an incredibly nasty reference to the late C. Wright Mills, see Seymour Martin Lipset and

as "an intellectual celebration of apathy" which has collapsed reasoning into reasonableness, attacks the Bell-Lipset emphasis on strictly factual analysis:[10]

The disclosure of fact . . . is the rule. The facts are duly weighed, carefully balanced, always hedged. Their power to outrage, their power truly to enlighten in a political way, their power to aid decision, even their power to clarify some situation—all that is blunted and destroyed.

Facts, of course, do not in themselves have the power to outrage, enlighten, or clarify. And perhaps for this reason C. Wright Mills' argument is in need of some elaboration. A brute empiricist, devoid of any "passion," is no more capable of describing the world *as it is* than is an ideologue who views the world around him solely through the lens of his ideological *Weltanschauung*. The hope, or the belief, that the end of the ideological cast of mind will permit us to view the real world uncolored by any value judgments is nothing but the delusion of an unsophisticated positivism; which is, in essence, a flight from moral responsibility. For facts are themselves the product of our viewing "reality" through our theoretical preconceptions which, in turn, are conditioned by the problems confronting us. And the theoretical precepts which determine the relevant facts of a particular view of "reality" are not themselves entirely value-free. Social theories, in short, are the result of our concern with specific problems. And social problems, at bottom, are concerned with ethical goals. Social theorists, furthermore, differ in their value judgments and thus differ in their theoretical constructions of "reality." They differ, that is, in the problems they see, or, what amounts to the same thing, they see a given problem in different ways. Consequently, they differ as to the facts relevant to a given problem. There is, in other words, a selectivity of facts in the analysis of social problems. Some facts included in one approach are excluded in another; and even those held in common may, and usually do, differ in the weight given to them and in their theoretical and causal interrelations.

All this, of course, raises the following possibilities: that the theory of verification in the social sciences is of a different order from that found in the other sciences; that the moral preconceptions of social theorists unavoidably determine the shape of their theories, the classification systems they employ, and their concepts

Neil Smelser, "Change and Controversy in Recent American Sociology," *The British Journal of Sociology*, March 1961, reprinted by the Institute of Industrial Relations, Reprint No. 164, Berkeley, 1961, n. 12, pp. 50–1.

[10] "Letter to the New Left," *New Left Review*, September–October 1960.

and hypotheses; and that objective criteria of relevance for the evaluation of competing constructions of social reality, therefore, may not exist. Perhaps the best we can hope for is some form of objective relativism. But however that may be, it is clear that those who would suggest that sociological analysis is a pure science objectively concerned with pure "facts" are indulging in an ideological positivism uniquely their own; a *wertlos*[11] positivism which amounts to nothing more than an unthinking apologia for whatever is. And their value judgments, because of their implicit subconsciousness, are all the more inflexible and rigid. Their pronouncements, moreover, do not admit of compromise and take on an *ex cathedra* quality found only in those who believe they have somehow secured *the* truth—or *the* good society. In this respect they parallel the more extreme ideologues of their analysis.

Along these lines, C. Wright Mills would have agreed that the end of ideology makes a fetish of empiricism and entails an ideology of its own—an ideology of political complacency for the justification of things as they are, and the celebration of modern society as a going concern. Utopian thought, or left-wing criticism, according to Mills, is concerned with a "structural criticism" of the institutions of society and with the formulation of programs for reform and fundamental change. It need not entail an apocalyptic or dogmatic vision. The choice is not between the wild-eyed fanatic and the cool, uncommitted pragmatist who is willing to take his progress piecemeal, if at all. Ideology need not, as Bell sometimes tends to do, be equated with chiliastic fanaticism. Its major function is to apply intelligence—the fusion of passion and critical reason—to the problems of the modern world. And intelligence can never lie down with itself in a passionate embrace of self-love. It must be concerned with the human condition and its betterment in an always imperfect world. Its justification for being is, in a word, progress.

Whether or not it is true that progress in the past has been exclusively the result of ideological conflict, it is nevertheless true that progress, as distinct from mere change, can be defined meaningfully only in terms of some "vision." For progress, as Santayana has observed, "is relative to an ideal which reflection creates." And it is here that, perhaps, the most serious criticism of the end of ideology can be made.

[11] Max Weber distinguishes between science as *wertfrei* and *wertlos*. *Wertfrei* is defined as being free from prevailing passion and prejudice; free, that is, to create its own values. *Wertlos*, on the other hand, is applied to the falsely objective or "scientistic" approach to social problems.

The modern politician is viewed, appreciatively by Bell and Lipset, as a noncommitted individual skilled in the art of compromise. The ideologue, on the other hand, is committed to some pattern of institutional change which, in terms of his values, becomes transformed into social progress. It is irrelevant whether one agrees with the vision of a particular ideology. The important point is that freedom, in the philosophical sense, and a social commitment which transcends the status quo are interrelated and interdependent.

Rejecting the notion of man tied to a merciless fate which robs him of his future, we are left to regard him free and immersed in the process of becoming. Man is, in other words, a potential, and his willingness or ability to seize life by the throat, as it were, and force it to serve his needs is a measure of his freedom. Freedom, in short, excludes a complacency which rests on past or present achievements, or which nurtures the illusion of having already achieved the best of all possible worlds where progress, in any meaningful sense is, by definition, no longer possible. If man, living as he does in a grossly imperfect world, is not uniquely determined by his past and is nothing but a potential in terms of his impending future, then the act of commitment is a prior requirement for the realization of his freedom and thus his future. And if modern democracy is predicted on the end of ideology, that is, on the end of commitment, then it negates itself and becomes the very denial of freedom. If it has any commitment at all, it is the false commitment to itself—to the narcissistic approval of itself as it is—with the net result that it has retreated from the problems of the world about it.

IV

Another objection to the end of ideology lies in its inability to make the fundamental distinction between what it considers to be the good society and a social theory which has become obsolete as a result of the changing values and problems of succeeding generations. Confusing the two and still obsessed and blinded by the orientations of the 1930s, it looks at the current situation and declares that the problems of the Great Depression have been, by and large, satisfactorily resolved.

Bell's book was accurately subtitled, *On the Exhaustion of Political Ideas in the Fifties*. Indeed, we have been, and continue to be, faced with a bankruptcy of political ideas at a time when cer-

314 CHALLENGES TO REVISIONISM

tain critical developments have been taking place in the United States—developments for which the end of ideology is in large measure responsible. On the international front there is the tendency to apply a splintering empiricism to our international problems, and on the domestic front there is inability to cope with, let alone, admit, the economic malaise that has seized the American economy since the end of the Korean War.

Concerning international matters, Hans J. Morgenthau writes of our "surrendering piecemeal to the facts of foreign policy . . . of thinking and acting as though there were nothing else to foreign policy but this [or that] particular set of empirical facts" concerning this or that foreign policy problem.[12] The latter-day pragmatists, in Morgenthau's opinion, are basically antitheoretical, and antiutopian empiricists who pride themselves on having "no illusions about the facts as they are nor any grand design for changing them." Indeed, their crowning achievement, in their own view, is their "courage to look the facts in the face and . . . deal with each issue on its own terms." Underlying their entire approach is their profound belief that "the problems of the social world [will] yield to a series of piecemeal empirical attacks, unencumbered by preconceived notions and comprehensive planning." As a result foreign policy lacks an overall cohesiveness and has degenerated into a series of unrelated operations not always consistent with each other, and often far removed from the realities of the situation which the facts, of their own accord, are supposed to make clear. Thus, according to Morgenthau, in trying to escape the Scylla of utopianism we are foundering on the Charybdis of empiricism. In the name of "facts" we are reduced to approaching the major problems of our existence as though they were mere matters of technical manipulation. What is obviously needed is an ideology to interpret the "facts" of a social situation and to suggest meaningful solutions in terms of a particular reading of these self-same "facts."[13]

[12] "The Perils of Political Empiricism," *Commentary*, July 1962.
[13] Hans Morgenthau denies the existence of unalloyed facts as follows: "Facts have no social meaning in themselves. It is the significance we attribute to certain facts of our sensory experience—in terms of our hopes and fears, our memories, inventions, and expectations—that creates them as social facts. The social world itself, then, is but an artifact of man's mind, the reflection of his thoughts and the creation of his actions. Every social act (and even our awareness of empirial data as social facts) presupposes a theory of society, however unacknowledged, inchoate, and fragmentary. It is not given to us to choose between a social philosophy and an unconditional surrender to the facts as they are. Rather we must choose between a phi-

In a similar vein, others deny that there is anything substantively wrong with the American economy. It is their unwillingness to engage in any form of structural criticism, and their tendency to look upon those who do as vestigial appendages of modern democratic society, that compels them to regard the existing tools as adequate for the correction of what they consider to be a temporary and fleeting imbalance. They deny the necessity for any structural reorganization of society and insist that it is all a matter of mere technical adjustment within the existing canons of responsibility. This ability of the end-of-ideology approach to blur understanding and lead to inaction is magnified out of all sensible proportions by the internal economic problems of the United States since 1953. The phenomenon of the business cycle has not disappeared from the American scene. Since the end of World War II the American economy has continued to experience alternating periods of expansion and contraction. The postwar boom of 1946–8 involved a huge spending spree by households and business firms for long-denied consumers' and producers' durable goods. And the liquid assets accumulated by both groups during the war provided the means for financing the boom. The 1948–9 recession which followed was quickly reversed by the outbreak of the Korean War, and with the cessation of hostilities in Korea the American economy dipped into the trough of 1953–4. These two initial postwar booms are easily understood. What is not so easy to understand is the grossly inadequate performance of the economy since the end of the Korean War.

Since 1953 the number of quarters from trough to cyclical peak has steadily declined. And while these post-Korean recoveries have become progressively abortive and of shorter duration, the rate of unemployment has virtually doubled as we have moved from one cyclical peak to another—from 2.7 percent of the civilian labor force during the second quarter peak of 1953 to 5.2 percent for the latest cyclical peak of 1960–2. It is not surprising, therefore, that in our successive peaks of economic activity both the average duration of unemployment and the amount of long-term unemployment have increased. A corollary to this rise of chronic unemployment is the slowing down of the annual growth rate (computed on a peak-to-peak basis) from 4.8 percent for the

losophy consistent with itself and founded on experience which can serve as a guide to understanding and an instrument for successful actions, and an implicit and untested philosophy which is likely to blur understanding and mislead action."

period 1948–53 to 2.5 percent for 1953–60—a drop well below the long-term historical rate (1890–1959) of 3.2.

An alternate method of illustrating the seriousness as well as the magnitude of the problem currently facing the American economy is to compute the difference between what the economy could have produced at a given point in time, assuming a full employment use of its resources, and what it actually did produce. This can be done by adopting the technique of the President's Council of Economic Advisers. Assuming a long-time potential growth rate of 3.5 percent (comprised roughly of a 1.5 percent increase in the labor force and a 2 percent increase in the productivity of labor) and an unemployment rate of roughly 4 percent (assumed, on the basis of mid-1955, to be compatible with relative price level stability), the gap between potential and actual output amounted to approximately $34 billion for the third quarter of 1962 on an annual basis and in constant 1954 dollars. If we accept the President's call for a higher growth rate of 4.5 percent, the gap increases to $70 billion. And if we set a 2.4 percent unemployment rate as our definition of full employment, then at the increased growth rate of 4.5 percent the gap jumps to over $100 billion of output lost irretrievably.

It seems reasonable to conclude on the face of this evidence that the American economy is suffering from a noncyclical slack of chronic proportions—despite arms expenditure which pumps into the economy an average of $50 billion a year. To argue that in spite of these developments things are not as bad as they were in the 1930s is to judge and compare business cycles solely in terms of their statistical differences, rather than the potential consequences which would follow from a protracted failure to maintain an adequate growth rate. Undue emphasis on nonideological, "factual" analysis and statistical comparisons can breed an unthinking empiricism which ignores the context of the data and hence their meaning. It becomes unhistorical and short-sighted.

Stripped to its bare essentials the crisis facing the United States in the 1960s involves two gaps—the *internal* gap between the actual and potential output of the American economy, and the *external* gap between the growth rates of the United States, the Common Market, and the Soviet Union. The closing of the internal gap and the narrowing of the external gap is of paramount importance if the United States is to survive as a major power in the long run. It should be made clear, however, that the closing of the internal gap does not necessarily imply a closing of the external gap. A closing of the internal gap would require a significantly larger increase in the short-term growth rate than we have been experiencing in the last decade. But once closed, the economy would then proceed along its now inadequate long-term growth rate of 3.2 percent. It is, therefore, of importance that, aside from the internal policies needed to close the internal gap, as measured by the Council of Economic Advisers, additional measures be undertaken to increase the long-term rate of economic growth; which would then require a still larger increase in the short-term rate.

What is desperately needed is a marked change in the American public's assessment of the role of government in a democratically oriented society. If we are to meet the joint problem of the two gaps, long-range planning on a governmental level is imperative and the present division between the private and public sectors of the economy must be looked upon as unrealistic. We must not engage, as has the Council of Economic Advisers, in historical extrapolations from the past which supposedly show that nothing has changed and that our old tools are as good as new. Nor does this necessarily imply the adoption of socialist planning. It is rather a question of what changes are needed to make the capitalist system viable in a power world. The internal gap, for example, may be a structural rather than merely a technical problem in cyclical instability. If so, then the indirect Keynesian controls of monetary and fiscal policy may no longer be fully adequate. For one thing, it must be kept in mind that business cycles and wars induce, however subtly, irreversible changes in the underlying institutional structure of a modern society. And our theoretical constructions of reality, if they are to have any meaning at all, must absorb these changes over time. Insofar as existing social theories do not take these structural developments into account, they become obsolete and hence invalidated.

One of the problems of the postwar period has been the emergence of inflationary depressions attributable to the relative mildness of the periodic American recessions and to the emergence of oligopolistic concentrations of market power in both commodity and factor markets. With the economic pressures thus emanating from the supply side more so than from the demand side, serious doubt has been cast on the ability of monetary and fiscal policy to achieve a full employment use of resources, even at an inadequate long-term growth rate based on a 4 percent unemployment rate. And it is a bit ludicrous to suppose that, by riding things out with inadequate policies derived from inadequate theories, it is only the timetable and not the path of an economy which will be affected. It may be that no changes exist, under these circumstances, which would make American capitalism, as we know it, viable.

But it is at least incumbent upon us to determine if this is so and not slide into a doctrinal rigidity which would ensure its defeat. The problem facing the United States may not be a purely technical one. We need to determine this and if the traditional tools are found to be inadequate, then what will be needed is a re-evaluation of the institutional framework and the value premises upon which it is based. It is time, therefore, that the graduate departments of major universities become rather more than just places where competent technicians are trained.

V

It has been agreed that Bell's and Lipset's account of the end of ideology in the West is, in large part, accurate. There is, nevertheless, a judgment to be made apart from the accuracy of their account. Bell and Lipset regard the end of ideology as good. Our point here is that it must be judged contextually, and that under the *present* conditions it borders on the disastrous. This can be illustrated by comparing the two supreme technicians of American politics—Franklin D. Roosevelt and John F. Kennedy. Both are supreme examples of the noncommitted, nonideological politician acting out of political expediency. Both placed the highest value on political success at the polls and regarded such success as the *sine qua non* of their existence. And neither had any fixed vision of the good society. Yet though they are similar in all these and other respects, the consequences of their common and purely "political approach" to politics are not the same. The 1960s are, obviously, not the 1930s. And it is in the context of each of these two periods of crisis that the end of ideology common to both Roosevelt and Kennedy must be judged.

The crisis of the 1930s gave rise, through the New Dealers, to a new wave of hope, and to the conviction that by social engineering things could be put aright. The flood of social legislation in the early days of the New Deal was an extraordinary attempt to bring about the needed institutional changes. This passion for pragmatic social experimentation was rooted deeply in the belief that human nature was highly, if not infinitely, plastic. It was in other words, basically optimistic and full of hope in a time of crisis. It was, above all, an age of critical thought, of regeneration, of faith in man's power to change the institutional complex within which he lived. It engaged, unstintingly, in a fundamental criticism of man and the institutional melange within which he had entrapped himself. Society, in short, was to be reconstructed in the image and in the interests of the so-called common man. But there was no over-all blueprint. It was an empirical approach to democracy. If there was no ideological cohesion, there was at least general agreement that something had to be done and a clear understanding of the problem in personal terms. It was there, staring at them—the breadlines, the hunger, the Hoovervilles, the closed factories, the ugly tear in the social fabric of a once prosperous society. The crisis of the 1930s was readily understood by the man in the street. It was a part of his everyday experience and affected or was a direct and frightening threat to his continued well-being. And it was on this stage that the end of ideology entered in the form of President Roosevelt. The political coloration and social innovations of the New Deal were largely the result of political expediency in a country where political success counts for all. The tune of the New Deal was played by ear and the end of ideology in the guise of a charismatic President served to make the vast power of the presidency responsive to the public will.

The 1960s are an entirely different matter. The current situation is not immediately understandable in direct, personal terms by the ubiquitous man in the street. The threat of nuclear annihilation numbs his sense of credulity and is so vast as to be beyond his conceptual capacity. The problem of disarmament is also much too complicated to be fully comprehended. Despite the poor performance of the economy since 1953 and the growth of unemployment, the affluent society continues to maintain its image unimpaired. There are no breadlines, as in the 1930s, and the economic problem has not yet pierced the individual's consciousness since, for most people, it is not yet a direct threat. And if one major aspect of the economic problem is the long-run power threat implied by the disparate rates of economic growth between the United States and the Soviet Union, then surely this is the most remote of his immediate concerns. In short, the problems of the 1960s are much too abstract for the limited social vision of the common man.

It is in this totally different context that a nonideological man like President Kennedy operated. It is not the kind of crisis which confronts the individual with understandable, let alone meaningful problems to which he can respond politically. So when President Kennedy wet his finger and held it up to the political winds, he found them blowing simultaneously in all directions. There is no coherence; no well-thought-out sense of purpose, as Hans Morgenthau has pointed out, in foreign policy, and as is even more obvious with respect to domestic policy. Above all, and unlike the 1930s, there is no general consensus in the body politic to which the President can respond out of sheer political expediency, in a clear and consistent manner. In short, there is no limiting frame of reference within which to innovate, and lacking one of his own, he flounders, compromises, and tries to be all things to all men. Indeed, like Lipset, he rationalized the emptiness of modern society and declared that it *is* the good society and that all the problems which do remain are purely technical. Two of Kennedy's recent talks more than amply demonstrate this. In his remarks before the Economic Conference held in Washington on May 21, 1962, the President distinguished between myth and reality in these words.

I would like also to say a word about the difference between myth and reality. Most of us are conditioned for many years to have a political viewpoint, Republican or Democrat—liberal, conservative, moderate. The fact of the matter is that most of the problems, or at least many of them that we now face, are technical problems, are administrative problems. They are very sophisticated judgments which do not lend themselves to the great sort of "passionate movements" which have stirred this country so often in the past. Now they deal with questions which are beyond the comprehension of most men.

A month later at his 1962 commencement address at Yale University, the late President further elaborated on this theme.

Today . . . the central domestic problems of our time are more subtle and less simple. They do not relate to basic clashes of philosophy and ideology, but to ways and means of reaching common goals—to research for sophisticated solutions to complex and obstinate issues.

What is at stake in our economic decisions today is not some grand warfare of rival ideologies which will sweep the country with passion but the practical management of a modern economy. What we need are not labels and clichés but more basic discussion of the sophisticated and technical questions involved in keeping a great economic machinery moving ahead.

. . . Political labels and ideological approaches are irrelevant to the solutions.

. . . The problems of . . . the Sixties as opposed to the kinds of problems we faced in the Thirties demand subtle challenges for which technical answers—not political answers—must be provided.

Though we do not agree with this position, it must be admitted that the President had the good sense to limit it to domestic issues. At no point would the President, or any other sensible person, have argued that our differences with the Russians were purely technical. Neither have Bell and Lipset.

VI

Bell and Lipset are of one mind. Whereas the old ideologies of the West have become exhausted by the march of Western progress, new ideologies have arisen in Asia and Africa—the ideologies, according to Bell, of industrialization, modernization, pan-Arabism, color, and nationalism. The new ideologies, unlike the old, are not being fashioned by the intellectuals along universal or humanistic lines. Rather, they are instrumentally parochial and employed by political leaders who have created them for purposes of rapid development and national power. And the disoriented Western liberals have desperately embraced the new ideology of economic development to "wash away the memory of old disillusionments" (pp. 397–8). In this sense, Lipset believes there is "still a real need for political analysis, ideology, and controversy, *within the world community,* if not within the Western democracies," and the Western ideologue, stripped of issues in his own back yard must now focus his attention on this new area. Though ideology and passion are no longer necessary in the affluent and advanced democracies of the West, they are very much needed in the less affluent countries of the world. In the underdeveloped countries, we should encourage the radical and socialist politicians because, according to Lipset, "only parties which promise to improve the situation of the masses through widespread reform . . . can hope to compete with the communists" (p. 416). Therefore, the disaffected liberals of the West, the unreconstructed intellectuals, the trade-union leaders (at least those who are still liberal), and the socialists have a positive role to play—abroad, where their vision and their need to criticize can be put to good use in developing free political and economic institutions.

This is, indeed, a remarkable argument. The Lipset and Bell position is that the end of ideology exists only in the West, but that ideology has still an important role to play in the underdeveloped countries if only like some Sorelian myth, to meet the three conditions and purposes of ideology as set down by Bell, *viz.* (1) to simplify ideas, (2) to establish a claim to truth, no matter how specious, and (3) to demand a commitment to action. Furthermore, the displaced ideologues of the West, those disenchanted intellectuals in need of a vision to sustain them, can be used to further and to speed up the role of ideology in the underdeveloped countries, and thus forestall a takeover of these areas by the communists.

In time, if we are successful, the underdeveloped countries will become developed and as they, too, solve all their pressing political, social, and economic problems, ideology will wither on their vines. Then peace will break out in an enlarged West and international relations and disputes will, like purely internal problems, be governed by an *international* ethic of responsibility.

Lipset and Bell are, in effect, arguing that the nations of the world are all racing toward a static state of equilibrium. Only some countries have had a head start. A few have already achieved the good society. Others are fast approaching it. And still others, the underdeveloped countries, have only just begun their ascent. In time, all will have arrived, but until such time it will be the responsibility of those already at the pinnacle to reach down and help the others up. In all this, it would seem, dynamic change is a transitory phenomenon and all of human history, in all its turmoil and in all its travail, has been moving, inexorably, toward this supreme goal of universal peace. At bottom, what Bell and Lipset are giving us is a philosophy of history—if not of the past, then certainly of the future.

for further study

ANTON, THOMAS J. "Power, Pluralism, and Local Politics," *Administrative Science Quarterly*, Vol. 7 (March 1963), 425–457.

BACHRACH, PETER. *The Theory of Democratic Elitism*. Boston 1967.

BARRY, BRIAN. *Political Argument*. New York, 1965, Ch. 14.

BURNS, JAMES MACGREGOR. *The Deadlock of Democracy*. Englewood Cliffs, N.J. 1963.

CRICK, BERNARD. *The American Science of Politics*. Berkeley 1959, Ch. 7.

GOLDSCHMIDT, MAURE L. "Democratic Theory and Contemporary Political Science," *Western Political Quarterly*, Supplement, Vol. 19 (September 1966), 5–12.

GUSFIELD, JOSEPH R. "Mass Society and Extremist Politics," *American Sociological Review*, Vol. 27 (February 1962), 19–30.

KARIEL, HENRY S. *The Promise of Politics*. Englewood Cliffs, N.J. 1966.

MAY, JOHN D. "Democracy, Organization, Michels," *American Political Science Review*, Vol. 59 (June 1965), 417–429.

McCOY, CHARLES A. and JOHN PLAYFORD (eds.), *Apolitical Politics: A Critique of Behavioralism*. New York 1967.

PARTRIDGE, P. H. "Politics, Philosophy, Ideology," *Political Studies*, Vol. 9 (October 1961), 217–35.

PERROW, CHARLES. "The Sociological Perspective and Political Pluralism," *Social Research*, Vol. 31 (Winter 1964), 411–22.

SCHATTSCHNEIDER, E. E. *The Semisovereign People*. New York 1960.

part four ❧

strategies for normative, empirical, and analytical work

The writers represented in the preceding part of this volume, Part Three, make evident how extensively the ideals of democracy highlighted in Part One have been revised. Revisionists such as Michels, Schumpeter, Dahl, Almond, and Berelson, having taken their bearings by the prevailing practices in the more developed nations, focus on political stability, large-scale industrialism, and political consensus. They thus tend to regard the existing order of facts as the very criterion of democracy. To this new "realism," the contributors to Part Three take exception by challenging the methodological assumptions of the "realists."

It is still far from clear, however, to what extent a conception of democracy more oriented by potentialities than actualities might be a tenable one, how it may be made persuasive, and how it may be tested by empirical work. In any case, the writers contributing to the final section of this volume, while questioning the adequacy of the prevailing "realism," seek at the same time to enlarge the sphere of politically relevant reality. There would seem to be agreement among them on one point: to determine whether the constraints under which men act today are truly ineluctable it is essential to reconceptualize what is alleged to be reality. Alternative realities must be posed and subjected to empirical tests. Experimental action must jeopardize the alleged "inner logic" of industrialism, the "necessities" of economic development, the "iron law" of oligarchy, and the "inevitability" of the historical process. To what extent contemporary constraints on men will yield to new visions may be discovered by hypothesizing states of affairs *contradicting* experience, by stipulating that modern man need *not* be victimized by industrialism, the economy, oligarchical organization, or what is still occasionally said to be a destiny manifest in events.

To move ahead, the following writers implicitly postulate the individual as agent, as self-directed, as active political participant. They postulate a political system that fully makes room for such individuals. And they postulate a model for political analysis and research that accommodates free individuals in a free society. However different their accents, they would have us attend to currently concealed phenomena—namely human needs, interests, and aspirations that have not become manifest, that orthodox research designs treat as peripheral or dysfunctional. They would regard both public action and work in the social sciences as successful to the extent that individuals are thereby enabled to realize the democratic ideals affirmed in the opening part of this volume.

26 ❦ BEHAVIORAL RESEARCH AND THE THEORY OF DEMOCRACY

CHRISTIAN BAY

"The only reason for making a buzzing-noise that I know of is because you're a bee." Then he thought another long time, and said: "And the only reason for being a bee that I know of is making honey." And then he got up, and said: "And the only reason for making honey is so that I can eat it."

A. A. MILNE, *Winnie the Pooh*

Winnie the Pooh appears to be steeped in the philosophy of Aristotle, for whom the plants exist for the sake of animals and animals for the sake of men. Aristotle, of course, was the more systematic and universalistic philosopher, for whom the provision of honey or its hedonistic equivalents by no means sufficed to satisfy the purposes he attributed to man's evolving nature.

The point I want to stress is that Aristotle's whole view of life and the universe was teleological: all natural phenomena, physical and biological, exist for the purpose of serving man. Consequently, for him the natural sciences, being concerned with phenomena relatively removed from man, were inferior to the social sciences. The master science was political science, which used the rest of the sciences: "The end of politics is the good of man"—of man in the city or community or nation, of course. "The attainment of the good for one man alone is, to be sure, a source of satisfaction, yet to secure it for a nation and for states is nobler and more divine." This was the aim, as he saw it, of political inquiry.

The progress of political thought had to wait for almost twenty centuries, till the advent of Thomas Hobbes, before the Aristotelian view of political science was effectively challenged. True, Machiavelli may be credited with having been an early behavioralist, but it remained for Hobbes to argue, essentially, that political inquiry should begin with the empirical study of human nature and the human condition as they actually exist, and seek to develop predictions about what normative political principles may become vindicated by the acid test of their facilitating, first of all, sheer physical survival for human beings. To find out how to get away from a state of affairs in which human lives tend to be "nasty, brutish, and short" was for Hobbes the basic task of political inquiry; man's ennoblement or moral improvement was to him at best a secondary concern.

Grim as the Hobbesian solution of the Leviathan state was, Hobbes should be credited with at least one indispensible contribution to the evolution of liberal political thought: he introduced the concept of individual *right,* natural *right,* as a crucial normative foundation for his reasoning about politics. He based his concept of natural right on realistic observations about behavior and on unassailable inferences about the individual's apparently crucial interest: staying alive, physically unharmed, was seen as the individual's most urgent interest and therefore as his crucial natural right. Political theory became to Hobbes not so much a queen science or the noblest science as it became the most practically compelling concern, a kind of how-to-survive-in-a-cruel-chaotic-world line of inquiry. Gone was the Aristotelian assumption of a benign, preordained social order in which the laws of nature imposed duties on the individual but no rights.[1]

The Aristotelian and Hobbesian approaches to politics have been contending for support, and the different normative assumptions in the two views continue to make representatives of each camp talk past one another. Worse still, many a modern political scientist seems to exhibit mild schizophrenic tendencies in his failure to resolve this dilemma in his own mind. In this paper I hope to bring out this failure of communication and of acceptable conflict resolution in the particular field of democratic theory in its confrontation with modern behavioral knowledge. And I hope to contribute toward a synthesis, that is, to reach a number of tentative conclusions that would seek to make democratic theory more attuned to the findings of empirical research, while at the same time seeking to make behavioral research, or some of it, more geared to the task of serving, in Aristotle's phrase, "the good of man."

I shall first sum up, in a few words, what I take to be the essential differences, at least for my present purposes, between the Aristotelian and Hobbesian approaches to political inquiry. Then (II) I will sketch some stages in the development of democratic theory, culminating in today's fashionable pluralistic stance; and then (III) briefly describe what I take to be some essentials of the behavioralist assumptions guiding the major trends of empirical political research today.

[1] *Cf.* Leo Strauss, *Natural Right and History* (Chicago, 1965), esp. pp. 181–184.

Next (IV) comes a few comments on the most apparent contradictions inherent in the simultaneous commitment to behavioral research and to democratic pluralism—quite a common orientation today. In the last two sections I shall propose (V) a different type of commitment to democracy and (VI) a different or at least an expanded or a complementary perspective on behavioral political research.

What separates Aristotle and Winnie the Pooh from Hobbes and contemporary heroes like the Hardheaded Businessman is not that Aristotle was concerned with norms and values while Hobbes was not. Both were concerned with values but in different ways. Aristotle held values to be empirically ascertainable, like (other) facts, and from this false premise, in my opinion, drew the logically correct inference, again in my opinion, that it is possible to determine scientifically the precepts of morality and politics. Hobbes was more modest in his claim to moral knowledge. He thought he knew the supreme value of one thing, namely human life itself, and quite sensibly, in my opinion, proceeded to develop a body of political theory geared to the preservation of this supreme value. There are structural faults at higher levels in the impressive if forbidding edifice he built, but his empirical foundation is sound and has been built upon by later generations of empiricists. What is particularly sound in Hobbes is that he did not assume a universe with a plan for mankind; his point of departure was the more earthy one of aversion to violence. His ambition was to think through the all-important problem of how human lives can best be protected by way of a political order tailored to the human condition such as it is, not as it might be or ought to be according to the will of the gods. He faced up to the fact that there may be many reasons why bees make honey, and that the taste buds of men or bears are unlikely to have much bearing on the behavior of bees.

II

The term "democracy" has had a checkered career in the long record of human semantics.[2] Some of the earliest Greek philosophers, like Democritus and possibly Solon, held the term in high esteem—or what it stood for. Plato and Aristotle, on the other

[2] See Jens A. Christophersen, "An Historical Outlook on the Different Usages of the Term 'Democracy,' " in Arne Naess et al., Democracy, Ideology, and Objectivity (Oslo, 1956).

hand, were both opponents of what they called "democracy"—
meaning, roughly, unrestrained majority rule; this jaundiced view
of "democracy" prevailed not only throughout the Middle Ages but
almost to the twentieth century. Indeed there are some in the
United States today who will argue vehemently against the common characterization of that country as a democracy; it is not,
they insist, it is a republic.[3] By this term they wish to emphasize
and identify themselves with the concern of most of the Founding
Fathers to avoid the hazards of democracy in the Greek sense, *i.e.*,
unrestrained majoritarianism. Historically these contemporary
conservatives are quite right: the American Constitution sought
to forestall, not only by its Bill of Rights but first of all by its
elaborate division of constitutional powers, every effective exercise
of tyranny by any majority. So elaborate are its safeguards against
bad government that it may well be argued that good government,
too, has been made difficult and improbable.[4]

Yet the ideology of democracy has been victorious in the United
States, as it has throughout the Western world. At the very least
it is clear that the *term* "democracy" is almost universally favored
and that it is utilized to bolster almost any cause. It is true that
fascists have tended to scorn the term, but everybody else, from
conservatives and Roman Catholics to socialists and communists
consider themselves democrats in some sense or other.

And in North America the consensus appears to extend much
beyond the *term* "democracy." It is my impression that politicians,
political scientists, and most other mortals on this continent also
tend to favor the *concept* of a pluralist democratic system—
roughly speaking, a system of representative government based
on free elections from time to time, a fair amount of free speech,
assembly, and organization, a free press (at least for editors or
those who can keep editors in business), and at least two competing political parties. A final but crucial item in the apparent
mainstream of North American thought today is a belief in private
enterprise or, conversely, in considerable limitations in the power
of political governments to interfere with private business decisions. It is true that the government's right to tax, even tax heavily,
seems to have become widely accepted, but at the root of the con-

[3] These sentiments are common on the extreme right. For example, see
H. L. Hunt, *HLH Columns* (Dallas: HLH Products, no date [1966 or 1967]),
p. 47: "Our Founding Fathers gave us a republic because they knew that
only a republic can preserve liberty. If we abandon their constitution, in
the name of democracy or any other name, we shall lose our liberty."

[4] *Cf.* my paper "Liberalism: Human Rights and Behavioral Science,"
Centennial Review 4 (1960), 331–353, esp. pp. 338–343.

cept of pluralism lies precisely this notion that there should be a wide variety of nongovernment interests capable of challenging the government. It appears widely believed that such a challenge would be less than real without strong private business.

Advocates of modern representative democracy, from John Locke on, have believed in democracy as a sort of contractual arrangement between the rulers and the ruled. C. B. Macpherson has shown, at least to my satisfaction, that Locke believed in individual rights only, or at least primarily, for members of the better classes and would have recoiled from the idea of universal suffrage.[5] But given the electorate that he contemplated, he believed that the best hope for a just government rested with a constitutional order in which political discussion was left fairly free and was given some impact on the course of legislation. Unlike Hobbes, Locke emphatically believed the social contract to be binding on the rulers as well as the ruled, and favored the right to advocate revolution as a last resort. Far from formenting anarchy such a right would, he believed, give governments a further incentive to respect the constitutional rights of the people.

With the Manchester liberals and the utilitarians came the idea of the free market, in ideas as well as in goods, and democracy came to be viewed as a way of reasoning together. James Mill thought of abuse of government power in a representative democracy as almost a contradiction in terms. John Stuart Mill, perhaps the most influential of all nineteenth-century champions of liberal democracy, was firm in his belief that the best ideas would win out in free competition, at least in the long run.

There is no space to discuss the many subspecies of democratic theory within this broad liberal tradition. Names like Burke, Schumpeter, T. V. Smith, Maritain, Niebuhr, Hallowell, Walter Lippmann, S. M. Lipset, and Robert Dahl, to mention only a few, suggest some of the variety of positions within the mainstream of liberal democratic political thought.[6] Some, like Burke, Maritain,

[5] See his *The Political Theory of Possessive Individualism* (Oxford, 1962), chap. V and *passim*.

[6] See Louis I. Bredvold and Ralph G. Ross (eds.), *The Philosophy of Edmund Burke* (Ann Arbor, 1960); Joseph A. Schumpeter, *Capitalism, Socialism, and Democracy* (New York, 1942); T. V. Smith, *The Democratic Way of Life* (Chicago, 1926); Smith with Edward C. Lindeman, *The Democratic Way of Life: An American Interpretation* (New York, 1951); Jacques Maritain, *Man and the State* (Chicago, 1951); Reinhold Niebuhr, *Moral Man and Immoral Society* (New York, 1932); John H. Hallowell, *The Moral Foundation of Democracy* (Chicago, 1954); Walter Lippmann, *The Public Philosophy* (New York, 1955); Seymour M. Lipset, *Political Man* (Garden City, N.Y., 1960); and Robert A. Dahl, *A Preface to Democratic Theory* (Chicago, 1956).

Hallowell, and Lippmann, are more Aristotelian than others, in their faith in the wisdom of the species or their belief in an objective natural law as a source of duties. Others, like T. V. Smith and to a lesser extent Lipset and Dahl, are in many respects relativists and empiricists; the two latter are in principle committed to research as a way of clarifying if not resolving many problems of democracy. Yet Lipset and Dahl too, I shall argue, are implicitly Aristotelian in their assumption that our Western, and more particularly, the United States type of democracy makes the best of all possible worlds, which must and will be preserved for the benefit of future generations.[7]

While unquestioned commitment to existing institutions of pluralist democracy is maintained by otherwise fact- and research-oriented behavioral political scientists, their own work has tended to leave their ideology out on a limb, as I shall try to show in the next two parts of my argument. Let me at this point only stress the tendency of many political scientists to stress the value of pluralist democracy as an instrument of social *stability* while showing a disinclination to investigate alternate possible objectives that might be less well served—for example, elementary welfare for the less articulate and the less well organized strata of society.[8]

III

If "research" is understood very loosely, research in political behavior dates back to the Greeks. In the stricter sense, gathering of empirical facts with which to test hypotheses, Robert Michels' study *Political Parties* (1915) was one of the first projects of research in political behavior (although there were no tables and no quantitative data in his book).[9] But it was the techniques of attitude scaling and of opinion survey research that made large-scale study of political behavior possible. Later and complementary techniques have been quantitative content analysis of documents, participant observation of role behavior, experimental and other observation of role behavior, experimental and other observation of small groups, measurement of decision processes and outcomes in bureaucracies, other large organizations, and communities, and so on. As a major field of scientific inquiry, research in political

[7] See especially the last chapters in Lipset, *op. cit.*, and in Dahl, *op. cit.*
[8] For a powerful plea for transcending the politics of the status quo, see Henry S. Kariel, *The Promise of Politics* (Englewood Cliffs, N.J., 1966).
[9] Robert Michels, *Political Parties* (Glencoe, Ill.: Free Press, 1949).

behavior in the United States dates back to the 1930s, with Harold D. Lasswell and Paul F. Lazarsfeld, each in his own way, among the leading pioneers.

But the behavioralists have drawn on a rich store of empirical theory from several social science disciplines. Max Weber, Emile Durkheim (whose empirical study *Suicide* [1897][10] presented a brilliant methodological model decades before it was rivaled by other studies), Pareto, Mannheim, Marx, Simmel, and Tönnies have all had their major works translated and have found their American students and sometime spokesmen. Themselves influenced above all by Weber and Durkheim, American sociological theorists like Talcott Parsons and Robert K. Merton have exerted a powerful influence on contemporary political behavior theorists, who at the same time have drawn on pragmatist and logical positivist philosophy.

In this part of my argument I am interested in the kinds of knowledge established by behavioral research, not in the theoretical orientation of our leading behavioralists. And let it be said that very impressive results have been achieved in three decades; we may really speak of a revolution of knowledge in this field. I don't mean merely that a large *quantity* of hypotheses have been confirmed; a few years ago Gary Steiner and Bernard Berelson in their inventory of scientific findings on human behavior listed 1,045 different hypotheses for which there is a good amount of scientific evidence![11] Most of these propositions would be applicable to political as well as to other human behavior.

The behavioral research revolution has produced much chaff, but much vital insight also. First comes to mind the many massive voting studies, each of which as a rule has probed more deeply or with more sophistication the range of stimuli that lead individuals of various kinds to vote a particular way or perhaps not vote at all. The despair of Graham Wallas about man's tendency to be rational and forward looking in his political decisions has been amply confirmed.[12] On the other hand, many processes of political influence have been uncovered; most voters are not irrational in the sense of having no cognitive reasons or reasons based on their own experience for voting as they do.

Apart from voting studies perhaps the most important contribu-

[10] Emile Durkheim, *Suicide* (Glencoe, Ill.: Free Press, 1951).
[11] Gary Steiner and Bernard Berelson, *Human Behavior: An Inventory of Scientific Findings* (New York, 1964).
[12] Graham Wallas, *Human Nature in Politics* (Lincoln, Neb., 1962, first published in 1909).

tions have come from students of organizational behavior and of decision making. Michels' discovery of tendencies toward elitism in social democratic organizations has been extended to encompass virtually all organizations, as a perhaps inevitable dimension of the life of every organization with formal or informal objectives about which its leadership feels strongly. Philip Selznick has shown how conflicts of interest between leaders and members are bound to emerge in every organization, with the leadership, which controls the supply of information, usually in the stronger position to protect its interests.[13]

Murray Edelman in his recent book, *The Symbolic Uses of Politics*,[14] by way of summarizing his own and much other research concluded that conflicts of demands on government between large but loosely organized groups—say, consumers—and small but well-organized lobbies usually are resolved in this manner: legislation or regulations are issued that offer tangible benefits to the well-organized groups, which have the information and ability to judge what they get, while largely symbolic satisfactions are given to the larger but less sophisticated or less well-organized groups. In most federal regulatory agencies some amount of favoritism is essential to their political survival, argues Edelman, and reviews in his book some of the "built-in tendencies" that reduce the chances that the agencies will do the job they ostensibly were set up to do.

There is not space here to survey the whole field of behavioral research that bears on our theories of democracy. Studies of power on the national scene have been scant, and the controversy over C. Wright Mills' *The Power Elite*[15] has not benefited from ambitious empirical inquiry. Studies of local decisions and of local power structures have been more plentiful and instructive, with major contributions from political scientists and sociologists as diverse in background and approach as the Lynds, Floyd Hunter, Robert Dahl, Robert Presthus, and Robert Agger and associates. While Mills' thesis about the national scene remains a plausible hypothe-

[13] See especially his "Foundations of a Theory of Organization," *American Sociological Review*, 3 (1948), 20–30. A large literature has subsequently developed in this field.

[14] Murray Edelman, *The Symbolic Uses of Politics* (Urbana, Ill., 1964).

[15] *Cf.* Robert S. and Helen M. Lynd, *Middletown* (New York, 1929); also, their *Middletown in Transition* (New York, 1937); Floyd Hunter, *Community Power Structure* (Chapel Hill, 1953); Robert Dahl, *Who Governs?* (New Haven, 1964); Robert Presthus, *Men at the Top* (New York, 1964); and Robert E. Agger, Daniel Goldrich, and Bert E. Swanson, *The Rulers and the Ruled* (New York, 1964).

sis, there is a mass of evidence that Edelman's more modest propositions are valid in local as well as national government: money and organization, not majority interest, are likely to sway the decisions of the governing elites; only in exceptional situations, as when it develops intense feelings on some issues and has strong and sophisticated leadership, is it likely that the majority will have its way. F.D.R.s victory in 1932 is an example. I do not know of many others, at least not in the Presidential elections.

The fact that the mass media by and large are controlled by conservative businessmen is another circumstance reducing the likelihood that majority needs under normal circumstances will prevail over minority interests. As Edelman and others have shown, by their power over symbols most elites are able to influence both the self-perceptions and the political goals of the majority, let alone their anxieties and fears. But just how these processes operate is a problem area in need of much more research.

Without taking the time for further discussion of behavioral work that has shown the classical theories of democracy to be largely inoperative in modern large-scale democracy—at least in the United States but surely in other countries too—let me conclude this part of the discussion by suggesting that our behavioral researchers should have accomplished for our political beliefs what Dr. Kinsey accomplished for our sexual beliefs: a shocking realization that traditional norms are far removed from current practices.

I will now discuss how the culprits themselves—not the sexual but the political behavioralists, a far more timid breed—have tended to handle their discovery. In conclusion I will, speaking for a minority of at least one, develop some of my ideas on how the conflict ought to be handled, first in terms of democratic theory and then in terms of the further development of behavioral research.

IV

The confrontation of behavioral knowledge with democratic theory has as yet not produced what may be called the moment of truth. The usual response has been to try to have it both ways, in my judgment—on the one hand to acknowledge that, realistically speaking, our system is in substance hardly a government "of the people, by the people, for the people"; on the other hand, to hold that all men who are good and true must proclaim their unreserved allegiance to our "democratic" form of government and stand up for it as doggedly as if we were in fact living today by its classical principles. In short, having first persuaded us that our traditional empirical reasons for owing allegiance to our constitutional system and to the politics of our pluralist processes are largely false, at least on the national level, most political scientists in the next breath assure us of their own unswerving allegiance to our "democratic" form of government.[16] There is nothing wrong with allegiance to the system under which one lives; in fact, it can be a very good thing, as it promotes stability. But as political scientists we should not need the crutches of false reasons for defending our political beliefs.

In recent behavioral literature one of the most illuminating, and influential, confrontations occurs in Berelson, Lazarfeld, and McPhee's 1954 volume *Voting*.[17] We are promised in the Introduction a "confrontation of democratic theory with democratic practice" as one of the two themes of the book, the other theme (or, rather, the first theme) being the empirical problem of how voter preferences are in fact formed. Yet all we get is a curt dismissal of the traditional democratic theory to the extent that it requires the citizen to be interested in politics, to be knowledgeable, and to be rational. The dismissal seems merited, but the authors are cavalier about what to put in the old democratic theory's place. There is no explicit discussion of what if any part of the old theory might be rescued. All we get is a facile discovery, or, I would say, a facile claim, to the effect that our present system of democracy in the United States actually works rather well; we are not informed of the criteria on which this and similar judgments are based, however. Nor are we told with any precision just how well, in what respects, or what aspects of the system works better than others.

In their recent monumental study, *The Civic Culture*, Almond and Verba[18] take over where Berelson *et al.* left off, and are even more explicit about making "the political culture in the two relatively stable and successful democracies, Great Britain and the

---

[16] Many go further than this and think of our American political system as a model for less developed countries to emulate. For example, see the discussion of the concept of civic culture below.

[17] Bernard R. Berelson, Paul F. Lazarsfeld, and William N. McPhee, *Voting: A Study of Opinion Formation in a Presidential Campaign* (Chicago, 1954).

[18] Gabriel A. Almond and Sidney Verba, *The Civic Culture: Political Attitudes and Democracy in Five Nations* (Princeton, 1963). Also see Almond and G. Bingham Powell, Jr., *Comparative Politics* (Boston, 1966).

United States"[19] their normative yardstick for measuring the political achievement of less favored countries. The idea of a civic culture (to which the British and American democracies are the closest approximations) is the authors' substitute for the traditional idea of a democratic form of government. The actively concerned citizen may be a menace to political stability, they argue; in the two most successful democracies we find, significantly, a more balanced "parochial-subject-participant" orientation. The need for democracy must be tempered by the need for authoritative government. "The need for elite power requires that the ordinary citizen be relatively passive, uninvolved, and deferential to elites. Thus the democratic citizen is called upon to pursue contradictory goals; he must be active, yet passive; involved, yet not too involved; influential, yet deferential."[20]

Called upon by whom, and on what grounds? This is like a page right out of Aristotle, with the perhaps significant difference that Aristotle was in favor of constitutional government, not democracy. Since the ultimate norm justifying the civic culture as a model is stability, or more precisely the stability of the British-American kind of social order, one wonders whether "constitutional government" would not be, as it was for Aristotle, the more fitting label for the Almond-Verba ideal of government.

Common to these authors and to Aristotle is a strong preference for middle-class domination as conducive to stability. As the golden mean is seen to be virtuous, so is excess of any kind seen as a vice—including excessive passion for social justice? Perhaps the deepest problem with Aristotle's politics and with Almond-Verba's conception of the civic culture, as I understand it, is the lack of explicit concern with what happens to the least privileged and to the sanctity of life (*their* lives too) once political stability based on pluralist inequality has been achieved.

Aristotle was quite content to live with slavery and the subjugation of women. Obviously, this is one area in which all modern liberal democrats in our profession differ with him. Another area is in their empiricism—in their insistence on empirical study as a prerequisite for realistic political thinking, in the Hobbesian tradition. And yet the normative point of departure for the mainstream theorizing about democracy in our profession strikes me as more Aristotelian than Hobbesian. The most basic norm appears to be

[19] Almond and Verba, *The Civic Culture, op. cit.,* p. 473.
[20] *Ibid.,* pp. 478–479.

not the survival or welfare of the individual (whether the least privileged one or, as with Hobbes, the citizen of means) but, it would seem, the continuance of the established social order with most of its blemishes, including the de facto subjugation of the underprivileged and the destitute. Not that modern liberal democrats are not against such blemishes as individuals; my point is that many of our colleagues too readily gear their normative thinking about democracy to the convenient banner of stability, not to the humane task of expanding the liberty of individuals according to standards of social justice.

My description of the encounter between behavioral research and democratic theory has been limited to two examples, but I believe these are rather representative of much of the best work in this area. Elsewhere, I have discussed other works from the same perspective.[21] My indictment is by no means proved valid by the present sketchy documentation, but I believe there is ample evidence for my principal conclusion: that our leading behavioralist researchers deserve credit for their demonstration that democracy in the traditional sense is largely inoperative, at least on the national scene, and perhaps always has been, but that they should be blamed for in effect abandoning the objectives to be served by democracy as advanced by its early proponents: social justice, the common good, the best ideas emerging from free and open encounter, and so on. The civic culture or a stable British or American or Canadian social order may present a worthy model for less fortunate lands, but neither is an adequate substitute for the *summum bonum,* and neither can have any claim to our uncritical allegiance. Much less can this American image of the civic culture lay claim to provide viable ideals for the intelligent Burmese, Brazilian, or Vietnamese in his search for a model of the good society.[22]

---

[21] "Politics and Pseudopolitics: A Critical Evaluation of Some Behavioral Literature," *American Political Science Review,* 59 (1965), 39–51. See also Jack L. Walker, "A Critique of the Elitist Theory of Democracy," *American Political Science Review,* 60 (1966), 285–295, which appeared after the completion of the present paper. Both papers are reprinted, along with others of related interest, in Charles A. McCoy and John Playford (eds.), *Apolitical Politics: A Critique of Behavioralism* (New York, 1967).

[22] A contrary assumption seems clearly implied in Lucian W. Pye's *Politics, Personality, and Nation Building* (New Haven, 1962)—to name but one example of an admirable study in some respects.

V

Democratic theory badly needs restructuring and new perspectives. First of all, we need a theory of democratic institutions as a means to substantive ends. By "substantive" I mean meaningful to individuals and capable of being maximized, so that we may develop yardsticks for measuring how well particular democratic institutions work in terms of what values or what human needs. In this field, incidentally, The Civic Culture offers, as does Almond's theorizing in other works, interesting data and leads for further measuring the sense of participation in various political input functions and of benefit from various output functions.[23] And in his current project in comparative politics Verba has chosen as one of his main dependent variables a truly substantive concern in the sense just suggested: the extent of actual political and social rights that exist and are acknowledged by ordinary individuals in local communities in five different countries.[24]

My own basic approach to democratic theory is to analyze the proper scope and limits of majoritarianism and constitutionalism as instruments for the maximization of individual freedom, with priority for those who at each time are least free. I have tried in my book, The Structure of Freedom, to sort out some of the issues and propose some priorities among possible aspects of freedom that lend themselves to expansion.[25]

On this occasion let me give only a bird's eye view of my approach, for I would also like to take the time to touch on one or two issues raised by that other school of democratic theory—the truly orthodox, natural-law-oriented, self-professed Aristotelians among us; and the topic of natural law will make it necessary also to consider briefly the problem of civil disobedience in a mass democracy.

I take it to be the task of what we call human rights, or civil rights, to establish and protect the most basic freedoms first, for

[23] See also Almond, "Comparative Political Systems," Journal of Politics, 18 (1956) 391–409; Almond and James S. Coleman (eds.) The Politics of the Developing Areas (Princeton, 1960); and Almond, "A Developmental Approach to Political Systems, World Politics, 17 (1965) 183–214; and Almond and Powell, op. cit.

[24] This project, sponsored by the Ford Foundation, includes simultaneous field research in India, Japan, Mexico, Nigeria, and the United States.

[25] Stanford, 1958, and New York, 1965. I am very much aware of many shortcomings in my attempt, in addition to those insufficiencies imposed by the magnitude of the task.

all individuals. "Human right" in my vocabulary refers to any freedom that empirically can be enjoyed by all, without conflict, as distinct from "privilege," which refers to freedoms that in fact diminish as they are shared. I am not against privileges but admit to a normative stand implied in the use of the laudatory term "human right" for freedoms that do not diminish by being shared, like freedom of worship or freedom of political inquiry and speech. I adopt the view that no majority or minority should be authorized to diminish anybody's freedom except when someone else's more basic freedom may require it. Human rights should, once established or proclaimed, never be subject to curtailment, only to gradual expansion as conditions permit. To determine empirically *when* conditions permit must in a country such as the United States be up to the Supreme Court. It must not be left up to the Congress, although priorities among possible avenues of rights expansion may pose normative issues subject to legislative choice. The U.S. Supreme Court may not be ideally equipped for deciding rationally and empirically, for example, the extent to which extreme kinds of dissent *can* be permitted without serious violations of liberty to others; but assuredly it is better equipped for such a task than Congress.

Generally speaking, I see the proper scope of democracy as an instrument of freedom delimited by two types of decisions that should be removed from majoritarian control. First, the basic commitment to the principle of increasing the freedom of all individuals as much as empirically possible by way of human rights expansion; this decision I see as underlying our Constitution and indeed as being the fundamental credo of any nation aspiring to freedom and human dignity for all. Secondly, the purely empirical type of decision, including empirical decisions about whether freedoms in fact have been violated, or are in conflict, or can be expanded; this is a type of decision best handled by the courts, ideally with guidance from behavioral scientists.[26] Other kinds of decisions should be made democratically, or as democratically as possible; when values and interests are in conflict, and there is no one right or wrong answer, the ballot remains the most feasible way, in the long run, and perhaps the only way compatible with the dignity of sharing in self-government.[27]

[26] Some provocative ideas on how to improve on and expand the political usefulness of U.S. courts are advanced in Harvey Wheeler, *The Restoration of Politics*, an "Occasional Paper" published by the Center for the Study of Democratic Institutions, Santa Barbara, California.

[27] This general problem is discussed at greater length in my paper, "Liberalism: Human Rights and Behavioral Science," *op. cit.*

But what are the most basic freedoms to be considered as human rights? With Hobbes I take survival and physical inviolability to be the most basic human rights. The first objective of government should be to protect all lives and forestall or reduce all physical violence. Government coercion is justifiable to the extent that it forestalls or reduces the amount of worse (more extreme) kinds of coercion. Next comes the protection of health, including mental health. After that it becomes more difficult to determine generally acceptable priorities.

In order to resolve this problem we desperately need further advances in our psychological knowledge of human development. This is the only feasible way to develop a viable, empirically useful theory of freedom. How important, for example, is freedom from fear compared to freedom from want, and from which fears and which wants? Individuals differ, obviously, and yet have something in common—a basic if empirically elusive human nature,[28] and possibly also elements of a national character and fragments of an in-principle universal education in a given society. No really precise positive model of the fully developed person can or should be developed; human beings are not that much alike, even potentially, and one flirts dangerously with totalitarianism if one makes such an assumption. On the other hand, a negative model of some stages in the process of individual development toward full humanness is available, and can be improved upon.

I am thinking of the Katz and Sarnoff model, or the Smith, Bruner, and White model.[29] Briefly, both models see the individual mind in various stages of development toward the full use of the rational faculties. Individuals cowed by anxieties about their worth as human beings may be doomed to lives of self-hatred and authoritarian bigotry toward others. Those worried about being socially accepted may be induced to entertain only palatable and therefore shallow views about themselves and their social order; likewise, when people are preoccupied with career anxieties. In this perspective the developed human being is he who is sufficiently free from anxieties about self to be capable of rational thought about life and about society, and capable of natural empathy with

[28] See James C. Davies, *Human Nature in Politics* (New York, 1963), esp. chap. 1.

[29] *Cf.* Irving Sarnoff and Daniel Katz, "The Motivational Bases of Attitude Change," *Journal of Abnormal and Social Psychology,* 49 (1954) 115–24; M. Brewster Smith, Jerome S. Bruner, and Robert W. White, *Opinions and Personality* (New York, 1956); and Daniel Katz, "The Functional Approach to the Study of Attitudes," *Public Opinion Quarterly* 24 (1960), 163–204.

others, especially with victims of violence or other oppression.

When Rousseau wrote about democracy as being fit for gods only and distinguished between the general will and the will of all, I believe he anticipated a developmental model of man somewhat along the lines suggested above. Albert Camus has carried this idea much further in his great work, *The Rebel*.[30] The positions of both Rousseau and Camus can be contrasted with the conventional commitment to democracy in our profession in the emphasis on man's potentiality for development. Drawing on the work of modern psychologists, I believe it is possible to say that the civic-culture model of democracy is a static one that assumes that most individuals are capable of developing no further toward political responsiveness, toward concern with morality and justice, than today's average American or British voter. From the developmental perspective just outlined, on the other hand, it would seem that the civic-culture type of democracy is only a way station on man's long development from barbarism toward humanity—a way station at which the minority of upright public-spirited individuals are invariably outvoted (though not always out-influenced) by the majority of their fellows, who remain to a large extent the prisoners of their own failing self-esteem, anxieties, fears, lack of knowledge and ability or incentives to inquire, or of their desperate desire for economic affluence or security or the kind of social status and pseudo self-esteem that goes with affluence.

But what of the modern defenders of natural law as a basis for democratic theory? It is easy to sympathize with an exasperated critic of Leo Strauss who at a recent meeting of the American Political Science Association accused the master of drawing knowledge out of his nose, and added, "Why should it be *his* nose?" There is in the Straussian school little concern with assembling evidence from our contemporary situation as a way of testing the present applicability, at any rate, of Aristotelian eternal verities, and little concern with developing empirical propositions with sufficient precision so that others might subject them to possible tests. Indeed, Strauss shows his contempt for the very idea of empirical research in statements like: "The new political science puts a premium on observation which can be made with the utmost frequency, and therefore by people of the meanest capacities."[31]

[30] Albert Camus, *The Rebel* (New York, 1956).
[31] Leo Strauss, "An Epilogue," in Herbert V. Storing (ed.), *Essays on the Scientific Study of Politics* (New York, 1962), p. 326.

A still more serious objection is that natural-law theorists of this school tend to mistake some of their individual political prejudices for eternal verities; too frequently their versions of natural-law function are an in-group sanctification for their particular, usually conservative, and strongly anticommunist beliefs. Thus, Strauss is scornful that "the new political science has nothing to say against those who unhesitatingly prefer surrender [read compromise under terms of peaceful coexistence] . . . to war."[32] The implication would seem to be that those who differed with his "better dead than red" stance (at that time, in 1961–1962) deserved to be ostracized from the profession, if he had his way. Or take a more recent book by Walter Berns, a student of Strauss's, which is one long diatribe against the U.S. Supreme Court for its defense of freedoms that the author does not value. Characteristically, Berns recommends a reinterpretation of the First Amendment as if it read "Congress shall make no law abridging the freedom of *good* speech."[33] To determine what speech is good is presumably a matter for Berns to settle, drawing, of course, on his Aristotelian vision.

And yet, if we were to throw all of natural law out with the improbable claims advanced by writers like Strauss and Berns, we might well lose the baby with the bath water. For these writers have a point when they charge the behavioralists with having no viable conception of the public interest and "no objective criteria of relevance" for distinguishing the important from the unimportant.[34] Behavioralists do occasionally assert boldly that there is no such thing as "the public interest."[35] In opposing this view, the editors of *The Public Interest* state ironically in their introduction to the first issue of that journal that they doubt that the American Political Science Association can be defined adequately as a self-seeking organization; when political scientists meet they surely "have the sense that they are quite disinterestedly (if passionately) concerned with truths that bear upon something like 'the public interest.' "[36] There surely must be a place in the theory of democracy for such a concept as Walter Lippmann defines: "The public interest may be presumed to be what men would

[32] *Ibid.*, p. 317.

[33] Walter Berns, *Freedom, Virtue, and the First Amendment* (Baton Rouge, 1957), p. 251.

[34] Strauss, *op. cit.*, p. 317.

[35] For example, see James M. Buchanan and Gordon Tulloch, *The Calculus of Consent: Logical Foundations of Constitutional Democracy* (Ann Arbor, 1962), p. 12.

[36] "What Is the Public Interest?" *The Public Interest*, 1 (1965), 5.

choose if they saw clearly, thought rationally, acted disinterestedly and benevolently."[37]

I believe in a probable comeback for natural law in democratic theory. But the dogmatic teachings of Strauss and his followers and also of some of the neo-Thomist theorists[38] will be replaced by, or at least supplemented by, advances in research on human development. Strauss is right, in my opinion, when he asserts that "man has natural ends—ends toward which he is by nature inclined" and that, as Hobbes saw, "self-preservation is the most important natural end."[39] But the way to determine what the rest of these ends or basic inclinations may be is surely to develop better methods for observing the profundities and not only the surface aspects of human behavior. If we are to determine the dictates of a realistic natural law today we must first of all study nature, *i.e.*, human nature and the nature of our human and social condition.

Until such knowledge is forthcoming, it seems to me, any claim to restrict liberties in the name of natural law must be resisted as an attempt to impose an intolerant ideology on people with other commitments. Now, it may well be that the development of a new natural law based on sound psychological research provides no better basis than the old one for restriction of liberties; if freedom is to be the end, even perverse (if harmless) freedoms must be welcomed. But this kind of new and more realistic natural law would accomplish at least one thing: it would make it easier to decide in cases of conflict which possible *new* human rights should take precedence over possible alternatives in a given society at a given time. For example, should the right to choose retirement age take precedence over the right to choose how many days a week to work? Should the right to free dental care take precedence over free services from opticians and optometrists? Up to what age level (if any) should formal education be compulsory, if available resources permit a free choice? Improved knowledge of the development of human needs cannot dictate but can surely guide the resolution of issues between competing freedom demands.

[37] Walter Lippmann, *The Public Philosophy* (New York, 1956), p. 40.
[38] See especially Jacques Maritain, *Man and the State* (Chicago, 1951); Yves R. Simon, *The Philosophy of Democratic Government* (Chicago, 1951); and John H. Hallowell, *The Moral Foundation of Democracy* (Chicago, 1954). This last work includes some hard-hitting criticism of some of the orthodox democratic ideas discussed in this paper.
[39] Strauss, *op. cit.*, p. 325.

Rousseau and Graham Wallas have been proven only too right in their belief that pluralist liberal systems of alleged representative democracy are unlikely to guarantee, or even to make probable, public-spirited governments and political decisions in the public interest. As private interests have tended to prevail at the public's expense, it has made matters worse for the underprivileged citizen who has been effectively taught to respect and honor his government's policies in the name of "democracy," with all the traditional myths about democracy as legitimizers. Tocqueville expressed his astonishment at the arbitrary powers sometimes exercised by "American functionaries" on the strength of the apparent political mandate won by the party in power, and he warned that in this way "habits are formed in the heart of a free country which may some day prove fatal to its liberties."[40] It is hard to convince citizens to demand their freedom once they have been convinced that they are free already; and to the extent that our present so-called democracy is revered as if it embodied our traditional democratic ideals, the prospects for advancing those ideals in the United States will remain dim.

Perhaps it is time to replace the Aristotelian faith in our system of checks and balances as providing the best of all possible political worlds with a Hobbesian determination to base our political thought on the real state of affairs. If we extend Hobbes' premise that the first task is to preserve (all) lives and state that the first task of government is to preserve (all the people's most basic) liberties as well, then we must conclude that certain objective norms must be given a validity more compelling than any contrary norms that may emanate from the authority of the government, or from the allegedly democratic processes as we know them. The norm that forbids the taking of lives is an obvious example.[41]

To put it more generally, our advancing behavioral knowledge underscores our need for at least a few "objective" or consensual standards with which to judge decisions emanating from the legal processes of mass democracy. We need certain standards of justice, whether we want to associate them with natural law in some sense or not. And we need to qualify our allegiance to demo-

[40] Alexis de Tocqueville, *Democracy in America* (New York, 1945), Vol. 2, pp. 272–273.

[41] Or, *at least*, the taking of lives without demonstrable necessity, that is, compelling proof that only such an extreme measure can save a much larger number of lives. No such proof has even been marshaled in justification of capital punishment, certainly, or even in justification of most acts of war.

cratic policy decisions with a prior allegiance to at least one or two elementary principles of justice.

The principle of equality under the law is one example of such an elementary standard of justice. Most majorities are poorly equipped to remedy, or to feel strongly about remedying, inequities suffered by racial minorities, for example. Courts may be better equipped, but they too need to be instructed about the depth of resentment and alienation at the receiving end of racial discrimination. In the United States, particularly in the South, we have observed that it has taken the breaking of laws by participants in the civil rights movement, and the threat of further law violations, to force even the federal courts to change the laws (and indeed the substance of the Constitution itself) so as to reduce inequities long imposed against the Negro.

There is a general principle I would like to derive from this observation and from the previous argument: if the purpose of government is to protect and expand liberty on the basis of equal fundamental rights, then laws and government policies that flagrantly discriminate should be disobeyed, no matter how impeccably constitutional (or formally "democratic") the origins of such laws or policies may be. If the majority is firmly bigoted, then the wronged minority should not in the name of democracy be asked to wait. They might have to wait for a hundred years, as the American Negro has done.

Perhaps in a mass democracy acts of civil disobedience are a necessary way of bringing the most intense grievances of a minority to the urgent attention of a relatively apathetic and previously untroubled majority; perhaps even the grand old men of the Supreme Court occasionally need this kind of instruction. One thing is certain: progress toward freedom, in the sense of broader human rights, or broader freedoms for the least free, is unlikely to be originated by either popular or legislative majorities, or even by distinguished lawyers elevated to high judicial office.[42]

The superior right of conscience over positive law has in our time been proclaimed by an eminent authority who has some claim to represent the most orthodox natural-law tradition. Pope John XXIII made no distinction between democratic and authoritarian

---

[42] The U.S. Supreme Court does deserve credit, however, for at least one great freedom-expanding decision that was not made under the pressure of demonstrations or possible riots: *Brown vs. Board of Education*, the historic decision of May 17, 1954, which declared segregated schools unconstitutional.

regimes when he stated in his *Pacem in terris: "For to safeguard the inviolable rights of the human person and to facilitate the fulfillment of his duties should be the essential office of every public authority.* This means that, if any government does not acknowledge the rights of man or violates them, it not only fails in its duty, but its orders completely lack juridical force."[43]

Our pluralist political system is not all bad; in our fallible world we know worse systems only too well. My point is that our profession should no longer idealize this system, but judge it strictly as a means to the ends of freedom and study more actively how its inbuilt inequities and shortcomings can be remedied. We must not blithely assume, as some of our most influential colleagues have tended to do,[44] that we have already arrived in the good society or in as good a society as men are capable of producing.

VI

Behavioralists have taught us much about how men actually behave under our system, and have mapped out at great lengths popular attitudes, opinions, and other proclivities. We have learned much about how groups, organizations, and whole communities function. They have taught us much about power and decision processes. They have taught us much that we need to know about the wants and demands of various socioeconomic and sociocultural strata under different conditions.

But the main emphasis in political behavior research has been on sociological rather than psychological determinants of demands. In relevant theory too it is worth noting that political sociology has become an established discipline, while we only intermittently hear of a field called political psychology.

I won't go into the hen-or-the-egg-first type of question here. A mutually reinforcing relationship exists between a research emphasis on the social as distinct from psychological basis of political behavior, and a democratic theory that emphasizes manifest wants and demands rather than latent needs.

To study human needs is almost infinitely harder than to study wants and demands (I take "want" to refer to the sense of perceived or felt need, and "demand" to a want for which remedies are

---

[43] Glen Rock, N.J., 1963, paragraphs 60, 61; emphasis added.
[44] See note 7 above.

being actively sought). Socrates stressed how easily what seems good is mistaken for what is good, and what seems true for what is true. But he devoted his life to striving to sort out false images so that he might come nearer the real thing.

My most fundamental objection to much of the theorizing around behavioral work today and to virtually all pluralist democratic theory is that there has been an abdication of the search for the real thing—man himself and his real needs. Pluralists generally write as if articulated wants and demands are all we need be concerned with; if so, majoritarianism or even government by way of Gallup polls might well make sense. But apart from the fact that overprivileged groups are able, generally, to articulate and press for satisfactions of *their* wants more effectively than other strata, the equally stubborn fact remains that the less privileged that particular people or strata are in our socioeconomic order, the less likely it is that their manifest aspirations and wants (beyond matters of food and shelter) are really their own. For the less educated and less prosperous a person is, the more vulnerable, statistically speaking, he is to being taken in and influenced, even in his conception of himself, by advertising or propaganda or demagogues who falsely claim to be the spokesmen for his interests.

Yet, even if it has been shown and can be shown that many wants and demands are artifacts imposed on individuals and groups from the outside, the difficult question remains: How can a person's (or a category of persons') genuine, internally rooted *needs* be established empirically?

Only at the most basic level is this a simple task: the elementary biological needs, including sexual and some parental drives, are by and large of such force that they cannot be suppressed by indoctrination. Outside this sphere our empirical task is formidable. But it is not in principle an impossible task, and it is surely a bit premature to give it up.

Empirically I would start out with defining "human need" as referring to any tendency whose continual suppression or blocking leads to pathologies. "Pathology" cannot be defined precisely either, but it is possible to list some widely accepted examples: schizophrenia, suicide, homicide, alcoholism, drug addiction. Destruction of self or others, whether fast or slowly, presumably indicates a pathology, which by the present hypothesis is believed to derive from a severe deprivation of some kind; *i.e.*, the frustration or blocking of some essential need—unless, of course, the pathological behavior can be traced to brain damage, body chemistry change, or drug use.[45]

Our hypothesis asserts that for each tentatively defined pathology, with the exceptions noted, there is a corresponding frustration or blocking of some genuine human need. The test of the hypothesis, over the long run, will be whether therapists can identify the hypothetical need and, by way of providing for its recognition or satisfaction, make the pathology go away. From this perspective it may be suggested that the study of misusers of alcohol or narcotics should provide a potentially fruitful approach toward a better understanding of the structure of human need priorities in relation to typical patterns of need denial or frustration in a particular social order. What kinds of people tend to be most vulnerable to drug pathologies, depending on what patterns of life experience?[46]

Maslow has developed a hypothesis about a hierarchy of universal human needs, starting with the biological, and James C. Davies has tried to apply this hypothesis in the study of politics.[47] Neither Maslow nor Davies has succeeded so far in developing verifiable knowledge about the nature and sequence or priorities of human needs, or about how needs determine behavior, perhaps because they have been too bold and ambitious; I believe that slower, more painstaking research is necessary, research that attempts to add a Maslovian dimension or theoretical framework to the normal behavioral concern with surface behavior.

Let me by way of illustration throw out several suggestions about possible areas in which I believe it is possible and profitable to add new psychological and normative dimensions to mainstream behavioral research or to apply more directly to the study of political behavior work that goes on in neighboring fields:

1. There needs to be more study of the genuine public-spirited minorities, or individuals, in different communities and so-

[45] In the last instance, the taking of drugs may itself tentatively be defined as pathological behavior, or partly so, if as a result of an addiction process it has become partly a result of body chemistry change.

[46] Possible approaches toward the empirical study of human needs (as distinct from wants) are discussed at greater length in my paper, "Beyond Pluralism: The Problem of Evaluating Political Institutions in Terms of Human Needs," *Canadian Journal of Political Science* 1 (1968), 241–260.

[47] Abraham H. Maslow, "A Theory of Human Motivation," in Philip L. Harriman (ed.) *Twentieth Century Psychology* (New York, 1946), pp. 22–48; also see Maslow, *Motivation and Personality* (New York, 1954); and James C. Davies, *Human Nature in Politics* (New York, 1963).

cieties, wherever such people can be identified (there are, also of course, neurotics and careerists among practicing idealists and fighters for social justice). What do they have in common? How can we grow more of them?

2. Political socialization is a relatively new but immensely promising area. What types of childhood and youth experience go with what kinds of predispositions toward government and toward issues of freedom and justice? More so, of course, if comparisons can be made with studies of socialization within different social systems—like Joseph Fiszman's current work on Czech and Polish schools as agencies of political socialization.[48]

3. Studies of student development in this and other cultures can usefully include data on political and intellectual development and at the same time data on anxieties, self-perceptions, and types of ambitions for the future. College-student populations may well be the best ones possible if we are looking for substantial minorities of relatively articulate and relatively "idealistic" but not yet narrowly career-socialized individuals.

4. Improved dogmatism scales (improved over Rokeach's[49]) can perhaps yield very rough indications in varying populations of levels of suppressed anxieties, guilt, etc., and so give indications of degrees of ego defensiveness as basis for opinions and attitudes, and perhaps for degrees of distance between wants and basic needs.

5. Measures of preoccupation with conventional career goals and/or social acceptance, correspondingly, may become improved and with increasing apparent validity indicate something about the extent to which salient opinions and attitudes serve these desires rather than cognitive needs, or needs for understanding reality "like it is."

6. Historical and geographical studies of men and movements in the service of high principles can, if enough facts are

[48] Dr. Fiszman's project is sponsored by the United States Office of Education. A classic study (which also coined the term) in this new field is Herbert Hyman, *Political Socialization* (Glencoe, Ill., 1959). For a valuable recent symposium, see Roberta Sigel (ed.), "Political Socialization: Its Role in the Political Process," *Annals of the American Academy of Political and Social Science*, 361 (1965).

[49] *Cf.* Milton Rokeach, *The Open and Closed Mind* (New York, 1960). Rokeach's dogmatism scale is composed of various subscales along different dimensions, it would seem; I particularly would like to remove worry-type questions, replies to which indicate *acknowledged* anxiety level, from what I take to be more genuine dogmatism or closed-mindedness questions.

available with which to combat myths, also help uncover sources of relatively disinterested devotion to the public interest or to some just cause.

These are only a few examples of ways to add to and influence behavioral research toward greater serviceability in the cause of man's freedom. Let me add that I also consider coordinated philosophical analysis, including logical development and analysis of norm systems, as an essential part of this broad and long-term endeavor.

Let me summarize my hopes for the future of behavioral research in political science in relation to theorizing about democracy as follows: I would have us stop limiting our major efforts to seeking data on how our pluralist political system, such as it is, now operates, and also have us stop assuming that it will not or ought not to change. Rather than adjusting the classical ideals of democracy to present realities and preaching that we must nevertheless be loyal supporters of our democracy, let us do more research on kinds of citizen behavior that, if more widespread, would make the classical ideals of democracy more nearly realizable, and seek knowledge about how such citizens can be developed in greater numbers in our various agencies of socialization. Above all, let us never forget that democracy as we have it has no claim to be considered sacrosanct; man himself surely ought to have the prior claim. For me, this means that the crucial test for judging a democracy or any other system of government is the extent to which its decision processes favor the protection and expansion of human rights, or the expansion of the freedom of those strata that at a given time are least free—whether their chains are made by economic or cultural impoverishment, political disenfranchisement, or lack of equality in the courts of law.

This position I see as the most appropriate modern synthesis between Aristotle's and Hobbes' basic approaches to political theory. Let us with Hobbes start out with the human condition such as it is and be concerned first of all with the most essential human needs, such as physical survival for all. But let us raise our sights to the extent possible, and follow Aristotle in his quest for the kind of society that lets men develop their natural potentialities for becoming more civilized and humane.

Let us avoid the Hobbesian pessimism about man's ability to change and develop and someday govern himself. But let us also avoid the Aristotelian faith in some benign power, a sort of cosmic

Christopher Robin, who will see to it that all will go well—or will seem to go well—if we somehow stick to the democratic or constitutional principles and institutions of our forefathers, and somehow refuse to be subverted by new ideas or even by new knowledge established by our own behavioral research.

Democracy too can be a dangerous system unless we remain vigilant on behalf of the basic humanistic values like freedom and human right, and the sanctity of human lives and individual potentialities for growth. There *is* no cosmic Christopher Robin who will keep us, the overfed nations, safe so long as we are God-fearing and "democratic," in a world of starvation and exploitation. As members of a profession, political scientists have far too long been supportive of our people's conventional liberal self-righteousness, adorned with a fine democratic phraseology as a cover for the American establishment's cruel defense of the strong against the weak on a world-wide basis. In short, we have in fact served our corporate rulers instead of justice and the dignity of man. We have accepted much of the *Leviathan* in return for the safety of our own academic soapboxes, but without matching Hobbes' humanistic aversion to violence.

27 🙚 RESEARCH ORIENTATIONS: SOME PITFALLS AND SOME STRATEGIC SUGGESTIONS

MURRAY EDELMAN

This paper explores some of the social-psychological and semantic processes through which distortions in research findings, conclusions, and value implications are systematically induced. It then suggests an orientation intended to encourage more flexible,

[This paper is a revised version of one the author presented at a symposium on Normatively Oriented, Empirically Based Political Research, Northwestern University, May 1966.]

realistic, and imaginative political-system metaphors than those commonly employed in research. A central objective of the suggested strategy is to assure attention to the sense in which governmental acts, pronouncements, and policies themselves shape public wants, values, and expectations, in contrast to the optimistic assumption that popular demands and supports are the system inputs and the key independent variable.

It is certainly one function of research on political processes to suggest avenues through which people can achieve values they prize. Kurt Lewin once observed that "nothing is so practical as a good theory." Research results are practical in the measure that they call attention to data that are relevant to a group's concerns and in the measure that the data are incorporated into a framework that adequately defines the ties between alternative courses of political action and results.

Such adequacy is not easily achieved, and no neat formula for attaining it is likely in the forseeable future. At the same time it is possible to identify some characteristics of commonly employed research approaches that subtly confine attention to only a part of the relevant consequences of political actions or that arbitrarily make assumptions about the causes of observed behaviors or about the direction of cause-effect relationships. Any of these shortcomings detracts from the effectiveness of groups that rely upon the research for strategic guidance just as they systematically mislead academic investigators about the dynamics of political interactions; for they unjustifiably constrain investigation of the range of both independent and dependent variables.

The serious and interesting, because subtle, pitfalls in the design of research stem from inadequate definitions of the dimensions and the dynamics of the system under study: the range of variables and of their consequences that need to be considered. To look at some of the results of such inadequacy is to conclude that the converse of Lewin's dictum also holds: nothing is so impractical as an inadequate theory.

I

Whether a normative orientation is conscious or unconscious, failure to take steps to ensure that the unintended consequences of political acts and institutions will be observed and studied can be serious and distorting. The point is clearer and the trap possibly more tempting when there is a conscious normative orientation; and some examples of studies with conscious normative orientations are therefore considered first.

Concern about inflation has been almost chronic in recent decades, and periodically it becomes intense and widespread. When it is intense, governments feel strong pressure to do something about it; and in all countries they have repeatedly taken measures ostensibly designed to deal with it. What kinds of anti-inflationary measures particular groups favor has been closely related to their ideologies and norms, and the extant research on the subject serves rather neatly to support the policy predilections either of liberals or of conservatives. In the face of steep price rises liberals are likely to favor direct price controls and conservatives to favor indirect controls through credit restriction or tax increases with a regressive effect. Liberals are eager for commitment by the government that it will directly and openly restrict the right of businessmen to charge what the traffic will bear while conservatives are eager to avoid such direct intervention in what they regard as private business decisions.

In some comparative research on the politics of wage-price decisions[1] Fleming and I found strong evidence that liberals (whose general orientation we both shared) frequently defeat their own purposes by taking it for granted that the problem is adequately defined as "How do we get direct controls?" rather than "What range of functions do direct controls and indirect controls respectively serve?" Once the second question is seriously posed, some disconcerting findings are reached fairly easily and confidently: that direct controls in times of really strong upward pressure on prices are likely to be accompanied by black markets and gray markets that go far toward nullifying their effects or that raise prices even more than market forces do; that for political reasons control agencies frequently serve largely to rationalize price increases and permit them to occur in response to market forces or even faster than the market would raise them;[2] and above all, that the establishment and publicized functioning of direct

[1] Murray Edelman and R. W. Fleming, The Politics of Wage-Price Decisions: A Four Country Analysis (Urbana, 1965).

[2] The Wage Stabilization Board during the Korean War was sometimes dubbed by insiders the "Wage Stimulation Board"; the economists who studied the wage effects of its activities concluded that there was some justification for the wisecrack. See Clark Kerr, "Governmental Wage Restraints—Their Limits and Uses in a Mobilized Economy," in Proceedings of the Fourth Annual Meeting of the Industrial Relations Research Association, Boston, December 28–29, 1951, pp. 28–29; Benson Soffer, "Cost-of-Living Wage Policy," in the same Proceedings; and Richard A. Lester, "Wage Troubles," Yale Review, 41 (1951), 54–65.

price-control programs serve an important political function: they reassure people who are worried about inflation that the government is protecting their interests, even when, for the reasons just suggested, there is good ground for skepticism about their effectiveness.

By concentrating their attention upon bringing about direct controls of doubtful utility, liberals leave the manipulation of credit controls in the hands of central banks and other conservative groups; and it is these *indirect* controls that are demonstrably effective. The tightening of credit means that price pressures are eased regardless of the willingness of businessmen and labor to cooperate, although such cooperation is obviously necessary to make direct controls effective.

The failure of those with liberal norms to adopt a sufficiently broad conceptual framework and to look at all the relevant political and economic dimensions of the economic stabilization system thus leads them to a self-defeating course of action. In this instance, as is often the case, the really crucial part of the research lies in asking the right questions in the first place. Once this is done, it is usually not difficult to find the answers, most of which are already available in published studies; and the answers point strongly to the conclusion that some cherished liberal assumptions about the functions served by controls are dubious. Public demands and supports are largely a function of the wage-price control arrangements already in effect.

A somewhat similar state of affairs exists with respect to the evaluation of American programs to regulate business activity and the war on poverty. These are programs that are clearly "liberal" in motivation, and judgments as to whether they are effective or ineffective hinge on whether the observer is concentrating upon these motivations or upon objective research regarding their functions and system effects. As Thurman Arnold pointed out long ago, liberal politicians like Senator Borah built their careers upon advocacy of antitrust legislation that was almost wholly ceremonial in effect. Liberals and spokesmen for liberal administrations conventionally take it for granted that utilities commissions keep rates down; that the Federal Communications Commission regulates broadcasters in the interest of listeners and viewers; that the Federal Trade Commission is a thorn in the side of businessmen tempted to engage in unfair trade practices; that the poverty program takes money taxed chiefly from the wealthy and aids the poor; and so on. Conservative businessmen and the academic literature on government and business often make the same assumption. We therefore have liberals supporting these measures and conservatives opposing them because both these groups assume that the ostensible purposes of such public programs are equivalent to their actual effects: in short, that they are *effective*.

But there are also liberals who oppose them as *ineffective* and conservatives who view them as ineffective or pointless rather than as regulatory. These groups with opposing norms thus reach a common conclusion regarding the facts; and it is the opposite of the conclusion reached by the liberals and the conservatives discussed in the last paragraph. The difference, I suggest, lies in the fact that those who think these programs are effective concentrate upon motivations and formal purposes while those who think they are ineffective concentrate on empirically observable functions. The first group has tended to limit its research to studies of the history and political background of regulatory legislation. These studies then become heroic tales of the forces of righteousness battling the forces of darkness, though which side is which depends upon one's norms. In any case such studies serve to reinforce the values of those who undertake them or use them. They are bound to do so, for the consequences of public acts are taken for granted and remain unexamined while attention is concentrated upon the formal rhetoric that states their intentions and purposes and upon the political battles to shape the rhetoric so that it will amount to a status victory for those who espouse them.[3]

The second group examines the empirically observable effects of these regulatory programs, and these studies have concluded, with impressive uniformity, that the regulatory agencies fall under the influence of those they are supposed to regulate. Fairly early in their histories they stop promoting the values of the consumer and other unorganized groups they are ostensibly established to protect;[4] or the empirical studies conclude that poverty programs or aid to small businesses often serve chiefly to bring lucrative contracts and other financial resources to large, well-established business concerns, as do the highway construction programs in Appalachia or the lending activities of the Small Business Administration.[5]

The final link that keeps this system of policy making in equilibrium appears from research on the psychological and symbolic

[3] See Joseph Gusfield, *Symbolic Crusade* (Urbana, 1963); and Murray Edelman, *The Symbolic Uses of Politics* (Urbana, 1964).
[4] This literature is summarized in Marver Bernstein, *Regulating Business by Independent Commission* (New York, 1955), chap. 3.
[5] Harmon Zeigler, *The Politics of Small Business* (Washington, 1961).

effects of regulatory legislation: the conclusion that the political and legislative battles for these programs and the publicity regarding the activities of the official regulatory agencies serve as symbolic reassurance to the groups they are intended to protect, even if these groups derive little or no tangible economic benefit from them.[6]

In the light of these findings the focus and the function of the research on legislative histories and on legal phrases becomes even clearer. Such research, while largely empirical, concentrates only upon those aspects of the policy-formation process that provide symbolic reassurance to the holders of one set of norms; it ignores those facets of the process that deny tangible benefits to this same group.

We thus have a fairly complete picture of the balance of claims and payoffs, of demands and inducements, that comprise the systems in operation in these various policy areas. It is worth emphasizing that zealous reliance upon empirical findings and objective procedures cannot in themselves prevent research from carrying misleading connotations about the norms realized or realizable through particular courses of action and can easily create and emphasize the misleading connotations. Only a sufficiently comprehensive definition of the system of decision making under study and care in observing unintended as well as intended consequences of actions can serve as a protection against this hazard. In the case of programs like those just considered, one common kind of empirical research suggests that objectives are achieved when they are not; another, rather less common kind suggests that one should be skeptical about the economic value of these programs to their ostensible beneficiaries, but fails to enlighten us as to how they retain their political vigor indefinitely and what forms of noneconomic benefits they afford.

II

In the examples just discussed it was assumed that the norms to be achieved by the public programs in question were accepted and shared by the public officials responsible for establishing them.

Another, more subtle kind of methodological issue often arises in the case of research explicitly designed to promote stated norms. It is based upon ambivalence between the ostensible norms of a

[6] Thurman Arnold, *The Folklore of Capitalism* (New Haven, 1937); Murray Edelman, *op. cit.*

358 STRATEGIES FOR WORK

public program and counternorms, and it is expressed through language styles that both reflect the counternorms and help the investigators tolerate the ambivalence. In suggesting this possibility I am certainly being somewhat speculative, but there is a strong basis for this view both in psychological theory[7] and in the brilliant work on motives by Kenneth Burke.[8]

The McCone Report on the Watts riots in Los Angeles[9] illustrates rather clearly a conflict between the ostensible norms of improving the conditions of the Negroes in large city ghettos and thereby avoiding future riots and the personal values of members of the McCone Commission.

The report employs in a particularly blatant way some linguistic devices that frequently help researchers with strong norms to disguise from themselves and their audiences the bias in their findings and recommendations. When calling attention to the instances of violence in Watts, the style of the report is grandiloquent and flowery: "a devastating spiral of violence"; "marauding bands"; and the title of the report itself, *Violence in the City*. This kind of language inevitably reveals something important about the motives, the perspective, and the audience of those who use it. It is the language of propaganda, not of research. It signals that the function of these sections of the report is to arouse anxieties and suggest conclusions, not to examine data. This language style, like other distinctive ones, defines and selects its audience. It alerts serious students of social conditions that it is not intended for them at the same time that it appeals to a mass audience to adopt a particular emotional and intellectul perspective and to bring pressures on the politicians to do so as well. In this instance it serves to emphasize one of the major themes of the report: that the Negroes in Watts can be aroused to violence by a small group of irresponsible leaders because they have recently come from rural areas, are disoriented and disorganized in the city, are influenced by "real and supposed" grievances emphasized in civil unrest in other places and hence have potentially lawless traits,

[7] Some of the leading strands of psychological theory contributing to this view appear in: George Herbert Mead, *Mind, Self and Society* (Chicago, 1934); Leon Festinger, *A Theory of Cognitive Dissonance* (Evanston, 1957); Bronislaw Malinowski, "The Problem of Meaning in Primitive Languages," in *Magic, Science, and Religion and Other Essays* (New York, 1948); and Susanne K. Langer, *Philosophy in a New Key* (New York, 1942), chap. 4.

[8] Kenneth Burke, *A Grammar of Motives* (New York, 1945).

[9] California, Governor's Commission on the Los Angeles Riots, *Violence in the City—An End or a Beginning?*, 1965.

all of which justifies firm treatment by the police. The language thus concentrates attention on the violence. Even more important, it turns attention away from the economic, political, and social institutions that are a major facet of any full explanation of the violence: police harassment, lack of Negro representation and participation in government, and economic exploitation of Watts residents. The explanation of the violence, in short, is emphatically in terms of alleged Negro character traits rather than in terms of social institutions.

When the report does discuss the social institutions of Watts and Los Angeles, the language style is revealingly different. Rather than flowery and striking phrases there is a retreat to banal terms and clichés. George Orwell has suggested that banal political language serves to dull the critical faculties, both for the speaker and for his audience.[10] It seems to me a tenable proposition that banal language, in whatever context it is used, not only is a signal that critical thought is absent but also that its user is identifying with established norms and the established authority structure. The prevalence of administrative jargon and similar special vocabularies in various settings is thus not accidental, but predictable. I suggest that such modes of expression systematically reflect the accepted norms and help those who use them to avoid innovative thought and take the established authorities as their "significant others." They also help their audiences to take a similar loyal role and avoid criticism or serious re-examination of values. They therefore serve both as symbols of the accepted power structure and as catalysts by which personalities submissive to authority are molded, exactly as George Herbert Mead suggested that role taking both creates significant symbols and shapes the self.[11]

In the McCone Commission Report it is the existing norms of the police department, the municipal administration, and the business community that are treated in this way, with few departures. These institutions are found to be basically sound. No need is seen, for example, for a civilian review board to hear complaints about police harassment and brutality. A passage defending existing police practices can serve as an example of how this section of the report bristles with clichés:

Our society is held together by respect for law. A group of officers who represent a tiny fraction of one percent of the population is the thin thread that enforces observance of law by those few who would

10 George Orwell, "Politics and the English Language," in A Collection of Essays (New York, 1954), p. 172.
11 Mead, op. cit.

do otherwise. If police authority is destroyed, if their effectiveness is impaired, and if their determination to use the authority vested in them to preserve a law-abiding community is frustrated, all of society will suffer because groups would feel free to disobey the law and inevitably their number would increase. Chaos might easily result.

In prefacing its recommendations, which are for the most part viewed by liberals as timid or moderate, the commission returns to grandiloquent language. It calls its recommendations "costly and burdensome" and alleges that a "new and we believe revolutionary attitude toward the problems of our city" is required. As Kenneth Burke acutely observed, it is one function of political rhetoric to "sharpen up the pointless."[12]

The McCone Commission, like some other research discussed in this paper, creates normative implications by ignoring much of the political system it purports to analyze and assuming much that needs to be studied. I cite it chiefly, however, because it is a good example of the linguistic pitfalls of normatively oriented research.

It may be objected that it does not deserve this much attention because it is not serious social science research; yet it certainly presents itself as that and is discussed as if it is. In this respect it is not significantly different from a great deal of academic research. The *New York Times* declared, "The study is said to represent the most detailed analysis ever made of a civil disturbance." The commission had a professional staff of twenty-nine and employed twenty-six consultants. There was thus all the dramaturgy of serious social science research. I am suggesting that this dramaturgy in itself is a major determinant of a normative orientation.

III

The designs and strategies so far considered have involved research explicitly intended to realize particular norms. A considerable body of normatively oriented research does not fall into this class but rather presents itself as non-normative, and is conventionally accepted as such. The convention is probably quite reasonable, for it may be impossible to prevent value considerations from influencing research designs and findings. What matters is the use of every feasible device to minimize the normative effect. This very consideration, however, suggests the importance of recognizing the sources of normative effects.

[12] Burke, *op. cit.*, p. 393.

It should be noted parenthetically that the distinction between serious research that is explicitly normative in orientation and serious research that is not basic for our purposes, but it is convenient in organizing this paper. For reasons already suggested both types will fail to do what they are intended to do if the system of political behavior under study is not defined comprehensively enough and if the functions of the systems components are not adequately recognized.

I suggest that there is frequently an unconscious normative orientation in research deriving simply from the choice of subject matter to explore: from repeated and widespread emphasis on particular subjects that may be relatively unimportant in the perspective of their overall contribution to an explanation of who gets what, or of the authoritative allocation of values. In choosing subjects to study, political scientists are certainly guided by many considerations other than a theory of how one best explains who gets what. Some topics are dramatic and the objects of widespread public attention, and so they get a lot of detailed study from researchers who fail to ask themselves how they mesh with the overall system of value allocation. Some topics are peculiarly amenable to research by particular methods, such as quantitative ones or deductive inference, and so researchers who like these methods are prone to tackle subjects on which they can use them.

There is little reason to suppose that the amount of space devoted to specific subjects or hypotheses in the political science literature is a measure of the explanatory power of those subjects in understanding how values are authoritatively allocated (which, following Easton, I take to be what we are finally interested in doing). There is, rather, excellent reason to suppose that the choice of research subjects is typically made on essentially irrelevant (but not random) grounds of the kinds just mentioned. More than that, the very emphasis on particular subjects implicitly conveys to readers the untenable belief that those subjects are in fact the key explanations of value allocations. Therefore, because some subjects get undue attention as explanatory factors, we are sometimes led to place our bets on relatively ineffective courses of action as ways of improving the political system and of realizing the values on which there is widest agreement.

Let me cite studies of electoral behavior as an example, even though it is certainly a controversial example. Elections, more clearly than any other topic studied by political scientists, are objects of widespread public attention. They are dramatic, and we are taught from childhood that they give the people control over the government, that they make the difference between democratic and undemocratic government, and that they determine what policies the regime will follow. Voting behavior, as it happens, is also amenable to quantitative study. Many of the most competent political scientists have been drawn to the field for both these reasons, and it may well be the area of political science in which the most sophisticated work has been done, especially in the last two decades. It is certainly one in which a high proportion of the political science researchers are working and one to which the academic and popular journals devote substantial space.

Yet political scientists have good reason to be skeptical that elections do in fact serve the functions we ascribe to them in civics books, patriotic orations, and homilies about undemocratic foreign governments. The voting-behavior studies raise serious questions about the rational basis for voting and the quality of the information on which the voter acts. Legislative, administrative, and judicial behavior studies raise even more serious questions about the dependence of value allocations upon the outcomes of elections. Elections certainly serve as important rituals of communal and national identification (which goes far toward explaining their dramatic quality and the social pressures to participate in them); but the instrumental effect of elections upon policy directions and value allocations is far more dubious and tenuous. Elections are very likely not nearly as significant in this respect as the bargaining that goes on in the course of administrative and judicial decision making.

The point, of course, is that the decision to engage in voting-behavior research does not flow rationally from a general model of its place in the political process. Whether that general model should assign to voting behavior the place I have suggested it ought to have or a larger place, the intense concern with voting behavior in our research certainly carries misleading normative connotations. It implies that it is the chief influence upon how democratic a regime is and how likely groups are to realize their just claims through political processes; and this in turn suggests that concentration upon electoral reform is the most effective strategy for improving the operation of the system. If we are not sure that the electoral process really serves that function in the system, we clearly ought to learn about it through research rather than assuming what we do not know or choosing to engage in electoral behavior research because it is popular or because it can be studied rigorously. The very choice of a research subject upon an irrelevant but nonrandom basis rigs our conclusions about how to achieve values. It also suggests unjustified conclusions about democratic political systems, for it leads us to base such conclusions chiefly upon examinations of their electoral procedures.

It is easy enough to present other examples of this effect, and I will suggest two without making the argument in detail. Many economists believe unions have a relatively slight effect upon wage levels, the outcome of collective bargaining depending upon such national economic factors as labor supply and demand and influences upon price levels.[13] If this position is warranted, much of the extensive research by labor economists on collective bargaining not only amounts to a devotion to the trivial but carries misleading suggestions about the determinants of workers' living standards and serves chiefly to cement the loyalty of workers to union leaders rather than to explain wage changes.

There is considerable reason to believe that the international disarmament negotiations that have gone on intermittently and with almost complete futility for many years do not function primarily to reduce armaments or promote peace; but they do provide a convenient podium from which the major powers seek to influence world public opinion by asserting their devotion to disarmament and casting doubts upon the rival powers' dedication to peace. However, obstacles to disarmament agreements fade whenever external developments give the major powers serious interest in concluding a pact, as happened in the case of the moratorium on nuclear testing. To the degree that this assessment of the function of the negotiations is valid, the considerable body of research on disarmament negotiations conveys a misleading impression about their utility and their promise as a strategy for achieving an international detente.

As already suggested, the obvious strategy for avoiding this kind of bias in the normative implications of research is to base decisions about the weight and meaning of research findings in a specific area upon a general model that specifies the relation of the subject area to the entire system. Obviously, this procedure can be undertaken more confidently if there is consensus upon the character of a general model. But each example I have cited, and in others that might have been cited, available studies suggest that popular assumptions about the weight and meaning of research are incorrect because assumptions about the character of the general model are incompatible with research findings.

[13] The most thorough review of the evidence on this subject, which reaches the conclusion summarized here, is in H. Gregg Lewis, *Unionism and Relative Wages in the United States* (Chicago and London, 1963).

IV

Another common source of unintended normative orientations lies in the methods employed to gather, organize, and present research findings. Sometimes a project's conclusions are implicit in its methodological assumptions and procedures, so that the gathering of data is, in a sense only a specification in concrete terms of what has already been assumed. Another, perhaps overly skeptical, way to put this is to say that the method is essentially deductive in reaching general conclusions, though empirical work is relied on to fill in the details of the postulated general categories.

The continuing debate among social scientists as to whether community power structures are basically elitist or pluralistic seems to me based partly upon studies of this type on both sides of the debate. Indeed, the very failure to resolve the basic issue through research over a considerable period and the fact that studies continue to fall fairly neatly into one or the other camp suggest that the division between the contending groups hinges more upon different assumptions and methods than upon empirical developments.

This debate has been carried on in rather contentious fashion precisely because it does have normative implications. Given our democratic norms, studies that find that our cities are ruled by a power elite imply that existing power structures should be viewed with suspicion and that ways should be found to overthrow or modify them. By the same token, studies that find that pluralism prevails in municipal decision making imply that the status quo is acceptable, at least in its basic structure.

Floyd Hunter's book *Community Power Structure*[14] is probably the best-known example of a study in this field that concludes that there is a power elite, and it also exemplifies the relationship between method and conclusion that I have just posited. Among the "postulates on power structure" that Hunter lists in his Introduction as "self-evident propositions" are the assumptions that "power is structured socially, in the United States, into a dual relationship between governmental and economic authorities on national, state, and local levels" and that "power is a relatively constant factor in social relationships with policies as variables." He sees it as a corollary of the latter postulate that "wealth, social status, and prestige are factors in the power constant."[15]

[14] Floyd Hunter, *Community Power Structure* (Chapel Hill, 1953).
[15] *Ibid.*, p. 6.

Hunter's method of identifying "power personnel" was to ask community organizations in Atlanta to provide lists of leaders in community affairs, business, and politics and "society leaders and leaders of wealth." Fourteen judges then gave their opinions as to who were the top leaders on each of the lists; those individuals receiving the highest number of votes were taken to be power leaders.

It is crucial that Hunter's attention was not focused upon which interests consistently get the benefits of municipal decisions: on who gets what. It focused rather on who are alleged to play the key roles in decision making, on how well informants agree on who the leaders are, and on ties among the leaders. This is a perspective that necessarily leaves unanswered the basic question whether the decision makers, even assuming they are accurately identified and their influence properly weighed, consistently function as agents of their own interests, those of specific social or economic groups, or those of any continuing interests. Most important of all, it does not tell us to what extent those who are prominent in the decision-making process are constrained by social and political influences to accede to the claims of interest groups.

Hunter's method of identifying leaders and his concern for finding social, political, and economic ties among the leaders cannot fail to produce a finding that a limited number of people play prominent roles in the community. We need to know, however, whether these people are free to maneuver as they please whether they must be sensitive to a wide range of group claims to retain their positions, whether they are free to call the shots or only to reflect a wide or narrow spectrum of group interests. In short, despite his assumption that community power comprises a structure, Hunter fails to describe the crucial parts of the structure because he concentrates his attention upon reputations and avoids the political issue: the sense in which incumbents of key positions systematically reflect the claims of their followings or fail to do so.

It is thus possible, as the pluralists contend, that a suitably designed project would conclude that the system of power functions so as to allocate values to different groups, depending upon the issue, the organization involved, or some other variable. Hunter may be correct in his conclusion, but his study amounts to a simple assertion of the conclusion rather than evidence of its validity.

Robert Dahl's study of community power in New Haven[16] is

16 Robert A. Dahl, *Who Governs?* (New Haven and London, 1961).

probably the most widely discussed example of the pluralist school of thought. It seems to me to suffer from almost exactly the same kind of tie between its methodology and its conclusions as the Hunter approach, though the conclusions of the two studies are at opposite poles.

As Thomas Anton aptly points out in a critique of the pluralist research,[17] these studies assume that it is the individuals involved in decision making, not social structures, that count and that no group constitutes a power elite. Nelson Polsby declared in an explanation of the pluralist position, "If anything, there seems to be an unspoken notion among pluralist researchers that at bottom nobody dominates in a town."[18]

Whereas Hunter's attention is concentrated upon the ties and overlaps in community leadership, Dahl's is concentrated upon the differences among the individuals involved in decision making on different public issues. His method is to examine which leaders and subleaders engage in what activities with respect to specific areas of policy formation: political party nominations, urban redevelopment, and public education. Thus, by assumption and by procedure the emphasis is upon discreteness, upon the range of individuals prominent in different policy areas, and Dahl finds that for the most part different individuals play key roles in the three policy areas. The Dahl book is organized into discrete conceptual and empirical subjects: spheres of influence, specialization of influence, sovereignties, and so on. The emphasis is always either upon divergencies in interest and function or upon the complexity, ambiguity, and impossibility of reaching clear conclusions about the structure of power and influence.

If there is an oligarchic structure of power in some significant sense, this method of research and of organizing data is ideal for clouding the fact and focusing attention on discrete segments and ambiguities. The book is pluralistic in its form as well as in its conclusions, for it segments both conceptual and empirical topics.

Dahl's approach cannot fail to furnish evidence that a wide range of individuals participates in one or another kind of decision making and that public policy making is a complex universe. Like Hunter's, however, it is not a method that can demonstrate that either the elitist or the pluralist position is valid, for the two methods are essentially alike in that they concentrate upon the

[17] Thomas J. Anton, "Pluralism and Local Politics," *Administrative Science Quarterly*, 7 (March 1963), 425–457.

[18] Nelson W. Polsby, "How to Study Community Power: The Pluralist Alternative," *Journal of Politics*, 22 (1960), 474–484, 476.

individuals who play decision-making roles rather than upon the political structure that explains these individuals' behaviors. No more than Hunter does Dahl tell us whether the range of group interests to which public officials are sensitive is wide or narrow, whether these officials have to accede to group claims to retain their positions, whether the structure of power (as distinct from the list and offices of individuals involved) is pyramidal, or segmented and dispersed. It is hardly surprising that each procedure for research yields the conclusions it assumes, that there is little meeting of minds between the respective schools of thought, and that the dispute remains unresolved. Each points to the values inherent in its assumptions.

V

It may be suggested that the argument of this paper proves too much. Most of the studies discussed are certainly important contributions, deserving of the wide attention they have received, probably better than average as examples of political and social research. If these research efforts convey unintended or unwarranted normative implications, is there reason to suppose that such an effect can be avoided? Political scientists certainly differ on the answer to that question, but few are likely to contend that nothing can be done to minimize the unintended and misleading conclusions flowing from serious research.

These studies have in common an assumption that is widespread in current political science thinking and research formulations: that individual or group needs, demands, or supports constitute the basic determinant of public policies. Easton's systems theory, Almond's functional theory, socialization studies, the commonly employed forms of psychological theory (such as the political analyses relying upon balance theory and authoritarian personality theory), and even group theory rest on models that regard people's demands and supports as inputs and public policies as outputs. Group theory and some of the socialization studies do evince some interest in the genesis of people's demands in group identifications, but contemporary political science has accepted this basic model of the policy-making process with few reservations. The proposition applies to behaviorists as much as it did to the institutionalists, who saw elections and people's support for the constitutional system as the prime mover of the polity and the fundamental influence on government actions.

That this key assumption should remain largely unexamined (and only casually qualified by references to feedback) is curious in view of its inconsistency with much of the influential work in social psychology and anthropology. Mead and the symbolic interactionists, as well as the psychoanalytic and anthropological students of the tie between culture and personality, have focused upon the ways in which social interaction, and the symbols created through taking the roles of significant others, mold individual values and aspirations. Their interactionist formulation suggests the utility of starting research with the converse of the assumption that has been pervasive in political science. It supports the view that the interactions involved in formal government proceedings and the myths and rituals represented by such proceedings give significant shape to the people's demands and supports.

This reorientation would free political science research from some encumbrances that limit the range of both political explanation and political criticism. If it is taken for granted that public wants and demands are the independent variable accounting for policy choices, then criticism is confined to the adequacy of government procedures and communication: to how well and how efficiently public wants are converted into policies. Fundamental criticism of policy and the system for formulating it in terms of its impact upon individual personalities, values, expectations, and potentialities for change is discouraged. The outlook common to political science conceptualizing therefore amounts to an optimistic perception of the current regime. There can then be study and criticism only of the devices for converting demands to policies; there is no encouragement to examine conscious, unintended, or systemic manipulation of the demands themselves.

The research discussed in this paper illustrates the strong and close dependence of political demands on prior policies. Direct price controls evoke significantly more popular resistance than indirect ones. Token or ritualistic protection against economic threats to consumers evokes political quiescence. Government activity suggesting the threat of foreign aggression evokes support for a militant nationalist stance. Elections, even when rigged or ritualistic, evoke support and sanction for the regime.

Both empirical observations of this kind and elementary social psychology suggest the general outlines of a systems model less confining and heuristically richer than the essentially mechanical input-conversion-output-feedback metaphor. Not only would such an orientation generate questions about the conditions under which demands and supports are dependent variables, but even more fundamentally, it would recognize that actual inputs and outputs can be less crucial in policy formation than anticipations of inputs and outputs. It would therefore take full account of the sense in which individual perceptions, beliefs about political dynamics, aspirations, and assumptions about the shape of the future are part of the same transaction as the interpersonal social and political process, and it would encourage close investigation of this transactional process. An adequate model would thus rely less upon mechanical or organismic analogies suggesting interactions between independent and dependent variables than upon approaches for exploring organic ties among personality development, perception, and the group interplay and role taking that are synonymous with public policy formation. In such a formulation, conversion procedures could not be viewed as a discrete phase of the system but rather as an integrated part of the process of generating both inputs and outputs; for legislative, administrative, and judicial activities hinge upon anticipations of what will be the responses of interested publics: estimates of sanctions, the expression of group identifications, and so on.

This suggestion is obviously not a model, but only a comment on some directions for revision of current models in the light of pertinent social science theory and the kinds of empirical observations just cited. The comment reflects an orientation resting upon formulations in Mead, Sapir, Sullivan, Cassirer, and the Dewey and Bentley of *Knowing and the Known.*

It would provide scope for a rigorous political science that is also realistic, imaginative, and humane, for it would concern itself directly with how mass publics come to have the political outlooks they do, including the possibilities for manipulation of their outlooks and for unintended but systematic influence upon their demands. Political scientists could not be satisfied with the reassuring but untenable assumption that the activities of leaders reflect the interests of large publics. Nor could they assume that survey research findings about public attitudes represent stable or "hard" facts. Such findings would have to be viewed as instances among a range of possibilities, where the crucial fact is not the particular survey response (which is almost certainly ambivalent), but the process determining that one rather than another response occurs. If the process by which influence is exerted upon public opinions is crucial, then the substance of political demands as of any particular moment or survey is not crucial, but only illustrative and possibly episodic.

Such an orientation, focused upon the range of intended and

unintended ties among leaders, followers, and the structures within which they act, would represent a gain both in explanatory power and in social relevance.

28 ✿ DEMOCRACY AND THE CHINESE BOXES

ROBERT A. DAHL

I

I have a fantasy in which a modern Constitutional Convention assembles a group of fifty-five men or thereabouts whose commitment to democracy and whose wisdom are not in doubt. Their task is to design democratic institutions suitable for this small planet in the year 2000. And so they come to the problem of the unit.

Being learned, as well as wise, naturally they recall the city-state. Well, says one, since full civic participation is possible only if the number of citizens is small, let us arrange for a world of small democratic city-states. Let the unit of democracy, then, be the small city.

Ah, says another, you forget that the world of the 21st century is not ancient Greece. You even forget that ancient Greece was the setting for a highly defective international system. The trouble with the small city in the modern world is that there are too many problems it cannot cope with, because they go beyond its boundaries. Think of some of the problems of American cities: revenues, transportation, air and water pollution, racial segregation, inequality, public health . . . I would make the list longer, but it is already long enough to show that the small city is obviously an inappropriate unit and that we have to locate democracy in a larger unit. I urge that we consider the metropolis.

But, says a third, even the boundaries of the metropolis are

This is a somewhat modified and condensed version of an address, "The City in the Future of Democracies," originally printed in the *American Political Science Review*, 61 (December 1967), pp. 953–970.

smaller than the kinds of problems you mention. The legal boundaries of metropolis are an obsolete legacy of the past. What we need is metropolitan governments with legal boundaries extending to the limits of the metropolitan area itself, boundaries set not by obsolete patterns of settlement but by present densities.

Your argument is persuasive, says a fourth, but you do not carry it far enough. Demographers and planners now tell us that in the United States, to take one example, there is an uninterrupted urban area on the East Coast extending from Virginia to Maine. Even your metropolitan governments will be too small there. And in the future much of the world will surely be as densely settled as our Eastern seaboard. Consequently, I believe that we must design regional democracies, controlled by democratic governments responsive to the electorate of a whole region.

Well, says a fifth, I notice you have already bypassed such things as states and provinces, which is all to the good, since they are as anachronistic as the small city. But you will have to agree that even if you carve up the world into regional governments big enough, for instance, to cover the Eastern seaboard, you cannot expect these units to be adequate for very long. With the population of the world reaching six billion, or ten billion, most of the United States will soon be a vast, undifferentiated, urban mass. Other countries are headed in the same direction. There is, then, a good deal to be said for the only traditional unit that enjoys consensus and allegiance on a scale commensurate with the problems. I mean, of course, the nation-state. If we were to think of the United States as one city, as we shall have to do in the future, it is obvious that the proper unit to bound our sovereign electorate cannot be smaller than the United States. With minor changes here and there, the nation-state is probably good for another century or so. So let us proceed to make use of it by eliminating the powers of all the intermediate units, which are, after all, only obstacles that permit local groups to frustrate national majorities.

But, objects a sixth, you are still too much the victim of the past to think clearly about the future. Obviously our very existence depends on our capacity to create a government that will subordinate the nation-state to a larger legal order. Just as your villages, towns, cities, metropolises, and regions are too small to cope singlehandedly with their problems, so too is your nation-state, even one as big as the United States, the USSR, or China. The fatal flaw of the nation-state is its inability to eliminate interstate violence; and because of our genius for violence we can now destroy the species. Even prosaic problems are now beyond the control of the nation-state: the efficiencies that come from world markets, monetary problems, the balance of trade, the movement of labor and skills, air and water pollution, the regulation of fishing, the dissemination of nuclear weapons. . . . I know it is bold, but we must plan for a world government, and to us that surely means a democratic world government. The appropriate electorate for the 21st century is nothing smaller than the human race. The only legitimate majority is the majority of mankind.

At this point there is a tumult of objections and applause. Finally the first speaker gains the floor. Each speaker, he says, has been more persuasive than the last. But, he adds, I simply cannot understand how my learned friend, the last speaker, proposes to govern the world, if he has in mind, as I thought, a single world-wide electorate, a single parliament, a single executive, all attempting to represent that nonexistent monstrosity, a single world-wide majority. I say that even if it would miraculously hold together, which I doubt, a democracy with six billion citizens is no democracy at all. I, for one, do not wish to be only one six-billionth part of any government. One may as well accept a despot and have done with the Big Lie that what we have is a democracy.

Ah, the advocate of a democratic world government now replies, of course I meant that there would be subordinate governments, which would be democracies.

I thank my learned colleague for this important clarification, says the advocate of the small city-state. I now propose that these subordinate governments consist of units about the size of small cities.

Again there is tumult. The speaker who now gains the floor is the one who had earlier spoken in behalf of the metropolis. Hold on, he objects, if we are to have a subordinate unit, surely it must be one large enough to deal with the problems of an urban society. Obviously this unit should be the metropolis. . . .

Suddenly it becomes as clear to everyone at the Constitutional Convention as it has become to you that the argument over the unit has gone completely around in a circle, that it has now started all over again, that it has no logical terminus, that it could go on forever. Perhaps that is why we still talk about the city-state.

For the logic seems unassailable. Any unit you choose smaller than the globe itself—and that exception may be temporary—can be shown to be smaller than the boundaries of an urgent problem generated by activities of some people who are outside the particular unit and hence beyond its authority. Rational control over such problems dictates ever larger units, and democratic control implies a larger electorate, a larger majority. Yet the larger the unit, the greater the costs of uniform rules, the larger the minorities who cannot prevail, and the more watered down is the control of the individual citizen. Hence the argument for larger units does not destroy the case for small units. What it does is to make a seemingly small but radical shift in the nature of the arguments.

For we drop completely the notion so dear to the Greeks and early Romans that to be legitimate a unit of government must be wholly autonomous. With autonomy we also drop the belief that there is a single sovereign unit for democracy, a unit in which majorities are autonomous with respect to all persons outside the unit and authoritative with respect to all persons inside the unit. Instead we begin to think about appropriate units of democracy as an ascending series, a set of Chinese boxes, each larger and more inclusive than the other, each in some sense democratic, though not always in quite the same sense, and each not inherently less nor inherently more legitimate than the other.

Although this may be a discomforting and alien conception in some democratic countries where political tradition has focused on the overriding legitimacy, autonomy, and sovereignty of the nation-state and of national majorities, even in these countries the evolution of pluralistic institutions has vastly modified the applicability of monistic conceptions of democracy. And of course in democracies with federal systems, like Switzerland, Canada, and the United States, or in nonfederal countries like the Netherlands that inherit a political tradition powerfully shaped by federalism and the legitimacy of pluralist institutions, to see the units of democracy as a set of Chinese boxes is very much easier— though even in these countries it will take some rethinking and a vast amount of institution building before any of us can think easily about the nation-state as a Chinese box nested in yet larger ones of equal legitimacy.

Our imaginary Constitutional Convention, and our Chinese boxes do not, of course, bring us much closer to a solution to our original problem of the appropriate unit for democracy. But they do suggest that there is not necessarily a single kind of unit, whether it be city-state or nation-state, in which majorities have some specially sacred quality not granted to majorities in other units, whether smaller or larger, more or less inclusive.

A Frenchman, perhaps even an Englishman, or any strong believer in majority rule will tell me that surely in one of these boxes there must be a majority that is sovereign, or else conflicts between different majorities, one of which may in a larger perspective be only a minority, can never be resolved. I ask, very well, a majority of what unit? And my critic will say, the majority, naturally, of the nation. To which I reply, *why* is this more sacred than the others? Because it is larger? But I can point to still larger majorities in the making in this world. Will you remain faithful to your answer when your nation is a unit in a world polity? Or will you not, instead, revert to federalist conceptions? Anyway, I might add, in a number of federal countries, including some rather old and respectable representative democracies, citizens have grown moderately accustomed to the idea that national majorities—or rather their spokesmen—are not necessarily more sacred than majorities or minorities in certain kinds of less inclusive units. This is logically untidy, and it requires endless readjustments as perspectives and levels of interdependence change. But it makes for a better fit with the inevitable pluralistic and decentralizing forces of political life in nation-states with representative governments.

The hitherto unreported debate at our imaginary Convention also suggests that in a world of high population densities, ease of communication, and great interdependence, where autonomy is in fact impossible short of the earth itself, we confront a kind of dilemma that the Greeks could hardly have perceived. Let me suggest it by advancing a series of propositions:

The larger and more inclusive the unit, the more its government can regulate aspects of the environment that its citizens want to regulate, from air and water pollution and racial justice to the dissemination of nuclear weapons.

Yet the larger and more inclusive a unit with a representative government, and the more complex its tasks, the more participation must be reduced for most people to the single act of voting in an election.

Conversely, the smaller the unit, the greater the opportunity for citizens to participate in the decisions of their government, yet the less of the environment they can control.

Thus for most citizens, participation in very large units becomes minimal and in very small units it becomes trivial. At the extremes, citizens may participate in a vast range of complex and crucial decisions by the single act of casting a ballot; or else they have almost unlimited opportunities to participate in decisions over matters of no importance. At the one extreme, then, the people vote but they do not rule; at the other, they rule—but they have nothing to rule over.

These are extreme cases, and if they were all there were, it would be a discouraging prospect. But may there not be others in between?

Before we turn to this question, I want you to notice that our hypothetical Constitutional Convention and the Chinese boxes also hint at the possibility that we may need different models of democracy for different kinds of units. I see no reason to think that all kinds of units with democratic institutions and practices do, can, or should behave in the same way—no reason, then, why we should expect democracy in a committee, in a city, and in a nation to be the same either in fact or in ideal. If we expect that representative government in the nation-state is roughly equivalent to democratic participation in a committee then we are bound to be misled in our understanding of political life, in our hopes, and in our strategies for changing the world from what it is to what it ought to be.

II

If the nation-state is too immense, and if interdependence and population densities render the autonomous self-governing city-state too costly, are there units powerful enough, autonomous enough, and small enough to permit, and in the right circumstances to encourage, a body of citizens to participate actively and rationally in shaping and forming vital aspects of their lives in common? Is there, in this sense, an optimal unit?

There are a number of candidates for this position. Occasionally, for example, one still runs across a nostalgia for the village—a nostalgia strongest, I suspect, among people who have never lived in small towns. There are also suggestions going back nearly a century that we shift our search for the democratic unit away from the government of the state to the government of nonstate institutions, such as the workplace, business firm, corporation, or industry.[1] And lately there has been a resurgence of interest, especially among young political activists, in the old and recurring idea of reconstructing democracy around small units that would offer unlimited opportunities for participation.

Although I cannot possibly do justice here to these various alternatives, I would like to venture a few comments on each.

The fragmented and even shattered community in which modern man seems condemned to live tempts one to suppose that the

[1] See, for example, Peter Bachrach, *The Theory of Democratic Elitism* (Boston: Little, Brown, 1967), pp. 95 ff.

376 STRATEGIES FOR WORK

appropriate unit for democratic life might be the village or small town. Only there, it might be thought, could one ever hope to find a center of life small enough so that it permits wide participation, and small enough besides to foster the sense of unity, wholeness, belonging, of membership in an inclusive and solidary community which we sometimes seem to want with such a desperate yearning. Speaking for myself, I doubt whether man can ever recapture his full sense of tribal solidarity. Like childhood itself, there is no returning to the childhood of man. What is more, the attempt to satisfy this craving, if carried far on a densely packed globe, leads not to community but to those hideously destructive forms of tribalism that this century has already seen too much of.

Anyway, I suspect that the village probably never was all that it is cracked up to be. The village, including the preindustrial village, is less likely to be filled with harmony and solidarity than with the oppressive weight of repressed deviation and dissent which, when they appear, erupt explosively and leave a lasting burden of antagonism and hatred. I have not been able to discover much evidence of the consensual *Gemeinschaft* in descriptions of the small town of Springdale in upstate New York, or St. Denis in Quebec, or Peyrane, the village in the Vaucluse, or the small English town of Glossop near Manchester, or the peasant village of Montegrano in south Italy, or the Tanjore village in south India that André Bétéille recently described.[2]

Here, for example, is how Horace Miner saw political life in the French-Canadian parish of St. Denis thirty years ago:

Politics is a topic of continual interest and one which reaches fever heat during election time . . . The whole parish is always divided between the "blues" or Conservatives, and the "reds." Party affiliations follow family lines and family cliques and antagonisms. The long winter *veillées* are attended almost invariably by family groups of similar political belief. Constituents of each party have a genuine dislike for those of the other . . . Election time is one of great tension, of taunts and shouting as parishioners get their evening mail . . . Insults are common, and many speaking acquaintances are dropped. During the last election the minority candidate had to have one meeting in the parish

[2] Arthur J. Vidich and Joseph Bensman, *Small Town in Mass Society* (Garden City, N.Y.: Anchor Books, 1960); Horace Miner, *St. Denis, A French Canadian Parish* (Chicago: University of Chicago Phoenix Books, 1939, 1963); Laurence Wylie, *Village in the Vaucluse* (New York: Harper Colophon, 1957, 1964); A. H. Birch, *Small-Town Politics, A Study of Political Life in Glossop* (Oxford: Oxford University Press, 1959); Edward C. Banfield, *The Moral Basis of a Backward Society* (New York: The Free Press, 1958); André Bétéille, *Caste, Class and Power* (Berkeley: University of California Press, 1966).

in secret, another open but under provincial police protection . . . Campaigns reach their climax with the *assemblée contradictoire*, at which both candidates speak. Characteristically at these meetings there are organized strong-arm tactics, drinking, and attempts to make each candidate's speech inaudible . . .

The chicanery of politicians is a byword in the parish. Factional strife threatens the life of every organized association . . . On the whole the associational life of the community is weak. The people are not joiners.[3]

Thus village democracy before the demos was ruined by industrialization and urbanization!

If the democratic village seems hardly worth seeking in this industrial and postindustrial epoch, the prospect is all the more appealing that democracy might be extended to the place where most adult citizens spend most of their time—their place of work. Professional people with a great deal of autonomy, academics who enjoy an extraordinary amount of autonomy and a fair measure of self-government in our universities, executives and administrators who see authority relationships from above rather than from below, all are likely to underestimate the consequences for the average citizen in a modern industrial society flowing from the fact that at his place of work he is a rather low-level subordinate in a system of hierarchical relationships. Although the term democracy has been prostituted in the service of employee relationships, the fact is that practically everywhere in the world, the industrial workplace—the factory, industry, or corporation, whether owned privately or publicly—is no democracy in any sense consistent with our usage in the realm of the state. "The idea of a factory, nationalized or privately owned," it has been said, "is the idea of command."[4] The factory, the enterprise, the industry, the corporation is a hierarchy; it may be an aristocracy, an oligarchy, a monarchy, a despotism, but it is not a democracy. This is as true in socialist economies as in capitalist and mixed economies. A century ago Engels asserted that hierarchy would be necessary in the factory even under socialism, that even in a socialist enterprise the worker would lose his autonomy. Over the entrance to the factory, he said, recalling *The Inferno*, the words should be written: *Lasciate ogni autonomia, voi che entrate!*[5]

[3] Miner, *op. cit.*, pp. 58–61.
[4] Graham Wootton, *Workers, Unions and the State* (London: Routledge and Kegan Paul, 1966), p. 36.
[5] *Ibid.*, p. 36. The quotation is from Engels' essay "On Authority" in Lewis S. Feuer (ed.), *Marx and Engels: Basic Writings* (New York: Doubleday Anchor, 1959), pp. 481–484.

Whether the workplace should be democratized, and if so how and how much, are questions that need to be distinguished from the problem of regulating the enterprise, industry, or corporation to ensure that it accomplishes the social and public functions that are the only reason the rest of us are willing to grant its vast legal rights, privileges and immunities, and extraordinary power. If democratic states have become immense, so have corporations. There are privately owned corporations that have gross annual revenues greater than the GNP of most countries of the world, that spend annually sums greater than the entire budgets of the governments of most of the nation-states in the world.[6] To ensure that these immense resources and powers are used for public purposes is a staggering problem. But internal democracy in the factory, firm, industry, or corporation is not necessarily a more effective means of public control than regulating a hierarchically administered firm by competition and the price system, by a regulatory agency, by government ownership, or by various combinations of these and other possibilities. Indeed, even if the modern corporation were internally democratic, no matter whether it were public or private and no matter whether it were to operate in an economy predominantly privately owned or predominantly publicly owned, I do not think we any more than the Soviets or Yugoslavs would want to dispense entirely with such external controls as competition and the price system. In short, no system of *internal* control negates the need for a system of *external* controls that compel or induce those who exercise authority within the enterprise, whether these managers are chosen by and are accountable to stockholders,

[6] In 1966, the largest U.S. corporation, General Motors, had a gross income from sales of $20 billion, assets of nearly $13 billion, a net income of $1.8 billion, and three quarters of a million employees (*Fortune*, June 15, 1967, p. 196). Dollar figures for GNP are not available for most countries for that year, but in 1964 the gross receipts of GM were $17 billion. This was approximately equal to the Gross National Product of Sweden, which ranked about 15th in GNP among all the countries of the world. The revenues of GM were larger than the GNP of the Netherlands, Belgium, Brazil, Switzerland, and presumably all the 100 remaining countries of the world. In 1957, the latest year for which I have been able to obtain central government expenditures in U.S. dollars, the expenditures of GM ($9 billion) were larger than the central government of all except two non-Communist governments in the world—the United States and the United Kingdom. GM's outlays were larger than the central government of France ($8.5 billion), or West Germany ($7.5 billion), more than two and a half times those of India ($3.4 billion), nearly four times those of Sweden ($2.6 billion), five times those of Brazil ($1.9 billion). I am indebted to the Yale Political Data Program for these data. Data for GNP, 1957, for 122 countries are in Bruce Russett *et al.*, *World Handbook of Political and Social Indicators* (New Haven: Yale University Press, 1964), p. 152.

workers, or the state, to employ their power and resources for jointly beneficial purposes rather than for exploiting consumers.

But even if we can distinguish the problem of internal democracy from that of external control, the problem does not vanish. It is true that in many developed countries with representative governments, trade-union power has substituted bargaining for undiluted hierarchy in the control of wages and working conditions. But even where they are most powerful, labor unions have by no means created a democratic factory or industry; moreover, as a result more of apathy than of repression, few unions anywhere have developed a really high degree of internal democracy. Aside from a few scattered instances elsewhere,[7] the most massive, ambitious, and far-reaching experiment in democratizing the workplace has been taking place in Yugoslavia since 1950. Sober studies[8] suggest that while the system of workers' control has problems—some of them, like apathy and Michels' iron law of oligarchy, familiar to every student of democratic organizations—it might well prove to be a viable system of internal control. If it does, it will surely stand as an alternative with a very great appeal —at least in the long run—to workers in other industrial nations. If workers can participate in the government of their factories in Yugoslavia, and if these factories prove to be relatively efficient, surely the whole question of internal democracy will come alive in other countries.

Yet even if it should prove to be possible, efficient, and desirable, I do not believe that democracy in the workplace is a substitute for democracy in the state. For one thing, I doubt whether democracy in the workplace can be preserved indefinitely unless there is democracy in the state. Moreover, where an opposition party is illegal in the state, opposition in the factory has distinct limits.[9] Finally—and this is the most important point—the workplace is not as important as the state and with increasing leisure it may grow less so. To accept as a focus for self-government a type of unit that is and must be concerned with only a small part of the range of collective concerns would be to trivialize the democratic idea. I find it hard to believe that man's aspiration toward rational control over his environment by joint action with his fellow men

[7] Wooton, *op. cit.*, pp. 113–124.

[8] Cf. Albert Meister, *Socialisme et Autogestion, L'Expérience Yougoslave* (Paris: Editions du Seuil, 1964); and Jiri Kolaja, *Workers Councils: The Jugoslav Experience* (New York and Washington: Frederick A. Praeger, 1966).

[9] See the comments of Kolaja, *op. cit.*, pp. 7, 66 ff.; and Meister, *op. cit.*, 240–245, 263–278, 373.

will ever be satisfied by democratizing the production of aspirin, cars, and television sets.

III

Any form of political participation that cannot be performed more or less simultaneously but must be carried on sequentially runs into the implacable barrier of time. Time's relentless arrow flies directly to the Achilles heel of all schemes for participatory democracy on a grand scale. It is easy to show that any unit small enough for all the members to participate fully (where each member has the opportunity to present his views and have them discussed) cannot be larger than a working committee. If you doubt this, I ask you to sit down with pencil and paper and do a few exercises with various assumptions as to the time available for decisions and the time required for each participant to make his point or at least present his point of view.[10] You will quickly see how cruel is time's neutral guillotine. Or let me simply evoke your own experience with committees to remind you how quickly a committee grows too large for every member to participate fully. Or consider the experience of legislative committees, cabinets, regulatory commissions, judicial bodies. Would we not all agree that an effective working committee can have no more than—let us err on the side of generosity—thirty to forty members? Drawing on their own experience, most readers, I imagine, would cut these figures by a half or two-thirds.

Now if the great advantage of a unit the size of a working committee is that it allows full participation by its members, its great drawback, from a democratic point of view, is that unless it is a representative body or an agent of a representative body it ought not be given much public authority. Either the unit, though small, is granted authority because it represents a much larger number of citizens; or else, not being a representative body, it has little authority other than to recommend and advise; or else, if it has much power and is not a representative body, its power is illegitimate. In an interdependent society, any significant power wielded by a body the size of a working committee is bound to have important effects on citizens not sitting on that committee. Consequently either the committee is representative or its power is illegitimate.

[10] Cf. Bertrand de Jouvenel, "The Chairman's Problem," *American Political Science Review*, 55 (June 1961), 368–372.

We can hardly espouse the small, self-governing, fully participatory unit as a normative goal if it is illegitimate. If it is representative, then it is no longer a body in which all citizens can participate fully. We have run into a cul-de-sac, as you see, and so we must get back to the starting point.

Some of you may regard this as a pessimistic analysis. It is, I admit, a very large fly in the ointment. Like death, it may be a brutal and perhaps even a tragic limit on man's possibilities, but I do not see why this conclusion must lead to pessimism. The idea of democracy would never have gotten off the ground if enthusiastic democrats had not been willing to settle for something a good deal less than complete and equal participation by all citizens in all decisions. It is worth recalling that in Athens, where the opportunities for free male citizens to participate in running the city seem to have been about as great as they have ever been anywhere, citizens were chosen for what was probably the most coveted participation in the life of the polis—a seat on the Council of Five Hundred, the inner council, or the various administrative boards —by lot or, in the case of the Board of Generals, by election, and to that extent these bodies were instances of representative government and not direct democracy. Participation in the Assembly, which met about once a month, was scarcely the fullest flowering of participatory democracy. I have been to enough town meetings myself to know something of their limitations. If you think of a town meeting in which a quorum sometimes required the presence of 6,000 people, where maybe as many as 30–40,000 were eligible to attend, and where perhaps 4–5,000 were frequently present, it is obvious that most Athenian citizens must have lived their lives without once speaking to their fellow citizens in the Assembly. That, one judges from the reports in Thucydides, was a forum that gave preference to orators.

Nonetheless, I doubt—although we shall never know—whether many Athenians felt frustrated because their opportunities to participate were not as unlimited as their skies. Between the working committee and the nation-state there is, I think, a critical threshold of size, below which the opportunities for participation can be so great and so fairly meted out that no one feels left out and everyone feels that his viewpoint has been pretty fairly attended to. Athens was far too large for the democracy of the working committee; de facto it had to employ a certain amount of representation. Yet I suspect that it was below the critical threshold. And even if we now reject as unattainable the ideal of full, equal, and direct participation by all citizens in all collective decisions—the ideal of committee democracy—we can still search for a unit that remains within this critical threshold for widespread participation.

IV

We have travelled a long trail and turned into a number of branching paths in our quest but we have not found a unit that seems optimal for rational self-government. The journey would have been much longer had we taken the time to explore the by-ways as carefully as they deserve. Yet if we keep going, I think that we shall finally end up about at the place where the Greeks left off: somewhere within view of the democratic city.

Yet what we come to is not the Greek city, nor can it be; not the polis, then, but a democratic city that would be consistent with the presence of the nation-state, the institutions of representative government, a level of technology beyond anything the Greeks dreamed of, and huge populations densely spread over the face of our shrunken earth.

If the ancient Greeks were the first truly modern people, choice shaped by geography and historical accident made them also city people. So, too, choice shaped by demography and technology makes us a city people. But even if the Greeks were a city people and though they were modern in almost every important sense, our cities must differ in fact and in ideal from their actual and ideal cities. For one thing, the proportion of the residents of a modern democratic city eligible to participate in political life will be very much larger—something like half of the population, so that even a city of 100,000 will have around 50,000 adult citizens. Much more quickly than the Greeks, we reach the limits of direct democracy. Moreover, the citizens of a modern city will also be highly mobile. A resident of Athens was a citizen only if his ancestors were Athenians; in any modern city, many citizens are recent arrivals, or are about to move to another city. In 1960 more than one resident out of every six in American cities had moved there within the last five years.[11]

As a result of our mobility, socialization into the political life of the modern democratic city is enormously more difficult for us

[11] In 1960 the percentage of migrants from another county since 1955 for all U.S. cities 25,000 and over was 18.4 percent. The percentage ran slightly higher (19.7 percent) in small cities 25–50,000 than in cities over 150,000 (15.6 percent). See Jeffrey K. Hadden and Edgar F. Borgatta, *American Cities: Their Social Characteristics* (Chicago: Rand McNally, 1965), Appendix, Table 1, variable #19, p. 108.

than for the Greeks. Then, too, the Greek city was completely autonomous in ideal and pretty much so in fact. Our cities are not autonomous in fact nor would many of us offer total autonomy as an ideal. Finally, the citizen of a Greek city ordinarily had one inclusive loyalty to the city of his ancestors and to its gods. He invested in his city a kind of engagement in comparison with which patriotism in the nation-state must seem either shallow or strident. But the citizens of our modern cities will have no single loyalty and no single community; they will have multiple loyalties to many associations; and nowhere will they find the all-inclusive community.

If for these reasons a modern city cannot be a polis, we can nonetheless reasonably hope one day to achieve great democratic cities. As the optimum unit for democracy in the 21st century, the city has a greater claim, I think, than any other alternative.

To begin with, from now on into the next century man seems clearly destined to live in cities. If to live in cities is our fate, to live in great cities is our opportunity. Is it not of some significance that of the four great waves of experimentation in the West with popular government, during three of these—the Greek, the Roman, and the medieval communes of north Italy—popular governments managed to construct cities of exceptional and enduring beauty?

Yet during the fourth wave, that of representative democracy in the nation-state, we have so far failed most profoundly in our cities. Is it too much to hope that we might be on the verge of a fifth wave, the age of the democratic city within the democratic nation-state? By we, I mean of course, the whole of the Western democratic world and its offshoots. But most of all, I mean we here in the United States.

City building is one of the most obvious incapacities of Americans. We Americans have become an urban people without having developed an urban civilization. Though we live in cities, we do not know how to build cities. Perhaps because we have emerged so swiftly out of an agrarian society, perhaps because so many of us are only a generation or two removed from farm and field, small town and peasant village, we seem to lack the innate grasp of the essential elements of the good city that was all but instinct among Greeks, Romans, and the Italians of the free communes. Our cities are not merely noncities, they are anticities—mean, ugly, gross, banal, inconvenient, hazardous, formless, incoherent, unfit for human living, deserts from which a family flees to the greener hinterlands as soon as job and income permit, yet deserts growing so rapidly outward that the open green space to which the family escapes soon shrinks to an oasis and then it too turns to a desert.

One advantage of the city as a unit for democratic government is, then, that it confronts us with a task worthy of our best efforts because of its urgency, its importance, its challenge, the extent of our failure up to now, and its promise for the good life lived jointly with fellow citizens.

These considerations point to another asset of the city as a democratic unit. While the city is not and cannot be autonomous, the policies of city hall and the totality of city agencies and activities are so important to our lives that to participate in the decisions of the city means, or anyway can mean, participating in shaping not merely the trivial but some of the most vital aspects of our environment. I say shaping and not totally controlling because the city is only one of our Chinese boxes. But it is in the city and with the powers and resources made available to cities that we shall deal with such crucial problems as the education of our children, our housing, the way we travel to and from our place of work, preventive health measures, crime, public order, the cycle of poverty, racial justice and equality—not to mention all those subtle and little understood elements that contribute so heavily to the satisfaction of our desires for friendship, neighborhood, community, and beauty.

V

Yet if the city and its government are important to us, can the good city today be small enough to remain below that critical threshold for wide participation that I mentioned a moment ago?

The existence of a few giant metropolises here and there may mislead us as to fact and possibility. Only a modest percentage of the world's population lives even today in the giant metropolis. Indeed, in 1960 only one-fifth of the people of the world lived in cities over 100,000. It is true that in the most urbanized region of the world, North America, in 1960 six out of every ten people lived in cities over 100,000. Yet even in the United States, less than one out of every ten lived in cities over a million.

It will take some doing, but we do not have to end up all jammed together in the asphalt desert of the large metropolis—unless that is really what we want. And Americans pretty clearly do not want to live in the large metropolis but rather in cities of modest dimensions. For example, in a survey by Gallup in 1966 nearly half the respondents living in cities of 500,000 and over said they would like to live somewhere else—suburb, small town, farm; by contrast, few of the people living in suburb or town wanted to move to the big cities. About three out of four respondents were distressed by the prospect that their own community will double in population.[12] Census figures for the past several decades tell us that Americans have been acting out these preferences.

What, then, is the optimum size for a city? Although this question, which so far as I know was first asked by political philosophers in Athens over 2,000 years ago, is no longer a subject of discussion among political scientists, scholars in various fields have provided a considerable amount of analysis and evidence to bear on the question.[13] It is only fair to warn you that all answers are still highly controversial; yet a good deal of evidence supports the view that the all-around optimum size for a contemporary American city is almost surely far less than the size of our giant cities, very likely less than 1 million, and probably less than half that. Indeed, the possibility cannot be ruled out that a city under 100,000 could be, and perhaps often is, a more satisfactory place to live in for most people than something bigger.

The matter is, as I said, still highly debatable; yet it is interesting that there is no worthwhile evidence at present demonstrating, for example, that governments of cities over 50,000 manage to achieve any significant economies of scale. The few items on which increasing size does lead to decreasing unit costs, such as water and sewerage, are too small a proportion of total city outlays to lead to significant economies; and even these reductions are probably offset by rising costs for other services, such as police protection.[14]

[12] American Institute of Public Opinion release, April 24, 1966.

[13] The most extensive survey and analysis of the evidence seems to be the work of Otis Dudley Duncan. The findings of his Ph.D. dissertation, *An Examination of the Problem of Optimum City-Size* (University of Chicago, 1949) have been summarized in Otis Dudley Duncan, "Optimum Size of Cities" in Paul Hatt and Albert Reiss (eds.), *Reader in Urban Sociology* (Glencoe, Ill.: Free Press, 1951), pp. 632–645; and James Dahir, "What Is the Best Size for a City?" *American City* (August 1951), 104–105. Robert A. Lillibridge, "Urban Size: An Assessment," *Land Economics*, 38 (November 1952), 341–352, summarizes Duncan and others. In addition, see William Fielding Ogburn and Otis Dudley Duncan, "City Size as a Sociological Variable," in Ernest W. Burgess and Donald J. Bogue, eds., *Urban Sociology* (Chicago: The University of Chicago, Phoenix Books) pp. 58–76; Otis Dudley Duncan, "Optimum Size of Cities" in Joseph J. Spengler and Otis Dudley Duncan (eds.), *Demographic Analysis* (Glencoe: The Free Press, 1956), 372–385.

[14] I am indebted to Mr. Garry D. Brewer for undertaking an extensive survey of the writings and findings dealing with economies of scale in American cities. The relevant literature is extensive, but the most relevant studies appear to be Amos H. Hawley's seminal article, "Metropolitan Popu-

Per capita city expenditures increase with the size of city, at least in the United States. In 1960 the mean expenditure for U.S. cities over 150,000 was $123 per capita compared with $70 per capita for cities in the 25–50,000 range. Yet there is no evidence that these higher costs per capita provide residents of large cities with a better life, taking it in the round, than the life enjoyed by residents of smaller cities. If it costs more in a city of a million than in a city of 25,000 to build, maintain, and police a park within walking distance of every citizen, then higher per capita expenditures for parks in big cities hardly signify that their residents have better public services than residents of smaller cities. What is more, the outlays in larger cities are actually less for some key functions than in smaller cities. For example, even though larger cities employ more persons per capita in public administration than smaller cities, per capita employment in education is on the average lower in larger cities than in small cities.[15]

Roads and highways nullify the older economic advantage of the metropolis as a market and a source of specialized labor. A student of urban economics argues, for example, that

a half-dozen towns of, say, 25,000 population with two or three main industries each plus a dozen small one- or two-industry towns of half that size add up to a 300,000 population, extended local labor market, built on the moderately broad base of a couple of dozen separate industries.[16]

The oft-cited cultural advantages of the metropolis are also largely illusory. On the basis of his research on American cities, Duncan estimates that the requisite population base for a library of "desirable minimum professional standards" is 50–75,000, for an art museum, 100,000, "with a somewhat higher figure for science and historical museums." Yet, even though larger cities have larger libraries, the circulation of library books per capita markedly decreases with size of city. There is also a negative correlation be-

lation and Municipal Government Expenditures in Central Cities," *Journal of Social Issues*, 7, nos. 1 and 2 (1951), 100–108; Werner Z. Hirsch, "Expenditures Implications of Metropolitan Growth and Consolidation," *Review of Economics and Statistics*, 41 (August 1959), 232–241; Harvey E. Brazer, *City Expenditures in the United States*, National Bureau of Economic Research Occasional Paper no. 66 (New York, 1959). See also the analysis of the evidence of these studies in Wilbur R. Thompson, *A Preface to Urban Economics* (Baltimore: Johns Hopkins Press, 1965), ch. 7, "The Urban Public Economy" pp. 255–292.

[15] Data in the paragraph above are from Hadden and Borgatta, *op. cit.*, Appendix, Table 1, p. 110, variables 57, 58, and 65.

[16] Thompson, *op. cit.*, p. 34.

tween city size and per capita museum attendance.[17] Moreover, just as smaller cities can retain their collective identities and yet form a larger economic unit, thanks to ease of transportation and communication, so we have barely begun to explore the ways in which small cities by federating together for specific purposes might enjoy all of the cultural advantages of the large city and yet retain their individual identities, the pleasures of living in communities of lower densities and more open spaces,[18] and relatively greater opportunities for political participation.

When we think about the size of a city in which a high culture may flourish, it is instructive to recall that during the Renaissance the city that produced Machiavelli and, I think it fair to say, an outpouring of great paintings, sculpture, and architecture beyond anything we Americans have yet created, had a population of around a hundred thousand. This was probably about the population of the city of Venice during the Renaissance. When Michelangelo chiseled out his Moses and painted his frescoes in the Sistine Chapel, Rome may have had as few as 40,000 residents.[19]

Now what is strangely missing from the discussion of the optimum size of cities is the voice of the political scientist. The question is, of course, broader than the problem of what size of city may be optimal for a democratic political life. One might prefer a giant city to a smaller community even if the larger city were not optimal for democracy. But political life is not trivial. Surely political criteria have a place among the criteria for the optimum size of cities; and among these political criteria surely one of the most important is whether a city is beyond the threshold for widespread participation.

It seems obvious that if a city small enough to permit widespread participation were also optimal in other respects, then that unit would have a truly exceptional role to play in a democratic civilization. For no other unit, surely, would at once be so important and

---

[17] Duncan, "Optimum Size of Cities," *op. cit.*, p. 381.

[18] " . . . museums, professional athletic teams, complete medical facilities, and other accoutrements of modern urban life could be supported collectively. As the federated places grew and prospered the interstices would, of course, begin to fill in, moving the area closer to the large metropolitan area form. But alert action in land planning and zoning could preserve open spaces in a pattern superior to those found in most large urban areas." Thompson, *op. cit.*, p. 36.

[19] Estimates of the sizes of the great cities of the West at different historical periods are subject to such wide variations that one is compelled to take these estimates cautiously. I am indebted to Mr. H. E. A. Driessen of Leiden, Holland, for calling my attention to estimates conflicting with several I used in the original address.

so accessible: a unit that could be—indeed must be—clothed with great powers and considerable autonomy if it is to manage its problems, yet a unit small enough so that citizens could participate extensively in determining the ways in which the city's great powers could be used. Unlike almost every other unit of which I can think, the city need not be so huge that, like the nation-state, it reduces the participation of most citizens to voting, nor so small that its activities must be trivial.

The city has at least one more advantage: it has great potentialities as a unit for educating citizens in civic virtue. We are approaching a crisis in the socialization of citizens into the political life of the democratic nation-state, a crisis that the challenges of nation building, democratization, and overcoming the most blatant evils of industrialism have delayed or obscured. There are signs of malaise among young people, among the very citizens who shortly before the dawn of the 21st century will have become—to use the word that has now become a mindless cliché—the establishment. If the malaise were only American, one could put it down to television, overpermissive child rearing, the persistence of an unpopular and ugly war, or other causes more or less specific to the United States; but there are signs of this malaise among youth in almost all the democratic countries.

I am not going to try to explain here a phenomenon too complex for brief analysis. But a part of the phenomenon—I don't know how much it is symptom and how much underlying cause—is a belief that the government of the nation-state is remote, inaccessible, and unresponsive, a government of professionals in which only a few can ever hope to participate actively and a still smaller number can ever gain great influence after years of dedication to political life.

What we need, what they need, and what some of them are trying to create (often with incredible ignorance of elementary political wisdom) is a political unit of more truly human proportions in which a citizen can acquire confidence and mastery of the arts of politics—that is, of the art required for shaping a good life in common with fellow citizens. What Pericles said of Athens, that the city is in general a school of the Grecians, may be said of every city of moderate size: it is a marvelous school. I have no doubt that a modern city even of moderate size is a good deal more complicated than Athens was. It has a much greater need for highly trained professionals, permanent administrative agencies, full-time leaders. Yet in the main, its problems are, I believe, within reach of the average citizen. And I believe it may be easier for citizens to reason about the good life and the ways to reach it by thinking in the more immediate and palpable context of the city than in the context of the nation-state or international politics. Even if solving the problems of the city is not quite enough for the good life, it is a great, indispensable, and comprehensible prerequisite.

VI

What I have presented is not a program but a perspective, not a prophecy but a prospect. It is not a solution to the problems of the city or of democracy, but a viewpoint from which to look at the problems of democracy and the city. If it does not lead directly to the answers, it might nonetheless help one to see the questions.

I have already suggested one implication of this way of looking at things—if popular governments in the modern world are a series of Chinese boxes, then we obviously need different models, theories, and criteria of excellence for each. I may seem to be repeating only what was commonly said nearly two centuries ago as ideas about representative government began to develop, that we cannot judge representative government in the nation-state as if it were or could be democracy in a committee, or, for that matter, a town meeting. Yet it is interesting to me that we have made so little of these palpable and evidently inherent differences in the performance of different kinds of units, all of which we are prone to call democratic.

Yet if the democratic city lies somewhere between democracy in the committee or in the town meeting and representative government in the nation-state, then it would be important to know what the similarities and differences are, and what standards of excellence we can apply to one but not the other. Even the democratic city, I fear, cannot satisfy anyone who has a vision of leaderless and partyless democracy, for at its best the politics of the democratic city will be more like a competitive polyarchy than a committee; organized parties and interest groups are more likely to exist than the free and spontaneous formation and dissolution of groups for every issue; a full-time leader or activist will exert more influence than any of his followers; institutionalized conflict is more likely than uncoerced consensus. Yet these are hunches that do no more than point to new worlds that need exploring.

The perspective I have been describing also bears on the way we think about units of government intermediate between nation-state and city. An American obviously must take the fifty states into account. These are too solidly built to be done away with and I don't propose to break any lances tilting against them. Yet in the perspective I am suggesting the states do not stand out as important institutions of democratic self-government. They are too big to allow for much in the way of civic participation—think of California and New York, each about as large in population as Canada or Yugoslavia and each larger than 80 percent of the countries of the world. Yet an American state is infinitely less important to citizens of that state than any democratic nation-state is to its citizens. Consequently the average American is bound to be much less concerned about the affairs of his state than of his city or country. Too remote to stimulate much participation by their citizens, and too big to make extensive participation possible anyway, these units intermediate between city and nation are probably destined for a kind of limbo of quasi-democracy. They will be pretty much controlled by the full-time professionals, whether elected or appointed. Moreover, many of the problems that states have to deal with will not fit within state boundaries. It cannot even be said that the states, on the whole, can tap any strong sentiments of loyalty or like-mindedness among their citizens. Doubtless we shall continue to use the states as important intermediate instruments of coordination and control—if for no other reason than the fact that they are going institutions. But whenever we are compelled to choose between city and state, we should always keep in mind. I think, that the city, not the state, is the better instrument of popular government.

This argument also applies to megalopolis, to the city that is *not* a city, to the local government that is *not* a local government. The city of New York, for example, has about the same population as Sweden or Chile. It is twice as large as Norway, three times the size of New Zealand. To regard the government of New York as a local government is to make nonsense of the term. If the Swedes were to rule their whole country from Stockholm with no local governments, I am quite sure that we would begin to question whether the people of Sweden could rightly be called self-governing. Where, we might ask the Swedes, are your local governments? But should we not ask the same thing of New Yorkers: Where are *your* local governments? For purely historical and what to me seem rather irrational reasons, we continue to regard the government of the giant metropolis as if it were a local government, when we might more properly consider it as the equivalent of a state or a provincial government—and hence badly in need of being broken up into smaller units for purposes of local government. If it turns out that the government of a metropolis cannot be decentralized to smaller territorial units, then should we not quite openly declare that the metropolis cannot ever be made into a democratic city? This may be an inconvenient truth, but if it is true, it may be—like much truth—liberating in the end.

Yet I must admit that problems like these involving the metropolis demand more than we now know. The metropolis is a world to be explored, so let us explore it, hoping that we may discover how even it might be turned into a democratic city.

VII

There are many questions that I shall have to leave unanswered. I could plead lack of time, but the fact is I don't know the answers, nor perhaps does anyone else quite yet.

There is above all the question that now overshadows all else in American life of how we shall solve the problems presented by race, poverty, inequality, discrimination, and centuries of humiliation. No failure in American society has been as enduring, as profound, as visible, as corrosive, as dangerous, and as tragic as our refusal to enable black Americans to share in equal measure with white Americans the realities of the American dream. Now this problem has become central to the whole future of our cities and indeed to the future of the country. I scarcely need to say that unless and until it is solved neither we nor our children nor our grandchildren nor any future generation can have anything like a decent urban life.

There is also the question of how the city can acquire adequate resources, particularly funds, without becoming excessively subordinated to higher levels of government. The bloc grant is a very promising solution, but only if grants are made directly to the cities and not, as is often proposed, exclusively to the states. In the perspective that I have been suggesting, to think of the states as the natural and exclusive recipients of bloc grants is anachronistic; for if the autonomy that is promised by the bloc grant is desirable for states—those barely democratic units in the limbo— autonomy is all the more desirable, and indeed necessary, if citizens are to enjoy the power to shape their cities.

A third question is how to control the size of cities. If there is an optimum size as I have suggested further inquiry might show, then how can cities be maintained within this range—to say nothing

of breaking up the giant metropolis? Typically, the people who influence decisions about the future of cities have acted on the
simpleminded axiom: the bigger the better. This is most notably
true here in America, where the rational prospect of great gain encourages an almost pathological obsession with the virtues of sheer
bigness, as if the very bigness of the city, the height of its buildings,
and the crowds on its streets must somehow outweigh all squalor
and ugliness. There seems to be a fear, too, that the moment we
stop growing we start to die, a half-truth that overlooks the fact
that in nature the mouse and the sparrow have outlasted the bron-
tosaurus and the saber-toothed tiger. There are, I suspect, all sorts
of devices we could use to control the growth of a city when it
reaches the optimum range. These need to be explored, but they
will be of little use until we decide that this is what we really want
to do.

A closely related though much more formidable question is how
we can make the legal boundaries of a city coincide more closely
with what might be called its sociological boundaries. As I suggested earlier, our view up to now has been passive or defeatist: we
say that we must constantly change legal boundaries to fit social
boundaries. But as I tried to suggest with my fantasy of a Constitutional Convention, this way lies madness; for the legal boundaries
must be extended until they cover the whole globe, which whatever
else it may be, cannot be a complete substitute for smaller territorial units. In general, the political autonomy allowed a territorial unit is likely to be less, the higher the amount of interaction
with others outside the legal boundaries.

In building nations or international systems, the greater the
interaction, and consequently the less "real" the significance of
local boundaries, the easier the task. Yet if we are to build democratic cities with enough autonomy to permit their citizens to
participate extensively in significant decisions about their environment, we must somehow reverse the tendency for the legal boundaries of the city to lose all social and economic significance. Nor
can we simply go on creating separate authorities for each problem. Obviously different problems call for different boundaries,
and we may have to live in a network of authorities. Yet the in-
definite multiplication of units of government is bound to fragment
the control of the ordinary citizen over a broad range of policies.

The problem of fragmented authority touches closely upon another, the problem of decentralization of authority and power
within the city. Even in a city in the range from 50–200,000 political participation is reduced for most people to nothing more

than voting in elections—as it is in the representative government of the nation-state—unless there are smaller units within which citizens can from time to time formulate and express their desires, consult with officials, and in some cases participate even more fully in decisions. Unfortunately, I can only indicate the problem; I have no answers to it. There are a number of proposals floating around for creating smaller participatory units in the city, the oldest and most popular candidate being the neighborhood; and there are even some interesting experiments of this kind going on. So far as I know none of the proposals or experiments triumphs over the universal tendency for a few activists to engage in most of the overt activities while the rest participate only sporadically, symbolically, or not at all. Although this limitation seems to me to deflate rather cruelly the most grandiose and utopian claims for citizen participation, and in addition raises serious problems, I do not think it is a reason for rejecting these efforts and experiments out of hand, if we are aiming not for committee democracy but a degree of participation so great and so fairly spread about that no one feels neglected and everyone feels, with justice, that his viewpoint has been pretty fairly attended to. To aim for the point at which practically everyone in the city believes with good reason that his claims ordinarily receive a fair hearing, and decisions, even when adverse to his claims, have been arrived at with understanding and sympathy, is already so distant and so splendid a goal that I am quite content to leave the exploration of what lies beyond it to someone in the 21st century.

Finally, there is the extraordinarily difficult problem of how to reconcile diversity and autonomy among smaller units with standards that larger units, like the state or nation, feel called upon to impose. Probably no single conception of the good city will satisfy the diversity of tastes, wants, and demands that exist in a large country. Any attempt to incorporate all kinds of diversity in every city may not only be futile but undesirable: why should all cities have essentially the same character? Might it not be much better to build an urban civilization out of diverse types of individuals and families with different tastes and values? Yet *complete* autonomy could quickly produce a truly stifling homogeneity within each city, however different each might be from another. What is more, anything approaching complete autonomy would permit some communities to enforce standards that would outrage the most elemental standards held by many of us. Shall we, for example, allow different cities to meet the challenge of racial, ethnic, and economic diversity by establishing racially, ethnically, and economically homogeneous communities? By another route we come back to the problem of the Chinese boxes: the city is nested in a larger society. To what extent can, or will, or should that larger society grant autonomy to the citizens of a city to shape that city according to their own values, if this conflicts with values of larger majorities? Like the members of that hypothetical Constitutional Convention with which I began, we seem to have traversed a full circle.

If we have now reached the point from which we began, perhaps it is time to stop. Another tour around the circle would, I know, turn up more questions, more problems, more obstacles. We might even conclude that the fifth high tide of democracy, the age of the democratic city in the democratic republic, is not after all in our destiny.

Or it may be within the possibilities of other countries, but not our own, to achieve in the rest of this century what the Greeks did 2,500 years ago, to develop an urban civilization founded on the democratic city, only consistent this time with the imperatives of modern technology, the existence of representative governments ruling over huge populations and territories, and the extension of constitutionalism and the rule of law to vast areas of the earth— ultimately, perhaps, to the globe itself.

29 ✤ FORGOTTEN ROOTS

LEWIS LIPSITZ

Political scientists have now learned enough about orientations toward politics in more or less democratic countries to make clear the tragic inadequacies of public life in many of these countries. Our research alone should have shown us the direction a new democratic theory had to follow—a theory that would establish standards for democracy that transcend any existing political

Revised from Lewis Lipsitz, "If, as Verba says . . .," *The American Political Science Review*, June 1968. Reprinted by permission of the author and The American Political Science Association.

system. Yet very few political scientists have traveled this path, and sometimes it seems as if many are unaware that any serious problems have been uncovered. Maybe the preoccupation with political stability, a problem always very near at hand, has given the profession a case of normative myopia. At any rate, contemporary political science is in a state of philosophical poverty at a time when new insights that might stimulate the construction of more sophisticated democratic theory are available, though often hidden, in much empirical research. First, we need to begin drawing more sensible conclusions from research already done. Second, we need to begin doing other sorts of research—work directly related to a growing body of problems in democratic theory. Let me illustrate the present myopia and the future possibility of theory and research in two areas: political allegiance and the political role of the poor.

I

After President Kennedy was assassinated, many studies were made of public reactions to his death. Reviewing these studies, Sidney Verba drew some startling and important conclusions about the nature of "political commitment" in more or less modern societies.[1] His conclusions are important because they are imaginative and go deep. Moreover, they fit neatly with other recent work by political scientists. And, though Verba fails to see it, his conclusions illuminate a critical problem for democratic theory.

Verba's most fundamental and far-reaching conclusion is that the state in modern societies may function as a religion. He sees a "primordial" commitment to the nation-state and its symbols. In the United States, the President is the primary symbol. What this means is that, psychologically, sacred and secular become intertwined in the political world. The state inspires awe and deals with ultimate matters, or, as Verba puts it, "matters of death and life and the quality of life." He notes the thorough meshing of religious and political observances during the weekend after the assassination. And he observes that everywhere public reaction was deeply emotional and radically different from everyday political involvement, and certainly from everyday noninvolvement.

[1] "The Kennedy Assassination and the Nature of Political Commitment," in Bradley S. Greenberg and Edwin B. Parker (eds.), *The Kennedy Assassination and The American Public* (Stanford, Calif.: Stanford University Press, 1965), pp. 348–360.

Verba's conclusions, though speculative, have considerable support in the work of other political scientists. Research on the political socialization of children has shown the central role of the President in the child's early orientations toward politics. In a disturbing passage, David Easton and Robert Hess talk about the flag salute: "The fact that as the child grows older he may be able to sort out the religious from the political setting much more clearly and restrict the pledge to a political meaning need not thereby weaken this bend. The initial and early intermingling of potent religious sentiment with political community has by that time probably created a tie difficult to dissolve."[2] Robert Lane's extensive interviews with "common men" lead him to conclude that "in many ways belief in a powerful state is a psychological substitute for belief in a powerful God."[3] Fred Greenstein argues that reactions similar to those after Kennedy's assassination occurred at the deaths of other Presidents—the reactions often taking a somatic form involving headache, tenseness, insomnia, and rapid heartbeat.[4]

With that heart palpitation we can turn to Seymour Lipset's treatment of American nationalism written in the "haunted Fifties." Lipset tells us that Americans are not a tolerant people and that Americanism is a political creed, a "compulsive ideology," and not merely a patriotic spirit.[5] The religious infusion into American politics then seems to have two central tendencies: intense and often intolerant patriotism, and implicit reverence for the President, particularly in times of crisis.[6]

What does all this mean for democratic theory? It is important to note that one is not likely to find out from the men who have conducted this research or have drawn conclusions from it. Most prominently, if one asks Verba what importance his idea of "primordial" allegiance has for democratic life, he replies in terms of political stability without any acknowledgement that such allegiance is at all problematical. His article on the Kennedy assassination studies is a model of that style of thought that finds this the best of all possible worlds and everything in it is a necessary

[2] David Easton and Robert D. Hess, "The Child's Political World," *Midwest Journal of Politial Science*, VI (August 1962), pp. 238–239.

[3] Robert E. Lane, *Political Ideology* (New York: Free Press, 1962).

[4] Fred I. Greenstein, "Popular Images of the President," *American Journal of Psychiatry*, 122, 5 (November 1965), pp. 523–529.

[5] S. M. Lipset, "Sources of the Radical Right—1955," in Daniel Bell (ed.), *The Radical Right* (Garden City, N.Y.: Doubleday, 1963), p. 264.

[6] For a more complete treatment see my paper, "If, As Verba Says, the State Functions as a Religion, What Are We to Do Then to Save Our Souls?" *American Political Science Review*, June 1968.

evil.[7] Of course, Verba is not alone in this tendency. He concludes, as Shils and Young did fifteen years ago about the British coronation, that symbolic attachments, unquestioned and largely unconscious, are necessary for political stability.[8] They are what we've got instead of religion itself, providing that fundamental social cement that even the teeth of group conflict cannot tear apart. The question of the nature of public allegiance is, however, central to democratic theory and cannot be put blithely in the stability basket. It may be comforting to believe that the sort of "primordial" attachments to presidency and country we have right now are precisely what we need to ensure political stability, but why accept this on faith? A central strand of the libertarian tradition, after all, from anarchists to socialists to contemporary liberals, is a sharp questioning of the sort of consent the citizen gives to political authorities. For the libertarian the only legitimate consent is thoughtful and hard-headed, and excludes a worshipful attitude toward the state, regardless of how pleasantly and innocently that worship may be disguised.

We can gain some perspective on this question by turning for a moment to Henry David Thoreau, one of the great questioners of political authority in the libertarian tradition. He perceived the intertwining of political and religious strands in the public attitudes of his time. In his famous essay *Civil Disobedience*, Thoreau saw that the political realm is dealing with ultimate questions— matters of conscience. He saw in this not a useful social cement but twin disasters for the libertarian impulse: first, the loss of moral autonomy for the mass of men who abandoned their consciences to state direction; and second, ostracism or worse for the few who would not abandon their convictions and who became enemies of the state. Calling attention to this dilemma, Thoreau asked: "Can there not be a government in which majorities do not virtually decide right and wrong, but conscience?—in which majorities decide only those questions to which the rule of expediency is applicable? Must the citizen even for a moment, or in the least degree, resign his conscience to the legislator?" Thoreau's solution to the conflict between conscience and state direction (even a majoritarian direction) is the Christian solution: disobedience. It is not so much Thoreau's solution, though that is important here. What matters is that he offers us a normatively important perspec-

[7] This turn of phrase is taken from T. H. Bradley.

[8] Edward Shils and Michael Young, "The Meaning of the Coronation," *Sociological Review*, I, December 1953. Norman Birnbaum has a thoughtful critique of Shils and Young, "Monarchs and Sociologists," *Sociological Review*, 3 (July 1955), pp. 5–23.

tive within which we can reanalyze the problem of political allegiance. Thoreau sees that a state that deals in ultimate coin cannot be merely a matter of convenience, as Lockean liberalism would have had it. Such a state, by its very nature, violates the separation of sacred and secular. Viewed with awe, it threatens the individual's moral autonomy and corrupts the nature of consent. Thoreau's libertarian radicalism consists in his stubborn refusal to turn away from this problem. He argues that the libertarian must, with Locke, insist on voluntarism in sacred matters. When the state deals in such matters, the libertarian must speak for the rights of conscience. Political salvation should not be coerced. The right to opt out should be recognized as it would be in the case of a church. If politics is our religion, each man must nonetheless save his own soul, but this time on the terrain of the authoritative allocation of values. A contemporary Thoreau, now blessed with Verba's analysis and the findings of Lane, Greenstein, and others, would suggest that democratic processes and democratic theory need a revitalization, to be accomplished by a renewed interest in civil disobedience and a heightened consciousness of the meaning of consent.

Thoreau's position confronts us with several serious problems. It is not my intention to argue that Thoreau's resolution of the conflict between individual conscience and majority rule (or non-rule) is fully acceptable or thoroughly thought through. But his conclusions can stand for us in contrast to the bland hopefulness of so much contemporary research that proclaims its interest in democratic theory. Thoreau sees the dark side of the conflict: the growth of unconscious conformity and moral irresponsibility; the decline of citizenry and the emergence of subjects. These issues, as our research should have shown us, have not vanished in our time. Many have not seen them because, like Verba, they have chosen not to see them, because not the individual life but the nation-state has been our love.

This problem of consent, like a huge tree trunk floating in the air, needs to put down serious roots, spread out, crack the façade of established institutions, and throw off at least a few useful apples. Once we see that consent is a normative problem, not just a matter of ensuring political stability, we have to concentrate on its quality. The first root we send down must involve more research about the nature of consent: about the key consenting decisions individuals make, such as tax paying, draft induction, obedience to the law. We need to know about the texture of this consent, its knowledgeableness, its hard-headedness. We need to know more about the issue of symbols so central in Verba's analysis. Is he correct in speaking of primordial commitments—how correct, for whom, under what circumstances? And what are the limits of and alternatives to such commitments?

A second concern should grow out of the studies of childhood socialization—socialization in the family, the school, and the church. Here a critique of both the form and the content of contemporary practices should emerge. We should be able to measure what *is*, against a standard of socialization appropriate for a democratic citizenry. Then the flag salute will perhaps appear in a new light, and early reverence for the President as well. Can one imagine the difference if early socialization emphasized the Bill of Rights and the significance of majority rule? To the argument that these are matters too abstract and that children need personalized symbolic attachments, one can only reply that that is what the monarchy once argued.

The third root matter concerns the study of institutions presently undemocratic or nondemocratic. Here, the nature of work experience must be examined. We have already discovered enough to know that a man's work has deep personal and some political significance. Work is intrinsically important, but beyond this, it may be that if men can control their destinies in the day-to-day issues of the job they will become more involved and sophisticated politically. At any rate, we need to know about this and about the rewards and limits of democratizing the work process and the institutions connected with work—unions and corporations.

It should be unnecessary to say, but probably needs saying anyway, that educational institutions also need an injection of rule from below—and not just an occasional student riot or seizure of buildings, but steady participation, informed, procedurally secure, and an expected part of the educational process.

One immediate apple from this tree of democratic knowledge would tell us about a pressing contemporary issue: conscientious objection to a particular war. Most of the argument about selective objection has dealt with the conflict between the demands of individual conscience versus the state's need for soldiers. What has been left out of most of these discussions is a concern with the quality of consent. Probably only radical changes in our educational processes can affect the quality of the majority response to the draft, but a provision for selective objection would be an important gain in democratic education in itself. The legitimacy of claiming selective-objector status would make it clear that *obedience* as well as disobedience ought to involve moral choice and reflection. There are many difficult questions connected with particular war objection, most notably the question of why the draft is to be differentiated from other government compulsions. Rather than explore that argument here, let me note only that a persuasive case for the uniqueness of the draft has already been constructed and that, given such a case, the legitimization of conscientious objection to a particular war would be a significant gain.[9]

Finally, a last root: the extent of public sophistication about politics is critically important. Many have argued that politics is a burdensome and unrewarding business and that it is therefore no surprise that few men concern themselves with it. But this is a reflection not on men but on a social order that makes the stuff of politics seem too remote for the ordinary man. Clearly, people are anxious to grasp the essentials of political matters once they perceive that politics touches their lives and that they can touch the political world. Political scientists who profess an interest in "democracy," if they take their own professings seriously, ought to be holding their heads in their hands and wondering how to build political sensitivity into the process of growing.

II

This brings us to the poor: the people without much money and with little education. These are the "Don't Knows," those who cannot tell you what it is they want, who are often suspicious of interviewers, and whose opinions are perhaps not really their own at all. Reading the literature of survey research, it is clear that poor poeple know little about politics, seem to care little, and certainly do very little.[10] How are we to understand this?

Much of the literature in political science tells us that the apathy of many of the poor is probably appropriate for the moment. Herbert McClosky, for example, tells us that given the relatively undemocratic attitudes of large numbers of ordinary people, their relative apathy prevents antiliberalism movements from succeeding.[11] Lipset's thesis concerning working-class authoritarianism, although it steers clear of prescription, leaves a similar impres-

[9] Michael Harrington makes a strong argument along these lines and also persuasively differentiates the draft from similar issues. See his article, "Strategies for Opposition: The Draft—Tax Refusal—'Resistance,'" *Dissent,* March–April 1968, pp. 119–130.

[10] See, for example, Robert E. Lane, *Political Life* (New York: Free Press, 1959), chap. 16.

[11] Herbert McClosky, "Consensus and Ideology in American Politics," *American Political Science Review,* 58 (June 1964), pp. 361–382.

sion.[12] If the poor are more undemocratically inclined than others, then perhaps others, particularly the upper middle class and the political activists, ought to be left without intense pressure from below.

Let's look more closely at this argument. It is based on two assumptions: first, that we have already achieved "democracy"— McClosky, for example, uses this term throughout his article to describe contemporary (1964) America; second, that the anti-democratic impulse comes from mass movements, not from elites. Neither of these assumptions is correct. How strange that political scientists, rabid for quantification and methodological refinement elsewhere, have not found a more exact way of discussing "democracy." Clearly, or perhaps hopefully, McClosky and others who have taken a similar position (Prothro and Grigg,[13] Almond and Verba[14]) would not claim that America is now a 100 percent democracy. It is considerably short of that. If we agree then that we are not talking about democracy versus nondemocracy but about degrees of democracy, then the argument becomes far more complex. With America, let us say, only 50 percent democratic, where can we place the responsibility for the missing 50 percent? So long as we assumed democracy was a quality we already possessed, the existing distribution of attitudes and political involvement was hard to condemn. Once the degree of democracy becomes problematical, however, neither elites nor masses are clearly the villains. Certainly it becomes very hard to claim that the democracy we do not have is a result only of the relatively undemocratic attitudes of poorer, less educated people. How could this be the case when these are the people least likely to be politically active? McClosky does not face this issue squarely. Instead he makes the second assumption mentioned above: that undemocratic movements are mass movements. He cites in particular the McCarthyism of the 1950s and the Impeach Earl Warren movement. But how can either of these be described solely as mass movements? McCarthy's prestige and influence cannot be dissociated from his usefulness to the Republican Party and from a generally repressive atmosphere among both elites and masses. Those who would impeach Earl Warren also drew sustenance from that significant

[12] Seymour M. Lipset, *Political Man* (New York: Doubleday, 1960), chap. 4.

[13] James Prothro and Charles Grigg, "Fundamental Principles of Democracy: Bases of Agreement and Disagreement," *Journal of Politics*, 22 (1960), pp. 276–294.

[14] Gabriel Almond and Sidney Verba, *The Civic Culture* (Boston: Little, Brown, 1965), chap. XIII.

portion of the political elite that revile the Supreme Court. The elite-mass dichotomy is simplistic, ignoring the emergence of new elites and the steady interaction between groups with different degrees of political involvement.

The definition of democracy itself is also at stake. If we take McClosky's word for it, democracy involves free speech, due process, and political rights. He avoids the main issues of the day by refusing to include social and economic equality within his definition. That may seem intellectually neat, but it defines away findings that don't fit. McClosky's own surveys showed that on questions of radical and ethnic equality elites and nonelites had very similar distributions of attitudes—with thorough nonconsensus in both groups. Moreover, on questions of economic equality, nonelites are far more equalitarian than the political elites. This finding, of course, would be all the more true for the poorest of the population. Had McClosky seen social and economic equality as a part of what he called democracy he would have been forced to reassess who was creating what, when, where, and how.

III

Looking back now on the survey literature of the 1950s and early 1960s and the conclusions drawn from that research, it is shocking to see how badly the empirical mark was missed. We could not, from that literature, have predicted anything like the civil rights movement, the riots, the revolt against welfare, nor, of course, anything like student movements against the Vietnam war. The poor, particularly the black poor, proved to possess a potential for action beyond our capacity or imagination to measure. Much of this failure was due to a conception of society that was too static, too elitist, and too complacent. It shows in our work.

We should have realized that the political ignorance of the poor (even if it were complete ignorance) and the political apathy of the poor (even if it were complete apathy) have profound normative significance. If these people were inarticulate and ignorant, isn't this of first importance to a serious democrat? Only a deep fear of mass action could override and obscure this. But the poor were never wholly apathetic or wholly ignorant.

Philip Converse's epic article, "The Nature of Belief Systems in Mass Publics,"[15] argues that most people know little about politics

[15] This article is in David Apter (ed.), *Ideology and Discontent* (New York: Free Press, 1965), pp. 206–263.

and that what views they have alter over time. Indifference is the rule. But there are two problems with this description. First, it is based on the probably aberrant period of the 1950s. Second, it fails to touch the normatively important questions: Are poor people apathetic because they feel their political efforts will be futile, or because they don't care about politics? Are they ignorant of specific issues because they have not been mobilized by leaders or because they really have no latent sentiments to mobilize? Actually, these are empirical questions that have not been asked clearly enough. Even if poor people were indifferent and without political feeling, which is usually not the case, that in itself would be a sorrowful commentary on our "democracy" that only a determined myopia could overlook.

Suddenly the poor have become important to us. They march. They speak of jobs and freedom. They riot. But our own work should long ago have induced us to advocate those economic and social reforms that would set men on a more equal footing and thereby make democracy more meaningful. Now the needed intensive research on the opinions and behavior of the poor is beginning to be done.

To be meaningful, to address itself to the larger issues, this research must go deeper in its efforts to see what people are and what they might be, must look for latent energies and buried directions. We cannot be satisfied when the welfare recipient in public housing tells us that he does not know anything about those candidates for President; we cannot be satisfied when the sharecropper in Mississippi is unclear about the nature of anti-poverty programs; we cannot be satisfied when the unskilled worker in a small Midwestern town wants taxes lowered and simultaneously favors more government spending; we cannot be satisfied when the unionized factory worker cannot tell us which is a more important issue, race relations or medical care. Beyond these uncertainties, the hesitations and ignorance, there are lives and worlds, expectations and disappointments, rages and hopes—tart apples we cannot be satisfied with until we bite.

30 ❧ THE USE OF
SOCIAL SCIENCE IN
DEMOCRATIC THEORY

DENNIS F. THOMPSON

It is no longer possible to discuss democratic theory adequately without giving serious attention to the findings of behavioral social science. But when these findings are brought to bear on democratic theory, the traditional concerns of that theory must be respected: it is essential that democratic theory retain its perspective of evaluation and prescription. The justification and revision of democratic theory in light of behavioral social science, therefore, must be conducted so that due weight is given to the value standards in the theory as well as to the behavioral evidence that is now available.

In this essay I examine two approaches or tendencies that discourage a fruitful encounter between democratic theory and behavioral social science; argue for recognition of both a disparity and an interplay between value standards and evidence; and propose an outline of the principal types of standards in democratic theory and their relation to behavioral evidence. The value standards to which I refer are evaluations and prescriptions that are explicitly or implicitly contained in the writings of democratic theorists who are at least as much concerned with evaluation and prescription as with description and explanation.[1] The appropriate evidence could be drawn from any of the empirical studies that follow the prevailing orientation in the social sciences, inelegantly called behavioralism. It is characterized most prominently (though not exclusively) by the use or proposed use of quantitative tech-

This essay is partly based on the author's forthcoming book, *The Democratic Citizen* to be published by Cambridge University Press, copyright Cambridge University Press.

[1] Twentieth-century British and American theorists who share a concern for improving the extent and quality of citizen involvement in politics seem most suitable for this purpose (*e.g.*, John Dewey, Leonard T. Hobhouse, A. D. Lindsay, Robert M. MacIver, Charles E. Merriam, Yves Simon, T. V. Smith, and Harold J. Laski, excluding his most doctrinaire Marxist views). Elitist democratic theorists (such as Walter Lippmann and Joseph Schumpeter) should also be considered. With twentieth-century theory, it is not necessary, as it would be with earlier theory, to speculate what a particular theorist *might have* said when faced, for example, with the consequences of universal suffrage.

niques that allow, as far as possible, findings about empirical phenomena to be controlled and to be replicated by other investigators.[2]

The ultimate aim of such an encounter between democratic theory and behavioral social science should be a full-scale theory of democracy that would integrate value standards and evidence so completely that the theory could not properly be called either empirical or normative. This aim is frustrated by the currently popular division of the study of politics into normative and empirical branches. Moreover, if the aim is taken seriously, it is not sufficient merely to point out that empirical research has normative implications.[3] Such implications must be analyzed within the context of a systematic theory of democracy. This essay suggests an approach by which such an analysis could be conducted.

Prescriptivism and Descriptivism

Faced with an apparent conflict between democratic theory and behavioral evidence, many writers tend either to discount the evidence or to give up the theory. Prescriptivism represents the first tendency, descriptivism the second. Neither constitutes a satisfactory approach.

Prescriptivism in its extreme form maintains that the value standards of democratic theory should be treated as prescriptions

[2] The term "behavioralism" is not only inelegant but also misleading if it suggests exclusive study of behavior strictly conceived or a unified school of social scientists who agree on methods (even on quantitative methods). Nevertheless, the term is so widely used (usually with apologies) at least as a description of the prevailing outlook or mood in the discipline that to resist it seems futile. In any case, it has now acquired that form of legitimacy that is most difficult to resist, having been sanctified by use in the titles of research institutes, divisions of foundations, and names of journals. The best discussions of the meaning of the terms are: Robert A. Dahl, "The Behavioral Approach in Political Science: Epitaph for a Monument to a Successful Protest," *American Political Science Review* (December 1961), pp. 763–772; and David Easton, "The Current Meaning of 'Behavioralism'" in James C. Charlesworth (ed.), *The Limits of Behavioralism in Political Science* (American Academy of Political and Social Science, October 1962), pp. 1–25. For democratic theory, the voting studies seem to be at present the most promising source of evidence because these constitute the most sustained investigation of problems relevant to a theory that focuses on the role of citizens in a democracy.

[3] See *e.g.*, Jack L. Walker, "A Critique of the Elitist Theory of Democracy," *American Political Science Review* (June 1966), pp. 285–295 and his "Reply," pp. 391–392; and Charles Taylor, "Neutrality in Political Science," in Peter Laslett and W. G. Runciman (eds.), *Philosophy, Politics and Society*, third series (Oxford, 1967), pp. 25–47.

that are immune to challenge by evidence from the behavioral sciences. The most important standards in democratic theory, it is said, are "prescription[s] for a worthwhile polity which should be sought after." Only if we can obtain evidence that would prove that men *by nature* cannot do what the prescriptions assert would the prescriptions be undermined.[4] But the concept of human nature contains an irreducible element of potentiality: no evidence about what people have actually been able to do under all past conditions would refute a claim about what people might be able to do in the future. On this view, democratic theory therefore remains immune to empirical evidence.

The trouble with prescriptivism is that it overlooks the fact that most democratic theorists insist that *some* of their value standards are closely tied to present political reality. John Stuart Mill believed that his theory was worth holding because the ideals he presented in it were likely to be realized. He wrote that "governments must be made for human beings as they are, or as they are capable of speedily becoming."[5] Many democratic theorists share Dewey's view that in seeking "a measure for the worth of any given mode of social life," we should not

set up, out of our heads, something we regard as an ideal society. We must base our conception upon societies which actually exist, in order to have any assurance that our ideal is a practicable one. . . . The problem is to extract the desirable traits or forms of community life which actually exist, and employ them to criticize undesirable features and suggest improvement.[6]

While prescriptivists would construe democratic theory as expressing standards that are unaffected by behavioral evidence, descriptivists would go to the other extreme. Descriptivism in its pure form asserts that behavioral evidence refutes or supports the

[4] Lane Davis, "The Cost of Realism: Contemporary Restatements of Democracy," *Western Political Quarterly* (March 1964), p. 39; and Graeme Duncan and Steven Lukes, "The New Democracy," *Political Studies* (June 1963), pp. 156–77. Also *cf.* Giovanni Sartori, *Democratic Theory* (New York, 1965), pp. 63–68, 79–82.

[5] John Stuart Mill, *Considerations on Representative Government* (Everyman: New York), chap. 6, p. 253.

[6] John Dewey, *Democracy and Education* (New York, 1961), p. 83. Also, Dewey and James Tufts, *Ethics* (New York, 1932), pp. 301, 387–388; Charles Merriam, *Civic Education in the United States*, Part IV (New York, 1934), pp. 182–183; Yves Simon, *Philosophy of Democratic Government* (Chicago, 1951), p. 116; Harold Laski, *Introduction to Contemporary Politics* (Seattle: University of Washington Press, 1939), pp. 35–41; and Leonard Hobhouse, *Liberalism* (New York, 1964), p. 30, and *The Metaphysical Theory of the State: A Criticism* (London, 1918), pp. 17–18.

standards of democratic theory in just the way such evidence would refute or support a descriptive or explanatory proposition. For instance, it has been argued that since electoral studies show that most voters do not consider the public good, the proposition that they should do so is somehow falsified.[7] The trouble with descriptivism is that it ignores the fact that democratic theorists do not offer this proposition or any other value standard as a description or explanation of anything. The value standards in democratic theory, though affected by evidence, express evaluations and prescriptions that cannot be treated as empirical generalizations.

Few democratic theorists can be charged with adopting prescriptivism or descriptivism in their extreme forms. Nevertheless, many theorists tend toward prescriptivism by attaching too little significance to behavioral evidence in framing their value standards. This tendency is not simply the result of such evidence being unavailable; it is often inherent in their general approaches. Some democratic theorists in the Thomist natural-law tradition, for example, consider the question of how far democratic ideals are actually realized to be casuistry, not genuine political philosophy, which deals with first principles.[8] Social democrats, such as Harold Laski in his non-Marxist moods, usually deal in broad historical generalizations susceptible to historical evidence but not to the findings of less sweeping inquiries normally conducted by social scientists. Furthermore, many theorists assume at least an attenuated doctrine of progress that encourages them to discount behavioral evidence, especially unfavorable items.[9] This doctrine suggests that the distant future will be brighter than the past and

[7] Bernard Berelson, "Democratic Theory and Public Opinion," *Public Opinion Quarterly* (Fall 1952), pp. 327–328. Also, *cf.* T. V. Smith, *The Democratic Way of Life* (Chicago, 1939), p. 203; C. W. Cassinelli, *The Politics of Freedom* (Seattle: University of Washington Press, 1961), pp. 13, 82; William Buchanan, "An Inquiry into Purpose Voting," *Journal of Politics* (May 1956), pp. 284–285; and Gabriel A. Almond and Sidney Verba, *The Civic Culture* (Princeton: Princeton University Press, 1963), pp. 475–476.

[8] M. J. Adler and Walter Farrell, "The Theory of Democracy," *The Thomist* (July 1941), pp. 347–398. For a qualification, see pp. 130–131.

[9] See Merriam, *The New Democracy and the New Despotism* (New York, 1939), p. 96, and *Prologue to Politics* (Chicago, 1939), pp. 74–75; Simon, *Community of the Free* (New York, 1947), pp. 122–136; and *Philosophy, op. cit.*, pp. 287–288, 318; Hobhouse, *Morals in Evolution* (London, 1929), pp. 609–611; and *Social Evolution and Political Theory* (New York, 1928), pp. 1–16, 127, 149–165; Robert MacIver, *The Web of Government* (New York, 1947), pp. 434–436; and Dewey, *The Public and Its Problems* (Denver, 1927), p. 146.

the present—brighter than the world portrayed by empirical studies. This retreat to the future borders on prescriptivism, despite some of these theorists' hopes that some of their ideals are realizable.

In formulating and assessing value standards other democratic theorists tend toward descriptivism by placing too much weight on behavioral evidence. One of the most common manifestations of this tendency is the view that the ideals or standards of orthodox democratic theory should be interpreted as myths because behavioral evidence indicates that they are unrealized. Myths, such as those about high degrees of popular participation, are very useful, these theorists maintain, because so long as political leaders believe them, government and other organizations will be more likely to respond to popular demands.[10] But if empirical research exposes the falsity of such beliefs without providing some hope and help for realizing the ideals that such myths express, leaders may eventually cease to believe the myths. This eventuality does not seem likely if one assumes either (1) that the academic study of politics and the practice of politics are so divorced that the conclusions of the former almost never affect beliefs in the latter; or (2) that leaders' beliefs are so resistant that no good evidence will persuade them to give up believing in myths.

Few democratic theorists or political scientists would be prepared to accept the complete irrelevancy of their activities. V. O. Key, who stresses the mythic functions of democratic ideals, rejects the first assumption, arguing that some academic theories about voting behavior have in fact affected the way politicians think about citizens' political competence (though the academic theories are distorted and simplified in the process).[11] The second assumption would be self-defeating for most of the theorists who interpret ideals as myths because it suggests that political leaders suffer from the same crucial defects for which these theorists indict ordinary citizens. It is desirable, therefore, to avoid descriptivist tendencies that would transform ideals into myths at best. Ideals and other standards in democratic theory should be taken seriously as evaluations and prescriptions that can be affected but not straightforwardly falsified by behavioral evidence.

[10] Sartori, *op. cit.*, p. 85; Robert Dahl, *Who Governs?* (New Haven, 1961), p. 280; V. O. Key, *Public Opinion and American Democracy* (New York, 1961), p. 547; and Cassinelli, *op. cit.*, p. 112. See also Almond and Verba, *op. cit.*, p. 486; and Lester W. Milbrath, *Political Participation* (Chicago, 1965), p. 152.

[11] Key, *The Responsible Electorate* (Cambridge, Mass., 1966), p. 6.

In assessing the value standards in democratic theory in light of behavioral evidence, we should therefore strike a balance between the two extremes of prescriptivism and descriptivism. We must stress, as descriptivism does too little and prescriptivism too much, the *disparity* between factual evidence and value standards. At the same time, we must emphasize, as prescriptivism does too little and descriptivism too much, the *interplay* between the evidence and the standards.

The Disparity Between Facts and Values

The disparity between factual evidence and value standards in democratic theory is merely a manifestation of the more general difference that many philosophers find between judgments of fact and judgments of value (or more roughly, between facts and values). Simply put, a judgment of fact is one that is expressed by a proposition that primarily describes or explains certain phenomena. A judgment of value is one that is expressed by a proposition that primarily evaluates phenomena or prescribes an attitude or action regarding phenomena. It is evident, at least *prima facie*, that evaluating and prescribing are kinds of linguistic activities different from describing and explaining, however mingled these activities may be in actual discourse. It is not so clear, however, exactly how the differences between these activities should be characterized, how important they are, or what implications follow from them. This set of problems is enormously complex and has occupied English-speaking moral philosophers more than any other in this century.[12] Fortunately, it is not necessary to settle this set of problems here. To explain the disparity in the sense I intend,

[12] The classic discussions of the fact-value distinction are still worth reading: David Hume, in L. A. Selby-Bigge (ed.), *A Treatise of Human Nature* (Oxford, 1960), Book III, Part I, Sec. 1; Max Weber, " 'Objectivity' in Social Science and Social Policy," in E. Shils and H. Finch (tr. and ed.), *The Methodology of the Social Sciences* (Glencoe, Ill., 1949), pp. 50–122; and G. E. Moore, *Principia Ethica* (Cambridge, Eng., 1959), pp. 1–58. For good modern discussions see Karl Popper, "What Can Logic Do for Philosophy?" *Proceedings of the Aristotelian Society*, supplementary volume xxii (1948); R. M. Hare, *Language of Morals* (Oxford, 1952), pp. 27–31, 79–93; Patrick Horace Nowell-Smith, *Ethics* (Oxford, 1957), esp. pp. 21–31, 43–54, 157–159; Alan Montefiore, *A Modern Introduction to Moral Philosophy* (London, 1958), pp. 105–132; Richard Brandt, *Ethical Theory* (Englewood Cliffs, N.J.: 1959), pp. 37–55, 151–270; and Phillipa Foot (ed.), *Theories of Ethics* (Oxford, 1967), pp. 16–114. A history of earlier modern arguments about the fact-value distinction is in Arnold Brecht, *Political Theory* (Princeton, N.J., 1959), pp. 207–258.

I need indicate only that judgments of fact and of value require different procedures of justification.[13]

The justification of a judgment of fact always depends on an observational test (or on other factual judgments which are subject to such tests). The justification of a value judgment depends not only on observational tests but also on a human decision to accept the judgment (or some higher principle from which the judgment follows). It might be objected that factual judgments even in the natural sciences presuppose the acceptance of certain principles, such as the principle of induction or the laws of logic, which cannot themselves be established by observational tests. But such principles must also be taken for granted in valuational inquiry, and in neither kind of inquiry are the principles normally questioned. But in justifying value judgments, there are *additional* principles or standards that require a decision not based on observation—for example, the principle of equality. Such principles or standards are typically in dispute; indeed, unless they were, the problem of justifying a value judgment probably would not even arise.

This contrast between the two kinds of justificatory procedures should not be taken to imply that the two kinds do not share certain features; they do. Nor should the contrast suggest that value judgments are not made in the process of justifying facts, and vice versa; they are. If the disparity exists in the sense I intend, it implies only that no value judgment can be completely justified by reference to any set of factual judgments alone, such as the evidence from behavioral studies.

---

[13] Models proposed in recent years by many moral philosophers of varying meta-ethical views to characterize the justification of value judgments differ significantly from models for the justification of factual judgments (though not necessarily in the way I describe in the text). See, for example, Herbert Feigl, "Validation and Vindication: An Analysis of the Nature and the Limits of Ethical Arguments," in W. Sellars and J. Hospers (eds.), *Readings in Ethical Theory* (New York, 1952), pp. 667–680; Stephen E. Toulmin, *An Examination of the Place of Reason in Ethics* (Cambridge, Eng., 1953), pp. 121–165; P. H. Nowell-Smith, *Ethics* (Oxford, 1957), pp. 43–54, 85–159; Paul W. Taylor, *Normative Discourse* (Englewood Cliffs, N.J., 1961), pp. 3–188, 255–259; and R. M. Hare, *Freedom and Reason* (Oxford, 1963), esp. pp. 86–111. Philosophers who, without identifying valuational and factual justification, stress their parallels, include: John Rawls, "Outline of a Decision Procedure for Ethics," *Philosophical Review* (April 1951), pp. 177–197; Kurt Baier, *The Moral Point of View: A Rational Basis of Ethics* (Ithaca, N.Y., 1958), pp. 47–84; and Paul Edwards *The Logic of Moral Discourse* (Glencoe, Ill., 1955), pp. 139–223. Also see Orval L. Perry, "The Logic of Moral Valuation," *Mind* (January 1957), pp. 42–62.

The Interplay Between Facts and Values

To recognize the disparity between facts and values is not to deny that values affect the selection of problems and the interpretation of data.[14] If we are to allow for an interplay between facts and values, not only must evidence affect the way we formulate and appraise value standards in democratic theory, but also the standards must influence what evidence we consider and how we interpret it in the process of justifying or revising the standards.

If democratic theorists who are prone to prescriptivism have discouraged the interplay between facts and values, many social scientists must also share the blame. In contemporary social science, the disparity between facts and values is blown up into a rigid dichotomy that inhibits any interplay between facts and values. Many social scientists have taken only too seriously Max Weber's strictures against confusing facts and values. They have shunned systematic evaluation and prescription, and have refused to apply their empirical findings to valuational theory.[15] It is often forgotten that Weber himself rejected the view that social scientists must eschew evaluation and prescription.[16] It is usually admitted that social scientists can in a straightforwardly empirical way investigate the origins, content, and consequences of values that people hold and the means for attaining them. But it is less often recognized that social scientists could also apply their conclusions to a systematic democratic theory that is primarily evaluative and prescriptive rather than explanatory and descriptive.

While it is true that the value standards in such a theory must ultimately rest upon human decisions that are not based on facts alone, it is also true that an intelligent decision results only from a complex process of reasoning that hardly can be said to yield arbitrary conclusions.[17] A value judgment must be justified by

[14] The best discussion of the whole issue of objectivity in the social sciences is Ernest Nagel, *The Structure of Science* (New York, 1961), pp. 447–502. Also see Weber, " 'Objectivity,' " *op. cit.*, and "The Meaning of 'Ethical Neutrality' in Sociology and Economics," in *The Methodology of the Social Sciences*, pp. 1–112; Gunnar Myrdal, in Paul Streeton (ed.), *Value in Social Theory* (London, 1960), pp. 47–87; and A. J. Ayer, "Man as a Subject for Science," in Laslett and Runciman, *op. cit.*, pp. 6–24; and Quentin Gibson, *The Logic of Social Enquiry* (London, 1960), pp. 47–87.

[15] See Christian Bay, "Politics and Pseudopolitics: A Critical Evaluation of Some Behavioral Literature," *American Political Science Review* (March 1965), pp. 39–51.

[16] Weber, " 'Ethical Neutrality,' " *op. cit.*, pp. 20–22.

[17] For the view that the fact-value distinction renders value judgments

reasons, in accordance with some systematic procedure that should show, for example, whether the judgment is consistent with other value judgments and whether it is supported by empirical evidence. In this process, properly conducted, an interplay between facts and values is inevitable.

How then can factual evidence from behavioral social science support or weaken a value standard in democratic theory? In general, there are two ways. First, such evidence can show whether a standard is realized or is likely to be realized. If, for example, evidence suggests that the changes meant to realize a prescription for greater citizen participation in present social conditions are not likely to do so, the prescription, though not refuted, becomes less tenable. Exactly why the prescription should be thus weakened is not easy to explain, but it no doubt arises from the assumption, built into at least some uses of our concept of choice, that we cannot sensibly be asked to choose to do something that is likely to be impossible. It is true that not all moral or political prescriptions are confined to the realm of what is possible or likely. The saints and heroes of moral life have their counterparts in the revolutionary radicals of political life. But a large number of prescriptions of democratic theory are intended to be realized. For these, evidence that indicates they are unrealizable under normal conditions, though not necessarily decisive, is damaging.

Unfortunately, it is not possible to specify in any precise way the degree to which a prescription is supported or weakened by a piece of factual evidence showing that it is unlikely to be realized, even if the evidence is realizable and quantitatively expressed. For it is not merely a matter of judging the probability of whether the means will realize the end posited by the prescription; the means themselves have to be judged by value standards. Moreover, the role of the standard in the whole theory must be taken into account. Although we can never say exactly how much a standard is weakened by being shown to be unlikely to be realized, we can certainly say that such a standard is less acceptable than if it were shown to be likely to be realized.

The second way in which factual evidence can be used to support or weaken standards is by showing what consequences would

---

arbitrary (and for other exaggerated views of its consequences), see Leo Strauss, "An Epilogue," in *Essays on the Scientific Study of Politics* (New York, 1962), pp. 307–327, and *Natural Right and History* (Chicago, 1953), pp. 35–80; and Eric Voegelin, *The New Science of Politics* (Chicago, 1952), pp. 1–26. For a critical discussion of such exaggerations, see Brecht, *op. cit.*, pp. 117–135; and Nagel, *op. cit.*, esp. pp. 485–502.

follow from realizing (or from not realizing) the standard. The consequences may follow either from the practice specified in the standard itself (for example, greater participation) or from means thought to be necessary to realize the standard (for example, greater social equality). In either case, if the consequences that follow from realizing the standard are less desirable than not realizing the standard, then normally the standard is not acceptable, or is at least weakened. Here again, there is room for imprecision, not only in weighing the probabilities of the consequences but also in weighing the consequences themselves.

This account of the general ways in which factual evidence affects value standards does not fully represent the interplay of facts and values that should occur in justifying a value standard. It is not simply a matter of clarifying a particular value standard and deciding, after using evidence in these two ways, whether the standard is acceptable. Consideration of evidence, as well as conceptual analysis of the standard, often opens up new possibilities or difficulties that may not be apparent when a standard is considered by itself. These new possibilities or difficulties may force a revision of the standard, either because a revised standard seems more feasible, has more desirable consequences, or is more compatible with other standards and presuppositions in the theory. The revised standard then may require analysis and may call for further empirical investigation. At the same time, investigating unforeseen possibilities may turn up implications for other standards in the theory. These implications will have to be explored before we can be satisfied that the standard with which we began, even if it is revised, is justified. The procedure is often not complete for one standard until all the standards in the theory are similarly examined.

Only by actually demonstrating how standards are revised and assessed in a whole theory of democracy could the procedure for justifying standards be adequately explained. However, we are not therefore forced to abandon completely the hope for some general outline of a procedure. Specifying the major types of standards in democratic theory, and the ways in which evidence can affect each type, will give some indication of how factual evidence can be brought to bear on value standards in a way that recognizes both the disparity and the interplay between evidence and standards. Three principal types of standards in democratic theory may be identified—what I shall call conditions, constructive ideals, and reconstructive ideals.

Conditions

A condition requires that in particular democratic systems certain functions or objectives posited at least implicitly in democratic theory be satisfied. To decide if the functions or objectives are fulfilled, we judge on the basis of minimal or weak criteria whether behavioral evidence indicates that the functions are performed (1) in the manner that a democratic theory implies; and (2) to the extent that the theory implies.

In formulating and justifying a condition, we deliberately try to find criteria that preserve at least a minimum of the valuational content of democratic theory and that at the same time can be met in systems generally regarded as Western democracies. Formulation and justification of a condition is neither a purely empirical nor a purely evaluative operation, but requires an interplay, described in the previous section, between value standards and factual evidence. The condition is brought into conformity with the evidence, but in a way and within the limits set by the standards and presuppositions in the theory.

This process is more complicated than is usually assumed. The participation condition, for example, requires that citizens participate in such a manner and to such an extent that at least five functions can be said to be fulfilled in some sense compatible with the theory. Participation is supposed to prevent rulers from deliberately disregarding citizens' interests; ensure that all interests are expressed and considered in the political processes; enable citizens to develop knowledge of what their interests are; promote a sense of legitimacy; and foster individual self-development. To show that these functions are fulfilled would require a full analysis not only of the functions and the relevant evidence but also of other conditions such as discussion, rational voting, and equality.

The reason we should seek conditions that can be satisfied is to escape the distortion (and possible disillusionment) that would come from denying that systems commonly regarded as democratic do not exhibit democratic characteristics in any sense. There is little to be gained from the semantic possessiveness that would confine the word "democratic" to only those activities of which one fully approves. The reason we must stress that the conditions are based on weak or minimal criteria is to avoid the implication that the quality of democracy that has been achieved is completely satisfactory from the perspective of democratic theory. The need for further improvement thus implied by the conditions is made explicit by the ideals in democratic theory.

Political systems are sometimes evaluated according to how well they satisfy conditions that are supposed to be empirically necessary for the persistence of democratic systems.[18] These prerequisites or background conditions, such as the proper distribution of income or cultural or psychological traits, should not be the primary interest in a theory meant to evaluate democracy. The stability for which such empirical conditions are necessary is better treated in democratic theory as only one objective or function of the conditions posited in the theory. It is a subsidiary objective because most democratic theorists have properly been more concerned about the quality of democracy and how it can be improved than about how the system manages to persist at all.

Some political scientists employ empirical conditions to evaluate the quality of processes in developed democracies in a way that, for a different reason, is inadequate for a theory of democracy that emphasizes evaluation and prescription. The trouble is that these political scientists would transform the evaluation of citizenship into a purely empirical enterprise. Robert Dahl's eight minimal conditions for a polyarchy, for example, are arbitrary points on a continuum that could quantitatively express, for instance, the extent of voting or the extent to which citizens possess equal information about political alternatives. Dahl concedes that, to use his criteria or conditions to evaluate political systems, we may have to make judgments that at least at present cannot be expressed meaningfully in purely quantitative or even empirical terms. However, he apparently does not think that this difficulty represents an insurmountable obstacle to formulating in purely empirical terms a democratic theory that can be used to evaluate political systems.[19]

Certainly we should not disparage efforts to develop quantitative indices and weighting procedures for the purposes of evaluation. But if my argument about the inevitable interplay between facts and values is correct, the difficulties in operationalizing evaluative

[18] E.g., see Seymour Martin Lipset, *Political Man* (New York, 1960), pp. 27–86; and Almond and Verba, *op. cit.*, pp. 261–262 and literature cited there.

[19] Robert Dahl, *A Preface to Democratic Theory* (Chicago, 1963), pp. 63, 73–75, 87. Also, see Morris Janowitz and Dwaine Marvick, *Competitive Pressure and Democratic Consent* (Chicago, 1964). More recently, Dahl recognized some limits of the use of empirical techniques for evaluation: "The Evaluation of Political Systems," in I. Pool (ed.), *Contemporary Political Science* (New York, 1967), pp. 176–178.

criteria cannot be escaped by greater scientific sophistication. They are inherent in any democratic theory that recognizes that evaluation cannot be based on empirical evidence alone.

Constructive Ideals

An ideal pictures a state of affairs that is not yet realized; it may also, at least by implication, evaluate the present state of affairs and prescribe changes that would realize the pictured state of affairs.[20] The first of the two principal kinds of ideals in democratic theory is a constructive ideal, which pictures a state of affairs that is meant to be realizable by means of trends and nonradical reforms. Such an ideal expresses a stronger version of a condition, since the state of affairs that the ideal pictures would require either (1) a greater degree of whatever the corresponding condition stipulates, for example, more participation by more citizens; or (2) a stronger form or kind of whatever the condition stipulates, for example, more debate-like political discussion where the condition requires only nonmanipulated discussion.

A reform is radical if it requires a qualitative change in an existing economic, social, or political structure of a nation-state. A structure may be thought of as a regularized pattern of interrelated roles and processes. Such a pattern can be characterized by one of a pair of terms (x, y) marking the limits of a continuum. A structural change is qualitative if the new pattern that it generates is closer to limit x on the continuum than to limit y when the old pattern is closer to limit y than to limit x. For example, a radical reform would alter the power structure *from* (a) a pattern that is closer to extreme centralization than to extreme decentralization; *to* (b) a pattern that is closer to decentralization than to centralization. A reform would not be radical if it required merely a pattern that is more decentralized (less centralized) than the existing pattern. Thus, a dispersion of political decision-making power so that all citizens could directly share in it would be a radical reform because it would require a political structure

[20] The idea of an ideal proposed here is broader than the common notion of an ideal as the "best attainable." For any desirable state of affairs, even less than the best, may be the subject of an ideal so long as it is not realized. Nor does "ideal" as used here exclude, as some philosophers' use of the term would, claims based merely on interests or wants. See the concepts developed by Brian Barry, *Political Argument* (London, 1965), pp. 38–41;; and Hare, *Freedom and Reason*, pp. 137–156. Also see Abraham Edel, *Method in Ethical Theory* (London, 1963), pp. 323–353.

different from the present one. A change in electoral requirements to generate a significant increase in voting turnout need not be a radical reform because it could occur within the existing structure.

These formal guidelines indicate in undisputed instances why some reforms are considered radical and others are not. In instances about which there is a dispute whether or not the reform is radical, the guidelines would enable us to decide the dispute only if we devised operational criteria to mark the points on the continuum that characterizes the structure in question. It is probably not possible to discover objective criteria that would empirically distinguish radical and nonradical changes in all possible instances, for what counts as radical change naturally depends on the perspective from which one views the change and on what stakes one has in the change. Nevertheless, even without such criteria, the guidelines direct our attention to the structure in which a reform occurs, and this is not an unimportant consequence, for the question of whether or not a reform is radical is often confused with whether the rate of change is gradual or sudden or whether the way in which a change is implemented is peaceful or violent. It cannot be maintained *a priori* that nonradical reform is always peaceful and gradual, and radical reform always violent and sudden. These are largely empirical issues (though behavioral evidence may not be decisive in resolving them, as I shall indicate below).

To justify a claim that a constructive ideal is realizable, we seek evidence that can be used to (1) reveal trends that, if continuing, tend to realize the ideal; and (2) suggest that certain nonradical reforms, if effected, tend to realize the ideal. Since constructive ideals typically call for "more" democracy (*e.g.*, more participation) without specifying how much more, evidence about reforms and trends can and should indicate only the direction and kind of change, not the precise degree to which the change would satisfy or fail to satisfy the ideal. Usually an ideal is too vague to serve as a standard against which to measure the precise amount of change. If we were to restrict democratic theory to ideals that are capable of precise formulation, we would tie the theory too closely to present political knowledge.

Behavioral evidence about effects of trends and reforms on various aspects of democratic life is certainly plentiful, though very little effort has been made to interpret it systematically from the perspective of democratic theory. Constructive ideals that would call for more participation, discussion, and political equality would seem to be favorably affected by trends such as increases in educational opportunities, urbanization, exposure to media, and extension of government activities. Unfavorable trends that deserve examination include increasing specialization of politics and ethnic assimilation.[21] Nonradical reforms that might contribute toward the realization of constructive ideals are, for example, the simplifying of voting procedures and barriers to other forms of participation, making campaigns and elections seem more interesting and important, strengthening organized groups, and dispersing some decision-making authority within existing structures.[22] Evidence about these and other changes would have to be examined in conjunction not merely with one ideal but with a whole set of interrelated ideals in democratic theory.

In addition to evidence about reforms and trends, evidence may have to be used to show that promotion or realization of a particular constructive ideal would not be undesirable or would not conflict with other ideals. For example, evidence about the characteristics of nonparticipants would help answer (though could not completely decide) the familiar argument that greater citizen participation is neither necessary nor desirable.[23]

Constructive ideals escape the defects of both prescriptivism and descriptivism. Since such an ideal must be supported by findings showing that it is realizable or that its realization is desirable, it is not immune to empirical evidence, as prescriptivism implies all ideals are. But a constructive ideal is not fully determined or justified by empirical evidence, as descriptivism implies. In assessing a constructive ideal, we must allow for an interplay between behavioral evidence and value standards, which, as we have already seen, precludes a purely empirical approach.

[21] See Angus Campbell, Philip E. Converse, Warren E. Miller, and Donald Stokes, *The American Voter* (New York, 1960), pp. 405–408; 475–481; Bernard Berelson, Paul F. Lazarsfeld, and William N. McPhee, *Voting* (Chicago, 1954), pp. 248–249, 337; Lipset, *op. cit.*, pp. 187, 191–192, 194; Campbell and Robert L. Kahn, *The People Elect a President* (Ann Arbor, 1952), p. 109; Stein Rokkan, "Mass Suffrage, Secret Voting and Political Participation," *European Journal of Sociology* (1961), II, p. 152; Robert E. Lane, *Political Life* (New York, 1965), pp. 262–263.

[22] Stanley Kelley, Jr., Richard E. Ayres, and William G. Bowen, "Registration and Voting: Putting First Things First," *American Political Science Review* (June 1967), pp. 359–375; Campbell, "Surge and Decline: A Study of Electoral Change," *Public Opinion Quarterly* (Fall 1960), p. 398; Key, *Public Opinion, op. cit.*, pp. 504–506; Frank Bealey, J. Blondel, and W. P. McCann, *Constituency Politics* (London, 1965), p. 200; and Dahl, *Pluralist Democracy in the United States* (Chicago, 1967), pp. 198–202.

[23] *E.g.*, Campbell *et al.*, *op. cit.*, pp. 110–115; Lane, *op. cit.*, pp. 340–348; and Key, *Public Opinion, op. cit.*, pp. 187–188.

Reconstructive Ideals

Conditions remind us how much of democratic theory has been achieved, and constructive ideals suggest what more can be done within an existing structure. Reconstructive ideals point out how much more remains to be done. Unlike a constructive ideal, a reconstructive ideal pictures a state of affairs that (1) cannot be realizable without radical reform; or (2) may not be realizable with any reform. In either case, the ideal is justifiable with little or no reference to behavioral evidence. Hence, prescriptivism seems to be nearly true of reconstructive ideals, though it is mistaken if applied to other standards in democratic theory.

The reason that even those reconstructive ideals that are meant to be realizable can receive little support from behavioral evidence is that the ideals and the evidence refer to different structures. Since the evidence is based on studies conducted within a given present structure, it would be very risky to extrapolate from this evidence to conclusions about democratic activity in some reconstructed future society. Many factors assumed to be constant in behavioral studies would have to be treated as variables if we were to take into account the possibility of radical reform. The voting studies, for example, assume as constant certain features of the context in which voting decisions are made; for example, findings about voter behavior in national elections assume a relative salience of national parties and candidates, which is largely a result of a centralized political structure. Were we to try to transform such constants into variables so that the findings would be applicable to all structures, the findings would have to be presented in a form that would be either much less reliable or much less conclusive than they are now.

It may be possible from evidence about radical reforms in substructures of society (for example, decentralization in a particular factory or industry) to gain some hint of what effects analogous reforms in the whole structure would have. But even here, transferring findings in a subunit to a whole society may not be warranted. Evidence might show, for example, that citizens have a greater sense of efficacy in a factory where decision making is decentralized and shared. But it would still be possible that, if the whole society were decentralized so that there were no dominant points of power to which citizens could refer, citizens might have a lessened sense of efficacy with respect to politics. A reconstructive ideal characteristically is so forward-looking that there exists no exact instance or adequate analogy of its realization anywhere in the past or present. Lacking such instances and analogies, advocates of reconstructive ideals turn not to the techniques of behavioral social science but to the tools of historical, philosophical, and even literary inquiry. The justification of such ideals requires an exercise of imagination that goes far beyond what any scientific facts can warrant; it depends on an imaginative reconstruction of society and a vision of historical forces that cannot be fairly captured in any quantifiable generalization.

Similarly, behavioral evidence is misapplied if directed against two beliefs about the way in which radical reform is to be implemented. It is sometimes asserted that radical reform must overturn the economic structure since economic factors are the most fundamental determinants of social and political life. Even if we could unambiguously distinguish economic from other factors conceptually, the statistical problem of "multicollinearity" would stifle any efforts to show comprehensively that economic factors are, or are not, more significant determinants of particular phenomena than other factors. When a number of economic independent variables are highly correlated with noneconomic independent variables, it is often impossible to make reliable inferences about the relative contributions of the two sets of independent variables to the determination of the dependent variables.[24]

A second belief—that violence is necessary for radical change—usually stems either from a psychological reaction to repeated failure in trying to reform a system peacefully or from an interpretation of history that alleges that all significant radical change in the past has come by violent means.[25] Behavioral evidence cannot destroy even the historical grounds for this belief because its proponents can always deny, usually with good reason, that any such evidence is seriously incomplete and frequently misleading when applied to broad historical generalizations.[26]

If behavioral evidence is of little help when reconstructive ideals are proposed as realizable programs for radical reform, it is of

[24] See Hugh D. Forbes and Edward R. Tufte, "A Note of Caution in Causal Modelling," *American Political Science Review* (December 1968), pp. 1258–1264; and Donald E. Farrar and Robert R. Glaubner, "Multicollinearity in Regression Analysis," *Review of Economics and Statistics* (February 1967), pp. 92–107.

[25] Laski, *Parliamentary Government in England* (New York, 1938), pp. 163–164, and *The State in Theory and Practice* (New York, 1935), pp. 279–280.

[26] See Barrington Moore, Jr., *Social Origins of Dictatorship and Democracy* (Boston, 1966), pp. 509–523.

even less use when the ideals are presented as critical challenges that are not meant to be realizable by means of any reform. An ideal picturing complete decentralization of political decision making may be practically impossible in any social and political structure. The ideal may nonetheless serve as a reminder that democratic activity in present structures falls far short of what would be desirable; it may give impetus to efforts to reconstruct society for the radical expansion of democratic activities.

A dialectic is thus generated between the ideal and the existing political life. In such a dialectic, it is desirable to have an ideal that pictures a state of affairs as far removed as is coherently possible from existing political reality. The further removed the ideal is, the more ideological pressure it brings against the status quo, and if ideals have effects on men's minds, the more likely it is that some kind of reform will take place. Moreover, the further the ideal from the status quo, the further will be the resolution of the dialectic from the status quo. It follows, then, not only that a justifiable reconstructive ideal may be unrealizable but also that it may be more justifiable to the extent that it is more difficult to realize. If, for example, the pressures of coordination and planning in the present structure of industrialized society make decentralized organization more difficult, this is all the more reason that a reconstructive ideal picturing decentralization needs to be urged.

Although reconstructive ideals are relatively unaffected by evidence from behavioral social science, they may be challenged or supported in three ways. First, it may be alleged that even a partial increase in an activity urged by a reconstructive ideal would be undesirable. Here evidence can be presented to show whether the allegation is true. In such cases, the evidence cited to support the desirability of a reconstructive ideal often will be the same as that cited to support the desirability of the corresponding constructive ideal. Also, some very limited support for a reconstructive ideal may, as I suggested above, be received from evidence showing favorable effects of a reform analogous to the reform prescribed by the ideal, though on a smaller scale than, or in a different setting from, the reform. Second, a proposed reconstructive ideal may be challenged as internally incoherent. Here conceptual analysis can be used either to defend or to reject the ideal. Third, it may be charged that a reconstructive ideal conflicts with other ideals deemed equally or more desirable. Again conceptual analysis and appeal to higher standards in the theory are the appropriate techniques.

Without reconstructive ideals, a democratic theory is devoid of vision. It fails to serve as a guide for the radical changes that full realization of democratic ideals may require. By concentrating on constructive ideals, a democratic theory becomes too cautious and may miss opportunities for demanding desirable change. For example, Neil Reimer, whose theory stresses prudential ideas that in effect are constructive ideals, is led to say that racial integration in the United States was not "practically wise" until 1954. His test of prudence turns out to be *ad hoc* and hence unduly conservative.[27]

With *only* reconstructive ideals, democratic theory spells disillusionment. That is, for instance, the result of the shift in emphasis from constructive to reconstructive ideals at one point in Laski's political thought. Similarly, treating all democratic ideals as reconstructive ideals is the fault of Giovanni Sartori's analysis of the logical relations of ideals and reality. To say that all ideals are "predestined not to succeed" and that they are "not . . . designed to be converted into reality" is to ignore the role of constructive ideals.[28] This is prescriptivism run riot. Without the backing of the less visionary but more widely acceptable constructive ideals, democratic theory might be more readily dismissed. As Dewey observes, the habit of setting up ideals of "remote perfection" may result in either "blind passionate revolt which trusts to destruction of what exists to bring forth by some miracle a better estate of things, or, more commonly, in an esthetic disgust with the present which seeks refuge in what is aloof and which through a refusal to face existing conditions actually operates to perpetuate them."[29] Reconstructive ideals unsupported by constructive ideals are thus as inimical to a satisfactory democratic theory as are constructive ideals unsupported by reconstructive ideals. A balanced democratic theory should include both kinds.

Conclusion

In the encounter between democratic theory and behavioral social science proposed here, democratic theory will not emerge unaltered, as prescriptivists would hope. At least the conditions and constructive ideals in democratic theory will have to undergo revision, though in the process they may prove to be more acceptable in their new dress. Yet such an encounter, properly conducted,

[27] Neil Riemer, *The Revival of Democratic Theory* (New York, 1962), p. 62.
[28] Sartori, *op. cit.*, pp. 63–65.
[29] Dewey and Tufts, *op. cit.*, p. 382.

should not undermine the traditional evaluative and prescriptive concerns of democratic theory, as descriptivists would do. Thus, while we must recognize a disparity between behavioral evidence and value standards, we must also allow an interplay between the evidence and the standards if we wish to integrate democratic theory and behavioral social science.

31 ❧ THE SOCIAL SCIENTIST'S TASK

C. WRIGHT MILLS

Regardless of the scope of his awareness, the social scientist is usually a professor, and this occupational fact very much determines what he is able to do. As a professor, he addresses students, and on occasion, by speeches and by writings, publics of larger scale and more strategic position. In discussing what his public role may be, let us stick close to these simple facts of power, or if you like, to the facts of his powerlessness.

Insofar as he is concerned with liberal, that is to say liberating, education, his public role has two goals: What he ought to do for the individual is to turn personal troubles and concerns into social issues and problems open to reason—his aim is to help the individual become a self-educating man, who only then would be reasonable and free. What he ought to do for the society is to combat all those forces which are destroying genuine publics and creating a mass society—or put as a positive goal, his aim is to help build and to strengthen self-cultivating publics. Only then might society be reasonable and free.

These are very large goals, and I must explain them in a slightly indirect way. We are concerned with skills and with values. Among "skills," however, some are more and some are less relevant to the tasks of liberation. I do not believe that skills and values can be so easily separated as in our search for "neutral skills" we often as-

FROM *The Sociological Imagination* by C. Wright Mills. Copyright © 1959 by Oxford University Press, Inc. Reprinted by permission of the publisher.

sume. It is a matter of degree, with skills at one extreme and values at the other. But in the middle ranges of this scale, there are what I shall call sensibilities, and it is these which should interest us most. To train someone to operate a lathe or to read and write is in large part a training of skill; to help someone decide what he really wants out of his life, or to debate with him stoic, Christian, and humanist ways of living is a cultivation or an education of values.

Alongside skill and value, we ought to put sensibility, which includes them both, and more besides: it includes a sort of therapy in the ancient sense of clarifying one's knowledge of self. It includes the cultivation of all those skills of controversy with oneself that we call thinking, and which, when engaged in with others, we call debate. An educator must begin with what interests the individual most deeply, even if it seems altogether trivial and cheap. He must proceed in such a way and with such materials as to enable the student to gain increasingly rational insight into these concerns, and into others he will acquire in the process of his education. And the educator must try to develop men and women who can and who will by themselves continue what he has begun: the end product of any liberating education is simply the self-educating, self-cultivating man and woman; in short, the free and rational individual.

A society in which such individuals are ascendant is, by one major meaning of the word, democratic. Such a society may also be defined as one in which genuine publics rather than masses prevail. By this, I mean the following:

Whether or not they are aware of them, men in a mass society are gripped by personal troubles which they are not able to turn into social issues. They do not understand the interplay of these personal troubles of their milieux with problems of social structure. The knowledgeable man in a genuine public, on the other hand, is able to do just that. He understands that what he thinks and feels to be personal troubles are very often also problems shared by others, and more importantly, not capable of solution by any one individual but only by modifications of the structure of the groups in which he lives and sometimes the structure of the entire society. Men in masses have troubles, but they are not usually aware of their true meaning and source; men in publics confront issues, and they usually come to be aware of their public terms.

It is the political task of the social scientist—as of any liberal educator—continually to translate personal troubles into public issues, and public issues into the terms of their human meaning for a variety of individuals. It is his task to display in his work—and, as an educator, in his life as well—this kind of sociological imagination. And it is his purpose to cultivate such habits of mind among the men and women who are publicly exposed to him. To secure these ends is to secure reason and individuality, and to make these the predominant values of a democratic society.

You may now be saying to yourself, "Well, here it comes. He is going to set up an ideal so high that in terms of it everything must seem low." That I might be thought to be doing so testifies to the lack of seriousness with which the word democracy is now taken, and to the indifference of many observers to the drift away from any plain meaning of the word. Democracy is, of course, a complicated idea about which there is much legitimate disagreement. But surely it is not so complicated or ambiguous that it may no longer be used by people who wish to reason together.

What I mean by democracy as an ideal I have already tried to indicate. In essence, democracy implies that those vitally affected by any decision men make have an effective voice in that decision. This, in turn, means that all power to make such decisions be publicly legitimated and that the makers of such decisions be held publicly accountable. None of these three points can prevail, it seems to me, unless there are dominant within a society the kinds of publics and the kinds of individuals I have described. Certain further conditions will presently become evident.

The social structure of the United States is not an altogether democratic one. Let us take that as a point of minimum agreement. I do not know of any society which is altogether democratic—that remains an ideal. The United States today I should say is generally democratic mainly in form and in the rhetoric of expectation. In substance and in practice it is very often nondemocratic, and in many institutional areas it is quite clearly so. The corporate economy is run neither as a set of town meetings nor as a set of powers responsible to those whom their activities affect very seriously. The military machines and increasingly the political state are in the same condition. I do not wish to give the impression that I am optimistic about the chances that many social scientists can or will perform a democratic public role, or—even if many of them do so—about the chances that this would necessarily result in a rehabilitation of publics. I am merely outlining one role that seems to me to be open and is, in fact, practiced by some social scientists.

It happens also to be a role that is in line with both liberal and socialist views of the role of reason in human affairs.[1]

My point is that the political role of social science—what that role may be, how it is enacted, and how effectively—this is relevant to the extent to which democracy prevails.

If we take up the third role of reason, the autonomous role, we are trying to act in a democratic manner in a society that is not altogether democratic. But we are acting as if we were in a fully democratic society, and by doing so, we are attempting to remove the "as if." We are trying to make the society more democratic. Such a role, I contend, is the only role by which we may as social scientists attempt to do this. At least I do not know of any other way by which we might try to help build a democratic policy. And because of this, the problem of the social sciences as a prime carrier of reason in human affairs is in fact a major problem of democracy today.

What are the chances of success? Given the political structure within which we must now act, I do not believe it is very likely that social scientists will become effective carriers of reason. For men of knowledge to enact this strategic role, certain conditions must be present. Men make their own history, Marx said, but they do not

[1] In passing, I should like to remind the reader that, quite apart from its present bureaucratic context and use, the style of abstracted empiricism (and the methodological inhibition it sustains) is not well suited for the democratic political role I am describing. Those who practice this style as their sole activity, who conceive of it as the "real work of social science," and who live in its ethos, cannot perform a liberating educational role. This role requires that individuals and publics be given confidence in their own capacities to reason, and by individual criticism, study, and practice, to enlarge its scope and improve its quality. It requires that they be encouraged, in George Orwell's phrase, to"get outside the whale," or in the wonderful American phrase, "to become their own men." To tell them that they can "really" know social reality only by depending upon a necessarily bureaucratic kind of research is to place a taboo, in the name of science, upon their efforts to become independent men and substantive thinkers. It is to undermine the confidence of the individual craftsman in his own ability to know reality. It is, in effect, to encourage men to fix their social beliefs by reference to the authority of an alien apparatus, and it is, of course, in line with, and is reinforced by, the whole bureaucratization of reason in our time. The industrialization of academic life and the fragmentation of the problems of social science cannot result in a liberating educational role for social scientists. For what these schools of thought take apart they tend to keep apart, in very tiny pieces about which they claim to be very certain. But all they could thus be certain of are abstracted fragments, and it is precisely the job of liberal education, *and* the political role of social science, *and* its intellectual promise, to enable men to transcend such fragmented and abstracted milieux; to become aware of historical structures and of their own place within them.

make it under conditions of their own choice. Well then, what are the conditions *we* require to play this role effectively? What are required are parties and movements and publics having two characteristics: (1) within them ideas and alternatives of social life are truly debated, and (2) they have a chance really to influence decisions of structural consequence. Only if such organizations existed could we become realistic and hopeful about the role of reason in human affairs which I have been trying to outline. Such a situation, by the way, I should consider one major requirement for any fully democratic society.

In such a polity social scientists in their political roles would probably speak "for" and "against" a variety of movements and strata and interests, rather than merely address an often vague, and—I fear—dwindling, public. Their ideas, in short, would compete, and this competition (as a process as well as in its result at any given time) would be politically relevant. If we take the idea of democracy seriously, if we taken the democratic role of reason in human affairs seriously, our engagement in such a competition will in no way distress us. Surely we cannot suppose that all definitions of social reality, much less all statements of political ways and means, much less all suggestions of goals, would result in some undebatable, unified doctrine.

In the absence of such parties and movements and publics, we live in a society that is democratic mainly in its legal forms and its formal expectations. We ought not to minimize the enormous value and the considerable opportunity these circumstances make available. We should learn their value from the fact of their absence in the Soviet world, and from the kind of struggle the intellectuals of that world are up against. We should also learn that whereas there many intellectuals are physically crushed, here many morally crush themselves. That democracy in the United States is so largely formal does not mean that we can dodge the conclusion that if reason is to play any free part in a democratic making of history, one of its chief carriers must surely be the social sciences. The absence of democratic parties and movements and publics does not mean that social scientists as educators ought not to try to make their educational institutions a framework within which such a liberating public of individuals might exist, at least in its beginnings, and one in which their discussions might be encouraged and sustained. Nor does it mean that they should not try to cultivate such publics in their less academic roles.

To do so of course, is to risk "trouble"; or what is more serious, to face a quite deadly indifference. It requires that we deliberately present controversial theories and facts, and actively encourage controversy. In the absence of political debate that is wide and open and informed, people can get into touch neither with the effective realities of their world nor with the realities of themselves. Nowadays especially, it seems to me, the role I have been describing requires no less than the presentation of conflicting definitions of reality itself. What is usually termed "propaganda," especially of a nationalist sort, consists not only of opinions on a variety of topics and issues. It is the promulgation, as Paul Kecskemeti once noted, of official definitions of reality.

Our public life now often rests upon such official definitions, as well as upon myths and lies and crackbrained notions. When many policies—debated and undebated—are based on inadequate and misleading definitions of reality, then those who are out to define reality more adequately are bound to be upsetting influences. That is why publics of the sort I have described, as well as men of individuality, are, by their very existence in such a society, radical. Yet such is the role of mind, of study, of intellect, of reason, of ideas: to define reality adequately and in a publicly relevant way. The educational and the political role of social science in a democracy is to help cultivate and sustain publics and individuals that are able to develop, to live with, and to act upon adequate definitions of personal and social realities.

The role of reason I have been outlining neither means nor requires that one hit the pavement, take the next plane to the scene of the current crisis, run for Congress, buy a newspaper plant, go among the poor, set up a soap box. Such actions are often admirable, and I can readily imagine occasions when I should personally find it impossible not to want to do them myself. But for the social scientist to take them to be his normal activities is merely to abdicate his role, and to display by his action a disbelief in the promise of social science and in the role of reason in human affairs. This role requires only that the social scientist get on with the work of social science and that he avoid furthering the bureaucratization of reason and of discourse.

Not every social scientist accepts all the views I happen to hold on these issues, and it is not my wish that he should. My point is that one of his tasks is to determine his own views of the nature of historical change and the place, if any, of free and reasonable men within it. Only then can he come to know his own intellectual and political role within the societies he is studying, and in doing so find out just what he does think of the values of freedom and of reason which are so deeply a part of the tradition and the promise of social science.

If individual men and small groups of men are not free to act with historical consequence, and at the same time are not reasonable enough to see those consequences; if the structure of modern societies, or of any one of them, is now such that history is indeed blind drift and cannot be made otherwise with the means at hand and the knowledge that may be acquired—then the only autonomous role of social science is to chronicle and to understand; the idea of the responsibility of the powerful is foolish; and the values of freedom and of reason are realizable only in the exceptional milieux of certain favored private lives.

But that is a lot of "ifs." And although there is ample room for disagreement over degrees of freedom and scales of consequence, I do not believe that there is sufficient evidence to necessitate abandoning the values of freedom and reason as they might now orient the work of social science.

Attempts to avoid such troublesome issues as I have been discussing are nowadays widely defended by the slogan that social science is "not out to save the world." Sometimes this is the disclaimer of a modest scholar; sometimes it is the cynical contempt of a specialist for all issues of larger concern; sometimes it is the disillusionment of youthful expectations; often it is the pose of men who seek to borrow the prestige of The Scientist, imagined as a pure and disembodied intellect. But sometimes it is based upon a considered judgment of the facts of power.

Because of such facts, I do not believe that social science will "save the world" although I see nothing at all wrong with "trying to save the world"—a phrase which I take to mean the avoidance of war and the rearrangement of human affairs in accordance with the ideals of human freedom and reason. Such knowledge as I have leads me to embrace rather pessimistic estimates of the chances. But even if that is where we now stand, still we must ask: If there *are* any ways out of the crises of our period by means of intellect, is it not up to the social scientist to state them? What we represent —although this is not always apparent— is man become aware of mankind..It is on the level of human awareness that virtually all solutions to the great problems must now lie.

To *appeal* to the powerful, on the basis of any knowledge we now have, is utopian in the foolish sense of that term. Our relations with them are more likely to be only such relations as they find useful, which is to say that we become technicians accepting their problems and aims, or ideologists promoting their prestige and authority. To be more than that, so far as our political role is concerned, we must first of all reconsider the nature of our collective endeavor as social scientists. It is not at all utopian for one social scientist to appeal to his colleagues to undertake such a reconsideration. Any social scientist who is aware of what he is about must confront the major normal dilemma I have implied, the difference between what men are interested in and what is to men's interest.

If we take the simple democratic view that *what men are interested in* is all that concerns us, then we are accepting the values that have been inculcated, often accidentally and often deliberately, by vested interests. These values are often the only ones men have had any chance to develop. They are unconsciously acquired habits rather than choices.

If we take the dogmatic view that *what is to men's interests*, whether they are interested in it or not, is all that need concern us morally, then we run the risk of violating democratic values. We may become manipulators or coercers, or both, rather than persuaders within a society in which men are trying to reason together and in which the value of reason is held in high esteem.

What I am suggesting is that by addressing ourselves to issues and to troubles, and formulating them as problems of social science, we stand the best chance, I believe the only chance, to make reason democratically relevant to human affairs in a free society, and so realize the classic values that underlie the promise of our studies.

index